Industrializing English Law

Legal stasis in the face of rapid economic change poses serious challenges to deterministic and functional interpretations in the theory of law, institutions, and economic performance. This book explores a particularly important example: the slow and contradictory development in the law of business organization in England during the critical phase of the Industrial Revolution. Based on extensive primary source research, Ron Harris shows how the institutional development of major forms of business organization – the business corporation, the partnership, the trust, the unincorporated company – evolved during this period. He also demonstrates how this slow and peculiar path of legal change interacted with and affected the practice of individual entrepreneurs and the transformation of the English economy.

Ron Harris is Senior Lecturer of Legal History at the School of Law, Tel Aviv University, Israel. Harris has been awarded fellowships from the Rothschild Foundation and the British Council, and has published articles in various journals, including the *Journal of Economic History* and *Economic History Review*.

POLITICAL ECONOMY OF INSTITUTIONS
AND DECISIONS
Series Editors
Randall Calvert, *Washington University, St. Louis*
Thrainn Eggertsson, *Max Planck Institute, Germany,* and *University of Iceland*

Founding Editors
James E. Alt, *Harvard University*
Douglass C. North, *Washington University, St. Louis*

Other Books in the Series
Alesina Alberto and Howard Rosenthal, *Partisan Politics, Divided Government and the Economy*
Lee J. Alston and Joseph P. Ferrie, *Southern Paternalism and the Rise of the American Welfare State: Economics, Politics, and Institutions, 1865–1965*
Lee J. Alston, Thrainn Eggertsson, and Douglass C. North, eds., *Empirical Studies in Institutional Change*
James E. Alt and Kenneth Shepsle, eds., *Perspectives on Positive Political Economy*
Jeffrey S. Banks and Eric A. Hanushek, eds., *Modern Political Economy: Old Topics, New Directions*
Yoram Barzel, *Economic Analysis of Property Rights,* 2nd edition
Robert Bates, *Beyond the Miracle of the Market: The Political Economy of Agrarian Development in Kenya*
Peter Cowhey and Mathew McCubbins, eds., *Structure and Policy in Japan and the United States*
Gary W. Cox, *The Efficient Secret: The Cabinet and the Development of Political Parties in Victorian England*
Gary W. Cox, *Making Votes Count: Strategic Coordination in the World's Electoral System*
Jean Ensminger, *Making a Market: The Institutional Transformation of an African Society*
Kathryn Firmin-Sellers, *The Transformation of Property Rights in the Gold Coast: An Empirical Analysis Applying Rational Choice Theory*
Clark C. Gibson, *Politicians and Poachers: The Political Economy of Wildlife Policy in Africa*
Anna L. Harvey, *Votes without Leverage: Women in American Electoral Politics, 1920–1970*
Murray Horn, *The Political Economy of Public Administration: Institutional Choice in the Public Sector*
John D. Huber, *Rationalizing Parliament: Legislative Institutions and Party Politics in France*
Jack Knight, *Institutions and Social Conflict*
Michael Laver and Kenneth Shepsle, eds., *Cabinet Ministers and Parliamentary Government*
Michael Laver and Kenneth Shepsle, eds., *Making and Breaking Governments*
Margaret Levi, *Consent, Dissent, and Patriotism*
Brian Levy and Pablo T. Spiller, eds., *Regulations, Institutions, and Commitment*

Series list continues on page following Index

INDUSTRIALIZING ENGLISH LAW
ENTREPRENEURSHIP AND BUSINESS ORGANIZATION, 1720–1844

RON HARRIS
Tel Aviv University

CAMBRIDGE
UNIVERSITY PRESS

PUBLISHED BY THE PRESS SYNDICATE OF THE UNIVERSITY OF CAMBRIDGE
The Pitt Building, Trumpington Street, Cambridge, United Kingdom

CAMBRIDGE UNIVERSITY PRESS
The Edinburgh Building, Cambridge CB2 2RU, UK   http://www.cup.cam.ac.uk
40 West 20th Street, New York, NY 10011-4211, USA   http://www.cup.org
10 Stamford Road, Oakleigh, Melbourne 3166, Australia
Ruiz de Alarcón 13, 28014 Madrid, Spain

© Cambridge University Press 2000

First published 2000

Printed in the United States of America

Typeface Sabon 10/12 pt.   *System* DeskTopPro$_{/UX}$ [BV]

A catalog record for this book is available from the British Library.

Library of Congress Cataloging in Publication data
Harris, Ron, 1960–
Industrializing English law : entrepreneurship and
business organization, 1720–1844
/ Ron Harris.
p.   cm. – (Political economy of institutions and decisions)
Includes bibliographical references.
ISBN 0–521–66275–3 (hb.)
1. Business enterprises – Law and legislation – Great Britain –
History. I. Title. II. Series.
KD2049.H37 2000
346.42'065 – dc21   99-34663
CIP

ISBN 0 521 66275 3 hardback

Contents

PART I
BEFORE 1720

PART II
1721–1810

Tables

Acknowledgments

This book is the outgrowth of a 1994 Columbia University dissertation. My first debt is to my dissertation supervisor, David Cannadine, and to the second reader, Eben Moglen. Their encouragement and criticism throughout the research, the writing and the rewriting of the dissertation, and thereafter, was indispensable. The criticism was at least as important as the encouragement, was just as welcome, and had a considerable impact on the final outcome. The two, in addition to Michael Edelstein, who devoted a great deal of time to this project in its dissertation stage, exposed me to three distinct disciplinary outlooks: mainstream British history, legal history, and economic history. The three outlooks were not always easily reconcilable, but the attempt was invariably stimulating and challenging. The challenge forced me to embark upon a lengthy interdisciplinary project, which aspires to meeting the minimal standards of each of three quite dissimilar disciplinary discourses. The risk was of arriving at a final outcome which might be unintelligible to all three.

Comments from Larry Neal were insightful and knowledgeable. They caused me to reflect again, at the revisions stage, on my general arguments and on some specific claims I made, to organize the book better, to make it more accessible to economic historians, and to integrate some relevant literature that I had missed. Their effect on the final product is invaluable. Joshua Getzler followed this project a long way. His comments convinced me to read many more law reports than I had intended, demonstrated new ways to connect legal and economic history, and caused me to reformulate some of my arguments.

Several others read parts of the book in various stages, and made valuable suggestions: Elizabeth Blackmar, Tamar Frankel, Alon Kadish, David Lieberman, Joel Mokyr, Avner Offer, Ariel Porat, Wim Smit, and Omri Yadlin. During the past eight years, from the earliest archival survey to the final revisions, I have accumulated debts to many scholars for their counsel and guidance on various topics: Reuven Avi-Yonah, Lucian Aryeh Bebchuck, Omri Ben-Shachar, Michael Bordo, Stuart Bruchey, Forrest Capie, Jan De Vries, Lawrence Friedman, Terry Gourvish, Avner Greif, Julian Hoppit, Morton Horwitz, Robert Kagan, Pnina Lahav, David Landes, Assaf Likhovski, Peter Lindert, Peter Mathias, Menachem Mautner, Patrick O'Brien, Andrew Plaa, Harry Scheiber, David Seipp, Yoram Shachar, David Sugarman, Barry Supple, and Gavin Wright. I thank them all. Earlier versions of chapters in the book were presented at various workshops and seminars, including those at the law schools of Tel Aviv University, University of California at Berkeley, Harvard University, Boston University, and Columbia University and at the economics departments of the Hebrew University and Stanford University. Questions and comments from participants at those meetings contributed to the improvement of the book.

Gila Haimovic worked intensively, discerningly, and rapidly to make my style more readable, and as a by-product served as an editor in other respects as well. As an author for whom English is a second language, this was a most valuable and enlightening service for me. Hadas Liss, my research assistant during the final stages of the revision, saved me from many embarrassing citation errors while working on the footnotes and the bibliography. In addition she contributed considerably as a critical reader of the entire book.

Various librarians and archivists were most helpful and patient as I made my way through unfamiliar sources. Particular acknowledgment should be made to the librarians at the Goldsmiths' Collection, Guildhall Library, the House of Lords Record Office and the British Library in London; Bodlean and Bodlean Law Libraries at Oxford; the Business School Library, Law School Library, and Butler Library at Columbia University; and Boalt Hall Library at the University of California, Berkeley. I am grateful to Deborah Gold and other Law School librarians at Tel Aviv University who faithfully fulfilled endless odd requests on my part. The Institute of Historical Research served as my second home while in London, and I benefited greatly from its extensive open shelf library, its seminars, and technical facilities.

Financial support for this project was granted by the Department of History of Columbia University, the British Council, Yad Hanadiv-Rothschild Foundation, and the Cegla Institute and the Faculty of Law of Tel Aviv University.

I have always felt awkward thanking my family in print. I hope I do it in more meaningful ways elsewhere. But I will follow the convention after all. I thank my wife Hadas, who was encouraging and supportive throughout this project, even when this meant that she had to compromise her wishes for mine, and my sons Yuval, Guy, and Ido, who were born into this book.

Introduction

The preindustrial framework of business organization in England was formed over several centuries, from the late middle ages until the passage of the famous Bubble Act in 1720, and persisted up to 1844 when the process of industrialization was already well under way. This preindustrial framework allowed the formation of joint-stock corporations only by specific authorization of the State while outlawing other forms of joint-stock association. It permitted the spontaneous creation of partnerships, yet denied them the privileges of limited liability or of separate legal entity. It explicitly prohibited the establishment of new joint-stock corporations and large partnerships in the financial sectors: banking and marine insurance. After 1825, a gradual transformation ensued and the modern legal framework began to emerge. The Bubble Act was repealed in 1825; minor reforms took place in the 1830s; an Act of 1844 regularized free incorporation by registration and provided for the unobstructed formation of companies with separate legal entity and transferable shares; and, by 1855–1856, general limited liability was attached to incorporation. The framework that developed during this period is essentially the framework that prevails today.

For more than a century during which the legal framework was unchanged, between the passage of the Bubble Act and the mid-nineteenth century, England went through an economic and social evolution known as the industrial revolution, expressed in a profound structural transformation. England's population increased at an unprecedented rate, urbanization reached high levels, and new industrial towns emerged. The relative weight of agriculture in production and employment declined, while that of industry correspondingly increased. A newly developed transportation network, composed of canals and railways, was constructed during this period. New growth sectors – cotton, iron, and mining – changed more rapidly than other sectors in

1

terms of technological innovation, organization of production, outputs, and exports. Internationally, England rose to a leading position as producer, consumer, financial, and shipping center, and naval and global power. The aggregate increase in production, productivity, and capital formation, though not as dramatic as scholars previously postulated, was substantial (compared with that of contemporary economies), unprecedented, and sustained.[1]

The central theme of this book is the relationship between legal and economic developments in the context of England's industrial revolution and, more specifically, in the context of business organization. It addresses the apparent discrepancy between the developing economy of 1720–1844 and the stagnant legal framework of business organization during the same period. This discrepancy is particularly puzzling when comparing England with other nations of that time. During much of this period, the legal framework of business organization in England was more restrictive than in other, presumably less advanced, economies such as France, the Dutch Republic, some German states, Ireland, Scotland, New York and other American states, and even Russia.[2] England, which served as an example to foreigners fascinated by its industrialization, was itself seeking alternatives abroad as far as business organization was concerned.

The book revisits numerous primary sources not consulted since Scott, DuBois, and Hunt worked on their classic accounts sixty and more years

---

[1]Since the late 1970s, economic historians, and particularly cliometricians, have tended to stress the limits to the growth achieved between 1780 and 1820. Some even questioned the appropriateness of the term Industrial Revolution (with or without capital letters). This revisionist approach was in turn criticized in the 1990s by scholars who argued that measuring the rate of aggregate economic growth is not a meaningful approach to understanding the Industrial Revolution. Today, many (including myself) agree that though longer, more gradual, less integrated, and more restricted (both region- and sector-wise), a fundamental, unprecedented, and irreversible structural transformation did take place in the English economy, roughly between 1700 and 1850. For major contributions to this ongoing debate, see David Cannadine, "The Present and the Past in the English Industrial Revolution, 1880–1980," *Past and Present* 103 (May 1984), 131–172; N.F.R. Crafts, *British Economic Growth during the Industrial Revolution* (Oxford: Clarendon Press, 1985); E. A. Wrigley, *Continuity, Chance and Change: The Character of the Industrial Revolution in England* (Cambridge University Press, 1988); Pat Hudson, *The Industrial Revolution* (London: E. Arnold, 1992); Joel Mokyr, ed., *The British Industrial Revolution: An Economic Perspective* (Boulder: Westview, 1993); Roderick Floud and Donald M. McCloskey, eds., *The Economic History of Britain since 1700*, Vol. 1: *1700–1860*, 2d ed. (Cambridge University Press, 1994).

[2]In each of these legal systems, at least some of the following applied: availability of limited liability partnerships, and of partnerships with transferable shares; general incorporation legislation; no prohibition on incorporation in the financial sectors; and no legislation parallel to the Bubble Act.

ago.[3] It utilizes other primary sources not used by earlier scholars, particularly business records, records on parliamentary proceedings, contemporary pamphlets, and legal manuals. Monographs accumulated over the past fifty years, and which were not available when the early seminal accounts were written, contributed considerably to a new understanding of different aspects of the subject. Finally, modern debates on the interpretation of the political, social, legal, ideological, and economic history of England during the relevant period, as well as on legal and economic theory, provided new perspectives and new insights on the major themes of the present work.

This book concentrates on the period from 1720 to 1844. Elements of the early history of the joint-stock company are presented insofar as they are relevant to later developments. The debate in the 1850s and 1860s on general limited liability, a worthy subject, is beyond the time framework of the book. In this, the book breaks with the periodization created by the division of labor between Scott, DuBois, and Hunt, the first covering the period to 1720; the second, 1720 to 1800; and the third, 1800 to 1867. I wish to advance a periodization that stresses the continuity before and after 1720 and particularly from the eighteenth to the nineteenth century.

Much of the literature on the relationship between legal and economic developments in early modern and modern England falls into one of two paradigms or, rather, ideal types.[4] It usually perceives the law either as developing in isolation by autonomous internal dynamics or as functionally evolving with the rise of the market economy and of the middle classes, with the views of the classical political economists, and with industrialization.[5] The existing literature on the development of the

---

[3]William R. Scott, *The Constitution and Finance of English, Scottish and Irish Joint-Stock Companies to 1720*, 3 vols. (Cambridge University Press, 1912; rpt., Gloucester, Mass.: P. Smith, 1968,); Bishop Carleton Hunt, *The Development of the Business Corporation in England, 1800–1867* (Cambridge, Mass.: Harvard University Press, 1936); Armand B. DuBois, *The English Business Company after the Bubble Act, 1720–1800* (New York: Commonwealth Fund, 1938). The only book-length work that dealt with the period to 1844 and was published after 1938 was C. A. Cooke, *Corporation, Trust, and Company: An Essay in Legal History* (Manchester University Press, 1950). Many of the later articles on these subjects relied heavily on these early accounts, offering new interpretations but only scarce research into the primary sources.

[4]Donald R. Kelley, *The Human Measure: Social Thought in the Western Legal Tradition* (Cambridge, Mass.: Harvard University Press, 1990); Robert W. Gordon, "Critical Legal Histories," *Stanford Law Review* 36, nos. 1 & 2 (1984), 57–125.

[5]The legal history literature in the field of English business law within either of the paradigms is too immense to be listed here. A few examples in the fields of contract law and negotiable instruments are: J. Milnes Holden, *The History of Negotiable Instruments in English Law* (University of London, 1955); James Steven Rogers, *The*

framework of business organization can also, for the most part, be classified into one ideal type or the other. This is not to say that all of these historians were aware of their affiliation with one of these two ideal types or dealt expressly with the historical problem of the discrepancy. What follows is my classification of the literature in this field. I first present the two interpretative approaches that fall neatly into these two ideal types of autonomy and functionality. I connect each to the wider tradition out of which it arose. I then present a third interpretative approach that tries to mediate between the ideal types. This interpretation suggests that while the law-in-the-books was indeed autonomous, the law-in-action was, in fact, functional. Last, I present my own approach which is more pragmatic in the sense that it shifts between these ideal types according to changing contexts. This is not to say that I am the first to take such a pragmatic approach. I do think, however, that much of the literature on the history of the legal framework of business organization in England tends to be too dogmatic in the sense of leaning too rigidly toward one of the ideal types. I emphasize these ideal types as analytical tools to highlight my arguments and contrast them with the arguments of other historians. For this reason, I have made the tension between these ideal types a central organizing theme in the present book. The autonomy–functionality tension is more of a pretext and a metaphoric organizing theme for working on the twilight zone between narratives and disciplines than a domineering and mechanistic model.

The first interpretation attributes a high degree of autonomy to the legal system. According to this interpretation, the Bubble Act, the common law, and legal hostility to the share market played significant parts in hindering the development of the joint-stock company for more than a century. After the passage of the Bubble Act, unincorporated joint-stock companies were declared illegal by judges and their formation was harshly punished. Incorporation by the State was an expensive and complicated matter, granted only in exceptional cases. The legal framework was unresponsive to economic needs and delayed the progress of joint-stock companies in England until well into the nineteenth century.[6] Only

Early History of the Law of Bills and Notes: A Study of the Origins of Anglo-American Commercial Law (Cambridge University Press, 1995); A.W.B. Simpson, *A History of the Common Law of Contract: The Rise of the Action of Assumpsit* (Oxford: Clarendon Press, 1975); P. S. Atiyah, *The Rise and Fall of Freedom of Contract* (Oxford: Clarendon Press, 1979).

[6]Scott, *Constitution and Finance of Joint-Stock Companies*, vol. 1, pp. 437–438; William Holdsworth, *A History of English Law*, 17 vols. (London: Methuen, 1956–1972), vol. 8, pp. 219–222; H. A. Shannon, "The Coming of General Limited Liability," in E. M. Carus-Wilson, ed., *Essays in Economic History*, 3 vols. (London: Edward Arnold, 1954–1962), vol. 1, p. 358; Hunt, *Business Corporation*, pp. 6–9; A. H. Manchester, *Modern Legal History of England and Wales 1750–1950* (Lon-

in the mid-nineteenth century, when intellectual developments within the realm of law reached a certain maturity, did a new legal doctrine emerge. Its outcome is a significant legal constraint on the economy.

This interpretation comes out of a long isolationist tradition which explains the significant discrepancy between legal and economic developments by the relative autonomy of the law. The legal system had its own doctrines and concepts, developed within the legal institutions by legal professionals. Economic and social changes mattered only little to this autarchic system. This tradition dominated the practice of many lawyers writing legal history in the United States until the 1950s and 1960s, and is still an underlying assumption in some of the mainstream legal history literature written in Britain to this day. Autonomy paradigms seem more reasonable within the traditional common law system whose jurisprudence and reasoning, or at least rhetoric, were oriented toward the past. They limited the alleged role of the oracles of law, the judges, to the declaration of the old customs and rights of Englishmen, and to adjudication based on centuries-old forms of action and precedents. Furthermore, in the common law world, the legal profession, bench and bar, was socially separated from men of business. Legal education was separated from general university education and the law was supposedly an intellectually self-sufficient realm. The attribution of a high degree of autonomy to the law was quite natural in the context of this legal culture. The autonomy tradition thus has a reasonable foundation in the unique case of the English legal system, with its peculiar common law history.

According to the second interpretation, there was no real discrepancy between economic and legal developments. The scale of the undertakings and their capital requirements during the early stages of industrialization were modest. In this period, the sole proprietorship, the family firm, and the closed partnership sufficed to meet the needs of the English economy. Only with the coming of the railway in the 1830s and 1840s did things change, and by then, the legal framework was responsive and the joint-stock corporation became readily available.[7] Thus, the presumed discrepancy between economic and legal developments is not a real one. In fact, when the need for a change in the legal framework emerged in the

don: Butterworths, 1980), 348–349; Philip Mirowski, *The Birth of the Business Cycle* (New York: Garland, 1985), 271–278.

[7]P. L. Cottrell, *Industrial Finance: 1830–1914 – The Finance and Organization of the English Manufacturing Industry* (London: Methuen, 1980), 10–11, 34–35; Phyllis Deane, *The First Industrial Revolution*, 2d ed. (Cambridge University Press, 1979), 180–181. In fact, the implied assumption of many economic historians, that joint-stock associations were not common or relevant to economic development, is evident in the fact that they did not mention them at all when writing on this period. See Floud and McCloskey, eds., *Economic History.*

railway age, it was swiftly met by the legal system. The law responded functionally to the economy and placed no constraints on growth during the industrial revolution.

This second interpretation also relies on a wider tradition, one that maintains that the law was merely a functional element in a wider economic and social order. Ever since the nineteenth century, grand theories of the rise of capitalism as well as slightly more modest schools of jurisprudence have attributed to the law an instrumental and derivative role. The German historical school viewed the law as the product of a long historical process embodying the unique spirit of the nation in its formal norms.[8] For Marx, to put it very simplistically, the law was part of a superstructure whose content was shaped by the changes in the substructure, the material world. Weber viewed the legal systems of Western Europe as having distinctive rationalistic features which enabled them to develop along with the rise of capitalism and to instrumentally facilitate it.[9] Socioeconomic approaches to law, from Jehring and some of the American legal realists, to Willard Hurst and the Wisconsin school of legal history, to Morton Horwitz (in his first book), E. P. Thompson, and other left-wing historians, conceived the law as being shaped by social needs.[10] They differ only on the issue of whose needs are being advanced, those of the society as a whole or those of powerful and hegemonic classes. Some of the leading law and economics scholars regard the law, and particularly the common law, as an inherently efficient norm creator that will dynamically adjust to the new efficiency needs of the market, in order to promote optimal

[8]Otto Gierke, *Political Theories of the Middle Age* (Cambridge University Press, 1900; rpt., Cambridge University Press, 1958); Otto Gierke, *Natural Law and the Theory of Society 1500 to 1800* (Cambridge University Press, 1934; rpt., Cambridge University Press, 1958); Otto Gierke, *Community in Historical Perspective* (Cambridge University Press, 1990); Henry Sumner Maine, *Ancient Law: Its Connection with the Early History of Society and Its Relation to Modern Ideas* (London: John Murray, 1861); Michael John, *Politics and the Law in Late Nineteenth-Century Germany: The Origins of the Civil Code* (Oxford: Clarendon Press, 1989).

[9]Max Weber, *Economy and Society: An Outline of Interpretive Sociology*, ed. Guenther Roth and Claus Wittich, 3 vols. (New York: Bedminster Press, 1968); David M. Trubek, "Max Weber on Law and the Rise of Capitalism," *Wisconsin Law Review*, no. 3 (1972), 720; Anthony T. Kronman, *Max Weber* (Stanford University Press, 1983).

[10]James Willard Hurst, *Law and the Conditions of Freedom in the Nineteenth-Century United States* (Madison: University of Wisconsin Press, 1956); Lawrence M. Friedman, *A History of American Law*, 2d ed. (New York: Simon and Schuster, 1985); Morton J. Horwitz, *The Transformation of American Law, 1780–1860* (Cambridge, Mass.: Harvard University Press, 1977); E. P. Thompson, *Whigs and Hunters: The Origin of the Black Act* (New York: Pantheon, 1975); Douglas Hay et al., *Albion's Fatal Tree: Crime and Society in the Eighteenth-Century* (New York: Random House, 1975).

resource allocation.[11] The revived evolutionary legal and economic theorists argue that only those elements in the legal system that better fit their environment survive the natural selection process.[12] Institutional and new institutional economists believe that institutional change, including change in property rights, transaction costs, and legal institutions, correlates with economic performance, and thus conclude that the law in well-performing economies must have evolved instrumentally to growth.[13]

A third interpretation of the discrepancy offers a seemingly attractive combination of the first two. It argues for autonomy at the top – the formal-official judicial and legislative doctrine – and instrumentality at the bottom – the practice of businessmen and their attorneys on the margins of legality. The third interpretation acknowledges that the economic need for aggregate forms of business organization appeared in the eighteenth century, if not before. Yet despite the negative attitude of the State and the official legal system, the business community developed an adequate substitute for the business corporation in the private sphere. This substitute, the unincorporated company, was designed by shrewd businessmen and lawyers, and received from the courts of law the limited degree of recognition needed for practical functioning.[14] This interpretation fits the notions of those who advocate the importance of "law-in-action" and of writing legal history from below and stress the centrality of fictions, bypasses, and other flexibilities in the common law system (which would ease Weber's England problem).

The present book argues that neither the strict autonomous interpretation nor the strict functional one can fully explain the development of

[11]See, particularly, Richard A. Posner, *Economic Analysis of the Law,* 3d ed. (Boston: Little Brown, 1986).

[12]Robert C. Clark, "The Interdisciplinary Study of Legal Evolution," *Yale Law Journal* 90, no. 5 (1981), 1238; Robert C. Clark, *Corporate Law* (Boston: Little, Brown, 1986).

[13]Douglass C. North, *Institutions, Institutional Change and Economic Performance* (Cambridge University Press, 1990) and *Structure and Change in Economic History* (New York: Norton, 1981); Thrainn Eggertsson, *Economic Behavior and Institutions* (Cambridge University Press, 1990); Oliver E. Williamson, *The Economic Institutions of Capitalism: Firms, Markets, Relational Contracting* (New York: Free Press, 1985).

[14]F. W. Maitland, "The Unincorporated Body" and "Trust and Corporation," in *Maitland: Selected Essays* (Cambridge University Press, 1936), 128–140, 141–222; DuBois, *English Business Company,* 215 ff.; Cooke, *Corporation, Trust and Company,* 83–88; T. S. Ashton, *An Economic History of England: The 18th Century* (London: Methuen, 1955; rpt., London: Methuen, 1972), 119; Tom Hadden, *Company Law and Capitalism,* 2d ed. (London: Weidenfeld and Nicholson, 1977), 16–19; Gary M. Anderson and Robert D. Tollison, "The Myth of the Corporation as a Creation of the State," *International Review of Law and Economics* 3 (1983), 107–120. Of the above, only DuBois is clearly aware of the deficiencies of the unincorporated company.

the legal framework of business organization between 1720 and 1844. Stated briefly, I reject the functional interpretation by showing that there were needs and calls for reform in the law of business organization in some sectors of the business community, notably transport and insurance, as early as the 1760s, and these became widespread by the turn of the nineteenth century. However, the law was not responsive to these: Legal scholars, judges, and legislators ignored them, refused to remove past constraints, or even imposed new prohibitions. I reject the autonomy interpretation because there is no evident internal legal dynamic to, in itself, explain the eventual change in the period 1825–1844. Furthermore, nonlegal factors, such as pressure from litigants, lobbying of interest groups, and the rise of the share market do have a considerable role, in my judgment, in explaining the change. Unfortunately, I have to argue in the following chapters that the third interpretation, though more sophisticated than the first two, does not work well enough. Contract law could not provide legal personality or limitation of liability and its use involved high transaction costs; trust law was slow to adapt to the business context; and full incorporation privileges could be enjoyed only by resorting to the formal law-in-the-books system dominated by the State. The unincorporated company, the core of this third interpretation, could not, and did not, serve as an instrumental surrogate from below to the constraining legal framework.

This book therefore avoids postulating that the legal system had a great degree of autonomy, or that it was merely functional. I recognize that the complexity of the interaction between legal and economic change in our case goes beyond the distinction between an autonomous law-in-the-books and a functional law-in-action. Conceptual attempts at establishing such an intermediate path have been made in recent years by several legal historians.[15] The present book is inspired to some extent by these conceptual exercises and historical researches. I hope in the present book to demonstrate the advantages of abandoning the poles and moving toward the center. My interpretation does not offer a simple and coherent thesis, as this cannot be supported by the complex nature

[15]For some recent attempts to develop a theoretical construction to replace the traditional relative autonomy and functionalist approaches, see David Sugarman and G. R. Rubin, "Towards a New History of Law and Material Society in England: 1750–1914," in G. R. Rubin and David Sugarman, eds., *Law, Economy and Society, 1750–1914: Essays in the History of English Law* (Abingdon: Professional Books, 1984); Mark V. Tushnet, "Perspectives on the Development of American Law: A Critical Review of Friedman's 'A History of American Law,' " *Wisconsin Law Review*, no. 1 (1977), 81–109; Gordon, "Critical Legal Histories," 57–125; Rande W. Kostal, *Law and English Railway Capitalism 1825–1875* (Oxford: Clarendon Press, 1994). Joshua Getzler, *A History of Water Rights at Common Law* (Oxford: Clarendon, 2000). Kostal's and Getzler's are the only works which try to implement the new construction in a comprehensive historical research.

of the interaction. It is rather a pragmatic and dialectic approach. However, I try to be more concrete by drawing a preliminary map that attributes varying degrees of functionality and autonomy at different times and in different settings.

In terms of timing, I argue that until 1720, the interaction between legal and economic developments was closer to the functional pole of the continuum, whereas between 1721 and the early nineteenth century, it was closer to the autonomous pole, and subsequently it again moved closer to the functional pole. From a meager start in the mid-sixteenth century, the legal framework developed considerably during the first period, responding to the needs of merchant groups, royal financial needs and foreign policy aims, powerful moneyed companies, and the like. During the second period, the issue of business organization rarely reached the courts, was not placed on the agenda of either the cabinet or Parliament, and did not attract the attention of legal writers. Attempts to make the law-in-action instrumental to business had reached their limits. The gap between economic development and legal stagnation seemed to widen. During the third period, repeated shocks from the courts and the stock market intensified the interaction between the two spheres. The interest groups were arrayed in a manner more favorable to change. The number of middle-class members of the legislature was larger and they were more responsive. Cabinet, in some of its compositions, was willing to take a more active role in the economy and the legal system. The conflict within the judiciary, due to the institutional crises and social change, intensified, and this weakened its control over the field. Eventually both statute law and judge-made law began to respond to the mounting economic change. The above is a simplistic portrait of each of the periods. Qualifications and refinements come in the following chapters.

What can explain the tendency of the interaction between legal and economic developments to be more autonomous in nature during one period and more functional during another? To deal with this question, we have to go one step down on the general/concrete ladder, to the changing settings of the interaction in different periods. In terms of setting, there are too many minute details for them to be fully presented in an introduction. I make do with four examples: sectors, market structure, jurisprudence, and institutions.

Sectors: This setting focuses on the effects of sector-specific supply and production side factors, such as technology, capital, and the organization of labor, on the nature of the interaction between legal and economic change. In its legal framework of organization, the long-range overseas trading sector had new needs, particularly in terms of capital. Production sectors like iron and cotton, whose growth was based on the

gradual diffusion of new, mostly low-capital, technology, the extension
of the market, and the plowing-back of profits, found the legal framework relatively instrumental to their needs. The shipping and part of the
mining sectors, which operated within unique and separate legal regimes,
though in need of a finance-raising mechanism and risk-spreading,
placed no pressure on the general legal framework, and located instrumental microcosms that need to be analyzed in isolation. On the other
hand, sectors like transportation and finance had totally new needs: the
raising of huge lump-sum capital, the spreading of risks, and the limitation of liability. They were the first to clash with the autonomous legal
framework.

Market Structure: This setting focuses on the structure of competition
in the market (or industrial organization, in economists' terminology)
and its effects on the interaction. Markets with legally imposed entry
barriers into certain types of business organization experienced different
types of interaction than more open markets. Markets which tended to
enable the formation of natural monopolies, or markets with State-
conferred monopolies, affected the legal framework differently than
competitive markets. Generally speaking, open and competitive markets
were a better setting for functional evolutionary processes, whereas entry
barriers and monopolies enabled the legal status quo to prevail while
constraining the non-State-privileged parts of the economy.

Jurisprudence: The jurisprudential discourse and the positions of various normative and positive conceptions within it changed over time. I
do not wish to argue that the jurisprudential discourse dominated the
nature of the interaction between legal and economic developments.
There was a considerable gap between the high discourse and the actual
functioning of the legal system. Nevertheless, as discussed above, some
contemporary jurisprudential schools, such as religious and secular natural law and the declarative view of the common law, perceived the law
as more autonomous. Other schools, such as the utilitarian, positivist,
and reformist views of the role of legislation, and the historical view of
the common law, perceive it as more instrumental. Interaction that was
taking place in a period, or a setting, in which instrumental jurisprudential conceptions were more influential were more likely to lead to instrumental outcomes than interactions that were taking place in a period
and settings in which autonomous conceptions were more influential.
The Benthamite and post-Benthamite Parliament was more likely to feel
legitimized when legislating in spheres of law that were traditionally
considered as within the province of the common law. The same can be
said of judges. Those among them who held instrumental jurisprudence
positions, such as Lord Mansfield or Henry Brougham, were more likely
to be innovative in the field of business law. A judge who viewed his

job as one of following precedents, of retaining the coherency and systematization of legal doctrine, and of settling specific disputes was more likely to create a relatively autonomous law.

Institutions: The institutional setting of the interaction changed from period to period due to political and other factors that were in many cases external to the components of the interaction itself. The institutional setting shifted between the executive, legislative, and judicial branches of the State. It also shifted within each of the branches, from the King to his Privy Council to Cabinet, from the full House of Commons to private bill committees, from King's Bench to Chancery. The lower house of Parliament seems to have been a more functional institutional setting than the upper house; the committees more so than the full House; the Cabinet more than the King's Council; and the courts of common law more instrumental in some periods than Chancery. The interactions within some institutions were more functional in their nature than interactions taking place in other institutions due to institutional and related social, political, jurisprudential, and cultural characteristics.

Thus, the changing setting of the interaction from period to period, due to the changing weight of sectors with different legal needs and characteristics, the changing position of the State and competition in the markets, the changing jurisprudential discourse, and the change in the structure and role of legal and political institutions, to mention just four examples, had major implications on the place of the legal/economic interaction along the autonomous/functional continuum.

The last contours that I wish to add to the preliminary map of the continuum between autonomy and functionality are not as embedded in the characteristics of each given period as are the settings presented above. These contours can be labeled in economists' jargon as path-dependency, exogenous shocks, and contingency. Many historians have, in fact, been aware of such factors for quite a while, though without theorizing about them or giving them fancy labels. The unique legal features attributed to the concept of the corporation in medieval, if not Roman, times were carried into later periods, during which the fundamental economic and legal conditions were altogether different, and bounded the later history of the abstract conception and its practical applications. The order in which legal conceptions were employed for business purposes (whatever the causes), for example, first the corporation and only later the trust, may have given the corporation a considerable advantage later on, as a first mover which enjoyed a two-hundred-year lead in the learning and adaptation process. The situation in India that enabled the East India Company and its organizational model to flourish and expand (during the seventeenth and eighteenth centuries), and the independence of Spain's American colonies, initiating the market boom that led to the repeal of the Bubble Act (in 1825), are just two examples of spatially exogenous shocks that led to permanent changes in the course of development. Contingency is recurrent in history and in the present story. Two examples: The decision of an anonymous informer to revive the Bubble Act in 1807 (of all years) and the nomination of William Gladstone to the Board of Trade (of all possible Cabinet positions) had a considerable effect on the course of events. As these examples show, the preliminary map I have attempted to draw is already complicated and becomes more detailed and nuance-filled as the narrative unfolds.

The book is divided into three parts. Chapter 1 introduces the reader to three core legal conceptions: partnership, trust, and corporation, and the four central features of business organization: transferability of interest, limitation of liability, the existence of separate legal entity, and the entrance into these forms, and describes a spectrum of concrete forms of organization.[16] The two chapters of Part I deal, more or less chronologically, with the period up to 1720. Chapter 2 takes us from the first appearance of the business corporation in England in the sixteenth century, to the eve of the South Sea Bubble. It outlines the not-very-linear development from an early Stuart heyday to a post–Glorious Revolution heyday, a period during which many characteristics of the business corporation changed in several trends. It also provides the background for understanding the South Sea Bubble and the enactment of the Bubble Act, which are discussed in Chapter 3. The third chapter argues that the motivation for the passage of the Bubble Act was connected mainly to public finance and not to sentiments regarding the joint-stock company, and that it did not operate as a turning point in the development of this form of business organization.

Part II covers the period 1720–1810. The chapters are roughly arranged according to sectors and forms of organization. Chapter 4 deals with two sectors – transport and insurance – and with the emergence of a wide array of aggregate forms of business organizations within both. It explains the reasons for the process variation between the sectors and within each sector. Chapters 5 and 6 examine the features of the business corporation and the unincorporated company and their implications within the contemporary legal and economic context. They conclude that within that particular context, corporations gradually gained dominance while unincorporated companies were at a disadvantage. Chapter

---

[16]Other features of the company, which are also of importance, such as form of governance, directors' duties and authority, shareholders' rights, accountancy practices, holding of real property, and winding up, are only marginally discussed and deserve separate treatment.

7 demonstrates the progress of the joint-stock feature in a wide array of sectors, some not commonly associated with this form of organization during a relatively early period, prior to 1810. The period 1720–1810 is thus presented as a period of tensions, divergence and convergence, limitations and expansion, autonomy and functionality.

Part III is organized by spheres and arenas. Chapter 8 deals with the stock market, political economists, and the business community, Chapter 9 with the courts, and Chapter 10 with Parliament. They all cover roughly the same period: 1800–1844. It is argued that tensions during the previous period together with clashes within the business community and the revival of the Bubble Act in a series of court judgments and the stock market cycle between 1807 and 1812 destabilized the legal framework of business organization. The only way to settle the organizational crisis was to resort to the legislature, and Parliament, quite reluctantly, stepped in after 1825. A series of parliamentary committees and acts adopted diverse approaches to the problem and no coherent doctrine seemed to emerge. Only in 1844 was a general incorporation law enacted. An explanation of the concept, timing, and the relatively smooth passage of this act appears in the concluding part of this book. The conclusion also recaps some of the more general trends and arguments.

1

The Legal Framework

Much of the literature on the history of business organizations is the history of winners. It projects backward from the end of the story. The rise to dominance of the joint-stock limited corporation in the late nineteenth and early twentieth centuries led many historians to focus their attention mostly on this form of organization from as early as the sixteenth and seventeenth centuries. They neglected other forms of organization that did not win the day, assuming that the winning was in some sense inevitable from the outset. I argue that it is impossible to isolate the story of the business corporation from the stories of other forms of organization. Entrepreneurs employing these forms interacted and competed with one another in the commodities and financial markets. Lawyers, judges, and legislators shaping these forms copied features from others, and at times rejected features found to be problematic in relation to other forms. I further argue that the rise to dominance of the business corporation was not inevitable in any sense from the perspective of the year 1500 or even the year 1800. Its rise cannot be comprehended in a narrow context, by unfolding the story of the business corporation in a linear and deterministic manner.

This chapter surveys the legal framework of business organization in early modern England. It lays out the full range of possible forms of organization of enterprises available to business persons, from the sole proprietorship to the joint-stock corporation and beyond, and the legal constraints within which entrepreneurs and their lawyers functioned. The discussion, in the following chapters, on adherence to the framework, the attempts to bypass it, or pressures to alter it can be understood only in light of this framework. The purpose of this chapter is also partly introductory, to place readers of different disciplinary starting points – historians, economic historians, legal historians, and scholars of law and economics and of corporate law – on a common ground. Some of these disciplinary groups may well be familiar with parts of the material.

14

The discussion of the concrete forms of organization follows two preliminary steps. The first is a historical and analytical discussion of the three major legal conceptions applied to groups of individuals: the corporation, the partnership, and the trust. The second examines four features, related in different degrees to these abstract conceptions and attributed to concrete forms of business organizations: legal personality, transferability of interests, managerial structure, and limitation of liability.

In addition to the creation of a common denominator, I wish at this early stage to emphasize the historical burden, or path-dependence, of later developments. Understanding the medieval origins of the three legal conceptions – corporation, partnership, and trust – and the features attached to them at that formative stage is essential for analysis of later developments. Realization that some features, such as joint stock and limitation of liability, are of a later period and of different origin is also imperative. So is the comprehension that by the early eighteenth century, the starting point of this book, a wide spectrum of forms of business organization existed. The fact that the joint-stock corporation became dominant in the modern world is not the result of a lack of alternative conceptions, features, and concrete forms. On the contrary, it is the convergence, from the mid-nineteenth century onward, that is an unexpected and puzzling outcome in light of the diversity of the early eighteenth century.

To meet the above purposes, the time period covered by this chapter is longer than that of the following chapters. It goes back to Roman and medieval times, to the first appearance of the business corporation in the sixteenth century, and also deals with the later period of 1720–1800 which is the focus of the second part of this book. Geographically, as well, this chapter reaches beyond England to the continental origins of some of the conceptions and concrete forms.[1]

LEGAL CONCEPTIONS OF GROUP ASSOCIATION

This section presents three legal conceptions which, by the late Middle Ages, applied in one way or another to groups of individuals: the partnership, the corporation, and the trust. Potentially, these conceptions can define the association of individuals into collective frameworks for business purposes. While initially only the partnership was employed in

[1] One caveat to the structure of this chapter. It breaks the chronological sequence, to which the rest of the chapters generally conform, as it deals with forms that emerged in the sixteenth century, side-by-side with those that emerged some two hundred years later. Taking into account the hoped-for diversity of the readership and the nature of the argumentation, I believe that this is unavoidable.

business, the two others – the corporation and the trust – were adjusted for business purposes in the sixteenth and eighteenth centuries, respectively. I present the origins and basic legal characteristics of these forms here.

One of my main concerns throughout the book is why the corporation, and not the trust or the partnership, came to dominate business organization in England by the second half of the nineteenth century. It would not seem to have been the obvious winner from the perspective of the fourteenth or even the early sixteenth century. Until then, it was used mainly for religious and municipal purposes, whereas the partnership was used for business purposes. The corporation was controlled by the King, while the trust was developing dynamically out of his reach. Why then did the corporation adjust to business needs better than the other two conceptions? The present chapter broadly states the question. I hope that halfway through this book the answer surfaces and the connection between it and the autonomy/functionality paradigm, presented in the introduction, become evident.

The Corporation

Some historians trace the origins of the corporation back to the *universitas* of classical Roman texts, as codified in the sixth-century *corpus juris civilis*.[2] Others maintain that it was the fourteenth century commentators, with their liberal interpretative methods, who read into the Roman texts a well-defined concept of the corporation, foreign to the original authors.[3] Some scholars trace the origins of the corporation to the realities of the middle ages, particularly to institutions such as the guild and the city.[4] Others assert that the corporation owes its existence not to secular bodies but to Church institutions and canonist constitutional theory.[5] Some members of the Germanist branch of the German historical school are convinced that it grew out of the communal fellowships and *Volksgeist* of medieval Germanic clans.[6] I bypass the question of origins, and the other historical and jurisprudential issues related to it, and turn directly to sixteenth-century England. In this period, corporations of various sorts were widespread; the King himself, cities and

[2]P. W. Duff, *Personality in Roman Private Law* (Cambridge University Press, 1938; rpt., New Jersey, 1971).

[3]Reuven S. Avi-Yonah, "The Development of Corporate Personality from Labeo to Bartolus," Seminar Paper, Harvard University, 1989.

[4]F. W. Maitland, *Township and Borough* (1898, rpt., Cambridge, 1964). Scott, *Constitution and Finance of Joint-Stock Companies*, vol. 1, pp. 3–6.

[5]Harold J. Berman, *Law and Revolution: The Formation of the Western Legal Tradition* (Cambridge, Mass.: Harvard University Press, 1983).

[6]Gierke, *Political Theories*, *Natural Law*, and *Community in Historical Perspective*.

boroughs, guilds, universities and colleges, hospitals and other charitables, bishops, deans and chapters, abbots and convents, and other ecclesiastical bodies were organized into corporations. They were classified by Blackstone, in retrospect, into sole and aggregate, lay and ecclesiastical, eleemosynary and civic.[7]

Could corporations in sixteenth-century England be created voluntarily or only by the State and the law? Because this question is conveniently less controversial for the sixteenth century than for earlier periods, I take this period, on the eve of the appearance of the business corporation, as my starting point.

Blackstone and Kyd, writing in the second half of the eighteenth century, still found relics of two ancient modes of creating corporations: by common law (bishops, deans, and others) and by prescription (the City of London) which did not involve immediate State authorization.[8] But even these forms were considered, generally or implicitly, to lie within the embrace of King's consent, and in any event, they referred to ancient corporations whose creation was concealed in the mist of immemorial past. For contemporaries, they were more of an ex post rationale for formally legalizing well-established corporations than a historical explanation of their origins, and had not been used for creating new corporations since medieval times.

Another indirect form of creating corporations, by delegation of power (e.g., from the King to the Pope for ecclesiastical purposes), was discontinued by the end of the Reformation.[9] The decline of implicit and delegated incorporation was one of the outcomes of the strengthening of the centralized government and the royal court. By later Tudor times, the Church, the Universities, the City of London, and semiautonomous regions were giving way, not without resistance, to Crown authority.[10] This was expressed in many fields, among them, in our case, the disappearance of other incorporating authorities and the creation of an effective Crown monopoly over incorporation.

Thus, by the sixteenth century, an explicit, ex ante and direct authorization by the King became the only mode of incorporation. This authorization was normally given in the form of charter (or letters patent), and, occasionally, by way of Act of Parliament bearing the King's explicit consent, or a combination of an act and a charter. By this time, it

---

[7]William Blackstone, *Commentaries on the Laws of England*, 4 vols. (London, 1765– 1769; rpt., Chicago: University of Chicago, 1979), vol. 1.

[8]Blackstone, *Commentaries*, vol. 1, pp. 460–463; Stewart Kyd, *A Treatise on the Law of Corporations*, 2 vols. (1793–1794), vol. 1, pp. 39–41.

[9]Similarly, the creation of academic corporations by general delegation of powers by the King to the Chancellor of the University of Oxford became insignificant.

[10]Though the autonomy of boroughs from the rural surrounding was on the rise in this period, they were placed within the system of Crown-created corporations.

was considered that incorporation was an essential component of the King's exclusive and voluntary prerogative to create and grant dignities, jurisdictions, liberties, exemptions, and, in our case, franchises.[11] The law of corporations was classified by contemporaries as part of the law of the King, the core of the English Constitution. The employment of franchises in general, and specifically corporations, was subject to judicial review. This was done by way of the prerogative writs of *quo warranto* and *scire facias*, by which claimants were required to show by what authority they were exercising the franchise or the alleged corporation. Unauthorized corporations could be dissolved and abused charters could be forfeited by the court through these prerogative judicial writs.[12]

What were the consequences of incorporation? Incorporation involved the creation of a new personality, distinct from that of individual human beings. There is no evidence that sixteenth-century English legal theorists, insofar as there were such, were concerned with the debate on the basis of justification for that personality. The classical Roman law, the *corpus juris civilis* and the glossators' and commentators' interpretations of its dealings with corporate conceptions, and the canonist literature on these issues, did not offer solutions to practical problems within what was by then a crystallized common law system. The origins of the corporation within or without the law, and the timing and route of the importation of the corporation from the Continent into the common law, which has bothered legal historians since the nineteenth century, did not interest the practically oriented sixteenth-century English judges and lawyers. All they wanted was to solve, as they reached courts, the concrete daily disputes to which corporations were party. If one can nonetheless suggest a dominant abstract common-law conception of the corporate personality, without being charged with anachronism, it would be that of the State- or law-fabricated artificial person and not the spontaneously created natural person, or the contractually, voluntarily devised aggregate person. That must have been Hale's conception, when writing in the mid-seventeenth century that "every corporation must have a legal creation."[13] The personality of the corporation was instituted through a concession by the King to some of his subjects, and had no other justification.

---

[11]Matthew Hale, *The Prerogatives of the King* (London: Selden Society, 1976), vol. 92, chap. 19.

[12]John Bouvier, *Bouvier's Law Dictionary and Concise Encyclopedia*, 8th ed., 2 vols. (Kansas: Vernan Law Book, 1914), see "Quo Warranto" and "Scire Facias"; Holdsworth, *English Law*, vol. 9, pp. 65–67; J. H. Baker, *An Introduction to English Legal History*, 3d ed. (London: Butterworths, 1990), 166–167; Kyd, *Law of Corporations*, 395–439. The distinction between the two writs is discussed in the next two chapters.

[13]Hale, *Prerogatives*, 240.

The separate legal personality of the corporation had several implications. Its legal personality did not terminate with the death of any human individual; it was potentially immortal and subject to dissolution only in a strictly defined manner. A corporation could own (in the feudal sense) and convey land, at times with restrictions. Its perpetual existence conflicted with the feudal arrangements which held that the death of a landlord generated dues to the Crown. As a result, the Crown was opposed to land-holding by immortal legal persons such as corporations. Only by receiving a special license from the Crown in the charter of incorporation, or in a statute, to hold land in *mortmain*, could the corporation enjoy the privilege of perpetual ownership and exemption from dues.[14] The corporation did not have to litigate under its members' names, but could sue and be sued, for better or for worse, in its separate personality, in the same manner as individuals. A corporation had to have a common seal, a unique feature of incorporation, and could make bylaws to govern its internal affairs.[15] As a legal entity, a corporation could receive additional franchises, liberties, and exemptions from the State, usually in the incorporating charter or act itself.

The Partnership

The employment of partnerships for business purposes has its origins in antiquity and the early middle ages. From this early period, the partnership was closely linked to business purposes. Since classical times, the partnership had been viewed as a legally enforced contract, one of several categories of agreements recognized by Roman law and medieval law merchant. By the late middle ages, several forms of business partnership agreements, or organizations, could be distinguished in the North Italian cities. They were loosely related to the Roman *societas*[16] but each acquired its own distinct attributes based on medieval economic realities, more than on classical texts and their scholarly interpretations. Some historians identify three or more distinct prototypes. Here I introduce the origins and characteristics of the two basic, more generally accepted forms: the general partnership and the limited partnership.

The continental unlimited business partnership, *société generale* or general partnership, descended from the Italian *compagnia*. In its origins, the *compagnia* was a closed family partnership. Family members were

---

[14]See Bernard Rudden, *The New River: A Legal History* (Oxford: Clarendon Press, 1985), 230–236, for a discussion of the *mortmain*. As we see in the next section, trusts were also devised to circumvent the same feudal dues in different manner.

[15]*The Case of Sutton's Hospital*, 10 Co. Rep. 23a, 30b (1610); Edward Coke, *Commentary upon Littleton*, 19th ed., 2 vols. (1832), vol. 2, p. 250a; William Shepheard, *Of Corporations, Fraternities and Guilds* (1659); Kyd, *Law of Corporations*, 69–70; Blackstone, *Commentaries*, vol. 1, pp. 462–467.

[16]*The Institutes of Justinian*, 3, 25.

its partners for all purposes. They invested capital and labor, based on ability; shared profits, based on needs and customs; and took part in its management according to a generational hierarchy. In fact, the early *compagnia* was less a formal partnership in internal affairs than a legal organization in its relationship with third parties. These had to know both that not all family members could always bind it and that all its assets were liable for its debts. In time, the internal affairs of the *compagnia* also became more formally fixed.

Another type of partnership, the *commenda* (also known as the *societas maris*) was developed in maritime Italian cities with the revival of trade in the eleventh century. It was used as a partnership between merchants and ship masters for the purpose of conducting a specific voyage to an overseas destination. This type of partnership was characterized, due to its unique use, as the cooperation among a small number of partners for a specific and short-term purpose. It was an asymmetric partnership, in which one partner contributed capital while the other contributed labor, which meant there were two types of partners with potentially different duties and liabilities. The model of the *commenda* was adopted in following centuries, under different names, in north German ports and other parts of continental Europe. This line of development from the maritime partnership eventually led to the limited partnership, which was recognized in 1673 in France by Colbert's Ordinance as the *société en commandite*.[17]

The general partnership arrived in England from the Continent via the internationally accepted and relatively universal law merchant. It was gradually absorbed from the various commercial and local tribunals and courts into the center of the English legal system, the royal common-law courts.[18] The unlimited partnership, which was recognized throughout the Continent, was not adopted by English law. By the time the general partnership was absorbed, the common law had already been formalized and rejected the limited partnership. The concept of a partner immune to claims conflicted with basic common-law forms of action and with tort, contract, and agency doctrines, and was therefore blocked by the common law from entering England. It was recognized in English law by statute only in 1907.

---

[17]Olivia F. Robinson, T. David Fergus and William M. Gordon, *European Legal History: Sources and Institutions*, 2d ed. (London: Butterworths, 1994), 100–105; Carlo M. Cipolla, *European Society and Economy before the Industrial Revolution: 1000–1700*, 3d ed. (London: Routledge, 1993), 194–196; Charles E. Freedeman, *Joint-Stock Enterprise in France 1807–1869: From Privileged Company to Modern Corporation* (University of North Carolina Press, 1979), 3–5; Michael Postan, "Partnership in English Mediaeval Commerce," in *Mediaeval Trade and Finance* (Cambridge University Press, 1973), 65–91.

[18]This process is discussed further in Chapter 6.

Partnerships of both types, unlike the corporation, had no legal personality distinct from that of its members. The partners were the holders of the property; they were the party in contracts, and they had to be named in litigation. Lacking a separate personality, the partnership did not have an immortal or even a perpetual existence. The death, retirement, or change of personal status (insanity, bankruptcy, and the like) of even one of its members signaled the end of the partnership. The remaining partners, if all wished to and were able to reach a new agreement, had to reorganize in a new partnership. A partnership, unlike a corporation, could be created voluntarily, by way of agreement between the would-be partners, and did not require permission of the State. Unlike the corporation, which had constitutional law bearings, the partnership was a private law and a commercial law conception, mainly involving elements of contract and agency law. Another significant difference which should be reiterated is that until the sixteenth century, the corporation had been employed for public and semipublic purposes, whereas only the partnership served as a viable form of business organization.

The Trust

Unlike the partnership and the corporation, the trust was not imported from the Continent. It is a unique English conception whose roots are not to be found in Roman law, canon law, merchant law, or the tribal and customary laws of medieval Europe. It deals with a continuous, not totally predetermined, relationship between individuals based on confidence.

The trust grew out of the "use" that stemmed from the realities and constraints of the English feudal system. In crude modern terms, common-law proprietors held the formal title over the land for the use of beneficiaries who had an equitable interest in that same land. The creation of uses was mainly motivated by the prohibition in some religious orders from holding property, the difficulties of absentee landowners such as the Crusaders to perform their feudal role, and, in time, mainly the evasion of feudal dues at death.

The common-law system was unable to deal with the use that created equitable rights to land that did not coincide with the legal rights to that same land. For this reason, the arrangements regarding the use, and later the trust, were generally not recognized and not enforceable in courts of common law. As early as the fourteenth or early fifteenth century, the Lord Chancellor acquired judicial supervision over disputes concerning such arrangements. By the late fifteenth century, the use became a relatively coherent equitable doctrine. Cases regarding uses and trusts comprised a considerable share of the total litigation within the expanding jurisdiction of Chancery.

The trust is of interest to us because it had an element of perpetuity and of joint holding, potentially on the part of both the trustees and the beneficiaries, and because it offered a separation between two levels of control over the trust's assets. It was a much more complex concept than mere joint-ownership in land. The trust (and earlier the use) was a fast-growing legal conception with some aggregate elements. It was constructed casually and voluntarily by way of explicit or implicit agreement between individuals. By the sixteenth century, it had already developed considerably and had the potential for further employment, and possibly also for business purposes.

One of the enigmas to be confronted in this book, then, is why the more flexible, expanding, and less-regulated concepts, the trust and the partnership, did not win the day. This enigma makes it essential, in my view, to follow the history of all three conceptions in search of an explanation for the rise to domination of the concept of the corporation. This will be done in the following chapters.

FEATURES OF BUSINESS ORGANIZATIONS

The authors of most corporate-law textbooks in recent decades focused on four basic features in analyzing the differences between the various forms of business organizations. These are the nature and lifespan of the legal personality, the transferability of interests, the organization and function of managerial hierarchy, and the limitation of investors' liability. These writers usually argued that modern business corporations differ from partnerships in all four features. Corporations have the advantage of a separate legal personality, free transferability of interests, limitation of shareholders' liability, and hierarchical managerial structure, whereas partnerships in most cases lack all four features. Hence, the argument goes, the corporation is legally, and possibly also economically, more efficient than the partnership and other "inferior" forms of organization.[19] These four features explain, so the argument says, the

[19]See, for example: Clark, *Corporate Law*; L.C.B. Gower et al., *Gower's Principles of Modern Company Law*, 5th ed. (London: Sweet and Maxwell, 1992). This legal discourse is distinct from the economic discourse, which focuses on elements which affect the boundary between hierarchical activity within the firm, whatever its legal structure, and contractual activity in the open market; and from the law and economics discourse, which focuses on analyzing the business corporation within the setting of the separation of ownership from control and a relatively efficient share market. These discourses analyze agency and monitoring problems, information, risk bearing, contracting costs, and transaction costs in general. All of these are highly relevant for the study of the history of the corporation in the late twentieth century, and are

rise of the corporate form of organization to dominance in late industrial societies. Their discovery, in the wilderness of archaic medieval legal concepts, or their invention by progressive and enlightened jurists, are of phenomenal importance for the rise of modern industrial capitalism. It would not be a gross overstatement to compare the discovery, or invention, of these features, which led to the corporate economy, to the discovery of America or the invention of the steam engine.

Were these features discovered by turning to classical and medieval legal texts, or invented in the modern era? Were they linked together as a cluster, or did each have its own separate history? Were they considered by contemporaries to be superior, in terms of efficiency, as a group or individually, or was there an element of efficiency in not having certain features or in having different combinations of organizational features? Were they inseparable from the corporate legal conception, or could they alternately be attached to the partnership, the trust, or other legal conceptions? I return to all four elements later, particularly in Chapters 5 and 6, and examine their interplay with several concrete forms of business organization, in the changing intellectual and material realities. At that point I argue that the second alternative in each of the above four questions is no less viable than the first.

Legal Personality, Managerial Hierarchy, and Limitation of Liability

The legal personality and the managerial hierarchy were already briefly introduced in the first part of this chapter, because they were features of the corporation (ecclesiastical, municipal, academic, or guild) even before it was first employed for pure business purposes in the sixteenth century. These corporations enjoyed a considerable degree of separation of their legal personality from that of their human members. Most had a hierarchical structure, which included heads, officials, members, and assemblies (or at least some of these organs), and a formal decision-making process including the power to make bylaws, to hold internal tribunals, and the like. I elaborate on these at a later stage.[20] Limited

probably of some relevance for the historical research of periods since the fundamental transformation associated with the rise of big business in the late nineteenth century. I find them less relevant to the earlier setting and the more basic questions in which I am interested.

[20]This book deals with the formal institutional structure of managerial structure. It deals only briefly with the structure of share holding: the nominal price of individual shares, minimum and maximum limitations on holding of shares by individuals, voting rights attached to shares, and the actual spreading of shareholding in various types of associations. All of these are worthy subjects of study for those wishing to understand the control and management mechanisms of business associations. They undoubtedly deserve fuller treatment elsewhere.

liability was absent, at least as a coherent conception, from the English legal framework until the late eighteenth century. It did not play a significant role in business organization before that relatively late era. Thus I do not discuss it in this chapter, except to briefly mention the limited partnership, in which it functions differently than in the limited corporation. I return to it in Chapter 5. For now, I turn to the fourth of these features: the evolution and meaning of transferability of interests, which is closely related to the financial conception of joint-stock capital.

Transferable Joint-Stock Capital

Joint-stock capital was a novel financial feature. It borrowed older elements from the business partnership, particularly the marine partnership, added new elements in the sixteenth and seventeenth centuries, and was eventually associated with the conception of the corporation, to form the joint-stock business corporation. This association took place at a relatively late stage in the history of the corporation. Only in the sixteenth century, when the corporation was first used for business purposes, did the preconditions for the emergence of this new feature occur. Efforts were made to integrate the feature of joint stock with the partnership and the trust, but as I shall argue later, this integration proved, at least in England, not to be a feasible alternative to the joint-stock business corporation.

The notion of joint stock only appeared in 1553. It took another century or so for it to crystallize and become widespread. Thus, one cannot speak of integration of the old legal conception with the new financial feature until the mid-seventeenth century. The development of the conception of joint stock and its integration into the corporation cannot be discussed in general and abstract terms, as it took place within the specific context of a small number of mostly merchant corporations, and within a well-defined time frame.

The Russia Company, chartered in 1553, was the first corporation to trade in joint stock, as discussed in the next chapter. The Levant Company, incorporated in 1581, also traded in joint stock in the first two decades of its existence. However, much of the development of the concept of joint-stock capital took place within the East India Company, chartered in 1600. Experiments were made using both ad hoc capital and capital for a term of years, and at times, the first was more profitable than the second. Additional capital was sometimes raised by issuing new shares to new members, at other times by calling on existing shares, and in some cases by raising loans rather than additional equity capital. In some circumstances, the entire capital, if not lost, was divided at the end of a voyage; in others, capital was divided up to the amount of the initial investments while profits were reinvested for future use; and yet in others, only the profits were divided while the initial investment was retained by the company until the end of the joint-stock term. One can even find several models coexisting simultaneously within the East India Company.[21] Yet toward the middle of the seventeenth century, a general pattern of development can be identified within the dominant East India Company: from ad hoc per voyage capital (1–3 years, invested in specific ships), to capital for limited duration (8–15 years), and finally to permanent and continuous capital. Thus from the mid-sixteenth to the mid-seventeenth century, a mechanism was developed for raising money in return for shares, for dividing profits among shareholders, for transferring shares among members and to outsiders, and for keeping accounts of joint-stock concerns for long durations.

This new mechanism did not develop as a legal conception, neither an abstract scholarly conception nor a case-based common-law one. It was a pragmatic, entrepreneur-made conception inspired partially by the modes of marine-partnership finance, and later employed within the framework of the corporation. Eventually the concept of joint stock was separated from that of the corporation, as it was utilized by other forms of organization, including the unincorporated company.

Court Jurisdiction

The application of a given court jurisdiction is not a positive feature of a concrete form of business organization. It is rather a by-product of the legal building blocks used in its formation. Different forms of organization were litigated in different courts, and this factor had at times far-reaching consequences for the prospects of these forms. I now provide a nutshell survey of the court and jurisdiction structure of the English legal system in our period.

At the heart of the English judicial system were the courts of the common law. There were three common-law courts: Common Pleas, King's Bench, and Exchequer. They were institutionalized as distinct courts in the formative period of the common law (mid-twelfth to early fourteenth centuries). During that period, they both complemented each other (each having its own field of specialization) and competed with each other over litigants. By the early eighteenth century, the competition

---

[21]For example, in 1611, capital was raised for four separate voyages. A second joint stock was raised in 1617 and the first was dissolved only four years later. Capital was separately raised in 1628, 1629, and 1630 for three Persian voyages, when the second joint stock still remained. K. N. Chaudhuri, *The English East India Company: The Study of an Early Joint-Stock Company 1600–1640* (London: Frank Cass, 1965), 209.

eased, and in the main, for our purposes, we can view the three as one departmentalized institution. Most of the litigation concerning the conception of the corporation and its various concrete forms of organization, and some aspects of disputes concerning the partnership conception and its offspring, were subject to the jurisdiction of the common-law courts.

Chancery was initially a secretarial and administrative department which assisted the Lord Chancellor. In the late fourteenth and early fifteenth century, it gradually acquired judicial functions institutionalized within a one-judge court, the Court of Chancery. The Lord Chancellor was the sole judge of this court until well into the industrial revolution. The jurisdiction of Chancery was not predetermined but evolved historically in response to the formalistic rigidity of the common law and the growing demand of litigants petitioning Chancery. Because of this, the Court of Chancery became a strong competitor of the three common-law courts. The competition between them reached its climax in the seventeenth century, and was not totally eased in our period. Chancery as an institution developed a set of judicial norms and doctrines, at times competing with and at times supplementing those of the common law. These norms, called "equity," were at first more particularistic, and flexible enough to allow a just solution for each singular dispute. In time, they became more general, formal, and predictable. The conception of the trust was created, recognized, and regulated only in the jurisdiction of Chancery and the norms of equity, and was nonexistent in common-law courts. Several aspects of the partnership were also litigated only in Chancery. So were aspects of the unincorporated company, which combined elements of the trust and of the partnership. The duality of the English legal system, which was in fact composed of the competing systems, common law and Chancery – equity, each having its own jurisprudence, doctrines, and institutions, and each having its own life cycle of formation and decay, is a key to understanding the history of business organization in England.

The central royal courts, those of the common law, and later joined by Chancery, competed successfully with older courts. By our period, these courts (local, feudal, and tribal) together with other non-royal courts (ecclesiastical and merchants courts) were swallowed by the royal courts, and became extinct or were marginalized. Two exceptions are worth mentioning because they remained relevant for our needs. One was stannary courts. These were local courts in tin-mining regions that survived the expansion of the common-law courts, and applied regional mining customs. The other was the High Court of Admiralty. This was a central court originating in the fourteenth century which was a specialized court, dealing with maritime and mercantile litigation, and did not apply the common law but rather an internationally recognized merchant law. The quasi-joint-stock partnerships – the mining cost book partnership and the shipping part-ownership – were each within one of these jurisdictions, stannary and Admiralty, respectively. We come across these forms of organization and their jurisdictions in the next section and in more detail in Chapter 7.

FORMS OF BUSINESS ORGANIZATION

In this section, I present a wider range of concrete forms of business organizations. Each of these forms is based on one or more of the legal conceptions introduced in the first section: the partnership, the corporation, and the trust. Each form embodied, or lacked, some or all of the four features of organization: separate personality, managerial structure, transferability of interests, and limitation of liability. The following analysis provides an initial comparison of the various forms of business organization and serves as a point of reference, as we turn to the actual world, in the next chapter. It surveys a wide range of forms, ending with the more aggregate, profit-oriented, and complex ones. The aggregate forms receive more attention in this section, not because they were more popular in our period (which they were not), but because they are the focus of this book.

The Sole Proprietorship

The legal framework in which the sole proprietor conducted his or her business did not distinguish between business activities and activities in any other sphere of life. Business assets were owned, conveyed, and managed by an individual, under the same rules of law and usually with no separation from other personal and family assets. The sole proprietorship did not employ any of the three collective legal conceptions, raised no problems of common ownership, transferability of interests, or separation between ownership and control. The sole proprietorship was an important form of business ownership in this period, but since it does not raise questions associated with the more complex forms of ownership and of business organization, it does not fit the general course of the present work and is not discussed further.

The Closed Family Firm

The family firm was based on kinship and mutual faith. Normally, it did not rely on any of the three legal conceptions discussed above, nor on other external laws, but rather on family values and traditions.[22] Management was based on the generational hierarchy within the family. All family members contributed the whole of their labor capability to the firm and enjoyed the use of the family capital. Profits were distributed according to need and tradition, or plowed back into the firm. Interest in the firm was transferred from one generation to the next by way of succession, according to family and inheritance laws, and regional and class customs. Disputes between family members were expected to be resolved informally within the family. In most cases, the closed family firm did not resort to external legal frameworks, such as the conception of the partnership.

Even though the closed family firm was a major form of business organization in pre- and early-industrial England, it, like the sole proprietorship, lies outside the scope of the present work. When a family firm became more formal in the legal relationship among its members, and more prone to external intervention in its structure, it fell into the category of the *compania* on the Continent, and the general partnership in England, and as such is discussed here.

The General Partnership

The English general partnership, or the co-partnership as it was more often called by contemporaries, was rooted in the continental *compagnia* and *société*, a variant of the legal conception of partnership. By the seventeenth and eighteenth centuries, these roots blended into the chaotic mixture of the common law.

As mentioned above, forming a partnership in England at this time, unlike the case of corporation, did not require State sanction. No specific

---

[22]For an interesting work on the relationship between family and enterprise, with reference to organizational forms, see Leonore Davidoff and Catherine Hall, *Family Fortunes: Men and Women of the English Middle Class, 1780–1850* (London: Hutchinson, 1987), esp. chap. 4. For the renewed interest in the family firm in business history, in industrializing Britain and in general, see Peter Payne, "Family Business in Britain: An Historical and Analytical Survey," in Akio Okochi and Shigeaki Yasuoka, eds., *Family Business in the Era of Industrial Growth: Its Ownership and Management* (University of Tokyo Press, 1984), 171–206; Roy Church, "The Family Firm in Industrial Capitalism: International Perspectives on Hypotheses and History," *Business History* 35, no. 4 (1993), 17–43; Mary B. Rose, ed., *Family Business* (Aldershot: Edward Elgar, 1995). Though they do not directly deal with the family firm, the arguments of the present work have bearing on its role in the Industrial Revolution. If indeed joint-stock enterprise played a larger role than hitherto believed, could it be that the family firm also played a larger and more dynamic role, as some new literature argues? The two forms are not mutually exclusive, but an attempt to reconcile the two arguments will not be easy.

procedure or written documents were required. All that was necessary and sufficient for forming a partnership was the consent of the partners to a communion of profits. Statutory exceptions to the general common-law principle of free and voluntary formation of partnerships existed in three sectors of the economy: banking, marine insurance, and the coal trade. The act that renewed the charter of the Bank of England in 1707[23] precluded partnerships of more than six partners from engaging in short-term note-issuing banking. The Bubble Act of 1720[24] precluded partnerships from engaging in marine insurance. An act of 1787 excluded partnerships of more than five members from the coal trade.[25]

Legally speaking, it made no difference whether all partners contributed finance, labor, or other resources or whether all intended to take part in the management, to bear losses if such occurred, or to receive only a small share of the profits. The common-law framework of the partnership applied to all partners in any undertaking in which sharing of profits existed. This framework was shaped by the dominant concept that a partnership, unlike the corporation, was not a legal entity. Based on this concept and on the actual disputes that were brought before it, the courts provided the law regulating the relationship among the partners, and of partners toward incoming and outgoing partners and third parties; the regulation of the formation, management, and dissolution of partnerships; and procedures and remedies in court. The status of the partnership was determined by the status of its individual members. The death or bankruptcy of a member terminated the partnership. Transfer of interest, in the form of retirement or replacement of a partner, required the consent of all partners and reorganization of the partnership. All partners had to join court litigations, and these could not be conducted using a common name. The liability of each of the partners for the debts of the partnership was not limited; each could be liable for the entire debt of the partnership to his last shilling.

The Limited Partnership

The limited partnership is distinct from the general partnership by virtue of the existence of two classes of partners. In addition to the active, or general, partners, who share management and liabilities in the concern, another class, usually called the passive, or sleeping, partners, share investments and profits with the general partners, but do not share in management or have unlimited liability. Thus, the limited partnership

[23] 6 Anne c.22 (1707).
[24] 6 Geo. I c.18 (1720).
[25] 28 Geo. III c.53 (1787).

enables wealthy individuals to invest in business without being fully involved in its day-to-day management or being exposed to economic risk and the social stigma of the business.

By the late eighteenth century, the limited partnership, descendant of the *commenda* variant of the partnership conception, was recognized by the legal systems of continental Europe. Widely used on the Continent, it served as an important tool for channeling aristocratic capital into commerce and industry. It was well known in England as well, and appreciated by many English lawyers and businessmen. From time to time, its introduction into England was discussed. After the enactment of the Irish Anonymous Partnership Act of 1782[26] and Napoleon's widely publicized Code de Commerce of 1807, it made its way to the state of New York in 1822, and from there to other states in the United States. However, the limited partnership was not recognized by common law, either directly or via the mercantile law, and made no inroads into the English legal system itself until the early twentieth century. It was finally introduced into the English system by statute in the Limited Partnership Act (7 Edw. VII c.24) of 1907.

English lawyers attempted to form general partnerships with de facto limited liabilities, utilizing various legal structures, in an attempt to circumvent the general common-law rejection of the idea of having two classes of partners, one of which had limited liability. The lawyers used two major structures for this purpose.

In the first structure, sleeping partners were known only to their active partners and were concealed from third parties. Thus, they could not be joined in any action against the partnership, and debts could not be collected from them. The problem in this structure was that sleeping partners had no standing in court or in any other external arena against their active partners or third parties, and had no real guarantee that their names would not be revealed at a most inconvenient moment, subjecting them to full liability.

According to the second structure, dormant partners were presented as lenders who received interest on their investments and were not liable to losses. The problem with this structure was that the essence of the transaction was not one of a loan repaid with fixed interest, but rather one of profit sharing. Since the dormant partners wanted to receive a return on their investment according to the prospects of the undertaking in which they had invested, they were exposed to the usury laws (which did not apply to partners, but did apply to lenders) if the undertaking was profitable and they received more than the legal interest rate of 5 percent. On the other hand, this was considered to be sharing profits,

[26] 21 & 22 Geo. III (Irish) c.46, (1782).

which, according to partnership law, was the ultimate test for perceiving them to be partners in the undertaking and, as such, was subject to unlimited liability for the partnership's debts. In conclusion, both the common-law doctrine and accepted practice in England did not enable the limited partnership to play any significant role in the organization of business in the eighteenth and nineteenth centuries.

The Quasi-Joint-Stock Partnership

Partnerships with some elements of joint stock or transferable interests appeared on the Continent only in the nineteenth century, starting with Napoleon's Code. They were not recognized by the English common law. However, in England itself, at a much earlier period, forms that could be labeled quasi-joint-stock partnerships emerged outside the realm of common law, in the areas of shipping and mining. Because of their peculiar path of historical development and their distinct economic circumstances, shipping and mining had a unique legal framework for business organization: the part-ownership in ships and the cost-book partnership system in mining. The first developed within the realm of the Admiralty court and the second within stannary jurisdiction. Both of these forms are discussed in detail in Chapter 7; for now, suffice it to say that though they rested on different legal bases, the two forms had an element of joint stock and of transferable interests.

The Unincorporated Joint-Stock Company

The unincorporated company was not distinguished as a separate form of business organization until in the late eighteenth century it was expressly adopted by businessmen, and in the early nineteenth century, lawyers began to discuss it. No unanimous definition of an unincorporated company existed in this period. The unincorporated company included elements of the partnership, trust, and corporation conceptions and was intended to have all four features that characterized the joint-stock corporation: transferable interests, limited liability, managerial hierarchy, and a degree of separate personality. In practice, as I show in Chapter 6, these features were acquired only partially, and not to a sufficient extent for most entrepreneurs.

The question of the nature of the unincorporated company arose in two instances. In the first, partnerships were initially formed with, or gradually grew to include, a large number of partners authorized to transfer their interests in the undertaking relatively freely. In the second, if a charter or act of incorporation was sought by the promoters, but for one reason or another the incorporation was not achieved, the promoted joint-stock scheme nevertheless continued. In both cases an intermediary form of organization, between the general partnership and the joint-stock corporation, appeared. The legal status of this form, the unincorporated company, is thoroughly examined in Chapter 6.

The Regulated Corporation

The regulated corporation, which emerged in England in the sixteenth century, as we shall observe in the next chapter, was built on the old legal conception of the corporation. From a formalistic legal perspective, the business corporation, whether regulated or joint-stock, was an aggregate (not sole), lay (not ecclesiastical), and civil (not eleemosynary) corporation. This categorization held not only for business corporations (regulated or joint-stock) but also for municipal and district corporations, the corporate bodies of Oxford and Cambridge, the Royal Society, the Society of Antiquaries, and the guild-like companies of the City of London. All of these corporations, and to a considerable degree other sorts of corporations as well, could be incorporated in the same patterns, enjoyed the same powers, capacities, and privileges, and were subject to the same remedies.

The regulated corporation, like the joint-stock corporation, and unlike earlier corporations, was formed purely for business purposes and aimed at profit maximization. In this period it could be incorporated only by the State. It had features of a separate legal entity with hierarchically structured managerial powers. The liability of its members, like that of the members of the joint-stock corporation, was not materially limited in early stages, as I shall discuss in Chapter 5. It had transferable joint stock only in a confined sense. Members of the regulated corporation traded in their own stock, taking risks and liabilities individually. Regulated companies collected entrance fees, annual payments, and duties on imported and exported goods. Money collected in this way was used to provide facilities for members, such as factories, embassies and consulates, and convoys. Thus, while each member performed routine trading separately, on his own account, much of the infrastructure was common, or in the form of joint stock. Members shared the investment in this infrastructure. They shared the expected increased profit due to better trading facilities and to a more stable political environment, as well as the possible loss of the investment if the infrastructure were damaged or captured. In fact, the difference between the regulated and the joint-stock corporation in terms of the joint-stock feature is one of degree rather than kind. The regulated corporation still had some elements in common with the older guild: It regulated and disciplined the business activities of its members. However its nature was less social, religious, or ritualistic, and more purely profit-oriented than that of the guild.

Regulated corporations played a major role in the development of English overseas trade in the late sixteenth and seventeenth centuries. However, by the end of the eighteenth century, they were almost passé. Wars, foreign competitors, changes in market conditions, interlopers, and the rise of joint-stock corporations, notably the East India Company, all led to the demise of the regulated corporations. The rise and decline of the regulated corporation is discussed in Chapter 2.

The Joint-Stock Corporation

The early joint-stock business corporation was not distinguishable in its legal framework from any other corporation of that era.[27] However, it combined the well-known legal conception of the corporation with the novel financial feature of joint stock. The joint-stock corporation, like the regulated corporation and unlike other corporations, aimed at profit maximization. Unlike the regulated corporation, the joint-stock corporation traded in only one account. That meant that members shared not only overhead but all business activities of the corporation, that is, all profits and losses. In this, the joint-stock corporation was somewhat similar to the general partnership. But while interests in the joint-stock corporation were relatively freely transferable, in the partnership they were not. In addition to the feature of transferability of interests, the joint-stock corporation, like other corporations and unlike partnerships, was also characterized by separate legal personality and concentration of management. Limitation of liability became an inherent feature of the joint-stock corporation only relatively late, in the eighteenth century. Even without limited liability, the joint-stock corporation was fundamentally different from the partnership and substantially different in degree, if not in kind, from the regulated corporation. This form of organization is addressed in many of the following chapters.

The Mutual Association

The mutuals differed from joint-stock corporations in the nature of their economic activities, though not necessarily in terms of the legal framework to which they were subject. Mutuals could be organized under various schemes: as corporations or as unincorporated firms, with or

---

[27]Business corporations were mentioned only briefly in the major eighteenth-century treatise on corporations, written in 1793–1794: Kyd, *Law of Corporations*. They are also only briefly noted in the chapter on corporations in Blackstone, *Commentaries*, vol. 1, pp. 458–459, 462–464.

Table 1.1. *Collective forms of business organization and their characteristics*

Form of organization	Aim	Legal conception	Features	Jurisdiction	Restrictions	Diffusion	Chapter where discussed further
General partnership	Profit	Partnership	None	Common law / Equity	Large partnerships illegal in banking, marine insurance, and coal trade	Spread	6
Limited partnership	Profit	Partnership	Limited liability	None	Not recognized in England	None	10
Quasi-joint-stock partnership	Profit	Partnership[a]	Separate personality[a] / Hierarchical managerial structure / Transferable stock[a]	Admiralty / Stannary	Only ships and mines within stannary jurisdiction (in the south-west)	Shipping: part-ownership / Mining; cost-book partnership	7
Mutual	Profit[a]	Corporation/ partnership	Varies	Common law / Equity	Varies	Insurance / Milling / Building loans	4

Unincorporated company	Profit	Partnership Trust	Hierarchical managerial structure[a] Transferable stock[a]	Common law Equity	Illegal, depending on interpretation of Bubble Act[a]	Insurance Birmingham area West Riding wool	4, 6, 9
Regulated corporation	Profit	Corporation	Separate personality Hierarchical managerial structure	Common law	Can be formed only by state sanction	Commerce	2
Joint-stock business corporation	Profit	Corporation	Separate personality Hierarchical managerial structure Transferable stock Limited liability[a]	Common law	Can be formed only by state sanction	Commerce Transport Utilities	2–5

[a] Only partial conformity to the characteristic, as explained in the text.

without permanent joint stock. The major difference between mutuals
and joint-stock companies was that the owners of mutuals (as their name
suggests) were also the consumers or clients. In the second half of the
eighteenth and the first half of the nineteenth century, mutuals could be
found in insurance offices, in which the owners-insurers were also the
insured, in building societies, in which the constructors would also be
the residents of the dwellings they built, and in loan banking, in which
the owners were to deposit and borrow.

The Nonbusiness and Nonprofit Organization

From a legal point of view, these organizations can be divided into two
groups: nonbusiness corporations and organizations formed as charitable trusts and regulated by the royal government through the Statutes of
Charitable Uses of 1597 and 1601. The former included hospitals,
schools, and theaters; whereas among the latter were mainly endow-
ments with an element of permanence, whose fruits were to be used for
charitable purposes while the original fund was perpetuated. The first
group is of no particular interest to us. The second is of some interest
because it was related to the conception of the trust, and because the
mechanism of its formation antedated that of general incorporation
statutes of the nineteenth century.

Table 1.1 summarizes the legal conceptions and the features embodied
in the major aggregate forms of business organization. It does not include a few organizations in the transportation sector, such as river
improvement commissions and turnpike trusts. These were to a degree
branches of local government, and were at least in theory non-profit in
their aims. They are presented in Chapter 4.

The attempt to compress a complex reality into a table format by
necessity lacks precision. Yet it provides an overview that may have been
lost in the detailed description above. This chapter as a whole is an
essential starting point for viewing three alternative legal conceptions –
the partnership, the corporation, and the trust – which are present and
at times compete with one another throughout the book. The four major
features of aggregate associations – transferability, liability, management, and personality – evolve over time and interact with these three
conceptions. What emerges is a picture of the legal framework of business organization between the mid-sixteenth and mid-nineteenth centuries which was constantly changing due to the interaction among legal,
political, and economic ideas and between these abstract ideas and the
changing material reality of England.

PART I

Before 1720

2

The Pre-1720 Business Corporation

In the second half of the sixteenth century and during the seventeenth century, the corporation, a familiar legal conception, increasingly began to be used for a new purpose. Employed since medieval times for ecclesiastical, municipal, educational, and other public or semipublic purposes, the corporation or, as it was often called at that time, the body corporate or body politic, was increasingly used for profit-oriented organization of business. There had been other, earlier, business associations such as guilds, but these had considerable social elements, and served as fellowships or brotherhoods which controlled and ritualized whole aspects of their members' lives. Prior to the sixteenth century, a number of groups of merchants such as the Merchants of the Staple and the early Merchant Adventurers traded with nearby continental ports, but these were associations of individuals usually with no formal legal basis, neither incorporation nor even a royal franchising charter. The novelty of the sixteenth-century corporation lay in the combination of specific business purposes with a formal corporate form of organization, and the fact that many of these new corporations reached beyond Western Europe. This new utilization, in kind and in degree, of the corporation for profit maximizing resulted in no immediate change in its legal conception nor in the features which characterized it. To what degree did the conception and features adapt to the new use by 1720, the starting point of this book? Did the pre-1720 history of the business corporation have any relevance to its post-1720 development?

The historical roots of the business corporation coupled with a backward-looking perception on the part of contemporary lawyers and others, I argue, play an important role in the later development of this institution. The development of the business corporation was more path-dependent than that of some other economic institutions because it employed a medieval legal conception, and because the first use of that conception for business or profit maximization was nested in a mercantilist era, not an industrial or a free-trade period. I hope to demonstrate in the coming chapters that throughout the eighteenth century and well into the nineteenth century, this early history of monopoly, overseas trade, and public finance still echoed in the contemporary discourse on business corporations.

The present chapter aims to provide the historical burden and the constraining path which were in force in 1720. To this end, it follows the English business corporation from the time it first appeared, in the mid-sixteenth century, until the early eighteenth century. It examines the emergence of two types of business corporations, the interplay between the two, the internal development of features and characteristics within each, their evolving relationship to the State, and the influence of the emergence of these concrete profit-oriented forms on the more abstract legal conception of the corporation. I divide this long stretch of time into three periods: the 1550s to the 1620s, the 1620s to the 1680s, and the 1680s to 1720.

FROM ORIGINS TO HEYDAY: THE 1550S TO THE 1620S

The early business corporations took two forms, regulated and joint-stock. With the exception of the regulated Merchant Adventurers, which was incorporated in 1505, the two forms emerged at about the same time, in the second half of the sixteenth century. Before turning to the differences between the two forms, already mentioned in Chapter 1, I present features common to both.

Only a few of the early business corporations were involved in the domestic market;[1] most were incorporated for overseas trade. During this period, the establishment of corporations required State authorization, which normally meant a royal charter. In addition to explicit incorporating clauses, the charters of overseas trading corporations also included clauses which granted the corporation a monopoly over English trade with a specified territory abroad. Since most of the sixteenth-century investors in merchant companies were personally involved in overseas trade, they were well aware of the risks of the high seas and of foreign, unfamiliar, and even hostile countries, particularly at an age in which marine insurance had not yet made significant inroads into England. They wanted to be sure that after making the initial investment and accepting, at times, personal risks, they would be in a position to

---

[1]Scott lists the Mines Royal (1561), the Mineral and Battery Works (1565), and the New River Water Supply Company (1608) as the only domestic joint-stock companies formed before 1630. See Scott, *Constitution and Finance of Joint-Stock Companies*, vol. 3, pp. 462–470.

profit from future trade with the territory. The monopoly granted by the Crown could relieve at least some of their worries. These early groups of merchants did not settle merely for license from the Crown; they sought exclusive license. In modern economic jargon, they could be labeled rent-seekers.

I argue that monopoly became an almost inherent characteristic of the early business corporations, and a major factor in their future development. The typical charter of a business corporation limited its membership by demanding relatively high membership fees or a significant contribution to the joint stock of the corporation. It gave the corporation the power to govern the Englishmen residing in a particular area. In practice, that meant territorial monopoly of trade for members of regulated corporations, or for officers and employees trading in joint stock of joint-stock corporations, and a barrier to the admission of outsiders into company territory. The corporate trade monopoly not only gave permission to self-enforce the monopoly but also granted State enforcement of the monopoly against competition from nonmember Englishmen, as well as some degree of sponsorship by the State vis-à-vis indigenous rulers and competing European merchants. In these early days of the business corporation, monopolistic privileges were seen as almost integral to the act of incorporation because of the nature of the companies' activities.

From the point of view of the Crown, the evolving monopoly system was more than welcome. The payment received for granting monopolies contributed significantly to the Court's attempt to close the gap between its declining land revenues and its growing military and civil expenses.[2] What made the monopoly system most attractive for Elizabeth, James I, and certainly Charles I was the fact that, at a time when the constitutional idea of no taxation without representation had already gained recognition, this system enabled them to raise their income while avoiding the parliamentary supervision set on other sources of revenue, notably on taxes.[3]

---

[2]There are of course other possible explanations for the development of the monopoly system: as a means to conduct foreign policy, a mechanism for the encouragement of foreign trade or an attempt to gain State control over business activities. The historiography on the origins of mercantilism and the monopoly system is too immense to be covered here. See Eli F. Heckscher, *Mercantilism*, rev. ed., 2 vols. (London: G. Allen and Unwin, 1955), and Robert B. Ekelund and Robert D. Tollison, *Mercantilism as a Rent-Seeking Society: Economic Regulation in Historical Perspective* (College Station, Texas: A & M University Press, 1981), for two stages in this long debate.

[3]Michael J. Braddick, *The Nerves of State: Taxation and the Financing of the English State, 1558–1714* (Manchester University Press, 1996), 131–144, and references in it. F. W. Maitland, *The Constitutional History of England* (Cambridge University Press, 1908; rpt., Cambridge University Press, 1968), 251–275.

Thus, during the Elizabethan and early Stuart reigns, monopolies were granted to business corporations in return for payments to the Crown. The payments had various names and were made before, during, or after the grant of the monopolistic privileges. Payment was made in return for franchises, charters, and licenses.[4] In addition, direct involvement of the Monarch in the formation and ownership of joint-stock companies was not uncommon during that period. Such involvement may have been motivated by foreign policy considerations, but always involved the expectation of economic benefit, usually in the form of dividends.[5] Corporations were major importers and exporters of goods with a considerable share in the total custom payment to the Crown. Thus, they played a role in public finance not only as buyers of privileges but also as large taxable business enterprises. Furthermore, because during this period the system of collecting customs payments was based on farming, the companies became efficient agencies of collection, from their members, on behalf of the State.[6] During the Elizabethan and early Stuart reigns, the companies did more than contribute to the revenue side of the public budget. They played an important role in reducing expenses. Companies took upon themselves expenses otherwise carried by the State. They covered the expense of maintaining embassies and other overseas representatives as well as forts and other naval, military, and trade facilities.[7] Business corporations were also called on to cover expenses of the fleet that presumably protected their interests.[8] In conclu-

---

[4]These payments could be termed royalties, voluntary payments, or even bribes, but their purpose was the same. For one example, see Frederick C. Dietz, *English Public Finance, 1558–1641*, 2d ed. (London: Frank Cass, 1964), 159, 163, 166, 169, on the payments made by the Merchant Adventurers in 1614–17.

[5]For example, Elizabeth was involved in the first company of African Adventurers in 1561, James I had a share in the ownership of the New River Company after 1612, and Charles I tried to be admitted to the East India Company in 1628. See Scott, *Constitution and Finance of Joint-Stock Companies*, vol. 2, 5–8; Rudden, *The New River*, 15–17, 38–40, and appendices for transcripts of some of the original documents; Scott, ibid., vol. 2, pp. 109–110.

[6]For the disputes between the Levant Company and Elizabeth and the early Stuarts over the impositions on imported currants, see Dietz, *English Public Finance*, 88–89, 132, 252–254, 364–366. For the conflict of interest between the tax farmers and the Levant Company and other trading companies within a wider political and constitutional context, see Robert Ashton, *The City and the Court: 1603–1643* (Cambridge University Press, 1979), 129–141.

[7]That was the case with the Levant Company, which financed the embassy in Constantinople, and other consulates that served the interests of the trading community as well as the government of England. See Scott, *Constitution and Finance of Joint-Stock Companies*, vol. 2, pp. 86–87, and Alfred C. Wood, *A History of the Levant Company* (Oxford University Press, 1935; rpt., London, 1964), 80–94.

[8]In 1619, six great trading companies, East India, Merchant Adventurers, Levant, French, Eastland, and Muscovy (Russia), were levied to cover two years' service of

sion, the first generations of business corporations were linked to public finance in a wide variety of ways and were exploited by the Crown as an important source of handy, liquid, and politically accessible income.

The early business corporations, having the above-mentioned characteristics in common, took two organizational forms: regulated corporations and joint-stock corporations. Though they emerged simultaneously, the two forms diffused into distinct fields of operation. The short-distance trade to nearby Western European ports was organized in regulated companies: The Spanish Company, whose trade also covered Portugal, was chartered in 1577; the Eastland Company, for trading with the Baltic Sea and Scandinavia, was chartered in 1579; the French Company in 1609. The 1505 charter of the old Merchant Adventurers was extended from Flanders to the Low Countries and Germany at about the same time.

On the other hand, long-distance trade to the outlying frontiers of Europe and to other continents, only entered by English traders during this period, was initially organized in joint-stock corporations. The first of these was the Russia Company (also known as the Muscovy Company), founded in 1553 and chartered in 1555. The Levant Company (Turkey Company) was formed in 1581 for trade with Turkey and the Eastern Mediterranean. Other minor companies, for trade with Africa and other remote areas, were incorporated at about the same time.[9]

After 1606, another type of corporation, the colonial corporation, appeared to settle Virginia, Massachusetts Bay, and other regions in Atlantic North America. I do not elaborate on this type of corporation because its aim was not purely profit maximization, and in my judgment, it had only marginal effect on the post-1720 development of the business corporation in England. Its effects in colonial North America have received due attention by U.S. historians and are not be dealt with here.[10] In the long run, the most significant of these early companies was undoubtedly the East India Company, initiated in 1599 and chartered in

the fleet sent to suppress the pirates of Algiers. See Dietz, *English Public Finance*, 175.

[9]To extend the list, mention can be made of some abortive, short-lived, or otherwise minor companies: the Merchant Adventures for Guinea, the Senegal Adventures, the Gynney and Bynney Company, the Greenland Company, the Barberry (or Morocco) Company, the Canary Company, the Cathay Company, and the North West Company. For the history of the North East Company, which is typical of this category of minor companies, see Carole Shammas, "The 'Invisible Merchant' and Property Rights," *Business History* 17, no. 2 (1975), 95–108. The above list does not claim to be conclusive, as other companies may have escaped my search or left no trace in records.

[10]For colonial companies, see Scott, *Constitution and Finance of Joint-Stock Companies*, vol. 2, pp. 241–360.

1600. In its charter it was granted monopolistic trading rights from the Cape of Good Hope to the Straits of Magellan.[11]

The division of English trade between regulated and joint-stock corporations was not static. For a while, most of the long-range trade, from Russia and the Orient to Africa and Asia, was conducted by several joint-stock corporations. On the accession of the first Stuart King, James I, in 1603, the entire English short-range trade from the Baltics through Western Europe to Spain was divided among four major regulated companies. But the division between joint-stock corporations, regulated corporations, and open trade soon began to shift. The Spanish Company was deprived of its monopoly and dissolved in 1606. The monopoly of the French Company was attacked and that of the Merchant Adventurers limited. Two of the major joint-stock corporations were reorganized as regulated companies: the Levant between 1588 and 1595, and the Russia in 1622–1623. The further away the market of a corporation was, the more likely it was to retain its monopoly and its joint-stock form.

An interesting and often overlooked trend during this period is the reorganization of joint-stock corporations as regulated corporations. It is too often believed that the joint-stock form was invented later than the regulated, was instantly appreciated as more efficient, and as such, rapidly replaced the older and inferior regulated company. It is also claimed that, in itself, the joint-stock form evolved from ad hoc capital raised separately for each voyage, to capital for a period of years, and finally to permanent and perpetual capital, out of which only timely profits were distributed to shareholders. This was clearly not the case before the 1620s. The financial structure of the Levant Company, established on a joint-stock basis in 1581, was debated as the charter expired in 1588. The merchants opposing joint trade had the upper hand, and the new charter of 1592 incorporated the Levant as a closed regulated company with high admission fees.[12] The first joint-stock company, the Russia, retained its financial structure, permanent joint-stock, for thirty-one years. The initial, paid-up capital on shares did not cover the high expenses of establishing the new trade nor the losses of ships and cargo. This meant that, in later years, more calls were made on shares, with no

---

[11]For the history of the first two joint-stock companies, see T. S. Willan, *The Early History of the Russia Company 1553–1603* (Manchester University Press, 1956), and Wood, *The Levant Company*. For the early history of the East India Company and its transformation into the first joint-stock company with perpetual capital, see Chaudhuri, *East India Company*. For a recent survey of the finance of the early trading companies, focusing on the East India Company, see Jonathan Barron Baskin and Paul J. Miranti, *A History of Corporate Finance* (Cambridge University Press, 1997), 55–88.

[12]Wood, *The Levant Company*, 16–23.

dividends in sight. As a result, in 1586, the company was financially reorganized under the same legal form, but using short-term rather than perpetual capital organized in several separate accounts, each for a period of one to three years. Beyond the difficulty in collecting from the original shareholders, this change stemmed from the intention to raise money in wider circles, to give more discretion to traders, to pay dividends more frequently, and to simplify accounting.[13] By 1622–1623, this process had been taken one step further and the separate accounts were replaced by individual accounts. With this step, the Russia Company was in fact organized as a regulated corporation.[14] From the above, we can see that permanent joint-stock turned out to be a problematic and undesirable feature for the early business corporations. It survived only in the exceptional case of the East India Company, and in highly adventurous one-time voyages to the remote shores of Africa and the Atlantic. There was no hint in this period of the later rise to dominance of the joint-stock corporation at the end of the seventeenth century. This would come as a surprise to the Levant and Russia merchants who had resolutely abandoned it.

The first two decades of the seventeenth century can probably be characterized as the heyday of the initial age of the history of the business corporation. About forty companies, including short-lived ones, were founded during this period. These companies were granted monopolistic privileges over much of the known world. Total membership in these companies was almost 10,000.[15] They played a major role in the overseas expansion of England in terms of commerce, colonization, and naval power.

A typical business corporation of this first period combined the legal framework of the medieval semipublic corporation with the more capitalistic-mercantilist aims of contemporary merchants. Such a corporation was usually established by royal charter that, in addition to the traditional and inherent privileges of having corporate entity, also granted monopolistic privileges. It was, with but few exceptions, involved in overseas trade and occasionally also in settlement. The corporation was usually regulated, in some instances traded in joint stock, but had no permanent stock. Typically, such a corporation was deeply involved in matters of public finance. It relied on the State for privileges and protection, and the State relied on it as a major source of finance, especially in times of crisis.

[13]Willan, *The Russia Company*, 41–47, 211–216.
[14]Ibid., 273.
[15]Theodore K. Rabb, *Enterprise and Empire: Merchant and Gentry Investment in the Expansion of England, 1575–1630* (Cambridge, Mass.: Harvard University Press, 1967), 72–77, 104.

THE DECLINE: THE 1620S TO THE 1680S

The decline of the monopoly system and of the great trading companies began late in the reign of James I. James was in urgent need of nonparliamentary income, and was running short of salable land. Thus, on a much larger scale than Elizabeth, he developed the system of selling monopolistic privileges as a means of bypassing Parliament. He divided business activities under his realm into small segments and tried to sell monopolistic privileges for engaging in each. In this way, a large number of monopolies, not only for overseas trade but also for domestic and even regional trade and manufacture, were sold by the King to individuals and corporations.

The Statute of Monopolies of 1623 was passed during one of the peaks of the long conflict between the early Stuarts and the Parliament and common-law judges.[16] The original aim of the Statute of Monopolies, as designed by the dismissed Chief Justice of King's Bench, Edward Coke, was to deprive the King of his power to freely sell new monopolies. The passage of the statute was intended to block an alternative source of income and force the King to turn to Parliament for permission to raise more taxes.

The wider conflict was between the idea of absolute royal sovereignty on one hand, and parliamentary supremacy coupled with the notion of "no taxation without representation" on the other. The parliamentary camp tried to take advantage of James's financial and political difficulties in order to diminish his strength by refusing to approve additional taxes to finance an army to join the Catholic coalition during the Thirty Years' War.

Yet the final outcome was not as radical as Coke envisioned. The compromised Statute of Monopolies included exceptions to the above principle, pushed through by the King's supporters, one of which is relevant in the present context: It would not extend to existing monopolies or trade corporations.[17] Moreover, whether intentionally or not, the statute left a loophole which enabled the King to include in charters of incorporation the authority to make bylaws and hold jurisdiction over Englishmen within the boundaries of a given territory. This, in fact, empowered these corporations to prevent nonmembers from trading within these territories. Thus, the Statute of Monopolies, which seemed

---

[16]The conflict had many faces and phases, political and religious, social and legal, constitutional and institutional. I avoid entering into the immense historiographical debates on the origins of the Civil War (or Revolution). In this chapter, I selectively discuss only a few of the effects of this long conflict on business organization.

[17]21 Jac. I c.3 (1623), section 9. Another important exception related to granting monopoly for the use of inventions. Section 5 of the statute, which allowed granting such monopolies for a period of up to 14 or 21 years, was one of the origins of patent law.

at first glance to hinder business corporations, in fact gave them an advantage over individuals as they could be granted monopoly privileges in a manner in which individuals could not.

Shortly after his accession in 1625, Charles I, who was in conflict with Parliament, turned, among other measures, to the old practice of selling monopolies by exploiting to the utmost the exceptions and loopholes in the Statute of Monopolies. He sliced the potential economic activities of the realm, both domestic and overseas, into small segments, and planned to sell franchises to the highest bidder, generally in the form of incorporation. He based this on his constitutional conception that all economic activities of English subjects are subordinate to the King's prerogative. His intention was to establish a constant stream of income beyond the authority of Parliament. For a while, in the late 1620s and early 1630s, the King was able to raise an annual income of £100,000 or more from the sale of monopolies. However, in the long run, the political instability of the 1640s led to the frequent incorporation of new companies that rivaled established ones, to the expropriation or limitation of incorporation charters, the lack of enforcement of monopolies, and tacit encouragement of pro-King interlopers. With the instability, lack of enforcement, and inconsistency of the State, the market value of monopolistic charters deteriorated. Thus, from the later years of the reign of Charles I, through the Civil War, and to the Interregnum, the position of the business corporation as a viable form of business organization steadily declined.

The Merchant Adventurers, the Levant Company, and the East India Company were the three companies whose privileges suffered most from the policies of Charles I and from competition with his favorite merchants.[18] The Civil War was not the best period for corporations chartered by the King. The Commonwealth found it difficult to maneuver between stability, which meant ratifying the charters of older companies; loyalty to its supporters, which meant creating new corporations; and ideological commitments, which could mean the abolition of monopolies altogether.

The Interregnum was a period of uncertainty for overseas trade in general. Most companies suffered considerable losses during the Anglo-Dutch war, due to closures of markets, seizure of ships, and governmental pressure to invest in fortification, subsidize the Navy, and lend money to the Treasury. The Eastland Company claimed that the Commonwealth government, which was allegedly ideologically hostile to monopolies, did not give it the support needed to protect its privileges in foreign ports.[19] The Russia Company supposedly lost its rights because

---

[18] Ashton, *City and Court*, 121–141.

[19] R.W.K. Hinton, *The Eastland Trade and the Common Weal in the Seventeenth Century* (Cambridge University Press, 1959), 84–94.

the Czar identified it as anti-Royalist.[20] The East India Company was thrown into competition with the Dutch East India Company, and its monopoly was later suspended due to the pressure of traders who objected to the joint-stock method. In addition to these difficulties, it was forced to lend the government £60,000.[21] The Merchant Adventurers, who supported Parliament, had to lend the army and navy some £60,000 in the early years of the Civil War.[22] Whether they supported the Commonwealth or not, the trading companies' position deteriorated during that period.

The Restoration did not reverse the previous trend. In 1662, the monopoly of the Merchant Adventurers was limited to only two ports: Dordrecht and Hamburg. In 1689, after a short revival of its old monopoly, the company, now known as the Hamburg Company, lost its monopoly in one stroke when monopolies on wool export were altogether abolished by a general statute. The French Company's monopoly ended when the company itself was dissolved in 1667. In 1673 the monopolistic privileges of the Eastland Company for the western part of the Baltic – Sweden, Norway, and Denmark – were eliminated and the company itself opened to outside traders. The Dutch and French wars, which increased State involvement in trade to the region, made the company dispensable even to those of its members trading with the Eastern Baltic. The diminished Eastland Company was finally dissolved in 1689. The Russia Company, by now a regulated company, struggled during the Restoration to retain the monopoly in the hands of a few members. In 1698 it was forced by law to admit practically anyone who would pay £5 for membership, and thus it became an open regulated company and any remainder of its past monopoly disappeared. The Levant Company decayed more slowly. In the late seventeenth century, due to competition from the East India Company, which was able to buy many goods directly from its source in Arabia and Central Asia, the overland trade of the Levant Company became outdated. After 1689, its trade was doomed because its sea routes in the Mediterranean were taken over by competing French fleets and merchants. In 1753, following decades of diminishing trade, barriers of entry to the company were practically removed.[23]

[20]Rudolph Robert, *Chartered Companies and Their Role in the Development of Overseas Trade* (London: F. Bell and Sons, 1869; rpt., London, 1969), 62–63.

[21]Maurice P. Ashley, *Financial and Commercial Policy under the Cromwellian Protectorate*, 2d ed. (London: Frank Cass, 1962), 112–115.

[22]Ibid., 121–125.

[23]The admission fees to the company were reduced to £20 and the requirement that members be freemen of the City of London was abolished. However, the company officially surrendered its charter only three-quarters of a century later, in 1825. For the decline of the Levant Company, see Wood, *The Levant Company*, 136–204.

The Royal African Company and the Hudson's Bay Company, incorporated during the Restoration, seem to have developed in contrast to this declining trend. These companies are exceptional in several respects: Both were incorporated at a relatively late date and both operated in British America (thus receiving unproportional attention from modern North American historians). The former was also unique in that it traded in human beings, running a triangular trade, and thus not relying on England as the sole target market; the latter had an exceptionally small scale of operation. Was it these contrasts which explained their different fates during this second period?

The Royal African Company received a charter of incorporation from Charles II in 1672, which included a monopoly on the slave trade between West Africa and the West Indies. It flourished for a while, experiencing its heyday in the 1680s, when it accounted for more than two-thirds of the slave deliveries to the Indies. Yet it declined rapidly after the Glorious Revolution as it could not get parliamentary ratification of its royal monopoly. Only in 1698 was it able get an Act of Parliament which entitled the company to receive a 10 percent duty on all exports from the West Coast of Africa for the purpose of keeping up its forts in the service of all traders. However, this act expired and the trade became totally free in 1712, and from then until its final dissolution in 1752, the only activity of the company was running coastal forts for the government, subject to public finance. Interestingly, recent research in economic history suggests that even in the 1680s the company was not able to fully enforce its monopoly, as a result of political pressure by the planters. In addition, because of competition from the fringe – foreign traders, English interlopers, and the company's own agents (such as ship captains who boarded slaves on their own account side by side with company slaves) – it was not able to control supply and prices.[24]

The Hudson's Bay Company was chartered in 1670 as a joint-stock corporation. It was granted a trade monopoly over the Hudson Bay drainage basin and used it mainly for the fur trade. Its monopolistic charter was renewed after the Glorious Revolution because of the French political and commercial threat to the region. The small scale of its activities enabled the corporation to stay off the agenda when other corporate monopolies were abolished.[25] Its monopoly was finally inves-

---

[24]David W. Galenson, *Traders, Planters, and Slaves: Market Behavior in Early English America* (Cambridge University Press, 1986), 13–21; Ann M. Carlos and Jamie Brown Kruse, "The Decline of the Royal African Company: Fringe Firms and the Role of the Charter," *Economic History Review* 49, no. 2 (1996), 291–313.

[25]Scott, *Constitution and Finance of Joint-Stock Companies*, vol. 2, pp. 228–236; Ann M. Carlos and Stephen Nicholas, "Agency Problems in Early Chartered Companies: The Case of the Hudson's Bay Company," *Journal of Economic History* 50, no. 4 (1990), 853–875.

tigated by Parliament around the middle of the eighteenth century, but
was not abolished until 1869.

In conclusion, toward the end of the seventeenth century, with but a
few exceptions, trade by either joint-stock or regulated corporations
which enjoyed the privilege of overseas territorial monopolies almost
entirely disappeared. From Turkey through Spain, France, the Low
Countries, and Germany to the Baltic, Russia, and West Africa, markets
controlled by corporate monopolies in the heyday of the trading companies of the early seventeenth century were, by the turn of the eighteenth century, open to other traders. This was the result of opening
regulated corporations to outsiders, abolishing corporate monopolies,
and dissolving corporations altogether. The process can be explained in
several ways: It can be attributed to the political, constitutional, and
financial changes in the English State, which affected its links to business
corporations; to the inefficiency of the trading corporations, because of
problems in management, agency, and information, costly infrastructure,
or deficient legal features; to international factors; or to the unique
circumstances of each corporation. It was caused directly by individual
interlopers striving to invade the monopolies, by the struggle for privileges among the different monopolistic companies, by conflicts over
authority between the Crown and Parliament, by internal organizational
failure, by local crises in the markets, by foreign fleets, and by competition from foreign merchants. In my judgment, the timing of the decline
can best be explained by the political upheavals which caused considerable inconsistency in the granting and enforcing of monopolies. Whatever the reason and the course, it is the outcome that is more important
for the present argument: the decline of the great trading corporations.[26]

The collapse of the monopoly system coincided with the decline in
the importance of business corporations to public finance. The corporations' contribution to public finance had been based on the monopoly
system, and died with it. The causality in this case is two-sided, but
additional constitutional and financial factors accelerated the demise.
After the Civil War, parliamentary control over State incomes was more
effective, and the loopholes smaller. In addition, new parliamentary-
controlled sources of revenue were exploited and new taxes introduced
during these troubled times. The most significant of the new taxes, in

---

[26]It is interesting to connect their decline to the recent debate over the rationale for
the rise of the trading corporation. See S.R.H. Jones and Simian P. Ville, "Efficient
Transactors or Rent-Seeking Monopolists? The Rationale for Early Chartered Trading Companies," *Journal of Economic History* 56, no. 4 (1996), 898–915; Ann M.
Carlos and Stephen Nicholas, "Theory and History: Seventeenth-Century Joint-Stock
Chartered Trading Companies," *Journal of Economic History* 56, no. 4 (1996), 916–
924.

the long run, was the excise. It fell mainly on basic domestic consumption goods and thus taxed the poor. In a way, the excise substituted for revenues from the monopoly system, because payments that had previously been collected from the holders of the monopolies were now rolled onto the consumers and collected directly from them.[27] Another old-new source of parliamentary taxation was customs. Most types of customs were within royal prerogative until 1641. But in 1641 and again in 1660 this changed, and by the Restoration, Parliament had attained effective control over this source of income. This control, and the gradual rise in the value of imports by individual merchants, made customs income another good substitute for income seized directly from the merchant corporation. The elimination of the function of the corporation as an agency for collecting taxes, together with the abolition of farming as a tax collection method in the years 1671–1683 and the introduction of administrative tax collection, also contributed to its demise. The trend after the Restoration was from collecting lump sums in return for charters of incorporation once every seven to fourteen years (typically), through collecting moderate sums in return for short-duration tax farming rights, to collecting small sums per deal or season directly by the State. This enabled the State to smooth its flow of revenue and to receive a higher percentage of the taxable potential. In conclusion, the significance of monopolies and of business corporations to public finance eroded between the 1630s and the Glorious Revolution. This occurred not only because the monopoly system was collapsing and the ties of the corporations to public finance were damaged from within, but also because other sources of revenue were being developed and exploited and the relative importance of the companies as a source of revenue was reduced from without.

Around the time of the Glorious Revolution, the position of the business corporation was quite different from its position at its heyday early in the century. First, the general trend was one of decline. The business corporation was used much less frequently. Between 1631 and 1680 less than ten new companies were formed.[28] Second, within this general trend of decline, an internal trend that had begun earlier continued. Joint-stock corporations were transformed into regulated ones, while regulated corporations turned into open regulated and eventually into governmental or ceremonial entities. Third, following the successful model of the East India Company, the few joint-stock corporations

[27]C. D. Chandaman, *The English Public Revenue, 1660–1688* (Oxford: Clarendon Press, 1975); Braddick, *Nerves of State*.

[28]Scott, *Constitution and Finance of Joint-Stock Companies*, vol. 3, pp. 470–472. Of these, only four lasted for a considerable period of time, the Royal African, Hudson's Bay, York Buildings, and the Lead Company.

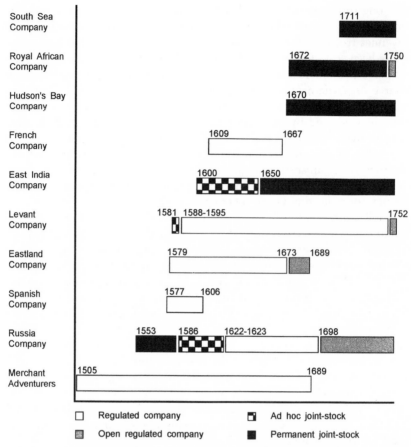

Figure 2.1. Organizational transformation in major trading corporations, 1505–1750.

formed in this period were organized with permanent rather than ad hoc and dividable capital. Fourth, monopoly privileges were no longer an essential part of every incorporation, and legal entity, capital, and other considerations could justify application for incorporation even without the grant of monopoly. Fifth, the two-way financial dependence between business corporations and the State diminished. Most of these trends are summarized in Figure 2.1.

Though many changes had occurred in the characteristics of business corporations and in the context in which they functioned, perception of these changes was slow. There were many in official circles, the legal profession, the business community, and the general public who still identified corporations with monopoly and its outcomes. Most of the seventeenth century was a downhill trip for the business corporation. The use of this form of business organization in novel and innovative ways was slow to come. But by the time of the Glorious Revolution, some new beginnings could be seen.

THE RISE OF THE MONEYED COMPANIES: THE 1680S TO 1720

After the 1680s, and particularly after the Glorious Revolution, four new trends can be identified, which justify the perception of the 1680s, or of 1689, as the beginning of a new, third period in the history of the business corporation. The first of these trends lies in the rise to dominance of three companies: the East India Company, the Bank of England, and the South Sea Company, which came to be known as the moneyed companies, and began to shape attitudes toward business corporations in general. They grew to be considerably different from other joint-stock corporations in their size, their role in public finance, and their economic and political importance. Second, after a prolonged decline, the joint-stock feature gained new popularity and in the 1690s many new companies were promoted on a vigorous stock market. This renewed popularity was coupled with the formation of numerous companies outside the overseas trade sector, that is, in domestic manufacture and trade. Third, the method for establishing corporations began to change as Parliament rose to dominance after the Revolution. An act of Parliament, or a charter coupled with an act, became the more common method of forming a company, while incorporation only by charter became rare. Last, in this period, for the first time, the joint-stock feature was employed without State incorporation in several, mostly not long-lasting, instances. Associations of individuals were formed within the framework of a new organizational form: the unincorporated joint-stock company.

The appearance of unincorporated companies after 1689 can be explained by the positive incentive found in the emergence of a booming stock market. On the negative side, it can be explained by the unwillingness of the newly organized Orange administration to fiercely enforce its prerogative over evaders of incorporation because such enforcement was identified with the absolutist Stuart tendencies of the seventeenth century. Attempts by the new monarch to prosecute unincorporated companies after the famous Stuart trial over revoking the charter of the Corporation of London in 1682 could prove highly unpopular.[29] We

---

[29]*The King v. The City of London,* 8 Howell's State Trails 1039 (1681–1683).

return to this novel form of organization in the next two chapters, when turning to periods in which it became more significant.

As the eighteenth century approached, the importance of the national debt and its management increased and, with it, the importance of the moneyed companies to public finance. During the Elizabethan and early Stuart reigns, the last resort in times of financial crises when tax revenues were not sufficient was selling of Crown and Church lands. The massive sale of land during that period and the Interregnum created a new reality for Restoration finance.[30] Since land was running out, Crown lands ceased to be a substantial source of annual income, and, worse, they could not serve as a reserve for emergencies.

Loans were of minor use to the Crown before the Restoration, mainly for short-term finance in anticipation of forthcoming tax revenues.[31] The business corporations, with but a few minor exceptions, were not involved in loans to the State during this period.[32] Strict parliamentary control over taxation after the Restoration forced Charles II to seek new lenders. Potential lenders had to have considerable liquid capital, and these included the Corporation of London and tax farmers, as in the past, but, in addition, also goldsmith-bankers and business corporations. Joint-stock companies were a better source of loans than regulated companies, because they had more ready cash in their possession. The larger and more successful a joint-stock company was, the more useful it was to the Crown. The East India Company, with its considerable permanent capital and its profitable commercial activities, soon became a primary source of loans to the Crown, lending it more than £230,000 in money and saltpeter between 1669 and 1678.[33] Thus, even before the Glorious

[30]The sale of land was approximately as follows: £813,000 by Elizabeth, £775,000 by James I, £650,000 by Charles I, £4,000,000 in Church and Crown land during the Interregnum. Charles II was able to sell lands to the value of £1,300,000. By this he practically eliminated land as a source of revenue, both in rents and in one-time sales. See Dietz, *English Public Finance*, 298–299, and Christopher Hill, *The Century of Revolution, 1603–1714*, 2d ed. (New York: W. W. Norton, 1982), 39–40, 125, 185.

[31]For the argument that short-term debt was devised and advanced as early as the 1650s, and thus that the Glorious Revolution should not be seen as the origin of the financial revolution, see J. S. Wheeler, "Navy Finance, 1649–1660," *Historical Journal* 39, no. 2 (1996), 457.

[32]For loans in general, see Robert Ashton, *The Crown and the Money Market: 1603–1640* (Oxford: Clarendon Press, 1960) and for the role of the companies, see, esp., 23. See also Scott, *Constitution and Finance of Joint-Stock Companies*, vol. 1, pp. 238, 242, 258.

[33]See Glenn O. Nichols, "English Government Borrowing, 1660–1688," *Journal of British Studies* 10, no. 1 (1971), 83; Scott, *Constitution and Finance of Joint-Stock Companies*, vol. 2, pp. 131, 133, 139. For a wider account of late Stuart finance, see Chandaman, *Public Revenue*.

Revolution, the East India Company had acquired a unique role in public finance.

After the Glorious Revolution, public finance went into a new phase. Expenses rose due to prolonged wars with France, and tax incomes, with the excise leading the way, increased, but an unprecedented degree of borrowing was nevertheless needed to bridge the deficit gap. The national debt grew steadily and its long-term component became larger. More sophisticated management of the debt developed, featuring attempts to lower the interest rate and to fund more of the debt. Parliament guaranteed debts to the State and thus created the distinction between the royal and the national debt. All the above changes and others amount to what is known as the Financial Revolution.[34]

Established in 1694, the Bank of England joined the East India Company in playing a central role in national finance. The two became known as the moneyed companies. They not only had enormous stock compared with other joint-stock companies and were deeply involved in the money market, but also had continuous involvement in national finance. This involvement began with a loan made to the Exchequer as part of the incorporation scheme. In the case of the Bank of England, half the sum subscribed as joint-stock, £1,200,000, was lent to the State. The New East India Company lent the Exchequer £2,000,000 when it was floated in 1698. The old and the new companies made a loan of an additional £1,200,000 when merging to form the United East India Company in 1708.[35] These long-term loans laid the foundation for a continuing financial and political relationship between the State and the companies.[36] Such a relationship had been less likely in earlier genera-

[34]The classic presentation of the Financial Revolution and the important role played in it by the national debt is in P.G.M. Dickson, *The Financial Revolution in England: A Study in the Development of Public Credit, 1688–1756* (London: Macmillan, 1967). In recent years, it has been argued that the importance of the national debt in public finance was overestimated. The central position of taxes in public finance and in the funding and structure of the national debt itself was shown by Peter Mathias and Patrick O'Brien, "Taxation in Britain and France, 1715–1810. A Comparison of the Social and Economic Incidence of Taxes Collected for the Central Governments," *Journal of European Economic History* 5, no. 3 (1976), 601–640; Patrick K. O'Brien, "The Political Economy of British Taxation, 1660–1815," *Economic History Review* 41, no. 1 (1988), 1–32; John Brewer, *The Sinews of Power: War, Money and the English State, 1688–1783* (Cambridge, Mass.: Harvard University Press, 1990), 88–134. My argument in this chapter focuses on the nature of the link between business corporations and the State regarding public finance, and not on the weight of the corporations in absolute terms in public finance. Thus, it is not necessarily weakened by the shift of attention from debts to taxation.

[35]Dickson, *Financial Revolution*, 46–57.

[36]The United East India Company made further loans of £200,000 in 1730 and £1,000,000 in 1744 to secure extensions of its charters. Ibid., 205, 217. For the role

tions, when one-time transfer payments, rather then a continuous credit relationship, were the standard solution in emergencies.

The links of the Bank of England to national finance were closer than those of the East India Company. The bank not only lent money to the State on the long term, but it also advanced short-term loans in anticipation of taxes, administered long-term borrowing by the government from the general public, and acted as underwriter for Exchequer bills. The bank first administered loans in 1715 and by the 1740s had completely taken over control from the Exchequer for administering these loans. After an early experiment in 1696–1697, the Exchequer issued bills totaling £5,600,000 in the years 1707–1713, and from that point on, the bank played a central role in this aspect of the financial system as well, by subscribing, circulating, and holding these bills.[37]

The South Sea Company joined the moneyed companies club with its incorporation as a joint-stock corporation in 1711 and followed the path of the East India Company in an attempt to establish overseas trade as its primary business. On incorporation, the South Sea Company received a trade monopoly for much of South America and additional lands to be discovered. The company hoped to capture some of the legendary wealth of that continent by entering both the general and the slave trade (by gaining the monopoly right, the *asiento*, from the King of Spain) of Spanish America via the West Indies. However, these hopes were not realized because of the war with Spain and her later reluctance, even after peace was achieved, to cooperate with an English company, and because the trade potential was lower than the company had originally estimated.

Thus, a few years after it was founded, the South Sea Company's ambitions, if such existed, to become mainly an overseas trading company came to an end. The company then focused its activities on the field of public finance in which it had been involved since its inception. The company's original capital, according to its Act of Incorporation, was to be exchanged for a portion of the national debt. The company opened subscriptions, and by the close of the subscription in 1713, came somewhat short of the specified amount with close to £9,200,000. By 1714, 39 percent of the national debt was owed to the three moneyed companies: the Bank of England, the East India Company, and the newly

---

of the East India Company as a moneyed company, see Lucy Sutherland, *The East India Company in Eighteenth Century Politics* (Oxford: Clarendon Press, 1962), 14–48.

[37]Dickson, *Financial Revolution*, 81–82, 373ff, 417–420. The full scope of activities of the Bank of England is wider of course and cannot be discussed in the present context. See a detailed presentation in ibid. and in John Clapham, *The Bank of England, a History*, 2 vols. (Cambridge University Press, 1944).

formed South Sea Company, and their share continued to grow in the following years.[38]

The involvement of the South Sea Company increased toward the end of the decade, and reached its profound and infamous apex in 1720 with the scheme for converting much of the national debt into its stock, in an episode that came to be known as the South Sea Bubble. This dramatic episode is discussed in detail in the next chapter.

The rise of the moneyed companies, and with them the market for government stock, was among the factors that contributed to the wave of formation of new companies that gained momentum after the Revolution, and to the share market boom of 1692–1695. More new companies were formed in the 1680s than had been in the previous five decades. William Scott estimated that by 1695 there were close to 150 joint-stock companies, only about 15 percent of which had been in existence prior to the Revolution, seven years earlier. He further estimated that the total nominal capital of these companies was about £4,250,000.[39] The sectoral spread of the newly formed companies is interesting. The overseas trading companies no longer dominated the scene, and new companies could be found in manufacturing, mining, banking and finance, fishing, and water supply.[40] The 1690s represented an important period of development and sophistication in the methods and practices of the stock market. A group of professional traders in stock could be distinguished, pamphlets on trading techniques were circulated, and the first price quotation lists were published.[41] The stock market boom also led to the first attempts at regulation of transaction methods and of the growing number of stockbrokers.

The peak of the 1690s was short-lived. Many of the companies promoted in the boom years disappeared shortly afterward. Although Scott noted the sharp increase in the capital of joint-stock companies, in the number of companies he noted a decline. He estimated the existence of some forty-six companies in 1703, but mentioned less than fifteen of them by name, as the rest were presumably insignificant. In 1717, he was able to gather information on only twelve companies. These figures

[38]Dickson, *Financial Revolution*, 80.

[39]Scott, *Constitution and Finance of Joint-Stock Companies*, vol. 1, pp. 327, 335–336; vol. 3, pp. 472–480.

[40]Ibid., vol. 1, pp. 330–333.

[41]Larry Neal, *The Rise of Financial Capitalism: International Capital Markets in the Age of Reason* (Cambridge University Press, 1990), 14–26; Dickson, *Financial Revolution*, 486–520. John Houghton's *Course of the Exchange* was first published in 1692 in London as part of a newspaper on economic issues. By May 1694, it listed fifty-two companies, but actually quoted prices for only about ten. In 1697, a new list, John Castaing's *Course of the Exchange*, began its publication. This list ran through the nineteenth century and is explored in the following chapters.

are even higher than the number of companies quoted in the *Course of the Exchange*, which listed only five for 1707 and six for 1717.[42] Furthermore, only four new joint-stock companies were reported to have been formed between 1700 and 1717.[43] The rise in the total capital of joint-stock companies can be attributed solely to the rise of the moneyed companies. Of an estimated £20.6 million share capital in English companies in 1717, £18.7 million, more than 90 percent, was attributed to the three moneyed companies. In conclusion, while the moneyed companies continued to gain in importance until 1720, the expansion of other joint-stock companies ended by 1700. For them, the boom, the first indication of which could be found in 1717, and which reached its peak in 1719–1720, was a deviation from the downward trend of the previous two decades. The events of the bubble year and the enactment of the Bubble Act, to which we turn in the next chapter, should be perceived in light of these longer-term trends.

Before moving on to the bubble year, I would like to pause at this point and ask what the relevancy of the pre-1720 period is to later developments. I hope that it is clear by now that the institution of the business corporation is not a product of industrialization, but rather of an earlier mercantilist era. My argument is that this early period is formative in several senses. The overseas trade sector was the leading sector in terms of incorporation during this period. As a result, the business corporation as an institution acquired several features, including stock structure, monopolistic rights, financial linkage to the crown, and public law regulation, which best suited the needs of this peculiar sector. By 1720, the linkage between the business corporation and overseas trade, the monopoly system, and public finance loosened, but the path created in the previous century and a half was already entrenched. In evolutionary terms, the features of this legal and economic institution were selected in a mercantilist environment. While this environment disappeared, the institution it gave rise to did not.

In fact, the period to 1720 can be divided into three distinct eras: the first, from the 1550s to the 1620s; the second, from the 1620s to the 1680s; and the third, from the 1680s to 1720, each with its own characteristics. Many of the institutional features were formed during the first era. The environment changed during the second. Thus, this was an era in which many of the companies formed during the first era were either dissolved or transformed. The institutional features were carried from the first era to the third by a handful of companies, notably the

---

[42] *Course of the Exchange.* See the first issue in January of each of the years.

[43] Scott, *Constitution and Finance of Joint-Stock Companies*, vol. 3, p. 480. These were the Sun Fire Office, the Company of London Insurers upon Lives, the South Sea Company, and the Company for Making Beech-Oil.

East India Company. They were not swiftly adapted to the new post-1688 constitutional and financial environment. The new enterprises that were being formed in growing numbers, and in a variety of sectors, in the period 1688–1720 utilized an institution that had been shaped several generations earlier in a different and by now forever lost context. As we shall see in the coming chapters, it took well into the nineteenth century for the legal framework, economic theory, and collective memory to partly escape this past mercantilist burden.

3

The Bubble Act, Its Passage, and Its Effects

The passage of the Bubble Act can be viewed as part of either of the two narratives that ended the previous chapter: the rise of the share market or the story of the moneyed companies and the national debt.[1] Most legal historians as well as historians of the business corporation recount the episode of the act as part of the ascent of joint-stock companies in general, and in particular of smaller, domestic, and unincorporated ones, the more speculative of which became known at the time as bubble companies. They view the Bubble Act as prohibitive and reactionary legislation aimed at impeding the rise of the joint-stock company as a legitimate form of business organization.[2]

Though many financial, economic, and political historians viewed the South Sea Bubble (the financial episode) as a central chapter in the story of the rise of the moneyed companies, the national debt, and the financial revolution, only a few considered the Bubble Act itself (the legal episode) as a relevant event in this well-known story.[3] If at all, they view the act as one of several measures aimed at contributing to the success of the financial scheme for the conversion and stabilization of the national debt.

From the narrower perspective of the first narrative, the Bubble Act is normally viewed as a watershed in the history of the unincorporated as well as the incorporated joint-stock company, from a status of recognition, popularity, and appreciation in the years 1689–1720 to one of

---

[1] An earlier version of this chapter was published as Ron Harris, "The Bubble Act: Its Passage and Its Effects on Business Organisation," *Journal of Economic History* 54, no. 3 (1994), 610.

[2] See Maitland, "Trust and Corporation," 208; DuBois, *English Business Company*, 437; Scott, *Constitution and Finance of Joint-Stock Companies*, vol. 1, p. 438; and see also Holdsworth, *English Law*, vol. 8, p. 221, for a statement similar to Scott's.

[3] John Carswell, *The South Sea Bubble*, rev. ed. (Dover: Alan Sutton Press, 1993), 114–15, 243; see also Neal, *Financial Capitalism*, 62; Brewer, *Sinews of Power*, 125.

mistrust and eclipse after 1720.[4] As one historian asserted, the act cast a shadow on the joint-stock company as a form of business organization for more than a century, and ultimately arrested its development.

The subject matter of the second narrative is national finance: the design of the financial scheme, its execution by the South Sea Company and the government, the share price crisis, and the reconstruction of the national debt. In this wider context, the act is a relatively marginal incident that did not considerably affect the blowing and burst of the bubble or the longer-term structuring of national finance, and if it transformed the joint-stock company form of organization, this was only incidental, a by-product.

In the present chapter, I argue that the motives and aims behind the passage of the Bubble Act can better be explained in the context of the second narrative, though the first should not be disregarded altogether. More concretely, I argue that the South Sea Company, which organized the national debt conversion scheme, also instigated the Bubble Act, but that it did so because small bubble companies had become an annoying factor in the stock market of 1720. I further argue that because this was the rationale behind the act, its immediate and longer-term consequences were relatively confined. In putting forward this argument, I connect the events of the bubble year with the developments of the period 1688–1719, surveyed in Chapter 2, and with developments up to the close of the eighteenth century, surveyed in the following chapters.

THE PROPER CONTEXT: BUBBLE COMPANIES OR NATIONAL DEBT

We follow the first narrative mentioned above, that of the rise of the share market, in terms of newly formed companies, prices, and volume of trade, until 1720. As shown in Chapter 2, after a heyday in the 1690s, the share market and joint-stock companies in general declined between 1700 and 1717. The market gathered new momentum toward the end of the 1710s. A few joint-stock companies, particularly in the insurance sector, were formed, and a few old charters of incorporation were bought by entrepreneurs to be employed in new undertakings in 1717–1719. But the real boom began in late 1719. Between the end of October 1719 and early July 1720 the share prices of the moneyed companies leaped: the Bank of England by about 170 percent, the East India Company by about 220 percent, and the South Sea Company by at least 820

---

[4]Scott, *Constitution and Finance of Joint-Stock Companies*, vol. 1, pp. 437–38; Holdsworth, *English Law*, vol. 8, pp. 219–222; Shannon, "Limited Liability," 358; Hunt, *Development of the Business Corporation*, 6–9; Manchester, *Modern Legal History*, 348–349.

percent. The rest of the share market followed, not only the established minor companies but also new company flotations. A few hundred new companies, many of them with highly imaginative business goals and dubious prospects, having nominal capital of £2–5 million per typical subscription and an enormous total estimated capital – £224 million – were formed within a period of just over six months (as compared with only four companies mentioned above between 1700 and 1717).[5] The vast majority of these newly created companies did not even bother to turn to the State for an act or a charter of incorporation, but simply opened up share subscription books in the city and collected deposits or partial payments. These small bubble companies, as they were called by contemporaries, were, in legal terms, unincorporated joint-stock companies with no State consent, and their legality was questionable according to common law. They were liable to prosecution for breaching the King's prerogative, under the ancient writs of *quo warranto* or *scire facias*. We leave this first narrative for the moment, with this undetermined legal question in mind, in the spring of 1720, and go back in time to 1689 to follow the second narrative.

The involvement of the new royal family, the house of Orange, in the costly Nine Years' War and the War of the Spanish Succession placed new and unprecedented demands on English public finance. The creation, after 1688, of a Parliament-backed national debt, distinct from the debt of the royal court; the establishment of the Bank of England, and later of the South Sea Company; and the creation of novel credit tools all allowed for the dramatic expansion of the national debt. The growth of the national debt was linked to the formation of an active bond market as well as to a complex network of public creditors, moneyed companies, the Exchequer, and Parliament. Between the Revolution and the end of the war in 1713, the national debt increased from less than £5 million to over £50 million. As the wars continued and the demand grew, the rate of interest the State paid its creditors increased from 5 to a high of 9 percent. When peace and the new Hanoverian King George arrived, the Exchequer was paying interest at a rate 2 to 4 percent higher than the peacetime market rate. However, much of the newly created national debt was, according to the original terms of the bonds issued to the public, irredeemable. This created a major burden on the English State from 1714 onward, and placed the reorganization of the national debt high on the government agenda.

The second narrative unfolded slowly between 1715 and 1719, as the Exchequer initiated several minor schemes for conversion of portions of the redeemable debt into lower-rate debt, but it seemed that only a

---

[5]Scott, *Constitution and Finance of Joint Stock Companies*, vol. 1, pp. 409–421.

scheme which would involve the moneyed companies would work for the irredeemable debt. This option gathered momentum in 1719 as the Bank of England and the South Sea Company vied for the design and implementation of a grand conversion scheme for the irredeemable debt. In early February 1720, Parliament, on the government's recommendation, accepted the South Sea Company's offer to the public creditors of the State to convert their irredeemable and redeemable bonds, some £30 million, into company shares in prices (terms of conversion) to be determined as the scheme unfolded.[6] The public was to gain by being offered attractive shares in a company whose share prices were on their spectacular way up, due to colossal expected profits in the near future, both in South American trade and in English high finance. The government was to gain both because the servicing costs of the national debt would be reduced considerably, and because the company agreed to pay at least £7.5 million to the Treasury in return for the privilege of performing the conversion. The gain for the company was based on the conversion ratio of bonds to shares; the higher the price of company shares at the time of conversion, the better for the company. In addition, the company intended to issue new shares and offer them to the general public at high prices that would be justified by the success of the scheme. Thus, in early 1720, the government and Parliament, the South Sea Company, the public creditors, and, in fact, all the investing classes were highly committed to the national debt conversion scheme. This scheme was unprecedented in English history in terms of sums of money, numbers of investors, and financial sophistication, and could be compared only to the Bank Royale scheme (known in retrospect as the Mississippi bubble), designed by John Law for the French government during the same period. The whole financial scheme had its legal footing in the South Sea Act, which received royal assent on April 7. During the following weeks, the scheme was unleashed, and the anxious nation watched it unfold into the summer.

In the spring of 1720, our two narratives were clearly connected. The entire share market was affected by the competition between the South Sea Company and the Bank of England, and then by the unfolding national debt conversion scheme. The bull market opened new opportunities to the bubblers to make easy money, and they did not hesitate to take a free ride on the success of the South Sea scheme. At this stage, when the two narratives are tightly linked, we examine how the passage of the Bubble Act can be explained in relation to each of them.

[6]In this chapter, references to days and months are based on the contemporary Julian calendar, whereas references to years are based on the modern calendar year which begins on January 1, and not on March 25, as was the case until 1752. See note 29 below for further clarification.

THREE EXPLANATIONS FOR THE PASSAGE OF
THE ACT

Modern literature provides three explanations for the passage of the Bubble Act. The first is most closely associated with the first narrative, that of joint-stock companies, and with the view of the act as a decisive downward turning point. This explanation is most commonly held, and most often quoted in textbooks, and can thus be considered as the orthodoxy regarding this issue. "The joint-stock system – 'pernicious art of stock-jobbing' – was the sole and sufficient explanation for the miseries of the country," says Scott in his trail-blazing work on the early joint-stock companies.[7] This explanation regards the act as hostile to speculation in the stock market and to joint-stock companies in general, and thus as attempting to limit both. While Scott's more sophisticated version of this explanation portrays the Bubble Act as a preemptive measure that predated the burst, a cruder version presents the Bubble Act as a remedy, motivated by the market collapse.

The second and most recent explanation for the passage of the act held by political scientists and economists stems from the public-choice approach and the rent-seeking interpretation of the legislation. According to this approach, the legislature, either as an institution or as individual members, sold legislative goods (in the form of regulation) to privilege-seeking entrepreneurs for a price: taxes, bribes, shares, and so on. More specifically, in the case of the Bubble Act, the government, or Parliament, "intended to prevent non-chartered firms from using the formal market," and they did so, according to Margaret Patterson and David Reiffen, to "enhance the importance of charters" and to protect their ability "to raise revenue through the issuance of charters."[8] Or, as Henry Butler put it, "the Bubble Act was a government-created entry barrier designed to put out of business (and hinder development of) all business associations which were competing with Parliament's chartering business."[9] This second explanation is also located within the general setting of our first narrative.

---

[7]Scott, *Constitution and Finance of Joint-Stock Companies*, vol. 1, pp. 436–437. It is cited, supported, and otherwise approved by Holdsworth, *English Law*, vol. 8, pp. 218–222; Shannon, "Limited Liability," 358; Hunt, *Development of the Business Corporation*, 6–9; Manchester, *Modern Legal History*, 348–349, to name but a few.

[8]Margaret Patterson and David Reiffen, "The Effect of the Bubble Act on the Market for Joint Stock Shares," *Journal of Economic History* 50, no. 1 (1990), 163, 171.

[9]Henry N. Butler, "General Incorporation in Nineteenth Century England: Interaction of Common Law and Legislative Processes," *International Review of Law and Economics* 6 (1986), 172–173. For the theoretical framework of this approach, see also Henry N. Butler, "Nineteenth-Century Jurisdictional Competition in the Granting of Corporate Privileges," *Journal of Legal Studies* 14, no. 1 (1985), 130–133. In fact, only the Crown granted charters, whereas Parliament passed specific incorpora-

The third explanation was more of a proposition or hypothesis than a full-blown thesis. According to this explanation, the South Sea Company initiated the Bubble Act because it believed that the wave of small bubbles competed with the company's conversion scheme and could endanger its own bubble. According to this view, the act was one of several attempts to hinder alternative investment opportunities and to divert more capital to South Sea shares.[10] Yet scholars holding this view to date were interested only in the story of the national debt and not in that of joint-stock companies, and thus did not make a detailed examination of the passage of the act and its impact, nor did they search for specific evidence to support their more general impressions. The present chapter concludes that this third explanation is the only one that is viable from all perspectives.

In fact, the first two explanations view the decades that led to the Bubble Act through the eyes of the joint-stock company and of the share market, whereas the third explanation focuses on the rise of the moneyed companies and the management of the public debt. The first two explanations assume that the spread of the joint-stock company, the growth of the share market, and the abuses caused by bubble companies and unincorporated associations after 1688 were the major incentives for the enactment. These phenomena are viewed in the third explanation as marginal, almost irrelevant to the legislative initiative. Central to this explanation is the rise of the moneyed companies after the 1690s, particularly the South Sea Company from 1710 to 1720, and the growing need to restructure the public debt that had increased dramatically in previous decades. According to the third explanation, these are the developments that led to the enactment of the Bubble Act and shaped its content.

This explanation of the background and intentions of the framers, together with the legal and economic effects of the act, minimizes the role of the Bubble Act as a turning point in the development of the joint-stock company. The present chapter provides us with an ex ante evaluation of the effects of the Bubble Act as viewed in 1720. An ex post evaluation of the effects of the act, as seen in 1825, the year of its repeal, is presented in Part III.

FROM BILL TO ACT

The committee that eventually recommended the Bubble Act bill to the House of Commons was formed on February 22, 1720. At that point, the South Sea Company's scheme for converting the national debt was

---

tion acts. Butler as well as Patterson and Reiffen must have wanted to include both in their explanations.

[10]Carswell, *South Sea Bubble*, 114–15; Dickson, *Financial Revolution*, 147– 148. See also Cooke, *Corporation, Trust and Company*, 82–83.

well on its way. The company's final tender, which had beaten the Bank of England's offer, was on the table, and its details were debated in Parliament and in the London press. By the time John Hungerford reported from the committee on April 27, 1720, the South Sea Act (6 Geo. I c.4) that authorized the scheme had already received royal assent. By May 27, when the Committee of the Whole reported on the amended version of the bill, the scheme was unfolding rapidly, and two money subscriptions and one offer of exchange had been completed. Furthermore, by late May, a new matter was included in the bill, the incorporation of two marine insurance companies, the Royal Exchange Assurance and the London Assurance. The two insurance projects (which had been under investigation by the committee for alleged improper private subscription) now received positive attention because of support by the Crown, after each offered £300,000 to pay off the King's Civil List debt.[11] The final version of the bill, which included these two unrelated and somewhat contradictory matters, was rushed through both houses and received royal assent on June 11. The King, eager to leave for Hanover, closed the session that same day, having approved no fewer than eighteen acts. By early June, the price of South Sea Company shares reached £750, more than five times their value in January. The shares reached a peak of £1050 on June 24, after the passage of the Bubble Act, and lingered at the level of £950–1000 at the end of July. Only at that stage, almost two months after the passage of the act, did the South Sea shares begin their rapid one-way journey downward. By December 1720, South Sea shares reached a bottom of £121, lower than their initial price in January. The entire market followed on the heels of this collapse: East India plunged from 449 to 145, the Bank of England from 265 to 132, London Assurance from 175 to 11, Royal Exchange Assurance from 250 to 9, and many small bubbles dropped to zero.[12] This sequence of events makes it clear that the act was not passed as a reaction to the crash of the bubble, as some mistakenly believe, but rather its initial bill was presented about six months before the beginning of the market collapse, and the act itself passed some two months before the crash.

The full title of the so-called Bubble Act (6 Geo. I c.18 (1720)) was "An Act for better securing certain Powers and Privileges, intended to be

[11]Barry Supple, *Royal Exchange Assurance: A History of British Insurance, 1720–1970* (Cambridge University Press, 1970), 30–32.

[12]Price quotations are approximate because there was no standard trade or reporting system. For versions of South Sea share prices, see Scott, *Constitution and Finance of Joint-Stock Companies*, vol. 3, chart inserted in a back cover pocket; Henry Roseveare, *The Financial Revolution: 1660–1760* (London: Longman, 1991), 57; Neal, *Financial Capitalism*, figs. 5.3 and 5.4; see the text that accompanies Neal's figures for an explanation of some of the variations among the different sources.

granted by His Majesty by Two Charters, for Assurance of Ships and Merchandize at Sea, and for lending Money upon Bottomry; and for restraining several extravagant and unwarrantable Practices therein mentioned." It is evident that only the latter part of the title refers, and only implicitly, to the phenomena at which the act is assumed to be directed, bubbles and speculations. The term "Bubble Act" is rarely found in eighteenth-century sources, and the nickname became popular only in the early nineteenth century. Modern use of the term "Bubble Act" led many to assume that this title indicates that the framers of the act perceived it as dedicated solely to fighting the bubbles. In addition, the use of the singular form, "Bubble," gave the mistaken impression that the act was specifically directed against the most famous bubble of 1720, that of the South Sea Company, rather than the small bubbles.

The first seventeen clauses of the act regulated the incorporation of the two marine insurance companies, and indeed most contemporaries referred to the act as "the act for establishing the two insurance companies." Only in Clause 18 do we find a description of the evils of speculation to be remedied and there the norm is set, first in general terms and then specifically:

All undertakings . . . presuming to act as a corporate body . . . raising . . . transferable stock . . . transferring . . . shares in such stock . . . without legal authority, either by Act of Parliament, or by any Charter from the Crown, . . . and acting . . . under any Charter . . . for raising a capital stock . . . not intended . . . by such Charter . . . and all acting . . . under any obsolete Charter . . . for ever be deemed to be illegal and void.

Clauses 19–21 set the penalties and remedies. Clauses 22 and 25 limited the extent of the new norm, which was not to apply to any undertaking established before June 24, 1718, nor to legal "trade in partnership." Clauses 23, 24, and 26–29 protected various interests of the South Sea Company, the East India Company, and the two newly established insurance companies. Of a total of twenty-nine clauses, only six, conceivably, deserve the moniker "Bubble Act." These clauses were ambiguous in some respects and their interpretation was problematic, as discussed below. On the other hand, clauses relating to the two insurance companies and to the South Sea Company were unambiguous. My impression of the wording of the act is that most of its clauses were the result of a compromise between two competing interest groups – the promoters of the two marine insurance undertakings and the directors of the South Sea Company – and only a few clauses represented an ambivalent attempt to confront some of the speculative activity of other undertakings.

Clause 27, which was added to the bill only on the day of the third reading, has been overlooked by most historians, yet it deserves special attention in the present context.[13] This clause states that any subscription made by the South Sea Company shall be valid. The clause was cited shortly after the burst in a pamphlet attributed to John Blunt, the South Sea director who promulgated the entire scheme, as proof that all actions of the directors were approved by Parliament, and thus the directors should not be punished for their role in the scheme:

> Parliament were pleased to pass a clause in the act for establishing the two insurance companies, confirming not only the subscription taken out but also all such subscriptions as should after be taken . . . assignable in law, which they would not have been without authority of Parliament.[14]

Thus, through the back door, the South Sea directors were able to legalize their departure from the original scheme.[15] This clause supports the assumption that the South Sea Company was behind the Bubble Act, or at least substantial parts of it, in two senses. First, there could be no other rationale for including this clause, except for serving the company's interest. Second, it demonstrates the company's ability to manipulate Parliament at will, even at the last moment.

THE SOUTH SEA COMPANY LOBBY

The South Sea directors believed, justifiably or not, that the "traffic [in bubbles] obstructed the rise of the South Sea stock."[16] They did not limit themselves to verbalizing their concerns but took action regarding this legislation. On May 6, the Court of Directors instructed the company's solicitor, the Committee of Correspondence, and all the directors who were MPs at the time, to keep track of the bill and represent the interests of the company regarding it.[17] This is one of the most crucial pieces of evidence for the depth of the South Sea Company's long in-

---

[13]*Commons' Journal* 19 (May 31, 1720), 368.

[14]*A True State of the South Sea Scheme* (1722), 24. This pamphlet is attributed to John Blunt, a senior director.

[15]The act authorized only the conversion scheme but not new subscriptions. See Dickson, *Financial Revolution*, 129, for a discussion of conflicting opinions on the question of whether the increase of capital by the company was legal. The assumption that contemporaries saw the point as controversial would probably be reasonable.

[16]Adam Anderson, *An Historical and Chronological Deduction of the Origin of Commerce*, 6 vols. (1764), vol. 2, p. 289. Anderson can be taken in this case as direct first-hand evidence, because he was a South Sea clerk at the time of the bubble. See also [Blunt], *South Sea Scheme*, 42, for a similar statement. Another pamphlet accusing the South Sea Company of an attempt to ruin smaller companies, the two insurance companies, and petite bubbles, in general, see *A New Year's Gift for the Directors, with Some Account of Their Plot Against the Two Assurances* (1721).

[17]Minutes of the Court of Directors, cited by L.C.B. Gower, "South Sea Heresy?," *Law Quarterly Review* 68 (April 1952), 217.

volvement in the legislative process. And indeed the company had many channels through which it could represent its interests and exercise its wishes.

Examination of the motives of the individuals most actively involved in this legislation points to close ties between them and the South Sea Company. The chairman of the committee on the bill, John Hungerford, was known by contemporaries to be connected to the company. The best evidence of his commitment to the company and its scheme is found in his call (in the midst of the collapse) in the Company's Court of Proprietors in September 1720 for a vote of confidence in the directors.[18] If he still supported them after the crash, when many deserted this sinking ship, he certainly served the company's interests while chairing the committee. The committee included, among others, James Craggs the Younger, who introduced and piloted the South Sea scheme in Parliament; Charles Stanhope, who was involved with Craggs in negotiating the scheme and drafting the South Sea bill; and Fisher Tench, a former director of the company and speaker for its interests in the Commons. Several other members of the committee received stock and speculated in it, or were kinsmen of directors and others with direct interests. Richard Hampden, Treasurer of the Navy, who speculated with navy funds in South Sea stock for personal profit, is an example of a member who, though not directly involved in the company, was willing to do whatever it took to serve its interests on the committee, as his fortune and career were at risk.[19]

Turning from the immediate circle of the committee to the political establishment as a whole, personal interest in the scheme can be seen everywhere. Twelve current or recent directors of the South Sea Company were sitting in the Commons in 1720, and many other directors held governmental and City offices, but that was only the tip of the iceberg.[20] On April 21, shortly before the Bubble bill was reported from the committee to the House, the General Court of the South Sea Company decided to empower the Court of Directors to lend money to individuals, upon security of South Sea shares, "as they shall see for the interest of the company." In implementing this decision, the Court of Directors fixed broad policy for the grant of loans for purchasing shares, but in fact breached even these policies, and distributed shares freely to

---

[18]*The Proceedings of the Directors of the South Sea Company* (1721), 28; and generally on Hungerford, in Romney Sedgwick, *The History of Parliament: The House of Commons,1715–1754*, 2 vols. (London: H.M.S.O., 1970), vol. 2, pp. 161–162.

[19]See the corresponding entry for each of the above MPs in ibid.

[20]The number and names are derived from the bibliographical appendix in Carswell's, *South Sea Bubble*, 244–255.

men of influence. It was discovered in 1721 by the Committee of Secrecy investigating the crisis that, at one point, the company offered £574,500 of its stock at favored terms to dignitaries in order to gain political support for its legislation, while making sure that these stock transfers were not recorded, or were recorded under false names, so as not to identify the politicians involved.[21] This striking piece of evidence shows that the company ran a well-planned full-scale operation for manipulating Parliament. The total number of MPs in both Houses taking part in at least one of the subscriptions of the company, on their own account, with company credit or as a gift, is amazing: 578, with shares valued at over £3,500,000.

The government was also well represented in the subscriptions. Nine ministers added their names to at least one subscription, and their total shares were valued nominally at over £650,000. The South Sea Company even made inroads into the royal court. Some of the King's favorite German mistresses acquired South Sea stock at irresistible terms through the services of Secretary James Craggs, and King George would have been severely embarrassed had the bubble burst and the facts come to light.[22]

THE ANTI-BUBBLES LOBBY

In addition to asking who was actually involved in the passage of the act, one can also ask who would be expected to be involved in initiating the act were it indeed intended to check speculations and bubbles, rather than to serve the interests of the South Sea Company. The most likely candidate to introduce a bill to that purpose in 1720 was certainly not John Hungerford, who was involved in the grand speculation of the South Sea Company, but rather Archibald Hutcheson. Hutcheson was the most prominent speaker in the House of Commons against speculation in exchange-alley bubbles, warning that they diverted the English people from productive activities and would lead to the country's destruction. He was also a major opponent of the South Sea Company scheme from its inception, saying that it was miscalculated and speculative, and called for alternative solutions to the burden of public debt. In addition to his parliamentary activity, in 1717 Hutcheson began publishing numerous pamphlets in an effort to bring his opinions to a wider

---

[21]*A Supplement to the Report of the Committee of Secrecy* (1721); *The Skreen Removed; A List of All Names Mention'd in the Report of the Committee of Secrecy* (1721); Dickson, *Financial Revolution*, 105–112, esp. tables 10 and 11.

[22]See Sedgwick, *History of Parliament*, vol. 1, the entry for Craggs; and Carswell, *South Sea Bubble*, 104, 256–261.

audience.[23] Yet Hutcheson had reservations about the concept of the Bubble Act. He attempted to prohibit speculative stock dealings through proposed amendments, which would eliminate futures transactions, require a minimum term of ownership before a stock could be resold, and mandate the logging of all stock assignments in company record books. He said:

> I am fully persuaded, that [such clauses] would have . . . suppressed all bubbles effectually . . . without the help of any penalty whatever; and it would also have prevented the turning of the stocks of companies, established by Acts of Parliament or charter for better purpose, into real bubbles, destructive to the public.[24]

To his disappointment, though he sat on the committee that drafted the bill, he found himself isolated in his opposition to the strong South Sea Company interest in the committee. The other committee members had no objection to the South Sea Company's stock becoming a bubble. A last-minute attempt to add a clause "for restraining stock-jobbing" to the final amendments of the Bubble Act in the House itself, after the committee stage, also failed.[25] Hutcheson had no real influence and his concerns found no expression in the final version of the Bubble Act, as it served different motives and aims. As a critical contemporary observer noted, "the South Sea managers were resolved to have the whole game of bubbles (so exceedingly profitable) to themselves only," and the act was "manifestly designed for [the South Sea Company's] service."[26] The connection between the company and the act, so evident to contemporary observers, was obscured in time.

THE PUBLIC AND THE GOVERNMENT

The very extensive pamphlet literature of 1720 reveals a public agenda shaped by the South Sea scheme. The debates initially revolved around the advantage of the scheme compared with other schemes for managing the national debt, and then around the profitability for investors and public creditors at each stage of the unfolding scheme. After the crash,

---

[23]Archibald Hutcheson authored at least thirty-four pamphlets between 1717 and 1723, fourteen in 1720 alone, all concerning the public debt, the South Sea Company, and the ongoing speculation in stocks. See John G. Sperling, *The South Sea Company: An Historical Essay and Bibliographical Finding List* (Boston: Baker Library, 1962), for a bibliographical list of pamphlets in four major collections, with references to Hutcheson's pamphlets.

[24]Archibald Hutcheson, *Several Calculations and Remarks Relating to the South Sea Scheme* (1720), 67.

[25]*Commons' Journal* 19 (May 27, 1720), 367.

[26]Thomas Gordon, *A Complete History of the Late Septennial Parliament 1722: In a Collection of Tracts by John Trenchard and Thomas Gordon* (1751), 63–64.

issues centered on the personal responsibility of the directors and politicians, their proper punishment, and on who would pay for reconstruction. The small bubbles received only minor attention in the pamphlet discourse of the period, and there is no indication that they were high on anyone's agenda. If they were mentioned at all, it was in the form of moral condemnation or satirical literature, rather than suggestions for concrete legal and economic measures.[27]

The government and Parliament were committed to the success of the scheme as it was approved by Parliament in the South Sea Act of April 1720, just two months before the passage of the Bubble Act. This interest was considerable as the scheme was to restructure the national debt to the State's advantage. The scheme offered to solve the problem of pressing irredeemable debt, from which the government had no other creditable way to disengage itself. It also promised payments by the company to the treasury of over £4 million, a sum which could reach as much as £7.5 million if the conversion offer turned out to be well received by the public creditors. And it would substantially reduce the interest paid by the State. The ministry and the nation as a whole had a lot at stake when the South Sea scheme unfolded, and every reason to contribute to its success. No other issue was as high on the public list of priorities in the first half of 1720 as the national debt and the scheme to reduce it, and no measures would have been taken to endanger its solution.

The atmosphere at the time of the passage of the Bubble Act is best manifested by the King's speech at the close of the session, on June 11, just after giving royal assent to the Bubble Act:

> The good foundation you have prepared this session for the payment of the national debt, and the discharge of a great part of them, without the least violation of the public faith, will, I hope, strengthen more and more the union I desire to see among all my subjects; and make our friendship yet more valuable to all foreign powers.[28]

To substantiate his satisfaction, on that same day, George made baronets of two South Sea directors: John Blunt, the financial mastermind

---

[27]The most comprehensive list of contemporary publications can be found in Sperling, *South Sea Company*. A simplified quantitative analysis of printed publications, mainly pamphlets, included in this list for the years 1720–1721 (ibid., 57–76) includes the following classification of topics: the public debt in general: 28; the South Sea conversion scheme: 61; investment in South Sea Stock: 27; personal responsibility of individual South Sea Directors and Officers: 64; post-crash financial reconstruction schemes: 32; financial affairs in France and Holland: 14; poems and satires on bubbles and speculations: 14; stock-jobbing and Exchange-Alley: 11; the small bubbles specifically: 5. The value of this quantitative analysis is obviously limited because classification of such items is tentative; there is no evidence of the circulation of different pamphlets; and some of the items appear several times in only minor variations.

[28]*Lords' Journal* 20 (1720), 359.

behind the scheme, and William Chapman. He then left to spend the summer in Hanover and did not return, or summon Parliament, until the crash.

CONCLUSION: WHY WAS THE BUBBLE ACT PASSED?

The first explanation for the passage of the Bubble Act, in its cruder manifestation, places the Bubble Act after the crash and as a reaction to it. This explanation, possibly originating in inconsistent use of the old and the new English calendars, has a long tradition.[29] It can be found as early as the 1760s in the famed legal writings of William Blackstone; it can be found in the early twentieth-century work of F. W. Maitland; and it can still be found in some modern textbooks.[30] Yet this explanation is chronologically baseless.

In its more advanced version, the explanation perceives the Bubble Act as a preemptive attempt to contain speculation in the stock market and to prevent a future disaster. This explanation is not found in contemporary sources, but first appeared in the early nineteenth century. At that point, the Bubble Act resurfaced on the public agenda because of a new speculative mania, and judges and pamphleteers used the crash of 1720 and the Bubble Act as a warning to their own generation not to engage in joint-stock speculation.[31] In the early twentieth century, the authoritative work of Scott gave new force to this explanation, and subsequent generations of scholars accepted his argument without close examination. This interpretation fueled the misconception that the title "Bubble Act" reflected contemporary intentions.

There were indeed some contemporaries who were deeply concerned with the unprecedented wave of new projects, subscriptions, and specu-

---

[29]By an act of 1751, England adopted the Gregorian Calendar, which was eleven days ahead of the Julian Calendar. Until 1751 the year had begun on March 25; this was changed by the act to January 1. The South Sea Company won the bid for the conversion scheme, and started blowing the bubble in February 1719, whereas the Bubble Act was passed in June 1720. In the contemporary calendar these were four months apart, but some later writers mistakenly placed the Bubble Act in the year that followed the bubble.

[30]See Blackstone, *Commentaries*, vol. 4, p. 117; Maitland, "Trust and Corporation," 208; J. H. Plumb, *England in the Eighteenth Century* (Harmondsworth: Penguin, 1968), 26; Eric Pawson, *The Early Industrial Revolution: Britain in the Eighteenth Century* (London: Basford, 1979), 89, for examples of this confusion, as repeated by different generations.

[31]See *An Account of the South Sea Scheme and a Number of Other Bubbles . . . With a Few Remarks Upon Some Schemes Which Are Now in Agitation* (1806); *The South Sea Bubble . . . Historically Detailed as a Beacon to the Unwary Against Modern Schemes . . . Equally Visionary and Nefarious* (1825); *The King v. Dodd*, 9 East 516 (1808). For discussion of later cases and of the debates in Parliament before the repeal of the Bubble Act in 1825, see Chapters 9 and 10.

lations in shares. There were those who were alarmed by the developments in France, where John Law's Mississippi scheme seemed to be spinning out of control.[32] The events in Paris in February and the capital flows coming from there were to some a harsh warning of the future of the London bubble. There were others, including Hutcheson and to some degree Walpole, who believed that the South Sea scheme was a mistaken and miscalculated approach to the national debt burden. But they were a small minority compared with the huge number of investors who, at least until the summer of 1720, crowded Exchange Alley from dawn to dusk and made fortunes by investing in anything from the smallest bubble to shares in the moneyed companies. In the days that preceded the Bubble Act's passage, public feeling was not of alarm in the face of a coming calamity, but rather of general optimism best reflected in the King's speech, the bullish market, and the success of the debt conversion scheme. This first explanation places the marginal phenomenon of small bubbles in the center and fails to connect it to the wider context, especially to the dominant position of the South Sea Company and the extreme importance attributed to a solution of the national debt crisis.

The second explanation, that the act was intended to raise revenue, departs from modern theoretical frameworks and does not emanate from thorough research of historical sources. It is too theoretical and abstract and there is no direct contemporary evidence to support it. It does not clearly specify the identity of those who were to benefit from the passage of the Bubble Act. Potentially these might have been either the English State (Parliament or the Crown), by increasing its budgetary income, or individual MPs, by putting additional revenues into their own pockets. In any event, this explanation relies on the premise that there were potential gains to be made by forcing unincorporated companies to apply for incorporation by way of an act or a charter. Both the social-benefit and private-benefit versions of this interpretation are examined below.

Could an increase in the volume of incorporation petitions increase the revenue of the State in any substantial manner? In the Elizabethan and early Stuart reigns, companies were essential contributors to public finance through a variety of channels. The most important of these, as

---

[32]After rising constantly from July 1719 to January 1720, the Paris stock market of February was much less stable and predictable. Alarmed by the course of unfolding of his scheme, John Law decided to close the Paris stock market but was forced by popular demand later in the month to reopen it. Speculators' capital began to exit Paris that month. Though the market had not yet collapsed in February of 1720, according to Neal, the burst of the rational bubble may have taken place as early as November 1719. See Neal, *Financial Capitalism*, 62–83; Carswell, *South Sea Bubble*, 65–81.

discussed in Chapter 2, were the payments and loans made to the Crown in return for the granting of incorporation and monopolistic privileges. However, the Civil War, the Interregnum, and the Restoration diminished the monopoly system while, concurrently, new sources of revenues developed. Thus by 1720, expenses on a new scale, a new tax base relying more on the excise, and a growing national debt, made all joint-stock companies, with the exception of the three moneyed companies, East India, Bank of England, and South Sea, almost irrelevant from the perspective of public finance.[33] Small undertakings could not have paid amounts remotely significant to the unprecedented needs of the Hanoverian State for the privilege of incorporation, and could not match the huge sums that the moneyed companies offered the State. Thus, to say that the act was intended to increase public revenue by blocking entry for those lacking charters does not fit the contemporary context of public finance in which the major revenues and loans came from totally different sources.

Could a boost in the volume of incorporation petitions increase the private earnings of individual MPs in any substantial manner? The nature of the legislative process during this period led to a variety of payments and costs at each stage that a bill had to pass. These included payments to the speaker, clerks of Parliament, counsel, solicitor-agents, printers, witnesses, and others. The total expenditure on a typical incorporation bill could have been £120, and there is no evidence that Members of Parliament were high on the list of those who shared in these amounts.[34] In any case, bills of incorporation could not be considered to be a significant business with potential for high private gains, either before the passage of the Bubble Act or afterward. Furthermore, the number of bills of incorporation around 1720 was negligible compared with bills of enclosure, turnpike trusts, naturalization, and estates. The real potential for private gain for MPs could be found in these bills and not in bills of incorporation.

Turning from the absence of potential increase in revenues to be derived from incorporation around 1720 to the actual effects of the Bubble Act, the same conclusion holds. The act did not cause entrepreneurs to stand in line with applications for charters or acts of incorpo-

---

[33]For the importance of business companies in Elizabethan and early Stuart public finance, for the changes in the structure of revenues and debts after the Civil War, the Restoration, and the Glorious Revolution, the decline in the importance of the joint-stock companies in general to public finance, and the rise of the moneyed companies, see Chapter 2 above.

[34]Brewer, *Sinews of Power*, 237. The South Sea Company, Bank of England, East India Company, and a few other large-scale enterprises paid much higher sums, but these were paid as part of a package that included monopolistic privileges and interest-bearing loans to the English State.

ration, and the number of incorporation bills remained as low after the enactment as it had been in previous years. Furthermore, the Bubble Act was followed by a policy of limiting the number of grants of incorporation, both by explicit decision of the Lords Justices to suspend chartering and by the reluctance of Parliament to pass further acts. To achieve the aim of increasing incorporation revenues they would have had to create an atmosphere which attracted petitioners by simplifying procedures, displaying positive attitudes toward petitions, and encouraging a wider stock market and investment in shares. Yet the opposite occurred, and as a result, the number of petitions to Parliament did not rise substantially but actually declined following the act's passage. Thus the Bubble Act could not and did not, in any significant way, increase the income of the State or the private gains of MPs, insofar as they are obtained from acts of incorporation.[35]

The Patterson–Reiffen version of this second explanation argues that "Parliament lost wealth that it might otherwise have captured because parties that could have successfully petitioned for corporate status chose instead to obtain used charters."[36] The rise of the charter resale market and the attempt to restrict this market are seen by Patterson and Reiffen as a major motive for the passage of the Bubble Act. However, the ancient writs of *quo warranto* or *scire facias* could be used to annul any charter that was abused, and no additional legislation was needed for that purpose. Indeed, actions taken shortly after the passage of the Bubble Act against charter abuses were based on the ancient *scire facias* and not on the new act.[37] Furthermore, only a very limited number of companies, probably no more than six, allegedly used charters for purposes other than those prescribed in their original grant. One of these companies, the Sword Blade Company, acted as a banker to the South Sea Company in 1720. There is no evidence of any intention to direct or enforce the Bubble Act against it, as this could have wrecked the entire South Sea scheme. Another such company was the Royal Exchange

[35]For the business of Parliament, procedures and quantities of private bills, and costs and earnings in legislation, see Sheila Lambert, *Bills and Acts: Legislative Process in Eighteenth-Century England* (Cambridge University Press, 1971); O. Williams, *The Clerical Organization of the House of Commons: 1661–1850* (Oxford: Clarendon Press, 1954); Orlo C. Williams, *The Historical Development of Private Bill Procedure and Standing Orders in the House of Commons*, 2 vols. (London: H.M.S.O., 1948–1949); Peter D. G. Thomas, *The House of Commons in the Eighteenth Century* (Oxford: Clarendon Press, 1971); Brewer, *Sinews of Power*.

[36]Patterson and Reiffen, "Bubble Act," 168.

[37]Though in earlier periods the *quo warranto* writ was considered to be more suitable and more popular, the *scire facias* writ was preferred in 1720. This may be explained by the despotic connotation of *quo warranto* after its use against the City of London in 1681. *The King v. The City of London*, 8 Howell's State Trails 1039 (1681–1683).

Assurance, which won the King's favor after taking on payment of his debts, and was legally incorporated by the first part of the Bubble Act. The role of four other companies, York Buildings, Lustering, English Copper, and Welsh Copper, in the active market of 1720 was negligible. Indeed, on August 18, the Lords Commissioners of His Majesty's Treasury guided the Attorney General to initiate *scire facias* proceedings against the four companies. This step might have been influenced by the Treasury's need, or the South Sea Company's interest, to complete the conversion scheme, but was not based on the Bubble Act. Furthermore, it was not the central measure undertaken to accomplish this goal, but only one quite marginal step out of many to manipulate the share market. Interestingly, the proceedings against all four companies were sooner or later abandoned.[38] In conclusion, these six cases of charter abuse could not, in themselves, serve as an incentive for passing a major piece of prohibitive legislation such as the Bubble Act.

Thus, the second explanation is also not supported by any direct historical evidence. It does not acknowledge the dominance of the conversion scheme or of the South Sea Company over the affairs of the bubble year. It does not offer a plausible account of the way in which revenues could be substantially increased by enacting the Bubble Act, other than those revenues that were linked directly to the debt conversion scheme or to the South Sea stock. This explanation does not fit into the great complexity of the bubble year and the wider perspective of that period.[39]

The third explanation – that the Bubble Act represented special-interest legislation for the South Sea Company, which controlled its framing and passage – has its roots in contemporary discourse, rather than in a later period. In practice, the Bubble Act did not divert substantial capital into investment in South Sea stock, contrary to its intended aim according to this third explanation. It did not attempt to bar investment in East India or Bank of England stock, the two major alternatives to South Sea stock. It did not prevent the speculation in bubbles of legally incorporated companies, including the two newly established insurance companies. The act could not prevent the movement of capital to foreign markets, most notably to Amsterdam. The impact of the act

---

[38]DuBois, *English Business Company*, 6–10.

[39]The theoretical framework on which this explanation was based, the analysis of rent-seeking and interest groups, could serve the third explanation adopted here, as well or even better. After all, the identification of the rent seekers and their methods is not determined by the theory, it is left to the detailed historical research. See William J. Baumol, "Entrepreneurship: Productive, Unproductive, and Destructive," *Journal of Political Economy* 98, no. 5 (1990), 893–921; Anne O. Krueger, "The Political Economy of the Rent-Seeking Society," *American Economic Review* 64, no. 3 (1974), 291– 303.

was only on a limited section of the market, and even there, speculative investments did not cease following its passage.

From the point of view of the South Sea directors, the Bubble Act was only one attempt of many to further blow their bubble. It was not a very well calculated measure, but many of the directors' actions were not well calculated, as they found themselves dealing with a highly complex scheme of unprecedented scale. The scheme unfolded rapidly and soon grew out of control. Thus, the fact that the act did not in fact serve the interests of the South Sea company should not be seen in retrospect as an indication that the company was not the prime force behind its passage. It was. The wording of the act, and the contemporary context of interests and discourses, support the third explanation.

THE BUBBLE ACT: A TURNING POINT?

There are several weaknesses in the commonly held interpretation that the bubble year was a decisive turning point in the history of the joint-stock company, from a period of progress toward an era of eclipse.

The wording of the Bubble Act was very broad and general. This raised doubts and questions among contemporary jurists and lawyers and diminished the effects of the act. Unincorporated undertakings were not recognized as corporations by common law. Acting as a corporate body without incorporation by charter or act was deemed illegal by common law prior to the act. Thus, such undertakings could not enjoy the capacities and privileges of corporations as legal entities, including perpetual succession, the right to sue and be sued in the corporate name, and the ability to purchase land.[40] It was not the act that deprived the bubbles of these privileges, but rather common law and constitutional conventions. As mentioned above, abuse of charters was prosecutable by the ancient common law writ of *scire facias*. To a considerable extent the Bubble Act only added new procedure and punishment to what had been sanctioned long before its passage by prerogative writs. But the general wording of the act led to interpretational uncertainties: Which stock is considered transferable? What about private subscription of shares? How would previously issued stock be divided? How would existing companies issue additional stock?[41]

The legal ambiguity of the Bubble Act, together with a weak enforce-

---

[40]See Blackstone, *Commentaries*, vol. 1, pp. 475–480. See also Coke, *Commentary*, vol. 2, p. 250. The question of whether by 1720 limited liability was an integral part of the privileges of incorporation is controversial; however, this controversy is not material to the present argument.

[41]See DuBois, *English Business Company*, 3–5, for a discussion of some of these points.

ment mechanism, the harsh criminal sanctions it embodied, and a widespread disregard of it by businessmen, made it practically a dead letter. Only one case of criminal prosecution based on the act was reported in the eighteenth century, that of *Rex v. Caywood* (1722), in which a project was floated to promote trade to the North Seas, a project whose similarity in name to the infamous South Sea bubble was enough to ensure its failure.[42] The act was revived in the early nineteenth century, more than eighty years after its enactment, by a new generation of law officers and judges, in a different setting of ideas and interests, and in the dynamic economic and legal context of the early industrial era.[43]

The actual effects of the passage of the Bubble Act on the stock market were very limited. The speculation frenzy ended, not because of the Bubble Act, but because of the crash which was brought about by a combination of complex economic factors: an overextended money market, tight credit, and external drains of capital to the Low Countries, to mention a few, together with the nervous behavior of inexperienced investors.[44] The Bubble Act did not prevent crashes and financial scandals in the longer term, either. It altered neither the mechanism of the market nor the practices of stock jobbers and stock brokers. A series of repeated attempts by Parliament to limit the growth of the stock market, to regulate it, and to check speculation, took place between the 1690s and the 1770s.[45] Acts of 1697 (8 & 9 Wm. III, c.32), 1708 (6 Anne c.68), 1734 (7 Geo. II c.8), and 1737 (10 Geo. II c.8) are the most significant of these attempts. The Bubble Act cannot be seen as part of this trend because it did not intervene in the market itself, as Hutcheson thought it should. It aimed at some of the companies whose shares were traded in that market, but not at others. Thus, the Bubble Act should not be seen as a major attempt to regulate the stock market.

The Bubble Act was only one measure among many that shaped the structure of business organization and the market for joint-stock shares. The decision of the Lords Justices, acting as Regents, to dismiss further petitions, limit the granting of charters in the following years, and prosecute charter abuse by *scire facias*, was legally unrelated to the Bubble Act and was a matter of policy rather than a new law or a new interpretation of the law.[46] This new policy was introduced in midsummer of 1720 in a different context, by different individuals, and with motives different from those for the Bubble Act. The structure of business orga-

[42]*Rex v. Caywood*, 1 Stranger 472 (1722).

[43]All of these are discussed in Chapters 8 and 9.

[44]For a full analysis of the reasons for the burst of the bubble, an analysis not attempted in this book, see Neal, *Financial Capitalism*, 106–112.

[45]Dickson, *Financial Revolution*, 516–520.

[46]Gower, "A South Sea Heresy?," 218–220.

nization in the financial sectors was considerably shaped by two other causes: the corporate duopoly in marine insurance granted to the Royal Exchange and London Assurance in 1720, and the corporate monopoly on issuing short-term notes, granted to the Bank of England in 1707, that excluded from this major aspect of banking not only joint-stock companies but also partnerships of more than six persons.[47] It was not the act alone, but rather a combination of measures, serving different interests and purposes, that shaped the map of business organization.

Modern historical research has shown that 1720 was not as disastrous a year in English history as Scott and his disciples would like us to believe. As recently shown by Hoppit, the number of bankruptcies did not jump following the bubble, and "[f]or the business community as a whole, through the length and breadth of England, the Bubble was not a catastrophe."[48] In Plumb's political perspective, the events of 1720 began an age of political stability at home and peace abroad.[49] According to Peter Dickson and John Brewer, who examined the public-finance perspective, the South Sea scheme was successful, solving the pressing problems of the national debt by lowering interest payments, putting the debt on a funded basis and attracting new public creditors. The trauma sent English public finance into a new era – more efficient, more financially sound, and less corrupted by private interests.[50] Taking an international capital market perspective, Larry Neal and Eric Schubert come to the conclusion that the South Sea bubble advanced the links between various financial markets in Western Europe, especially London and Amsterdam. In the long run, it thus facilitated the emergence, for the first time, of an integrated and efficient international financial market.[51]

[47]6 Anne c.22 (1707).

[48]Julian Hoppit, "Financial Crises in Eighteenth-Century England," *Economic History Review* 39, no.1 (1986), 39, 47–48. In the long run, counting bankruptcies poses data and methodological problems, yet in the short run one could expect a sharp rise in the number of bankruptcies throughout England had the bubble been a catastrophe. For an evaluation of the economic effects of the crash, which suggests a more mixed picture and even a depression, see Mirowski, *Birth of Business*, 231–235. His evaluation is based primarily on profit rates and share prices, rather than on bankruptcy records.

[49]J. H. Plumb, *The Growth of Political Stability in England, 1675–1725* (London: Macmillan, 1967), esp. 176–177, and J. H. Plumb, *Sir Robert Walpole*, 2 vols. (London: Crest Press, 1956–1960), vol. 1, chap. 8.

[50]Dickson, *Financial Revolution*, 134, 197–198; Brewer, *Sinews of Power*, 125–126.

[51]Neal, *Financial Capitalism*, chaps. 4 and 5, esp. pp. 79–80; Eric S. Schubert, "Innovations, Debt and Bubbles: International Integration of Financial Markets in Western Europe, 1688–1720," *Journal of Economic History* 48, no. 2 (1988), 299–306. It is appropriate to mention in this context that according to Mirowski, the English domestic share market peaked in prices, complexity, and efficiency in 1720

Thus, from other political and economic perspectives, even the bubble itself may not have retarded economic development.

In conclusion, the Bubble Act was intended by its formulators to serve the interests of the South Sea Company, as has been shown above. As such, it was intended to have an immediate short-term impact on the events of the coming weeks rather than to introduce a long-term change of course. The legal effects of the Bubble Act were not as radical as has been assumed. Insofar as the legal framework of business organization changed, this accrued from a variety of measures, most of them unrelated to the act. The Bubble Act was not as well defined a turning point as many have argued and its impact on the developments up to the end of the eighteenth century was minimal.

(Philip Mirowski, "The Rise (and Retreat) of a Market: English Joint Stock Shares in the Eighteenth Century," *Journal of Economic History* 41, no. 3 (1981), 559–577). That year was a turning point, and from then on, for the rest of the century, the market devolved and retreated. However, Mirowski does not relate the turning point to the bubble or the passage of the Bubble Act.

PART II

1721–1810

4

Two Distinct Paths of Organizational Development: Transport and Insurance

In Chapter 1, I surveyed a variety of organizational forms of business. In Chapters 2 and 3, I outlined the emergence, not without interruptions, of the joint-stock business corporation, from the mid-sixteenth century to the early eighteenth century. In the present chapter, I address the question of why the variety of forms persisted during the eighteenth century, whereas the joint-stock corporation did not gain dominance. In other words, why was a convergence process not observed, in which entrepreneurs transformed their existing undertakings, or at least their new ones, into joint-stock business corporations – obviously the natural candidates for this dominant position (particularly as we know the end of the story)?

Three major explanations for the persistence of this diverging path are explored in this and the following chapters. The first explanation is that the joint-stock corporation is not superior, in terms of efficiency, as some modern theoretical jurists and economists believe. The second is that the preconditions for exploiting its efficiency, an industrial economy with large-scale production and an effective share market, did not exist in eighteenth century England. The third is that there were legal, political, and other constraints that prevented businessmen from organizing in joint-stock corporations.

In the present chapter, I focus on two sectors, transport and insurance, and describe their divergence during the eighteenth century into two distinct organizational patterns: the first toward the joint-stock corporation and the second toward the unincorporated joint-stock company. I argue that the reasons for their divergence are rooted in systemic constraints. Thus, I support the third of the explanations suggested above, namely, that although entrepreneurs in both sectors realized that the corporation was a more suitable form of organization, those in the transport sector were able to employ it, whereas those in the insurance sector were, in the main, prevented from using it and had to resort to the unincorporated form.

The choice of transport and insurance is not random. Both are fascinating in terms of organizational experimentation, and both developed considerably during the eighteenth century and played a significant role in the early stages of industrialization.[1] Interestingly enough, both sectors, within this process of experimentation, transformed along different paths.

The present chapter examines the development of these two sectors throughout the century from the perspective of business organization, an aspect not comprehensively examined by economic historians in the past. It does so by utilizing business records, records that in the past have only rarely been examined by legal historians (who mainly rely on doctrinary records such as statutes, cases, and legal literature). It explores industrial organization, the structure of the market, and the competition within each of the sectors, and connects it to the legal organization these sectors sought and were able to achieve.

TRANSPORT

During the period covered by this part of the book, England experienced what some historians term the transport revolution. From a starting point of an erratic assortment of poorly maintained parish roads and mostly unnavigable rivers, the transport system expanded to a web of relatively well-kept turnpike roads and an extensive network of navigable rivers and newly constructed canals. I now examine the organizational aspects of this expansion, first with road transport, then with river navigation, and finally with canals.

The Emergence of the Turnpike Trust

The expansion and improvement of roads took place simultaneously with changes in the organization of their construction and maintenance.

---

[1]Rick Szostak, *The Role of Transportation in the Industrial Revolution: A Comparison of England and France* (McGill-Queen's University Press, 1991); Philip S. Bagwell, *The Transport Revolution*, 2d ed. (London: Routledge, 1988); Theo Barker and Dorian Gerhold, *The Rise and Rise of Road Transport, 1700–1990* (London: Macmillan, 1993); John A. Chartres, *Internal Trade in England, 1500–1700* (London: Macmillan, 1977); G. Clayton, *British Insurance* (London: Elek Books, 1971). Later works on transport were published by cliometricians, who model and quantify in order to estimate productivity gains and establish the claim that transport played a key role in the early stages of industrialization. The works on insurance are more traditional, and refer to rates of growth of the sector itself with no attempt to measure its effects on the economy as a whole.

This organizational development went through three stages. At first, there was no distinct organizational framework for roads; in the second stage, the framework was minimal and depended mainly on local administrators – the Justices of Peace; and only in the third stage was a distinct financial and administrative organization established for each road: the turnpike trust.

The poor conditions and the burden of maintenance of the King's highways had been problematic for many centuries, and various measures were taken at different periods to overcome the chronically poor condition of these roads. By the sixteenth century, the common solution (the first stage mentioned above) was to assign responsibility for upkeep on the parish level to local landowners, backed by regulations that enabled these landowners to enforce statute labor on their tenants. Parish surveyors were appointed to determine the necessary repairs. Each tenant was formally liable to serve for a certain number of days each year maintaining the local road, as determined by the surveyors. Sanctions could be levied on those who did not fulfill their duties. Roads were thus maintained by the local community, headed by the landlords. However, this system was not sufficient because the demand for road transport was evidently growing while the condition of the roads was deteriorating.

In the second half of the seventeenth century, a new solution based on the collection of tolls appeared. Tolls had been collected during earlier periods on some bridges and town roads. After 1663, the measure was used on a wider scale through an experimental form of business organization labeled in retrospect the "Justices of Peace turnpike." Each Justices of Peace turnpike was formed by a specific authorizing act. The act granted the local Justices of Peace the power to appoint surveyors, collectors, and other officers; to collect tolls; to raise money for the maintenance of the road by taking loans on the security of the tolls; and to end the toll collecting and open up the road again when it became well maintained.[2]

In the early eighteenth century, probably due to the growing duties of Justices of Peace and their lack of interest in road maintenance, a new

[2]A typical example of a Justices of Peace turnpike can be found in 1 Anne sess. 2 c.10 Pub. (1702) for the Thornwood–Woodford road. For a general discussion, see William Albert, *The Turnpike Road System in England,1663–1840* (Cambridge University Press, 1972), 14–29; Eric Pawson, *Transport and Economy: The Turnpike Roads of Eighteenth Century Britain* (London: Academic Press, 1977), 87–94; Sidney and Beatrice Webb, *English Local Government: The Story of the King's Highway* (London: Longmans, Green, 1913), 114–115. The Webbs, unlike later authors who stressed the innovative element, tended to see the Justices of Peace turnpikes as an extension of older forms of road maintenance.

organizational solution emerged: the turnpike trust. The turnpike trust was not an extension of the trust in its equitable sense, but rather something quite different that can be termed a statutory trust.[3] The first distinct Turnpike Trust Act was passed in 1706 and was characterized by appointed trustees with wide authority to demonstrate the trust's independent existence. Between 1706 and 1713, only six Justices of Peace turnpike acts passed, compared with fourteen trusts. One last Justices of Peace Turnpike Act passed in 1723. Thus, by 1714, the trust, a body outside the realm of the traditional local government structure, became the sole means of controlling a turnpike road. This third stage in organizational development went beyond the second stage mainly in terms of management rather than finance.

The process by which trustees replaced Justices of Peace in controlling turnpikes was more gradual than might seem from the above division into three distinct stages. The two forms existed side-by-side for a transitional period, during which time, within the turnpike trusts, trustees acquired wider powers and the role of the Justices of Peace gradually diminished. Several examples demonstrate this process.

In an act of 1702, Justices of Peace were empowered to appoint officers, supervise their activities, and inquire into their accounts.[4] An act of 1711 appointed some local notables including "all the Justices of Peace for the County" as commissioners (not yet trustees).[5] Both in terminology and personalities, this was an intermediate stage. An act of 1717 nominated "trustees for putting this act in execution."[6] This act still gave the Justices of Peace the role of checking accounts and surveying misapplication of money and abuse of powers. By 1728, trustees were empowered to conduct the day-to-day management of the turn-

---

[3]The legal concept of the trust as introduced in Chapter 1 is not really applicable to the turnpike trust. Its core is the equitable trust which is a personal relationship between beneficiaries and trustees, requiring no statutory sanction. Late eighteenth- and early nineteenth-century unincorporated companies used the equitable trust as a device in their organizational schemes (see Chapter 6). In the turnpike trust there was no such a relationship. There were no beneficiaries other than the general public, and the latter had no legal standing regarding the trust. The term trust was probably used because for some reason each act nominated officials called "trustees" for the execution of the purpose of the act, but they could just as well have been called "commissioners," as in river navigation acts, without altering the legal framework of the turnpike trust. Trustees as well as commissioners must have had some fiduciary duties because they were given powers by acts of Parliament, and such powers were generally linked to duties. Some historians have overplayed the importance of the trust conception when developing alternatives to the joint-stock corporation, by misleadingly linking the turnpike trust to the equitable trust and the unincorporated company.

[4]See 1 Anne sess. 2 c.10 (1702) for the Thornwood–Woodford turnpike.
[5]See 9 Anne c.33 (1711) for the Portsmouth and Sheet turnpike.
[6]See 3 Geo. I c.4 (1717) for the Islington, etc.–Highgate turnpike.

pike. The role of Justices of Peace was limited to warning the toll receivers under oath before the latter submitted their accounts to the trustees.[7] In an act of 1752, the Justices of Peace role was further limited to meditating disputes between the turnpike and neighboring landowners, and investigating complaints concerning the turnpike. This role is not easily distinguishable from their official tasks in the local community.[8]

The clauses of the turnpike trust acts became more uniform as the transition period (1700–1720s) ended. A typical mid-eighteenth century turnpike trust was based on the following organizational scheme: It was created by a specific act of Parliament which followed the private bill procedure in Parliament.[9] The act was limited in time, usually to twenty-one years. A renewal act (almost always routinely granted) had to be obtained for each additional period of time. Each act named the trustees and the powers conferred on them, the section of road to be turnpiked, the toll to be collected and the location of the toll gate, and the powers of the trust's higher officials – surveyor, treasurer, and clerk. Some of the earlier trusts had financial limitations on the amount to be borrowed and on the rate of interest payable on the loans. However, the general trend as the eighteenth century progressed was to ease the financial limitations of the trust and to expand the powers of the trustees in administering the trust and operating the road.

Can the turnpike trust be viewed as a substitute or forerunner of the joint-stock corporation in the transport sector? One way of approaching this question is by comparing the characteristics of the two. The governance powers were vested in the hands of a large number of designated trustees, usually local dignitaries, named in the act. The actual decisions, however, were taken by a small group of active trustees.[10] Thus, the decision-making process was not in the hands of formal representation of interested individuals or property, or on active voting to arrive at majority decisions, as in the joint-stock company. Though the trustees had the right to limit access to the road under trust, they were not the

---

[7]See 1 Geo. II c.11 (1728) for the Evesham–Worcester turnpike.

[8]See 25 Geo. II c.12 (1752) for the Worminster–Bath turnpike.

[9]Except that at some stages, such acts, unlike other private acts, were printed by the King's Printer in a manner similar to public acts. Lambert, *Bills and Acts*, 174–177.

[10]The quorum needed was only a fraction of the total number of trustees named in each act. Most of the trustees' names were included in turnpike acts to facilitate their passage through Parliament and to present a creditworthy image when applying for capital loans. For example, the Islington and Marylebone trusts had 399 trustees in 1756 but the average attendance at meetings was about thirty, and even this figure was high compared with other trusts. C. A. Allen Clarke, "The Turnpike Trusts of Islington and Marylebone: 1700–1825," M. A. thesis, University of London, 1955. See also Albert, *Turnpike Road*, 57.

owners of the road in any sense; it was a King's highway and not the property of neighboring landowners or local authorities represented by the trustees. The fact that the trusts had no legal owners can be viewed from a different aspect: that of profit. The trust's source of capital was borrowing, based on expected cash flow from the toll. Issuing shares was not within the powers of the trustees. Were trusts motivated by profit maximization goals, the way joint-stock corporations were? Theoretically, a turnpike trust's profits were invested in the upkeep of the road it governed. Surplus capital was directed to other needs in the same county, such as improving nearby roads and bridges. When these needs were taken care of, the tolls were to have been abolished, and the road opened to all passengers again. In practice, however, not many turnpikes were revoked, both because many of the trusts owed money and because trustees had an interest in continuing the turnpike. It was quite common for trustees to benefit by receiving a good rate of interest on loans to the trust, by the reimbursement of their expenses, by nepotism, and even by pure corruption.

In conclusion, though based on different legal foundations, the turnpike trust had much in common with the business corporation. It was a legal association created by the State. It had a hierarchical managerial structure. It had an economic purpose and an element of profit maximization motivation. It dealt with financial schemes, balancing of income and expenses, and accounting procedures. The experience of the individuals involved in it was in many respects similar to the experience of those involved in joint-stock companies. It was an experiment whose lesson would be studied by future generations of transport entrepreneurs who came to adopt the corporate form of organization.

The Organization of River Navigation Improvement

The improvement of the navigability of rivers went through an organizational transformation similar to that of road transport, yet it evolved one step further. It began as a matter for local authorities together with their other functions. It was then organized according to specific statutory authorizations, with finance based on the collection of tolls and management relegated to commissioners or trustees named in the act, in a manner similar to that of turnpike trusts. But river navigation further developed into statutory authorities financed by way of joint stock and invested in by quasi-shareholders. Later in the century, these projects became joint-stock navigation corporations.

Prior to the Restoration, only a small number of projects were undertaken for the improvement of the navigation of rivers or sections of rivers.[11] The authority for these projects was either granted by the Commissions of Sewers, royal commissions mainly concerned with drainage and flood prevention, or based on letters patent, granted by the Crown for the performance of a specific work. In both cases, the authority held by the promoters was limited in terms of both finance and negotiation with landowners along the river.

After the Restoration, and even more so after the Glorious Revolution, with the change in the political balance of power, economic development, and the rising demand for freight transportation, river navigation entered a new phase. Private acts of Parliament became the major, and later the only, source of authorization for river navigation projects. Acts of improvement of river navigation passed in four major waves: twelve between 1660 and 1670, ten between 1697 and 1705, twelve between 1714 and 1727, and twenty-two after 1750. Altogether, acts were passed for at least sixty-two rivers or parts of rivers.[12]

The typical river improvement act named the members of two bodies: the undertakers of the improvement and the commissioners of the navigation. The undertakers were those who actually carried out the project, initiated it and brought it to Parliament for authorization, executed the works for making the river navigable, and then administered the day-to-day running of the navigation itself. The commissioners were usually local dignitaries, who supervised the whole project and protected the interests of the general public. They also meditated between conflicting interests: those of the undertakers, landowners, merchants and other users, mill owners, boatmen, and so on.

In some cases, finance for the project came from municipal corporations or other groups with sufficient direct interest in the navigation and sufficient direct benefit from its improvement. In other cases, the undertakers invested in a project with the intention of collecting fees from the users of the river after the improvement, in the hope of profit. This form of finance resembles that used in road turnpikes. In most cases, the authorizing acts of Parliament specified the amounts to be invested and the maximum fees to be collected on completion of the project. In conclusion, a typical act specified the individuals involved in the project (undertakers and commissioners), the financial scheme (investments and fees), the initial settlement of some of the expected disputes between conflicting interests, the mechanism for mediating disagreements that might occur at a later stage, and some specification of the geography

---

[11]The survey in this and the following paragraph is based mainly on T. S. Willan, *River Navigation in England: 1600–1750* (Oxford University Press, 1936; rpt., London, 1964).

[12]Many of these acts were amended in subsequent years, thus the total number of acts relating to river improvement is substantially higher.

and engineering of the river improvement project. But economic realities, including a combination of growing financial needs, innovation, and imitation of other sectors, were strong enough to bring about a shift from this standard form of organization toward the joint-stock organization.

As attempts were made to make rivers with more problematic courses navigable, and as it became more common for individuals, rather than municipal corporations, to undertake river navigation projects, there was a growing need to share the burden of financing such projects. A standard act named undertakers and, in so doing, in fact, prohibited transferability of their interest to individuals not named in the act. A problem occurred when the financial resources of the undertakers ran out before construction was completed. Original undertakers may then have wanted to desert, to be replaced by new undertakers, or to add more undertakers to share the financial burden with them. A formal solution could be to amend each act when new individuals joined, but this solution was not very practical. A more practical solution was to ignore the authorizing status on this point and to transfer shares by agreement between the outgoing and incoming undertakers.

This seems to have been the course that was taken in several projects in the 1710s and 1720s. One case involved local undertakers named in a 1715 act for making the river Kennet navigable, who transferred their interests in the navigation to a group of London financiers a few years later, without specific authorization.[13] Early in 1720, an act was obtained by two undertakers to make the river Douglas navigable. Just two months later, as the South Sea boom was at its peak, they could not resist the temptation and issued 1,200 shares at £5 each. The share price soon jumped, with the rest of the market, and reached £70 per share; the undertakers sold quickly and made huge profits. This was done without any authorization in the act to transfer their interest or to divide it into shares.[14] In 1712, the Corporation of Bath obtained an act to make the river Avon navigable. Because it was not able to start the construction until 1724, it transferred its interest in that year to a group of thirty-two new undertakers.[15] This too was done without any legal base.[16]

---

[13]For the terms of the original act, see I Geo. I c.24 (1715); for the transfer of interest, see J. R. Ward, *The Finance of Canal Building in Eighteenth Century England* (Oxford: Clarendon Press, 1974), 10–11.

[14]6 Geo. I c.28 (1720); Charles Hadfield and Gordon Biddle, *The Canals of North West England*, 2 vols. (Newton Abbot: David and Charles, 1970), vol. 1, pp. 60–61.

[15]10 Anne c.2 (1712); Charles Hadfield, *The Canals of Southern England* (Newton Abbot: David and Charles, 1955), 40.

[16]Whereas evidence of legal arrangements in the stock of river navigation undertakings could be found in acts, as is shown below, evidence for the evasion of acts is

A more sophisticated solution was to prepare provisions in the original act for such cases. In an early case, the act of 1720 for making the river Weaver navigable gave the commissioners the power to add new undertakers to subscribe additional capital.[17] It is not clear whether they actually used this permission. In later years, this course of action was exploited to its extreme. Nathaniel Kinderley was appointed as single undertaker for making the river Dee navigable by an act of 1733. In this case, the actual entrepreneurs, Thomas Watts and Richard Manley, used a dual tactic: First, they used Kinderley only as a front man who acted as trustee while they were the beneficiaries, and second, they included a proviso in the act that enabled him to assign his rights to others. In the following year, they brought in ninety subscribers, raising £40,000 from them in 400 shares of £100 and, in return, nominating forty of them as assigned undertakers. Thus, while concealing their full intentions in Parliament, the two were able to turn the navigation from a nominally one-man undertaking into a joint-stock concern with transferable shares within one year, all based on the trust device and on the inclusion of a broadly framed clause in the authorization act.[18] The use of the equitable trust in this case suggests that it may also have been used in other navigation commissions which left no historical traces to accomplish a transfer of interests, before being employed for the structuring of unincorporated companies in the insurance sector, to which we soon turn.

More explicit measures could be taken when sufficient support was gained in Parliament. When London financiers lost money before making the river Kennet navigable, it became evident to Parliament that reorganization was unavoidable. An act was passed in 1730 for this purpose, reorganizing the undertaking into 300 shares of £100 totaling £30,000. The act de facto recognized the undertaking as a joint-stock company with transferable shares, but not as a corporation. However, one corpo-

---

found mainly in external documents. Thus, any estimate of the number of such cases is doubtful. 34 Geo. III c.37 (1794) for incorporating the Mersey and Irwell Rivers Navigation may be the tip of an iceberg. Its preamble referred to the fact the navigation was divided into 500 shares, a division not authorized in the original act, 7 Geo. I c.15 (1721). When and why this move to joint-stock took place was not specified. It may be that by the end of the century many of the river navigation undertakings, out of financial necessity and without authorization, turned to the joint-stock form. It is more likely that such organizational transformations became prevalent after the successful canal experiment in joint stock. The best way to study the scale of the unauthorized shift of river navigation undertakings to joint stock is probably by making a detailed study of their surviving business records.

[17] 7 Geo. I c.10 (1720); Hadfield, *Canals of North West*, 40.
[18] 6 Geo. II c.30 (1733); Joseph Priestley, *An Historical Account of Navigable Rivers, Canals, and Railways of Great Britain* (1831), 205–209; William T. Jackman, *The Development of Transportation in Modern England*, 2d ed. (London: Frank Cass, 1962), 196–200.

rate privilege was granted the company: the right to sue for tolls using a common name, without having to list all the shareholders. Interestingly enough, the act used the term "proprietors" and not "undertakers," which had been used in previous acts. The new term suggested a degree of ownership rights rather than execution on behalf of others.[19]

In 1740, long after a 1664 act for making the river Medway navigable was not exercised, a new act was passed in Parliament. The prospect of using the river for carrying timber for the navy probably facilitated its passage. The act authorized the proprietors of the river Medway navigation to raise £30,000, divided into 300 shares. Shares were to become transferable on the completion of the project. By this act, the Medway navigation, from its origins, was explicitly a joint-stock concern but still without privileges of incorporation.[20]

Financial difficulties were always a pretext for legal innovation. This was the case when the Company of Cutlers in Hallamshire and the Borough of Doncaster were not able to carry the financial burden of making the river Dun navigable, after obtaining acts for that purpose in 1726 and 1727, and were forced to turn to private resources. In 1733 they agreed that the powers they received in these acts would be vested in a newly formed business corporation. The act united the undertakers into one "Company and Copartnership" as a "Body Politick and Corporate."[21] It gave them a common, or corporate, name, "The Company of Proprietors of the Navigation of the River Dun." It even expressly listed specific privileges: perpetual succession, common seal, and the right to sue and be sued using the corporate name. The river Dun and the year 1733 were thus the first instance in which the joint-stock corporation was applied to a transport undertaking.

Other river navigation projects soon followed and adopted a corporate form. The need for reorganization of proprietorship due to capital shortage was the pretext for the bill incorporating the navigation of the river Dee. As mentioned above, in 1734 Nathaniel Kinderley was among the first to legally raise joint stock, without incorporation, for financing a navigation project. By 1740, this capital had been consumed and more money was needed for the completion of the construction. The shareholders decided to raise more money, but this time they did not settle for the authorization to raise an additional £52,000; they also petitioned

[19]3 Geo II c.35 (1730).
[20]13 Geo. II c.26 (1740); Willan, *River Navigation*, 67. DuBois, *English Business Company*, 158 n. 99, believed that this act incorporated the Medway navigation, but there is nothing in the act to support his claim, no corporate privileges were granted to the navigation, and even DuBois himself admitted that the clauses of the act "were on their face not free from ambiguity" (ibid.).
[21]The original acts are 12 Geo I c.38 (1726) and 13 Geo. I c.20 (1727). The incorporating act is 6 Geo. II c.9 (1733).

Parliament for incorporation.[22] The petition became an act that incorporated the company, specifying the privileges of the corporate entity to make bylaws and to purchase land.[23]

Economic realities in the second quarter of the eighteenth century made it impossible for many of the river navigation undertakings to maintain the form of legal organization used in the previous half-century. A process can be identified in which municipal corporations and single individuals were replaced by groups of individuals investing in joint stock, and finally by joint-stock corporations. Proprietors and shareholders were taking the place of undertakers. The process was gradual, developing from case to case. Up to the first decade of the eighteenth century, navigation projects were financed by individual undertakers and controlled by local commissioners. By the 1720s, de facto joint-stock undertakings without statutory authorization existed. In the 1720s, and more so in the 1730s, undertakers could pass acts that recognized transferable joint stock. In 1733, full incorporation was granted for the first time, and by the 1740s, several statutory navigation commissions were converted into joint-stock navigation corporations. Some navigations, such as the Dee and the Kennet, went through more than one organizational phase as they battled to complete their projects with limited financial resources.[24] The experiments of river navigations served as an important lesson for entrepreneurs, investors, solicitors, and Parliament in the canal era, to which I now turn.

The Coming of the Joint-Stock Canal Corporations

The experimental stage and the evolutionary process in the organization of canals were much shorter than in either road transport or river navigation. The first few canals were not organized as joint-stock corporations, for reasons examined below, but within twelve years of the first endeavor at canal building, a decisive turning point drastically changed the path of development of the canal sector into the corporate form. This section focuses on the context and reason for this turning point.

The first attempt at obtaining a bill for cutting a navigable canal in England was not the Duke of Bridgewater's celebrated act of 1759, or the less-known Sankey Brook bill of 1755. It was a petition brought to Parliament in January 1754 by residents of Manchester to bring in a bill

---

[22]*Commons' Journal* 23 (March 19, 1740), 597–598.

[23]14 Geo. II c.8 (1741); *Commons' Journal* 23 (March 19, 1740), 597–598.

[24]Most navigations transformed to joint-stock form eventually, but only a minority did so before the canal age. It seems that many of the later conversions to joint-stock corporations were influenced by the canal model. As suggested above, this issue should be further researched using business records of navigations.

for cutting a channel from Salford to Leigh and Wiggan. The channel was to be supplied by water from the river Irwell and used for carrying coal to Manchester and Salford. The bill was referred to a committee where it faced strong opposition. Within a week, seven petitions against the bill were submitted by owners of land bordering the channel and the river, by individuals with interests in fisheries and mills in the Irwell River, by the trustees of a competing turnpike, and others.[25] The bill was abandoned due to the strong opposition.

When the Sankey Brook scheme was promoted the following year, the Salford experience was still fresh. The promoters, financially and otherwise supported by the Liverpool Corporation, tried to keep a low profile. They did not want the novelty of their project to become known, and tried to represent it as one more river navigation improvement undertaking. They included a clause in their bill authorizing them "to dig or cut the banks . . . and to make new cuts, canals, trenches or passages for water . . . as they shall think proper and requisite."[26] This was a standard clause in river navigation acts of the time and did not attract any special attention. However, it provided the promoters with all the authority they needed to build a new canal. This must have been their original intention because the brook was too narrow in the first place and its improvement for navigation impracticable.[27]

When the Duke of Bridgewater began promoting his first canal bill in 1759, he was aware of the failure of the Salford bill in 1754 (a bill supported at the time by the Duke's guardians) and of the progress at Sankey Brook. He took into account strong opposition by the Mersey and Irwell navigation, whose water he intended to use in his canal. He must have been inspired by the Sankey Act to use some concealing tactics. He sent his bill through the private bill procedure, rather than the public bill procedure used in all the current river navigation bills and in the Sankey bill.[28] The private bill procedure attracted less attention and was easier for bill promoters to control. At that time, he introduced in the bill only a canal with a limited course that did not jeopardize the Mersey and Irwell navigation. He probably had no intention of carrying

[25]*Commons' Journal* 26 (1754), 905, 944, 968–969, 972–973, 977.

[26]28 Geo. II c.8 (1755).

[27]T. C. Barker, "The Beginning of the Canal Age in the British Isles," in L. S. Pressnell, ed., *Studies in the Industrial Revolution Presented to T. S. Ashton* (London: Athlone, 1960), 15–18. Barker is careful to emphasize that there is no conclusive evidence to support this "subterfuge" thesis, but it does seem to him more convincing than a later change of mind by the promoters.

[28]For the procedure taken by Bridgewater, see Frederick Clifford, *A History of Private Bill Legislation*, 2 vols. (London: Butterworths, 1885–1887), vol. 1, pp. 33–38. It should be noted that this description focused on the passage of his third bill in 1762 in the face of strong opposition by the Mersey and Irwell navigation, after two bills passed without opposition in 1759 and 1760.

it out at all, or planned to include it in a longer canal that was his final goal. Whatever the Duke's calculations were, they must have been well taken because his first canal bill passed with no opposition. This was indeed the first act passed which included express authorization to make a canal.

None of the attempts mentioned above led to the formation of a joint-stock corporation. The Salford scheme was blocked before it reached maturity, and there is no indication of an attempt to form a joint-stock corporation in this case. The Sankey Brook Act used the organizational form of standard river navigation improvement acts. There was no incorporating clause, and no corporate privileges were granted. The well-tried two-tiered structure of undertakers supervised by commissioners was employed for governance just as it had been in previous decades for roads and rivers. In fact, the Sankey promoters acted like many river navigation promoters of the 1720s and 1730s, and created joint stock without parliamentary authorization. The Liverpool corporation carried most of the initial expenses. A subscription for 120 shares was opened late in 1754, before a petition was made to Parliament.[29] Though the subscription predated the petition, it was not mentioned in the bill introduced in Parliament. The Duke of Bridgewater did not have to resort to joint-stock investment because he was able to finance 80 or 90 percent of the cost of his canals from his own resources.[30]

The dominant factor in the first decade of canal promotion was the urge to keep a low profile. The failure of the Salford scheme served as a harsh warning to the promoters of the Sankey canal and to the Duke of Bridgewater that many in influential circles were worried by the innovative spirit of the canal promoters and by the far-reaching economic and environmental consequences of canals. Thus, the attempts to represent canal building as continuing river navigation schemes, to conceal the fact that the project was actually a canal (Sankey), or to obscure its full course (Bridgewater), are understandable. In these circumstances, any attempt to include incorporation as part of a bill authorizing the construction of a canal could only increase the bill's chances of failure.

Thus the link between canals and joint-stock incorporation was formed not with the first canal scheme of 1754, but twelve years (and six bills) later, in 1766. In that year, bills were introduced in Parliament for two canal schemes which had reached maturity: the Trent and Mersey Canal and the Staffordshire and Worcestershire Canal. This was a critical moment from the point of view of the organizational form that was to be employed by future canals. Two alternatives were considered

---

[29]Ward, *Canal Building*, 26–27; Barker, "Canal Age," 15–17.
[30]Ward, *Canal Building*, 28.

by the promoters of the Trent and Mersey Canal: that of a trust, based on the turnpike trust model and the commissioner-controlled river navigation model, and that of the joint-stock corporation. This must have been a major concern for the promoters because "the rest of the year [from May 1765 on] was given to controversy upon whether the Trent & Mersey should be run by a trust or a company."[31] By February 1766, the decision had been made and a bill was presented in Parliament.

The Trent and Mersey bill was joined in Parliament by the Staffordshire and Worcestershire bill. These two bills, which passed through Parliament in April and May of 1766, created the lasting link between canal construction and the joint-stock corporation. At first glance, the two canals do not seem to have much in common. But close observation uncovers similarity in the acts that authorized them. They were passed in Parliament less than two weeks apart,[32] and received consecutive serial numbers: 6 Geo. III c.96 and 6 Geo. III c.97. Both were public acts, but for some reason neither was printed in the General Collection, and they were printed together and attached to the collection only many years later.[33] Neither was drafted by Robert Harper, the leading drafter of that era, who designed hundreds of bills, including the Sankey bill.[34] The general structure of the acts was similar, and the clauses that fixed their form of business organization and granted incorporation were almost identical.[35] It seems highly probable that the same solicitor, acting as a parliamentary agent, drafted both bills, and moved them in close proximity through Parliament.

Both acts included clear-cut incorporation clauses: "one body politic and corporate . . . shall have perpetual succession, and shall have a common seal, and by the name shall and may sue and be sued, and also shall and may have power and authority to purchase lands . . . without incurring any of the penalties or forfeitures of the Status of Mortmain."[36] Both acts then went on to specify the capital to be raised by each company, its structure, future calls, voting rights, assemblies and committees, bylaws, officers, and more. Thus, in one stroke, two companies

---

[31]Charles Hadfield, *The Canals of the West Midlands* (Newton Abbot: David and Charles, 1966), 23.

[32]See *Commons' Journal* 31 (1766), 354, 358, 368, 370, 397 for the Trent and Mersey; and 379, 383, 386, 389, 397 for the Staffordshire and Worcestershire.

[33]Both were printed in 1830 by George Eyre and Andrew Strahan, and placed in the British Library volume for 1766 after all the acts originally printed in 1766 (British Library, BS. Ref. 4).

[34]Lambert, *Bills and Acts*.

[35]Cf. sections 21–37 of 6 Geo. III c.96 (1766) – Trent to sections 25–41 of 6 Geo. III c.97 (1766) – Staffordshire.

[36]Preamble to both 6 Geo. III c.96 and c.97 (1766).

with complete corporate privileges and full joint-stock structure were established for the first time in the canal sector.

These two companies were to lead all further canal undertakings. From 1766 on, all canals were built on the same organizational model, that of the joint-stock business corporation. The Coventry Canal and Birmingham Canal Acts of 1768 and the Oxford Canal Act of 1769 were the first to follow.[37] The Leeds and Liverpool Canal promoters followed the path paved by previous canals when they decided late in 1768 "that application be made to Parliament this present session for an act to make and complete the same by a company of proprietors vested with the same powers and under the same conditions as the Staffordshire, Coventry and several other acts lately granted. And that a petition to Parliament be here signed."[38] Their petition was successful and in 1770 they obtained an act that authorized the construction of the most ambitious canal yet.[39]

Altogether, 122 acts for canals and river navigation undertakings were passed in the years 1755–1814. Most of the canal acts were passed in two waves, the first in the late 1760s and early 1770s and the second in the early 1790s (the canal mania). More than £17 million was raised by canal companies in the period before 1814. The Grand Junction Canal, the largest of all, required eighteen times more capital than the Staffordshire and Worcestershire (£1,800,000 compared with £100,000).[40] Its managerial and financial structure, as reflected in its act, was more complex.[41] However, the increase in the scale and scope of canal corporations, as canalization gathered momentum throughout the island, did not involve any change in the basic legal framework.

The year 1766, when the link between canal construction and the joint-stock corporation, not initially inevitable, was first formed, serves as a turning point. It occurred, I believe, due to a combination of long-term trends, time- and place-specific factors, and contingencies. As the transport network developed, entrepreneurs moved from easy and inexpensive routes to more ambitious and expensive projects, which could not be financed even by well-to-do individuals. By the 1760s, the orga-

---

[37] 8 Geo. III c.36 (1768); 8 Geo. III c.38 (1768); 9 Geo. III c.70 (1769), respectively.

[38] Public Record Office [P.R.O.], RAIL 846/1, Dec. 19, 1768.

[39] 10 Geo. III c.114 (1770). For general background, see J. R. Harris, "Liverpool Canal Controversies, 1769–1772," *Journal of Transport History* 2, no. 3 (1956), 158–174.

[40] Ward, *Canal Building*, 29–30, 43–46.

[41] 33 Geo. III c.80 (1793). For a case study of the organizational structure of two midsize canals, see John Hughes, "Organizational Metamorphosis, 1765–1865: A Study of Changing Practice and Theory in the Organization and Management of Transport Companies," Ph.D. thesis, Oxford University, 1983.

nizational experiments in road transport and particularly in river navigation were well known and their outcomes influenced debates among undertakers of the two canals on whether or not to aim at incorporation. But specific factors and chance, such as the problems of the two canals, the identity of their legal and parliamentary advisers, and the representation of relevant interests in Parliament were also of great importance in the final turning. Organization of canals could have taken a different path, but did not. The outcome was stupendous: Dozens of incorporation acts passed through Parliament, making MPs familiar with this sort of business organization; thousands of subscribers became familiar with business corporations and their functioning; and millions of pounds were invested in shares, leading to the development of active primary and secondary markets in shares throughout England.[42] Interestingly enough, this important turning point in the history of both the canal and the joint-stock corporation has been overlooked by economic and legal historians.

INSURANCE

The general path of development in the transport sector evolved throughout the century toward a relatively homogenous organizational model, involving the raising of joint stock, the separation of management from proprietorship, and in most cases also the use of the corporate form. To substantiate the divergence thesis presented in the introduction to this chapter, we now turn to the insurance sector. Here we find a different path, in which the corporate form did not dominate; in this sector, considerably more diversity in organizational form persists throughout the eighteenth century. This section outlines the path of the insurance sector and explains the reasons for its divergence from the evolutionary, progressive, and converging path of the transport sector.

The Early Companies: Before 1720

The concept of insurance made its first significant steps in England after the Great Fire of London.[43] Though a few short-lived pioneering insur-

---

[42]This is not to say that a national and liquid market in canal shares was created instantaneously in 1766. The markets were first local and provincial, with some networks connecting with each other and with London. The annual turnover of a sample of canals was 5–10 percent. Only gradually, with peaks during the canal mania of the 1790s and the speculative boom of 1807–1811, did the market become more national and liquid, and even then not as national and liquid is it would become in the railway age. See Ward, *Canal Building*, 82–87, 97–105, 174. See also my discussion in Chapters 5 and 8 below.

[43]Frank C. Spooner, *Risks at Sea: Amsterdam Insurance and Maritime Europe, 1766–1780* (Cambridge University Press, 1983).

ance projects appeared during the Restoration, the first long-lasting English assurance associations were not formed until after the arrival of the house of Orange and its financial innovations, in the years 1696–1720. These included Hand-in-Hand (1696), Amicable (1706), Sun (1710), Union (1714), Westminster (1717), London Assurance (1720), and Royal Exchange Assurance (1720). The heterogeneity in the forms of business organization that was to be a central feature of the sector in later periods was already apparent at this early stage. This also makes the insurance sector an attractive one for the present study. There were mutual fire offices: Hand-in-Hand, Union, and Westminster. In these offices, the insured policyholders were also the owner-partners. These offices had no permanent joint stock, and premiums, which were the basis for their capital, were divided by varied arrangements among the claimants when fire damages occurred. These offices were not incorporated and were formally established by deeds of settlement enrolled in Chancery.[44] The Amicable Society was also based on mutual principles, yet its object was life insurance. Unlike the fire offices, it was incorporated by a letters patent of March 25, 1706, that was revised on three occasions during the following century. The letters patent, in addition to granting the society the normal privileges of corporate bodies, common seal, right to sue and be sued, and to purchase land, limited the number of members to 2,000, and the number of shares per person to three, and regulated entrance payments, annual premiums, insurance coverage, and dividends. The Sun was based on proprietorship and joint stock, not on mutual principles. The insured persons were not necessarily members. Yet like its fellow fire offices, and unlike the Amicable, it was not incorporated but rather based on deed of settlement. The London Assurance and the Royal Exchange Assurance were both articulate examples of the joint-stock corporation. They were incorporated by the King on June 22, 1720, in charters that followed an authorization for incorporation by the Bubble Act (6 Geo. I c.18).[45] They had substantial permanent capital, divided into transferable shares, raised by subscription, and subject to calls until fully paid. Both companies were granted a monopoly in marine insurance, thus excluding any other corporation or partnership from this field. In 1721, the corporations were granted charters for monopolistic assurance of lives and fire by the King's prerogative (that is, without prior authorization by Parliament). The monopoly of these great marine insurance corporations did not exclude individuals

---

[44]Though partnerships could be formed by less formal means, partnership contracts were often formalized by the signing of a deed of settlement. The partnership basis coupled with the joint-stock finance element created what was in fact an unincorporated company.

[45]See Chapter 3 for the circumstances of their incorporation.

from the field, and individual marine underwriting developed considerably and was later organized under the umbrella of Lloyd's Coffee House. Thus, by the second quarter of the eighteenth century the insurance sector was probably the most diversified sector in the English economy from the point of view of business organization. In it one could find a wide range of business organizations: monopolistic corporations, incorporated mutuals, unincorporated joint-stock companies, unincorporated mutuals, and a syndicate of individual underwriters (Lloyd's). The passage of the Bubble Act in 1720 had no immediate effect on the unincorporated undertakings in this sector because they were established before 1718, and according to clause 22, the act did not extend to undertakings established before that date. Insurance undertakings established at a later period, discussed below, found themselves with different legal status.

The 1720s to the 1750s

For about four decades, from 1720 to 1760, the growth of the insurance market was absorbed by the existing concerns and Lloyd's, as no substantial and lasting insurance office appeared in this period. The Bubble Act had its dual effect on the insurance sector: the monopoly granted in marine insurance and the proclamation of the illegality of certain unincorporated undertakings, which applied to fire and life insurance as well as to marine insurance and other sectors. It is not clear to what extent this pattern of internal and relatively slow growth was a result of the Bubble Act, or of the demand for insurance in the market. Yet from 1760 to the end of the century and thereafter, a new experimental and pioneering era began.

The Equitable: In early 1756, persons interested in life insurance who had either been rejected by the Amicable Society due to old age or were dissatisfied members of that society initiated a new life insurance undertaking. "It was the opinion of the majority of the persons engaged in the design, that such design could not well be carried on without the sanction of a charter."[46] An agreement was reached between the projectors, a subscription was opened, and a society was formed for obtaining the charter. This society would be dissolved when the charter was obtained and the corporation established.

A petition for a charter of the Equitable Assurance was made on April 16, 1757. It was followed by three hearings before the Attorney and Solicitor General and a request for a written report, all of which resulted, after more than four years of effort, in a negative recommendation by

[46]*Equitable-Papers Relating to the Dispute Between the Members of the Equitable Society and the Charter-Fund Proprietors* (1769), 77.

the Law Officers in their report to the committee of the Privy Council on July 14, 1761. The report raised doubts as to the scheme's prospects of success because of the limited profits of other companies in this sector, low premiums, and the use of speculative tables of mortality. The report also mentioned the policy of granting charters only when a particular need for incorporation could be demonstrated by the undertakers, when the undertaking could not be carried out without incorporation, or when it was evident that incorporation would benefit the public.[47] It was argued, however, that the real reason for the negative report of the Law Officers was the pressure of the Amicable and the London and Royal Exchange, which were lobbying for protection of their unique corporate privileges.[48] It seems that the Crown did not formulate general policies regarding the desired role of joint-stock corporations in the economy, but rather arrived at ad hoc decisions, according to the apparent merits of the pending incorporation petition or the pressures exercised by affected interest groups.

After the promoters realized that a charter was out of their reach, some retired members joined with new members in a new subscription for an unincorporated association. On September 9, 1762, more than six years after the undertaking was initiated, a deed of settlement was signed for the Association of the Equitable Assurance.[49] The deed established the company on a mutual base, where the insured were also the proprietors. Yet there were provisions in the deed for entrance payments and calls which enabled the company to hold some permanent joint stock in accordance with its needs. The company's organization included a court of directors, a general court, and five trustees. Seven more years were to pass before all disputes between the original promoters and those who joined in 1762 were settled, and it can be said that only in 1769 did the Equitable overcome its organizational infancy.

The 1760s and the 1770s

Soon after the establishment of the Equitable, numerous new institutions for annuities for the aged and for life insurance were promoted. This wave of promotions was, for the most part, speculative and fraudulent in nature, and many projects disappeared just as rapidly as they had

---

[47]For a reprint of the full text of the report, see *On the Policy and Expediency of Granting Insurance Charters* (1806), appendix 4.

[48]See *A Short Account of the Society for Equitable Assurance* (1762) for the nature of the competition of Equitable Assurance with Amicable, Royal Exchange, and London Assurance.

[49]The original deed was printed and published in *The Deed of Settlement of the Equitable Society* (1801).

appeared. Between 1770 and 1771, many societies whose names have been lost and eleven whose names are preserved sprang up around London.[50] By this time, new fire insurance offices had begun to emerge throughout England. Nine new fire offices were established in provincial towns between the years 1767 and 1785: Bath (1767), Bristol (1769), Manchester (1771), Bath Sun (1776), Liverpool (1777), Salop (1780), Leeds (no later than 1782), Newcastle-on-Tyne (1783), and Norwich (1785).[51] These offices were much smaller than the well-established London offices and were more like members' clubs or closed partnerships than unincorporated joint-stock companies with transferable shares. Among them they held only a fraction of the market, and did not even consider applying for charters.

The Phoenix: The next major experiment in business organization in the insurance sector was initiated late in 1781, when a group of twenty-one London sugar refiners met and resolved to form a new fire insurance company, the Phoenix. Why they found it necessary to initiate this new project in 1781 and not earlier or later is not clear. What encouraged them to organize may have been the fading shadow of the Bubble Act, but they may also have been motivated by nonlegal factors such as specific insurance-coverage needs, growing wealth from the Atlantic trade in search of investment opportunities, or the fact that they spotted a niche in provincial insurance that had not yet been exploited by the leading London offices.[52]

For more than a year, the promoters of the Phoenix persisted in their attempts to obtain a royal charter. Only in February 1783, after the Attorney General, Kenyon, advised the King to refuse the Phoenix petition for a charter, did the promoters turn to an alternative form of business organization. The form that was adopted was that of the unincorporated company. As a model for their company the promoters purchased from Bristol Assurance a copy of its 1769 deed of settlement. The promoters modified the deed clause-by-clause to suit their needs, using the best legal advice of the time to rewrite some of the clauses. By August 1783, after long discussion, the final version of the deed was prepared for the subscribers' signatures.[53] The deed of settlement fixed the capital of the Phoenix, regulated its investment, established a commission of trustees with clear duties, and attempted to limit the liability of share-

[50]Francis Baily, *An Account of the Several Life Assurance Companies* (1810), 13–14.
    [51]Francis Boyer Relton, *An Account of the Fire Insurance Companies . . . Established in Great Britain* (London, 1893).
    [52]Clive Trebilcock, *Phoenix Assurance and the Development of British Insurance*, Vol. 1: *1782–1870* (Cambridge University Press, 1985), 9–11.
    [53]Ibid., 69–72.

holders.[54] Only at this stage, about two years after it was initiated, did the Phoenix open its doors to customers for the first time. This case is a good example of the preference insurance entrepreneurs had for the joint-stock corporation model, and indicates that the high transaction costs involved in forming unincorporated companies served at least partially to motivate this preference.

British Assurance: Two years later, in 1785, another project, the British Assurance Society, made its bid for a charter. This time, the chronology of organizational stages was different. The society was established and began to function in 1773. In 1779, a formal deed of association was drawn and enrolled in King's Bench. "The language of the deed seemed to be a conscious attempt to imitate a corporation's charter."[55] Apparently, when it was felt that the deed was not a sufficient legal base for the society, an application was made to Parliament for an act of incorporation. The major reason given for the need for incorporation in the application was the lack of capacity to sue and be sued as a society.[56] The petition was eventually rejected in the Lords.[57]

The undertakers of the British Assurance, like those of the Phoenix, tried various organizational forms. Yet, unlike the latter, they did not try to solve all organizational problems in advance. Instead, they began their insurance business and dealt with organizational and legal problems only when they arose. Differences in scale may explain the different approaches. The promoters of the Phoenix aimed at a larger concern and could afford the legal expenses involved in an attempt to ensure a proper legal base in advance.

Westminster Assurance: In 1789, another attempt at incorporation was made by the promoters of a new life insurance undertaking. They initiated a bill for the incorporation of the Westminster Society. The bill faced strong opposition in both houses of Parliament, due to a petition against the bill by the Amicable Society, which wished to preserve its leading position in the life insurance subsector. Opponents of the bill objected to "taking one hundred citizens [the shareholders], and separating them from the rest of the public, in order to give them such undefined and unlimited powers . . . without making their private fortunes responsible, or applying any restrictions to the use and appropriation of their capital whatsoever."[58] The limited liability seemed to be the most irritating component of the bill from the point of view of its opponents. The

---

[54]Ibid., 73–77.
[55]DuBois, *English Business Company*, 271. See also 250–251 for the charter petition.
[56]*Commons' Journal* 40 (March 8, 1785), 610.
[57]*Lords' Journal* 37 (1779), 340, 377.
[58]See Debrett's *Parliamentary Register* (1789), 567.

supporters of the bill said that a corporation could offer security to the insured superior to that which private insurers could, who were subject to frequent bankruptcies. They argued that competition in the business of life insurance was desirable and the opposition of the Amicable to the bill was due to their wish to monopolize the business. The bill was defeated, but three years later, in 1792, Westminster Life Assurance settled for second best and was established as an unincorporated company by a deed of settlement.[59]

The 1790s and the 1800s

Around the turn of the century, many new fire and life insurance undertakings were initiated: Pelican, Palladium and Norwich Union (1797), Minerva (1798), Globe (1799), Imperial (1803), Albion (1805), London Life and Provident (1806), Atlas, Rock, Eagle, Hope, West of England, Rainbow and Country (1807).[60] Some of those did not last, but most did, and became significant components of the insurance sector.

The Globe: The establishment of the Globe is a good example of the organizational alternatives and difficulties facing the insurance sector around the turn of the nineteenth century. In 1799, as a first stage in their scheme, the promoters of the Globe obtained an act to enable the King to incorporate them. At that time, they could not persuade the Law Officers of the Crown to recommend the granting of a charter. When, in 1802, the new Law Officers removed their objections, the Committee of the Privy Council itself decided that it was not expedient to grant the charter. The promoters then decided, in 1803, to establish the Globe as an unincorporated company based on a deed of settlement. In 1806, the Globe renewed its attempt to enter the marine insurance business with an attack on the monopolistic privileges of the London and Royal Exchange Assurance, and at the same time petitioned for incorporation, this time by act of Parliament, and not by charter. After facing strong opposition from the established companies, the Globe abandoned the bill and settled for a more modest measure, an act that would enable the company to sue and be sued using the name of one of the officers, which passed in 1807. This partial substitute for incorporation was copied by other concerns. By 1815, twenty-five such acts had passed in the insurance sector alone, and afterward this partial substitute spread in considerable numbers to other sectors as well.

The Globe is not really representative of the insurance companies

---

[59]Ibid., 566–570; *Lords' Journal* 38 (1792), 505, 507–508, 510–511.
[60]Thomas Tooke, *A History of Prices* (1837), 278–280; Baily, *Life Assurance Companies*, 15–18; Charles Babbage, *A Comparative View of the Various Institutions for Assurance of Lives* (1826), inserted table (before p. 1).

established around the turn of the century. Its promoter, Frederick Eden, was more ambitious, aggressive, and provocative than other promoters of his age, and in a way he was a pioneer. As such he experienced both failure and success, while the more cautious entrepreneurs that followed his path were able to avoid some of the failures by aiming at more reasonable targets.

Insurance: The End Point

By the early nineteenth century, the insurance sector was as diversified as it had been a century earlier. Substantial market shares were held by monopolistic and nonmonopolistic corporations, by unincorporated joint-stock companies, by mutual associations, by closed partnerships, and by syndicates of individuals. There was no general legislation or consistent policy toward this sector except for the Bubble Act, and each undertaking was treated by the State according to its merits, or, in fact, its ability to lobby. The Bubble Act itself played a peculiar role: on one hand, it placed an obstacle on the forming of corporations by creating a corporate monopoly in marine insurance, and, on the other, it motivated incorporation by limiting unincorporated joint-stock companies. There was, nevertheless, a definite tendency among newly formed insurance undertakings toward the unincorporated joint-stock form, the result of the way in which vested interests were able to block newcomers from full incorporation. The difference in this respect between the transport and insurance is discussed below.

CONCLUSION: TWO PATHS OF ORGANIZATION

The organizational development of the transport and insurance sectors throughout the eighteenth century involved several parallel features. Both sectors developed from a meager starting point, faster than most other sectors, and grew to play a leading role in the industrialization of the economy. The two sectors underwent an intriguing experimental and evolutionary process of learning by doing and by copying. Gradually, both adopted the features of joint-stock finance and the separation of management from proprietorship. The agents of change in both sectors were the businessmen. Development was achieved mainly through private acts promoted by parliamentary agents and interested lobbyists, and through contracts and deeds drafted by attorneys. It did not come from the high echelons of government or the courts of law, and was not reflected in general statutes or royal court decisions.

But the two sectors differed in one major aspect. Whereas in transport, the corporation with its unique feature of separate legal personality became the dominant framework of organization, in insurance it did not. The latter had to settle, in most cases reluctantly, for the second best alternative, the unincorporated company.

It is questionable whether the reason for this lies in the differences between the two sectors. The transport sector may have been considered by some to be more beneficial to the public at large and thus more deserving of the permissive incorporation policy by the State. This is debatable, however, because the transport sector did not produce public goods or free services to all, because it depended on fares collected. Moreover, in 1776, as high an authority as Adam Smith noted that both sectors were "of greater and more general utility" than other sectors, and equally deserving of joint-stock incorporation.[61]

More attempts were made by the insurance sector to incorporate by way of a royal charter than in transport, where incorporation was achieved only through Parliament. Insurance entrepreneurs were not refused incorporation because of miscalculation in turning to the wrong address, the Crown. They believed that the expensive and publicized procedure of parliamentary incorporation was less likely to result in a charter. Transport entrepreneurs, on the other hand, had no choice but to turn to Parliament, because they needed more than just incorporation, and the Crown could not provide the other sought-for privilege: land appropriation.

The two sectors also differed in their major motives for incorporation. In the insurance sector, the possibility of mass disasters and colossal claims motivated entrepreneurs to seek joint-stock investment, in order to spread the risk. Only incorporation could provide the ultimate protection through the related features of limitation of liability and separate corporate personality. In transport, the lump-sum nature of the required capital investment, which was beyond the means of individuals and small groups, forced entrepreneurs to raise joint stock. Since they had to turn to Parliament anyway to authorize eminent domain, many preferred to ask for full incorporation which would answer both these basic needs. Thus, while both sectors had good reasons to seek incorporation, it was the insurance sector which could not settle for the unincorporated form without giving up one of its major needs, the limitation of liability.

In conclusion, I do not believe that the differences between the two sectors in demand or desire for incorporation account for the final outcome: the widespread incorporation in the transport sector, in contrast to the mostly unincorporated insurance sector. This outcome can better be explained by differences in the structure of the interest groups and of

---

[61]Adam Smith, *The Wealth of Nations,* 5th ed. (London, 1789; rpt., New York, 1937), 714–715.

their markets. The legal framework created a narrow entry corridor to the corporate form. Vested interests were on guard for any incorporation petition that could affect their business. As soon as they identified such a petition they clustered together to block it. While in transport, each new undertaking seeking incorporation was a natural monopoly in its region; in insurance, such an undertaking competed directly with existing and established ones. However, this general statement deserves qualification: The insurance sector was divided into three subsectors – marine, fire, and life – which did not directly compete with one another, whereas in the transport sector a new undertaking of the same or of different nature – road, river, or canal – could divert traffic from an older one. In insurance, the clustering of vested interests accumulated in the late seventeenth and early eighteenth century created an impassable entry barrier, even in the individual subsectors. In the transport sector, in many cases the newcomer competed only marginally, if at all, with vested interests; even if there was more direct competition, settlements were more negotiable. Agreement could be reached between the limited and well-identified vested interests and the newcomers. Shares in a potentially highly profitable canal company could serve to buy off proprietors of nearby turnpike roads or river navigation undertakings. Tolls could be fixed and divided among various transport undertakings on the same line. Fair compensation could be offered to landowners to settle the routes of canals in advance. In insurance, a less predictable and more competitive sector, reaching settlements of this type was more complicated.

Whatever the causes for the different organizational paths, two distinct models emerged in the two sectors. The century that followed the Bubble Act is dominated by these two models, or forms of organization, the joint-stock business corporation and the unincorporated joint-stock company. Chapter 5 examines the legal characteristics of the business corporation, and the relevance of these characteristics to the specific economic context of early industrializing England. Chapter 6 examines the unincorporated company and contrasts it with the business corporation.

5

The Joint-Stock Business Corporation

My focus throughout the present work is on four features of the business organization: the nature of the legal entity, raising joint-stock capital and transferring interest, the degree of limitation on personal liability, and the existence of entry barriers. The present chapter examines the application of these features to the business corporation. I discuss the needs of the English economy in terms of capital, and how these needs could be fulfilled by raising joint-stock capital in the financial markets of the time. I then analyze the demand for limited liability in eighteenth-century England and the degree to which this privilege was available to business corporations. Finally, I examine the existence of entry barriers, in terms of costs and other obstacles, which could prevent incorporation and make the privileges associated with it unattainable. This chapter shows that by the beginning of the nineteenth century, both the joint-stock feature and the limited liability feature became more valuable and widely available, and as a result became the major motivation for seeking incorporation. It further shows that it was not Parliament, as such, which prescribed high costs for incorporation, nor did it place high entry barriers on the formation of new business corporations. Such barriers that existed resulted from the opposition of vested interests to newcomers and not from parliamentary policy.

LEGAL PERSONALITY

By the sixteenth century, if not earlier, long before our story begins, a corporation was a personality in English law. This meant that it had certain rights, was subject to duties, and had the power to perform actions with legal consequences. By the beginning of our story, it is also clear that it was a legal person, yet one that was different from human beings. Its birth and death were not natural occurrences, but occurred in the legal field, the result of an act of State. It was usually immortal and had perpetual existence.

Whereas on the Continent, relatively abstract and theoretical discussions on the nature of corporate personality evolved in the Romanist and Canonist schools from the fourteenth century onward, and with renewed vigor in the German historical school from the early nineteenth century, such discussions did not appear in common-law literature until late in the nineteenth century. Unlike high Continental law of early modern Europe, high English law of that period was not developed by scholars in secluded universities, interpreting old texts and drafting new comprehensive codes, having ample motivation and opportunity to discuss abstract jurisprudential issues. It was developed by a handful of overworked common-law judges and Lord Chancellors. Their agenda was shaped by the disputes that reached their halls and had to be settled within a reasonable time according to forms set generations earlier, during the formative periods of the common law. Only those aspects of corporate life that were subject to dispute and litigation were treated by English judges. More general and abstract questions were not part of the discourse between barristers and judges in the courtrooms. These could potentially be raised in the legal literature as was the case on the Continent. The common-law legal literature of the seventeenth and eighteenth centuries was not written by jurists of Oxford and Cambridge, who were totally devoted to the study of Roman and some Canon law, nor by teachers at the Inns of Court, who were practicing barristers with courtroom orientations and produced only moot trials and notebooks on forms of action. The limited English legal literature of this period was produced mainly by two types of authors: dismissed, exceptionally able, or early-retired judges such as Edward Coke, Matthew Hale, and William Blackstone; or underworked barristers on the margins of the profession, who aimed at supplementing their legal fees, or attracting clients, by writing and selling books.[1] There were some attempts at generalization, abstraction, and conceptualization within the first group. The sec-

---

[1]There were two other types of legal literature worth mentioning: books produced in Oxford and Cambridge by the Regious Professors of Civil Law, and the writings of political philosophers who touched upon law and jurisprudence, such as Hobbes and Locke. But books of the first type were mainly read on the Continent and in the universities themselves, whereas the latter were chiefly influential in the context of the political struggle and constitutional revolutions of the seventeenth century. Neither were part of the mainstream discourse of the common law. For the history of the English legal literature, see A.W.B Simpson, "The Rise and Fall of the Legal Treatise: Legal Principles and the Forms of Legal Literature," *University of Chicago Law Review* 48, no. 3 (1981), 632; David Sugarman, "Legal Theory, the Common Law and the Making of the Textbook Tradition," in William Twining, ed., *Legal Theory and Common Law* (Oxford: Blackwell, 1986), 26–61.

ond group produced mainly digests and abridgments of common-law cases loosely tied together, whose organization was usually modeled on the higher end of English literature, at times forced into Roman classification, and only rarely reflected the author's original framing for a narrow field.

Therefore, while the lower end of the literature is an important source, utilized elsewhere in this book, for acquiring the perspective of practical attorneys and understanding the constraints within which entrepreneurs felt they had to organize their business, it is not the place to examine theories of corporate personality. The higher end might be such a place. But, from Coke – who devoted only a few paragraphs to corporation – to Blackstone – who devoted a full chapter – the scheme was similar: classification of corporations, discussion of their modes of formation, and a list of the powers and capacities incidental to incorporation. The issue of the nature of the corporate personality was not touched on. Coke said that "persons are made into a body," while Blackstone, a century and a half later, speaks of the constitution of "artificial persons." Even Stewart Kyd, who wrote the first English legal treatise on corporations while in the Tower in 1793–1794, followed Blackstone's scheme.[2] The seventeenth- and eighteenth-century writers were brief not only on the personality of the corporation, but in their reference to business corporations as a whole. They did not consider two of its main emerging features: transferable joint-stock capital and limitation of shareholders' liability. There is no clear evidence that the increased diffusion of joint-stock corporations of their time affected their legal conceptualization in general, or regarding personality in particular. This lack of legal literature reflects the indifference of the higher legal writers toward the business world, and possibly also their autonomous conception of the law. This conception was detached from the economic reality and from the practical concerns of entrepreneurs and their attorneys.

As the eighteenth-century English corporate personality was not a part of contemporary English discourse, the only sources available are retrospective: a German or American perspective, Maitland's point of view in the late nineteenth century, or modern analyses. English corporations of this period can be seen in retrospect as entities made by the State, by way of franchise or concession of the King and later also Parliament. They were not conceived as being pre-State and pre-law natural persons, spontaneously created by the mere association of individuals, nor were they conceived as the aggregation of autonomous

---

[2]*The Case of Sutton's Hospital*, 10 Co. Rep. 23a, 30b (1610); Coke, *Commentary*, vol. 2, p. 250a; Shepheard, *Corporations, Fraternities, Guilds*; Blackstone, *Commentaries*, vol. 1, p. 455; Kyd, *Law of Corporations*.

individuals, contracting to form a new entity. With no competing theories in sight, and no ongoing theoretical discourse, there was no interaction between jurisprudence, corporate theory, and corporate doctrine analogous to that which could be found around the turn of the twentieth century. The franchise theory had been implicit and static ever since royal authority was centralized and consolidated vis-à-vis local authorities during the late middle ages, and vis-à-vis the Roman Church during the English Reformation of the sixteenth century.

Eighteenth-century English law had no explicit conception of the corporation as a private or a public person. The liberal distinction that became so central in American constitutionalism and corporate law, due to famous cases like Dartmouth College (1819) and the Charles River Bridge (1837), did not seem to bother English lawyers. Shares of business corporations of all sorts – financial, commercial, manufacturing, and transportation alike – were held by private individuals, not by the State. Some of these corporations were subject to State regulation or ad hoc State interference, but not based on an a priori distinction between public and private corporations. The larger the corporation and the more consequential the effects of its activities, the more likely was the State to interfere in its business at one point or another. Incorporation itself was not considered a protectable property right. The State could, at will, withhold an incorporation franchise which, in many cases, was of limited duration. Such withdrawal was not common, but it conformed to the Stuart conception of the constitution, which held that granting and revoking incorporation charters lay within the King's prerogative and discretion. It also conformed to the post-1689 constitutional settlement which made the Parliament supreme and, as such, free to enact and repeal incorporation acts according to changing circumstances or majorities. Like incorporation, monopoly was not considered protected private property. Corporations held monopolies of different sorts: on overseas territories, over specified business activity (such as note issuing), and on the corporate form in a given sector (marine insurance), as well as natural monopolies (infrastructure and utilities). Throughout our period, monopolies were granted and abolished, either directly or by inference.[3] There was no distinction in this matter between monopolies granted to private or to public corporations, though again, the larger a corporation was, the more likely it was to aim at monopoly and the more likely the State was to interfere with this monopoly at some point. Until 1844, there was no public/private distinction in another respect: that of offering shares to the public. There was a distinction between unincorporated companies, which were restricted by the Bubble Act in

---

[3]Ample examples of this can be found in Chapters 2 and 8.

issuing transferable shares, and corporations. But every joint-stock corporation was inherently allowed to open public subscriptions, within or outside of the Stock Exchange. Thus, the public/private distinction that seems so central to the crystallizing liberal political and constitutional ideology was not discussed in England in the context of the business corporation, and had no apparent influence on the development of the business corporation as a legal and economic institution.

THE RAISING AND TRANSFERABILITY OF JOINT STOCK

Transferable joint stock emerged in the seventeenth century as a unique and essential component of the business corporation. In this section, I examine the degree to which it was in demand by entrepreneurs, utilizable in the market setting of eighteenth-century England, and available within the legal framework. I begin by examining the demand for capital on the macro level as well as on the level of the individual enterprise, then turn to the supply of capital and to those intermediaries bringing together supply and demand in both the primary market of raising capital and in the secondary market of transferring shares, and finally investigate the law in respect to the stock market in general and to the holding and transferring of shares by individuals.

Capital Formation

Was capital accumulation a major cause of the industrial revolution? Or was shortage of capital a constraint on industrialization? In the 1950s, W. Arthur Lewis and W. W. Rostow made headlines with their "take-off" thesis, which viewed the dramatic increase in capital formation as a major cause of the industrial revolution in England, and of industrialization in general.[4] Rostow, and Lewis before him, held that the rate of capital formation, or the rate of savings, increased two- or even three-fold (from 4–5 percent to 10–15 percent) within a short "take-off" period. This presumed "take-off" serves as confirmation for the argument that the legal framework of business organization did not inhibit capital formation and economic growth. If that was indeed the case, capital considerations would not be expected to serve as a major motivation for incorporation.

[4]W. W. Rostow, *The Stages of Economic Growth: A Non-Communist Manifesto* (Cambridge University Press, 1960). See also W. Arthur Lewis, *The Theory of Economic Growth* (London: G. Allen and Unwin, 1955), for an earlier work arguing the same thesis.

The Lewis–Rostow figures were under constant attack during the 1960s and 1970s, attacks led by Phyllis Deane, W. A. Cole, Sidney Pollard, and Charles H. Feinstein.[5] Their basic tenet was that at the starting point of Rostow's "take-off," the rate of capital formation was higher than Rostow argued, whereas by the end of that period it was lower. Thus, capital formation increased only gradually during the industrial revolution. This revision could lead to two conflicting conclusions relevant to our problem. One, that capital was not a major factor during the industrial revolution. If capital was not in great demand because there were various ways to reduce the required investments, and if this demand could easily be met by traditional sources, then capital considerations were not likely to motivate incorporation or to put pressure on the existing legal framework of business organization. Another possible conclusion is that the increase in capital formation during that period was slow in spite of the fact that capital was an essential factor in industrialization. The slow increase in this case is explained by the supply side of the equation. There may have been a shortage of capital on the aggregate level, or there may have been legal constraints and capital market failures.

In the 1970s, and with greater vigor in the 1980s, the discourse on the role of capital during the industrial revolution finally branched out from the narrow occupation with the rate of capital formation forced on it by the Rostovian paradigm. A relatively wide understanding emerged: Regarding the macro level, there was no real shortage of capital prior to or during the industrial revolution. Compared with other countries in the early stages of industrialization, England enjoyed a relative abundance of capital. The increase in the rate of capital formation during the industrial revolution began at a relatively high level and was gradual; only in the railway age did the increase become more substantial. The linear and mono-causal explanations according to which acceleration in the rate of capital formation was the major cause, as well as the mani-

---

[5]Phyllis Deane, "Capital Formation in Britain Before the Railway Age," *Economic Development and Cultural Change* 9, no. 3 (1961); Phyllis Deane and W. A. Cole, *British Economic Growth, 1688–1959: Trends and Structure* (Cambridge University Press, 1962); Sidney Pollard, "The Growth and Distribution of Capital in Great Britain: c. 1770–1870," in *Third International Conference of Economic History, Munich 1965*, (1968); C. H. Feinstein, "Capital Formation in Great Britain," in P. Mathias and M. M. Postan, eds., *Cambridge Economic History of Europe*, Vol. 7: *The Industrial Economies: Capital, Labour, and Enterprise* (Cambridge University Press, 1978), part 1; Charles H. Feinstein, "Part II, National Statistics, 1750–1920," in Charles H. Feinstein and Sidney Pollard, eds., *Studies in Capital Formation in the United Kingdom: 1750–1920* (Oxford: Clarendon Press, 1988); Floud and McCloskey, eds., *The Economic History*.

festation, of the industrial revolution, were abandoned.[6] The most significant conclusion on the macro level was that this explanation had exhausted itself during the 1950s to 1970s and that new directions of research had to be initiated.[7]

While calling attention to the gradual growth of the economy as a whole, N. F. R. Crafts, in 1985, stressed structural change as an important phenomenon of the industrial revolution. He realized that the role of capital in the industrial revolution seemed minimal in the aggregate, yet at the same time, when focusing on the modernizing sectors, he noted that total capital, annual capital formation, and capital per worker rose significantly, together with productivity and output.[8] E. A. Wrigley, in 1988, said that "concentration on aggregate measures of capital investment, therefore, suggesting a relatively smooth acceleration, may predispose the unwary to regard as a unitary and progressive phenomenon something which was the result of two different growth paths with contrasting characteristics. . . . The [one] continued much as before during the century beginning in 1760; the [other] provided a new dimension to growth and some exceptional opportunities for investment."[9] Thus, both Crafts and Wrigley came to the conclusion that a fundamental structural transformation took place in the patterns of capital accumulation and investment, a transformation that occurred in other economic factors as well.

The structural transformation of the economy embodied a structural transformation in the patterns of capital investment. Based on Feinstein's estimates, both Crafts and Wrigley identified a considerable increase in industrial and transport capital formation (the mineral-based energy economy in Wrigley's terms) as compared with agricultural capital formation. In 1992, Hudson summarized the present state of the research: "Recent capital formation studies have indicated that the industrial revolution, although marked by moderate capital deepening, did involve major shifts in the magnitude, the nature and the sources of finance required to maintain a competitive footing in many manufacturing sectors."[10] Attention thus turned to the flow of capital between sectors,

[6]For a good summary of the early stages of this shift, see Francois Crouzet, "Editor's Introduction," in *Capital Formation in the Industrial Revolution* (London: Methuen, 1972).

[7]This new approach to the role of capital coincided with a new trend in the interpretation of the Industrial Revolution in general that began in the mid-1970s, a trend that stresses the limited growth and gradual change during the so-called revolution. For the sources and manifestations of this trend, see Cannadine, "English Industrial Revolution," 131–172.

[8]Crafts, *British Economic Growth*, 72–86, 122–125.

[9]Wrigley, *Continuity, Chance and Change*, 112.

[10]Hudson, *The Industrial Revolution*, 27. See also Larry Neal, "The Finance of Business During the Industrial Revolution," in Roderick Floud and Donald McClos-

especially from agriculture to industry and transport and to the utilization of new sources of capital supply in these growth sectors.

In some of the growth sectors of the late eighteenth and early nineteenth century, for example, canals and ship-building, insurance and banking, docks and gas-light, mining, and to some degree also iron and textiles, there was demand for capital. However, there were sufficient sources of capital outside of these sectors to supply the demand. This brings us back to Peter Mathias's persuasion two decades ago:

> This gives the institutional development of the financial structure of eighteenth-century England, as new intermediaries specialized out, a new significance. They institutionalized the means by which gaps between savers and borrowers became linked, drawing the threads of the capital market together.[11]

One such institutional development which bridged the gap between savers and entrepreneurs was the emergence of transferable joint stock as a financial device and of the share market as a meeting place for capital supply and demand. The transferability feature of the business corporation became central in the English economy of the industrial revolution not because of a leap in aggregate capital formation, which according to recent research did not take place, but instead because of the reapportioning of capital between sectors and regions, which was a core manifestation of the industrial revolution.

The Legal Nature of Corporate Shares

The invention, between the mid-sixteenth and the mid-seventeenth century, of joint-stock capital, divided into shares, was, as mentioned in Chapter 1, a financial and not a legal one. As a result, corporate shares, which began circulating during that century, were a phenomenon novel and strange to the law. The Bubble Act, discussed at length in Chapter 3, dealt with the legality of the primary market and the opening of subscriptions for companies with transferable stock. But what about the secondary market? Could shares be bought and sold freely on the market the way apples could, or was their transferability restricted socially and legally as landed estates were? Were shares a new form of property or quasi-property, or could they fall into existing classifications? Were they real or personal property? Did they give their holders rights in the corporation or directly in its assets? Were these rights in law or in equity? Answers to these questions are required in order to trace legal constraints on the transferability of shares.

key, eds., *The Economic History of Britain Since 1700*, Vol. 1: *1700–1860*, 2d ed. (Cambridge University Press, 1994).

[11]Peter Mathias, "Capital, Credit and Enterprise in the Industrial Revolution," *Journal of European Economic History* 2, no. 1 (1973), 125.

The answers remain ambiguous, however, because they were not considered directly, and certainly not in an abstract manner, by the courts until the 1820s.[12] Throughout the eighteenth century one could probably find no more than a handful of cases touching, usually only briefly, implicitly, or partially, on these questions. One could conclude, based on laconic citations, that the nature of the assets of a corporation determined the property classification of its shares. On three occasions, shares in land-dominated corporations, navigation, and water supply, were viewed as real estate.[13] This could lead to low transferability on the shares. Not much can be inferred from these at times conflicting cases. They definitely indicate the slow adjustment of English property law to the emergence of the joint-stock corporation. However, they did not pose a major threat to actual transferability for three reasons. First, because a standard clause in most incorporation acts declared shares to be personal property. Second, because transfer of shares was a simple selling transaction, normally completed smoothly, between two interested parties, under the auspices of the corporation, no room was left for legal disputes. Third, because the precedents were sufficiently ambiguous, they could be considered as applying to exceptional situations, ignored or manipulated for practical purposes.[14]

The spreading of shares and of share transactions may be the best indication of the irrelevance of these legal doubts. I turn now to an examination of the mechanism for raising capital by way of share subscriptions, the primary market, and for the transfer of these shares after the subscription stage, the secondary market. The availability of such a mechanism confirms the practical advantages of organizing into joint-stock business corporations, as far as capital considerations were concerned.

The Stock Market

The shares of joint-stock companies were first traded together with government stocks (bonds, in modern terms), commodities, insurance poli-

[12]See D. G. Rice, "The Legal Nature of a Share," *The Conveyancer* 21 (1957), 30; Rudden, *New River*, 224–248; Chantal Stebbings, "The Legal Nature of Shares in Landowning Joint Stock Companies in the 19th Century," *Journal of Legal History* 8 (1987), 25; Paddy Ireland, "Capitalism Without the Capitalist: The Joint Stock Company Share and the Emergence of the Modern Doctrine of Separate Corporate Personality," *Journal of Legal History* 17, no. 1 (1996), 40. Ireland's article offers an interesting new look at the legal redefinition of the share in the period 1835–1880 and its implications on corporate personality.

[13]*Townsend v. Ash*, 3 Atk. 336 (1745); *Buckeridge v. Ingram*, 2 Ves. Jun. 652 (1795); *Howse v. Chapman*, 4 Ves. Jun. 542 (1799).

[14]The first case referred to a corporation with a unique structure and the second to an unincorporated company.

cies, and foreign currencies on the Royal Exchange. Around 1700, as the halls of the Royal Exchange became overcrowded, some brokers moved their activities across the street to Exchange Alley.[15] The coffeehouses of Exchange Alley soon acquired a reputation as being meeting places for specialized traders: Lloyd's for marine insurance, Tom's and Carsey's for fire insurance, Garraway's for auctioning, Jonathan's for company shares and government stocks. In 1773 a new building was put up by the stock brokers in Sweeting's Alley behind the Royal Exchange and it was named the Stock Exchange. In 1801, £15,000 was raised among the brokers by way of share issuing for constructing yet another building, the New Stock Exchange.[16]

The London Stock Exchange of the eighteenth century was primarily a market for government stock. As the century progressed, the financial needs of the State increased. The national debt grew from just a few million pounds after the Glorious Revolution to £245 million by the end of the American war in 1783.[17] In a process known as the Financial Revolution, the construction and management of this debt became more efficient and sophisticated. Its administration was given by the State to the three moneyed companies, the East India Company, the South Sea Company, and, from around the middle of the eighteenth century, primarily to the Bank of England.[18] The Stock Exchange thus functioned as a secondary market for government stock, while the primary market for these stocks was with the moneyed companies.

Did the Stock Exchange also serve as a market place for the shares of joint-stock companies? It is undisputed that the shares of the three moneyed companies were regularly traded on the Stock Exchange. The moneyed companies were characterized by huge capital stock, by a high volume of trade in their shares compared to other eighteenth-century companies, and by their link to trade in government stock. It made sense that government stock and shares in the moneyed companies be traded under the same roof, since the same brokers and jobbers acted in both, practices were similar, and price changes in one type of security would inevitably influence the price of the others. The question should actually

[15]Fernand Braudel, *Civilization and Capitalism: 15th–18th Century*, Vol. 2: *The Wheels of Commerce* (London: Collins, 1982), 97–100, 106–110; E. Victor Morgan and W. A. Thomas, *The Stock Exchange: Its History and Function*, 2d ed. (London: Elek, 1969).

[16]Guildhall Library, Ms. 19,297/1, New Stock Exchange, March 4, 1801.

[17]Brewer, *Sinews of Power*, 115.

[18]In 1749, 28 percent of the redeemable national debt was owed to the three moneyed companies, and an additional 70 percent was administered by these companies, mainly the Bank of England. See Dickson, *Financial Revolution*, 80, 93; and 522–523, 232 for the growing share of the moneyed companies in the national debt. For the emergence of the moneyed companies and the early stages of this revolution, see Chapters 2 and 3 above.

be: Were corporate shares, other than those of the moneyed companies, traded at the Stock Exchange?

Evidence of stocks traded on the London stock market can be found in stock price lists. Several of these lists were published during the eighteenth century, most running for only a few years. The earliest and longest-running list was John Castaing's *Course of the Exchange*. First published in 1697, it changed hands several times. After 1786, it was published under Edward Wetenhall's name, and, beginning in 1803, it came out under the authority of the Stock Exchange.[19] It was a list of various foreign exchange rates, commodity prices, and stock prices, published twice a week. Though its format went through several changes, it continued to be a one-page list until the last issue of 1810. Most of the stock prices quoted were of various government stocks; only a few were of corporate shares. The list covers the entire period under discussion here. It was neglected by generations of historians until it was discovered a few years ago.[20] Finding a long-term series of prices is every economic historian's dream and the list has since served as the basis for some interesting studies. Table 5.1 shows all the corporate shares listed in the *Course* for the period between 1698 and 1810, in ten-year intervals. The table is a good indication of the scope and changes in the content of the list during the eighteenth century.

From the table, we can see that the number of companies whose shares were listed in the *Course* was very limited. A peak of nine companies was reached in 1727, but for most of the period, only four to six companies were listed. Besides the three moneyed companies, no more than three other companies were listed during most of the eighteenth century. Should we therefore accept Philip Mirowski's conclusion that the "the share market was increasingly not used as the 18th century progressed," or that "the English share market devolved over the course of the century"?[21] An unused share market may indicate that joint-stock incorporation was not such a desired privilege after all.

I argue that the *Course of the Exchange* provided only a partial view of the market for shares. From its inception by Castaing, the *Course* was directed at a specific group of readers, primarily merchants engaged in foreign trade and foreigners who were interested in exchange rates, commodity prices, and the prices of the major stocks.[22] They were interested in high finance and overseas trade, and not in the numerous minor

---

[19]Neal, *Financial Capitalism*, 21–26, 30–36; S. R. Cope, "The Stock Exchange Revisited: A New Look at the Market in Securities in London in the Eighteenth Century," *Economica* 45 (Feb. 1978), 18–20.

[20]Neal, *Financial Capitalism*, 35–36.

[21]Mirowski, "Rise of a Market," 576–577, and *Birth of Business*, 271– 276.

[22]Neal, *Financial Capitalism*, 25.

Table 5.1. *Shares listed in the* Course of the Exchange, *1698–1807*[a]

Share	1698	1707	1717	1727	1737	1747	1757	1767	1777	1787	1797	1807
East India	*	*[b]	*	*	*	*	*	*	*	*	*	*
Bank of England	*	*	*	*	*	*	*	*	*	*	*	*
South Sea			*	*	*	*	*	*	*	*	*	*
Hudson's Bay	*											
Royal African	*	*	*	*	*							
Million Bank		*	*	*	*	*	*	*	*	*		
Equivalent			*	*	*	*						
Royal Exchange				*	*	*	*	*	*	*		
London Assurance				*	*	*	*	*	*	*	*	
York Buildings				*								
London Dock												*

Source: Course of the Exchange, Guildhall Library and Goldsmiths' Collection.
[a] Listed in the first issue in January of the year mentioned.
[b] In 1707, both the Old and the New East India companies were listed.

shares that could be bought and sold in London. These were traded by Englishmen of more moderate means who got their information directly at the source, the coffeehouses of Exchange Alley, and later at the Stock Exchange itself.

The fact that the *Course* reflected only a small portion of the market can be easily demonstrated through several examples. The issue of the *Course* for May 31, 1720, at the height of the South Sea Bubble, when hundreds of bubbles were promoted and subscriptions were opening daily on Exchange Alley, listed none of these; the list was almost identical in its format to the issue of January 2, 1717.[23]

In addition, some well-known joint-stock companies, such as water companies, fisheries, and the new insurance companies, were not included on the list, and others, such as the Hudson's Bay Company, the Royal Exchange Assurance, and the London Assurance, were dropped from the list at one point or another although they remained in business.

It was only in 1811 that the conservative editorial policy of the *Course of the Exchange* with its traditional one-page format was considered totally outdated. The last issue of 1810 (December 31) included in its lists only six corporate share prices: those of the three moneyed companies and those of three newly established dock companies (London, West India, and East India). In the issue for the following day (January 1, 1811) no less than 64 company listings were included: 27 canals, 7 docks, 11 insurance, 8 waterworks, 3 moneyed companies, and 8 other companies.[24] By 1815, a second page had been added to the *Course*, company shares were dominant, and over 140 shares were quoted. Dozens of companies formed ten, twenty, and even fifty years before 1811 were added to the list in that one year. Only after the 1810s did the *Course* become more in tune with the actual extent of the share market. In light of the above, it is quite clear that the *Course of the Exchange* primarily reflected editorial preferences and not the full scope of the English share market in the eighteenth and the first decade of the nineteenth century.

Another window through which to view the contemporary share market was Thomas Mortimer's book *Everyman His Own Broker*, printed in fourteen editions between 1761 and 1807. It seems to have been a bestseller in its field. Like the *Course*, Mortimer's book concentrated on government bonds and on shares of the moneyed companies. The book did not discuss shares of other companies at all. Mortimer's advice was to invest in government stock and not in shares, not even those of the moneyed companies. He said that "there is no probability of India stock

---

[23]*Course of the Exchange*, Jan. 2, 1717, and May 31, 1720.
[24]*Course of the Exchange*, Dec. 31, 1810, and Jan. 1, 1811.

advancing in price in greater proportion than what may proceed from a rise of the government fund; while on the other hand, many events may take place . . . which would materially reduce the value of this stock."[25] Mortimer's hostility to stockbrokers and stockjobbers, as well as to speculation in stock, is evident throughout the numerous editions of the book. It seems to have been written for the conservative and passive investor. His readership may have come from groups who sought solid investments, possibly landed gentlemen, trustees, widows, and other rentiers. So, *Everyman His Own Broker* was no more representative of the contemporary share market than was the *Course of the Exchange*.

Whereas the *Course* was probably directed at the upper end of the market, at financiers and merchants, Mortimer's book was directed at the lower end, those who were remote from the world of business and wanted to avoid risk. Between these was another group, men with some means, possibly traders, manufacturers, professionals, and others, who were willing to invest modest sums in active businesses. In previous years they got the information they needed personally, but in 1796 a new guide, *An Epitome of the Stocks and Public Funds* by Thomas Fortune, was published. This guide, in tune with recent developments, stressed, as its title suggests, the availability of investment in corporate stocks and in public funds. Fortune, referring to Mortimer, said: "I mean to recommend a measure exactly opposite to that author's; and instead of advising every man to be his own broker, endeavor to persuade every man from being so."[26] While Mortimer was distrustful of corporate stocks, of professional brokers and jobbers, and of speculation, Fortune thought his readers should exploit them to the utmost. Fortune's book, printed in fourteen editions between 1796 and 1838, was soon to replace Mortimer's book (whose last edition was published in 1807). Thus, long before any legal reform occurred, the legitimization of investment in corporate shares was well on its way. The replacement of Mortimer's book by Fortune's both reflected and influenced the changing pattern of stock investment. In the years following, information about investment opportunities in corporate stocks became increasingly available. After 1811, investors could get up-to-date information from the *Course of the Exchange*. In the stormy year of 1825, several publications discussed the various schemes and stocks promoted in that year.[27] By this time, share

[25]Thomas Mortimer, *Every Man His Own Broker; Or, A Guide to Exchange Alley*, 13th ed. (1801), 30.

[26]Thomas Fortune, *An Epitome of the Stocks and Public Funds*, 8th ed. (1810), 16–17.

[27]Most notably, Henry English, *A Complete View of the Joint-Stock Companies Formed During 1824 and 1825* (1827). English circulated three separate pamphlets during the boom and consolidated them into one volume afterward.

market columns began to appear regularly in some of the leading daily newspapers, including the *Morning Chronicle* and the *Times*. In the 1830s, a new and most comprehensive guide was to replace Fortune's book. This was Charles Fenn's *A Compendium of the English and Foreign Fund, and the Principle Joint Stock Companies,* which went through twelve editions between 1837 and 1876.[28]

Where were the shares of joint-stock companies traded? A distinction should again be made between their primary and their secondary market. The inner circle of the primary market comprised a small group of entrepreneurs with personal associations and common business interests who were the initiators of a joint-stock corporation and who would offer shares in their proposed undertaking to a second circle of friends and relatives. If this was not sufficient, they would market their promotion to outsiders, by printing and distributing a prospectus, appointing agents and bankers outside their immediate vicinity, putting advertisements in local or other newspapers, and arranging for meetings in coffeehouses or pubs. Public offerings could be made during this period without prior approval of the Stock Exchange and outside its realm.

In most cases, the process of promoting a new undertaking and raising capital was not recorded, and thus cannot be studied by historians, because normally a company would open minute books only after it was officially established, as either a corporation or an unincorporated company, and not at the initiation stage. Two rare cases of records preserved from the initiation phase which allow us a glance at this fascinating process are presented below. They demonstrate the methods by which capital was raised for joint-stock companies in the period under discussion without resorting to the London Stock Exchange, in the first instance by a provincial company, and in the second, by a London company.

Following a notice in some regional newspapers, a first meeting was held in Bradford for raising subscriptions for the Leeds and Liverpool Canal Company. At this first meeting, on July 2, 1766, twenty-four subscriptions were obtained. At a second meeting, a month later, ninety-six additional subscribers were present. At subsequent meetings, a delegation of fourteen gentlemen from Yorkshire was appointed to confer with potential collaborators in Lancashire and to engage them in the subscription for the canal project. After creating the initial relationship between the Yorkshire and Lancashire investors, the effort turned to London, where absentee landlords with estates in the region were contacted, solicitors and agents in Parliament were appointed, and a "proper

---

[28]I was not able to locate a copy of the first edition, the date of which is unknown to me. The second edition was published in 1837.

gentleman" was sought to oversee the London interests of the new company. After more than two years of preparatory meetings in pubs in Bradford, Liverpool, and Burnley, and after subscribing the initial sum for covering a survey, a full-fledged effort was made. On December 19, 1768, it was decided to apply to Parliament for an act of incorporation, to open a subscription for the sum of £260,000, and to put advertisements in "all evening posts" and in the Liverpool, Manchester, York, Leeds, and Chester papers. Three weeks later, subscription books were opened in York, Leeds, Hull, Bradford, Sheffield, and other places.[29] Thus, a financial network that covered much of northern England, with some representation in London, was formed to raise capital for the Leeds and Liverpool Canal. This network did not rely on any formal capital market.

While the Leeds and Liverpool is an example of provincial raising of capital, the Atlas Insurance Company may be more representative of the London promotions. On December 19, 1807, at a meeting at Will's Coffee House, it was agreed to publish a prospectus for the formation of the Atlas and to put an advertisement to that effect in seven major London newspapers. Five London banking houses were appointed to handle the subscription. Three days later, an order was placed for 500 copies of a circular to be used by the Atlas committee members and their friends. The next step was a resolution by committee members to forward no less than 16,500 copies of the prospectus to twelve "great commercial towns" all over England, Scotland, and Ireland. Then, a list of recommended country bankers to handle the subscription and payments in the provinces was prepared. The London bankers for Atlas were asked to send the circular and the prospectus to their country correspondents. Letters were sent to Atlas subscribers encouraging them to contact friends and country bankers regarding the subscription. Several further rounds of advertisements were placed in London newspapers. Country bankers were asked to place advertisements, at Atlas's expense, in the press in their vicinity. Letters were sent to all members of both the House of Lords and the House of Commons calling on them to become proprietors and to support the plan. In addition, after the first meeting at Will's, an office was opened and Atlas commenced its business.[30] In this case, a network centered in London expanded to cover the

[29]P.R.O., RAIL 846/1, Leeds & Liverpool Canal Minutes of Subscribers, July 2, 1766; Aug. 2, 1766; Dec. 5, 9, and 19, 1768; Jan. 9, 1769.

[30]Guildhall Library, Ms. 16,170, Atlas Minutes, Dec. 19, 22–24, 26, 29, and 31, 1807; Jan. 5, 8, 12, 15, and 19, March 23, and April 6, 1808. Although the Atlas was never incorporated, at the initiation stage it aimed at incorporation and thus its promotion serves as an example for our purposes. The effects of the failure to incorporate, which are discussed in the next chapter, were felt in practice only as it entered active business.

entire country and to raise £200,000 immediately and up to £1,000,000 within months. Again, as in the case of the Leeds and Liverpool canal, the formal capital market, then at the New Stock Exchange, played no role in the subscription.

These examples demonstrate the variety of methods by which joint-stock companies could raise share capital. They also demonstrate the fact that the formal capital market was not the site of the action. The *Course of the Exchange* and other stock price lists do not uncover this fascinating world of corporate finance networking. They reflect only activities in government and other related stocks.

Like the primary market, the secondary market in corporate shares was also not concentrated under one roof, nor regulated by one authority. In London itself, shares could be traded at the Stock Exchange, but they could be traded as well in the coffeehouses of Exchange Alley or at any other coffeehouses or pubs in or around the City. They could also be traded at the East India House, at the South Sea House, or at the Bank of England where many brokers concentrated. Shares could be traded at any of the commercial banks of London. They could also be sold and purchased through at least one Inland Navigation Office in London, which specialized in trading canal shares.

Outside London, local pubs and country banks and similar places could serve as meeting places for sellers and buyers of shares. General meetings of proprietors of companies were used to close deals in shares. Attorneys played a major role in supplying information about the status of companies with whom they dealt and about potential buyers and sellers from among their clients.[31] By 1803, share prices of canal companies throughout the country were published, though not regularly.[32] There is no doubt that, at least after the establishment of the early canal companies of the 1760s, "a capital market was coming into being in England, outside of London and apart from the growth of the national debt."[33] This is not to say that it was an efficient market, in the sense of reflecting readily available and symmetric information, low transaction costs, and one quoted price for each company throughout England. But

[31]B. L. Anderson, "The Attorney and the Early Capital Market in Lancashire," in J. R. Harris, ed., *Liverpool and Merseyside: Essays in the Economic and Social History of the Port and Its Hinterland* (London: Frank Cass, 1969), 50–77; M. Miles, "The Money Market in the Early Industrial Revolution: The Evidence from West Riding Attorneys, c. 1750–1800," *Business History* 23, no. 2 (1981), 127–146; Peter Mathias, "The Lawyer as Businessman in Eighteenth-Century England," in D. C. Coleman and Peter Mathias, eds., *Enterprise and History: Essays in Honour of Charles Wilson* (Cambridge University Press, 1984), 151–167.

[32]In J. Phillips, *A General History of Inland Navigation* (1803), referred to in Ward, *Canal Building*, 82.

[33]Anderson, "The Attorney," 50.

it was moving in that direction. Provincial stock exchanges started to develop only in the 1830s and 1840s with the advance of the railway, and then the hitherto informal secondary market indeed become more organized and efficient.[34]

The issuance of corporate equity was certainly not the only form of finance in eighteenth-century England. Short-term credit and longer-term personal borrowing from banks, merchants and kin were common means of financing during that period. Even within the realm of corporate finance, corporate loans and preference shares played a role alongside ordinary shares.[35] But a general trend toward the wider use of share promotions, a better mechanism for attracting capital to these promotions, and the development of a more effective stock market can be found during the eighteenth century and accelerating toward the end of the century. These developments made the joint-stock form of business organization more attractive. The legal difficulties in the day-to-day management of the unincorporated joint-stock company (discussed in Chapter 6), combined with the constant threat of sanctions prescribed by the Bubble Act for forming unauthorized associations with transferable shares (discussed in Chapter 3 and which resurfaces in Chapter 9), elevated the business corporation to a preferred status. This is evident in the increasing number of petitions for incorporation in which the stated need to raise huge sums of money served as both motivation and justification for incorporation.

LIMITED LIABILITY

Limited liability was not a very relevant privilege for early corporations because they held most of their assets in immovable land; their tort liabilities were not expected to be considerable; they did not aim at profit, transact commercially, or have joint-stock capital; and for the most part they were not likely to be in deep debt. Only with the emergence of the business corporation in the sixteenth century, and of permanent joint-stock in the seventeenth, did limited liability become a relevant issue as far as corporations are concerned. Hence, I think that the question as to whether limited liability was an attribute of incorporation from the inception of the concept of the corporation is not really relevant. Therefore, I do not intend to examine this question for the period before the seventeenth century. There are scholars, including

[34] W. A. Thomas, *The Provincial Stock Exchanges* (London: Frank Cass, 1973).

[35] See John Reeder, "Corporate Loan Financing in the Seventeenth and Eighteenth Centuries," *Anglo-American Law Review* 2 (1973), 487–526; George Heberton Evans, *British Corporation Finance: 1750–1850 – A Study of Preference Shares* (Baltimore: Johns Hopkins Press, 1936).

Scott, Shannon, and Holdsworth, who argue that limited liability was embodied in the legal characteristics of the business corporation by the late seventeenth century.[36] Other scholars, most notably DuBois and Davies, note the very partial existence or the complete absence of limited liability in late seventeenth- and early eighteenth-century business corporations.[37] Some even argue that only the general limited liability acts of 1855 and 1856 created the basic link between limitation of liability and incorporation.

There are indications that some sort of limited liability already existed in the late seventeenth century. First, shareholders could not, in practice, be arrested for the debts of the company in which they held shares, thus they could not be forced to pay its debts. Second, an act of 1662 confirmed the exemption of shareholders of certain corporations from bankruptcy procedures.[38] Third, it could be inferred from a judgment of 1671 that when a corporation was not authorized to make further calls upon members, the debts of the corporation could not be collected from its members.[39] The question, then, is what kind of limited liability was available in the late seventeenth century?

The answer to this question, as well as a partial explanation for the controversy among scholars, lies in the confused and inconsistent definition of limited liability by both contemporaries and historians. When discussing the limited liability of shareholders in a business corporation, different lawyers and historians referred to different things.

At least three kinds of debts are described: those of shareholders to the corporation, those of shareholders to third parties, and those of the corporation to third parties. A separate issue was that of the mechanism, or procedure, for enforcing and collecting debts of shareholders. Could

---

[36]Scott, *Constitution and Finance of Joint-Stock Companies*, vol. 1, p. 270; Shannon, "Limited Liability," 358; Holdsworth, *English Law*, vol. 8, pp. 203–205.

[37]DuBois, *English Business Company*, 94; K. G. Davies, "Joint-Stock Investment in the Later Seventeenth Century," in E. M. Carus-Wilson, ed., *Essays in Economic History*, 3 vols. (London: E. Arnold, 1954–1962), vol. 2, pp. 282–283.

[38]13 & 14 Car. II c.24 (1662). Following a judgment in King's Bench in the case of *Andrews v. Woolward*, (1653), in which a knight who was a shareholder of the East India Company was found liable for a commission of bankrupts, the above act was passed in Parliament. It was intended to protect "noblemen, gentlemen and persons of quality." It exempted shareholders of the East India, Guiney, and the Royal Fishing Trade from bankruptcy procedures and made the abovementioned judgment of King's Bench void.

[39]*Salmon v. Hamborough Company*, 1 Chan. Cas. 204 (1671). In this particular case the charter of incorporation gave the company the power to levy on its members, and the company, on occasion, used that power. In view of this arrangement, judgment was given in favor of the debtor of the corporation. However, when such a power was not in the charter, no further calls could be made and a degree of limitation of liability existed.

shareholders, as such, be arrested for debts acquired on account of the corporation, and could they, alternately or in addition, be liable to bankruptcy laws as far as such debts were concerned? Timing was also of importance. Were shareholders liable for corporate debt only upon dissolution, or as soon as the unpaid debts were claimed? Also unclear was the actual portion of corporate debt that could be placed on shareholders. Were shareholders liable only up to the sum of their paid-up capital? Could calls also be made for the unpaid balance of the shares they held in order to cover corporate debts? Or could they be forced to pay debts even above the nominal value of the shares held, without any limit? Furthermore, what was the relationship between shareholders as far as debts were concerned? Were shareholders held in debt together or separately; that is to say, could the entire debt of a corporation be collected from one shareholder, or was each shareholder responsible only for his or her proportional share in the total debt? All these questions indicate that there was no coherent, well-defined conception of limited liability in late seventeenth-century England. This lack of coherence resulted in different people, contemporaries as well as historians, referring to different things when talking about limited liability. I think that to avoid confusion, it should not be assumed that the seventeenth or eighteenth centuries functioned under the modern perception of limitation of liability as a binary legal feature that a corporation or an era has or lacks. Limited liability in this period should not even be viewed as a continuum, but rather as a matrix with several dimensions, as evident from the questions above.

The path of development of the concept of limited liability throughout the eighteenth century is not altogether clear. It is not found in case law reports or in treatises, and only occasionally in the statute book, scattered among various specific acts of incorporation. It might better be sought in the changing business enterprises and their environs, and consequently also in the motives of entrepreneurs. But it is clear that by the turn of the century, limited liability had emerged as an integral part of incorporation and a major motive for it. DuBois provides us with an excellent survey of this development.[40] By the end of the century, it became clear that holding shares in a business corporation did not, in itself, turn a nontrader into a trader, subjecting him or her to bankruptcy law, even when the corporation (in its corporate capacity) did engage in trade. It also became clear that a corporation could not make additional calls for capital on its members, based on bylaws or directors' decisions, in order to pay its creditors, unless call-making powers were explicitly given to that corporation in its act or charter of incorporation. It also

[40]DuBois, *English Business Company*, 94–104.

became relatively clear by 1825 that incorporation by charter carried with it limitation on the liability of the shareholders.[41] In those cases when incorporation was granted by an Act of Parliament, rather than charter, limited liability was also available, provided that an explicit clause to that affect was included in the incorporating statute, and in fact, such clauses became common.[42] In both cases, the responsibility of each shareholder was limited to the amount actually paid and, only if further calls were authorized, to the amount that could be called by the corporation.[43]

The growing importance of limited liability is also evident in the fact that toward the end of the eighteenth century, it became a declared motive of entrepreneurs who petitioned for incorporation. These entrepreneurs explained, either in Parliament or to the Law Officers, that limited liability was essential for the success of their undertaking.[44] Montefiore in his *Trader and Manufacturer's Compendium* of 1804 may have been expressing this notion when he wrote that incorporation was obtained "principally for the purpose of exempting the shareholders from any responsibility as partners."[45] Thus, by the early nineteenth century, the limitation of liability joined, or even surpassed, the raising of a large amount of capital as the leading motive for incorporation.

Both the conceptualization and the appreciation of limited liability significantly progressed between the late seventeenth and the late eighteenth century. By the late eighteenth and early nineteenth century, unincorporated companies which could not benefit from limited liability were at a considerable disadvantage vis-à-vis the business corporation, as shown in the next chapter.

[41] We learn this in retrospect from the fact that in 1825 a specific legislative arrangement had to be made in order to make it lawful to grant charters without full limited liability, 6 Geo. IV c.91 (1825), section II. See also J. R. McCulloch, *A Dictionary of Commerce* (1832), 358. For the original intention behind this clause, see Chapter 10.

[42] Such clauses could be found in 4 Geo. III c.37 (1764), for the incorporation of the English Linen Company; 26 Geo. III c.106 (1786), for the incorporation of the British Society for Extending the Fisheries; 31 Geo. III c.55 (1791), for incorporating the Sierra Leone Company.

[43] The power to make additional calls upon shareholders was not as prevalent as in the past. But it still existed in many of the transportation projects, in which calls were made according to construction, and room was left for unplanned expenses.

[44] See DuBois, *English Business Company*, 94–98, for cases in the last third of the eighteenth century, in which limitation of liability was a declared motive for incorporation. These include, among others, the cases of Warmley Company, Albion Mill, Sierra Leona Company, and British Plate Glass Company. In the case of the Globe Insurance Company, early in the nineteenth century, the request for limited liability was the center of the debate. See *On the Policy and Expediency of Granting Insurance Charters* (1806), 2–7.

[45] Joshua Montefiore, *The Trader and Manufacturer's Compendium Containing the Laws, Customs and Regulations Relative to Trade* (1804), 235.

The significance of limited liability for those who could benefit from it is better understood when the alternative of doing business with unlimited responsibility is considered. In England of the eighteenth and early nineteenth centuries, insolvency and bankruptcy law were at the preindustrial stage, and reform was not to arrive before the mid-nineteenth century. The major weapon of a creditor was the arrest of his debtor.[46] A debt of £10 was sufficient to send a debtor to prison. This could easily be achieved even before trial, on mesne process. Arrest, even on mesne process, was expedient and quick, and could be achieved ex parte, based on summary proceedings and without any external evidence. Once in prison, the debtor's prospects were not good, because he had to cover his own imprisonment expenses, disease was rampant, and the bail required was much higher than the original debt. The some 10,000 individuals sent to prison annually for unpaid debts were a constant warning to any person who dared to take risks individually, on his own account, and served as a leading motive for seeking limited liability.

Traders faced an even worse fate than ordinary debtors during most of the period discussed in this book. From the late sixteenth century until 1861 only traders were subject to bankruptcy law. The considerable growth in the number of bankruptcies, to a total of over 33,000 during the eighteenth century, especially after 1760, made fear of bankruptcy momentous and must have increased the motivation of traders to limit their liability.[47] Eighteenth-century bankruptcy law clearly favored creditors over debtors, in substance as well as in procedure. Bankruptcy resulted in public examination, seizure of assets, and often also criminal prosecution. The law of bankruptcy bestowed on creditors control of the process, enabled them to take action even against landed property, and on the other hand, offered debtors the privilege of discharge only on rare cases. In fact, for nontraders, who were not subject to bankruptcy, landed property was relatively immune from creditors.[48] By the late eighteenth century bankrupt traders could find some ways of manipulat-

[46]Paul Hess Haagen, "Imprisonment for Debt in England and Wales," Ph.D. dissertation, Princeton University (1986); Bruce Kercher, "The Transformation of Imprisonment for Debt in England, 1828 to 1838," *Australian Journal of Law and Society* 2 (1980), 60; V. Markham Lester, *Victorian Insolvency: Bankruptcy, Imprisonment for Debt, and Company Winding-up in Nineteenth-Century England* (Oxford: Clarendon Press, 1995).

[47]Julian Hoppit, *Risk and Failure in English Business: 1700–1800* (Cambridge University Press, 1987), 42–55, 182–183; Sheila Marriner, "English Bankruptcy Records and Statistics before 1850," *Economic History Review* 33, no. 3 (1980), 350–366.

[48]M. S. Servian, "Eighteenth Century Bankruptcy Law: From Crime to Process," Ph.D. thesis, University of Kent at Canterbury (1985); Hoppit, *Risk and Failure*, 18–41; I.P.H. Duffy, "Bankruptcy and Insolvency in London in Late Eighteenth and Early Nineteenth Centuries," Ph.D. thesis, Oxford University (1973).

ing the process for their advantage. However, only from the 1820s onward was bankruptcy law reformed in a manner more favorable to debtors, and thus to traders. Only as the nineteenth century progressed did it become a privilege rather than a sanction.

In conclusion, limited liability emerged during the eighteenth century as a more narrowly defined legal concept and as a valuable economic benefit. Its major role in the development of the business organization can be understood only when viewed in the context of the unlimited liability of the partnership and the unincorporated company on one hand, and the cruel contemporary laws of debt and bankruptcy on the other.

ENTRY BARRIERS

There is a common belief that incorporation by specific act or charter was extremely cumbersome and involved considerable "trouble and expense," in the form of exceptionally high official fees, less official bribes, and other expenses and payments. It has been estimated that by 1855, the railway industry had spent some £30 million in and around Parliament.[49] It is often assumed that undertakers refrained from aiming at incorporation because of the high costs involved. This assumption is used to support the theory which claims that Parliament (and to a lesser degree the Committee of the Privy Council) controlled the entrance to the corporate form of business organization in order to increase its income from payments stemming from exercising that control.[50] This claim is influenced by the public-choice approach to economic regulation and by the conception of rent-seeking.[51] If expenses involved in obtaining incorporation were indeed so very high, the legal and economic advantages of the business corporation over other forms of business organization, such as the partnership and the unincorporated company, are merely theoretical. The cost of obtaining these advantages would offset or considerably diminish the benefits.

Fees at the House of Commons in 1700 for a private bill were fixed at £14.[52] The fee list remained in force, with but few modifications, until 1847. This amount included all the fees in the House from the Speaker to the Clerks Without Doors in the Committees to the Doorkeeper.

[49]Kostal, *English Railway Capitalism*, 126.
[50]Butler, "General Incorporation," 169–187.
[51]For the foundation of these theories, see George J. Stigler, "The Theory of Economic Regulation," *Bell Journal of Economics* 2 (Spring 1971), 3–21; Krueger, "The Political Economy," 291–303.
[52]Williams, *The Clerical Organization*, 300–303.

When a bill affected several individuals, double, triple, or even higher fees could be charged. After several inquiries into the multiple fees in the years 1827–1847, a new table, based on ad valorem charges, was drawn up.[53] No complete information exists on what fees were actually paid by applicants for incorporation bills, taking into account multiple fees, but they were certainly several times larger than the basic £14.

Fees in both Houses were only one part of the actual cost to the applicants. In addition to the fees in Parliament, applicants also had to pay fees to solicitors and to parliamentary agents, to cover the travel and lodging expenses of their representatives when these went to London, to pay for witnesses, arrange for petitions, and print bills. So the actual costs of the promoted company should be assessed, I believe, not through parliamentary records, but rather through the business records and account books of the company itself. Evidence of initial incorporation costs is scattered, because, as mentioned previously, in most cases, official records were kept only after incorporation. Nevertheless, a number of examples are available. The Portsmouth and Sheet Turnpike noted "Charges in and about obtaining the Act" totaling about £173 when it was formed in 1711. Two renewal acts in 1726 and 1742 cost the trust £167 and £200, respectively.[54] The costs of the passage of the original Islington Turnpike Trust Act were £152, and those of the first Marylebone Trust were £218.[55] The Weaver Navigation Bill of 1727 cost its promoters £386.[56] The Liverpool Corporation financed the Sankey Canal with £300 "towards securing the necessary Act of Parliament" in 1754.[57] In 1768, the Coventry Canal Company paid £1,002 in expenses concerning the Act of Parliament.[58] In 1769, the Leeds and Liverpool Canal collected 0.5 percent of its subscribed capital (£1,300 of £260,000) for application to Parliament and related expenses.[59] Equita-

[53]For example, companies with raised capital of up to £50,000 had to pay fees of £65. For companies with capital of £1.5 million to £2 million, the fees were fixed at £650. Frederick Clifford, *A History of Private Bill Legislation*, 2 vols. (London: Butterworths, 1885–1887), vol. 2, pp. 732–744.

[54]William Albert and P.D.A. Harvey, eds., *Portsmouth and Sheet Turnpike Commissioners' Minute Book: 1711–1754* (City of Portsmouth, 1973), entries for Oct. 17, 1711; Oct. 12, 1726; and Oct. 13, 1742, respectively. The figures in the text are rounded off and are the sum of several items.

[55]Clarke, *The Turnpike Trusts.*

[56]Lambert, *Bills and Acts*, 165. The various fees and expenses are itemized, but the expenses in the country are not included. Lambert estimated that "this may probably be taken as a minimum for an opposed local bill."

[57]Barker, "Canal Age," 16.

[58]P.R.O., RAIL 818/1, Coventry Canal General Assembly and Committee Minutes, April 14, 1768.

[59]P.R.O., RAIL 846/1, Leeds and Liverpool Canal Minutes of Subscribers, Feb. 2, 1769.

ble Insurance spent £734 in the years 1756–1762 in its futile attempt to attain incorporation by charter.[60] Generalizing from such a narrow and unrepresentative sample is clearly risky; nevertheless, it appears that the range of expenses surrounding such acts was between £150 for the simplest unopposed turnpike bill of the earlier period and £1,500 for the opposed bill of a large canal in later years. Application for incorporation outside the transport sectors, where eminent domain powers were not sought, could cost somewhere between these two extremes.

Was obtaining incorporation in fact expensive? It could be considered expensive for a small turnpike trust which raised an initial capital of several hundred or at most a couple of thousand pounds. However, it was not that much for a midsized canal company or for an insurance company that raised capital of several hundred thousand pounds. In these cases incorporation procedures would consume less than 1 percent of the total expenditure.

The fact that the legislative procedure, as such, was not extremely expensive, and that it did not, in itself, create a formidable barrier on entry can also be demonstrated by observing the flood of public and private legislation in many fields. The total number of acts passed in 1711 was seventy-four; by 1811 the annual number of acts grew almost six-fold and reached a total of 423.[61] Much of this increase can be attributed to private, local, and personal acts which comprised 295 of the 1811 total. The number of enclosure, turnpike, and divorce bills increased dramatically during the eighteenth century.[62] Matters of relatively low economic value such as change of name, naturalization, and divorce frequently reached Parliament. Stuart Anderson concluded his study of statutory divorce stating that "the cost of statutory divorce was less, and the range of those prepared to pay for it wider than anyone would have expected."[63] This conclusion seems valid for other sorts of statutory proceedings as well. Otherwise one could expect a very limited number of applications to Parliament rather than their dramatic increase. Why then was the number of incorporation acts so meager? After all, the type of legislation examined here generally involved considerably higher economic value than most other private legislation.

How can we reconcile the £30 million presumably spent by the railway industry in the race for obtaining incorporation acts with the low

[60]*Equitable-Papers Relating to the Dispute Between Members of the Equitable Society and the Charter-Fund Proprietors* (1769). Committee Accounts, Jan. 6, 1764.
[61]Lambert, *Bills and Acts*, 52.
[62]Clifford, *Private Bill Legislation*, vol. 1, p. 493; Albert, *Turnpike Road*, 201ff; Stuart Anderson, "Legislative Divorce – Law for the Aristocracy?," in G. R. Rubin and David Sugarman, eds., *Law, Economy and Society, 1750–1915: Essays in the History of English Law* (Abingdon: Professional Books, 1984), 415.
[63]Anderson, "Legislative Divorce," 444.

costs presented here? That huge sum was so unreasonably high that it unavoidably leads to the opposite conclusion: It does not actually reflect high parliamentary expenses. In fact, the explanation has two elements. The first relates to the new Standing Orders which applied to canal companies after the 1790s and, after the 1820s, to railway companies as well. These orders made it mandatory to include detailed maps, plans, and financial calculations in every petition for a canal or railway bill. From that point on, many of the initial costs of surveying, engineering, accounting, and so forth, clearly very high in such projects, were considered parliamentary expenses, though they were not actually of this nature. The second element is that very considerable sums were spent in an attempt to fight opposition from existing undertakers, competing promoters, or other vested interests such as landowners.[64]

The barrier on entry into the corporate world was not created by Parliament intentionally, nor was it to any considerable degree manipulated by Parliament, and it did not benefit the State as such. Parliament and the Committee of the Privy Council (in the case of charters) served only as the arena and set the procedural rules. The arena itself was left open to the active players in this game, the vested interests.[65] And it was the vested interests which created the barriers on entry. In the previous chapter, I exposed the way in which established vested interests in the insurance sectors, and to a lesser degree also older means of transportation, clustered to block newcomers. Examples of the activity of vested interests in other sectors can be found in later chapters. Attempts to form joint-stock companies in sectors controlled by individuals, such as flour milling and brewing, united all the individual manufactures against the intruder. Slave traders vehemently attacked the bill of the abolitionist Sierra Leone Company. The Bank of England prevented the formation of joint-stock banks. Many other examples of the same sort can be found.

If a legal framework had not been in existence requiring that each incorporation be granted separately and specifically in an act or a charter, vested interests could obviously not have controlled entry. This state

---

[64]We have seen in Chapter 4 that turnpike trusts and river navigation improvement undertakings had to be compensated by new canal promotions, in order to offset their opposing parliamentary lobbyism. The promoters of new railway projects had to do the same, that is, to spend money on buying off opposition from the vested interests in canals and turnpikes, as well as on blocking a novel and competing technology, steam engine carriages that were intended to run on roads rather than on fixed rails. For this interesting episode, see Paul Johnson, *The Birth of the Modern: World Society 1815–1830* (London: Weidenfeld and Nicolson, 1991), 188–192.

[65]For the important role played by special interest groups, pressure groups, and lobbyists in this period, see Brewer, *Sinews of Power*; Paul Langford, *A Polite and Commercial People: England, 1727–1783* (Oxford University Press, 1989).

of affairs had several implications: Entrance was blocked into some sectors but not into others, the structure of competition and the price levels in several sectors was influenced, and levels of production and growth of some sectors may have been affected, thus reducing, even if only marginally, the performance of the English economy.[66] A more precise and quantitative statement than this would have to rely on evidence of the economy as a whole which is beyond the scope of the present work. Yet because it was not Parliament as an institution which created the entry barriers, no clear policy or general criteria existed for incorporation during much of the eighteenth and early nineteenth century. Incorporation was granted or refused on the basis of the level of opposition of conflicting vested interests. Decisions were not based on the potential revenues to the State by granting the specific incorporation, nor on the need to limit supply in order to ensure high prices for each grant by the State. Unlike in Elizabethan and early Stuart times, corporations as such were not an important source of revenue to the State.

In this chapter, I have argued that separate legal personality was a well-established feature of the corporation from an early stage. This meant that the corporation was distinct from natural personalities and that it could come into being only by State and law. However, other theoretical and doctrinal implications of this feature were not yet altogether clear. I further asserted that due to changing economic and legal circumstances, both transferable joint stock and limitation of liability became, by the late eighteenth century, desirable features for entrepreneurs. By then, these features were closely linked to the business corporation. And last, I maintained that this bundle of privileges could apparently be obtained by way of an inexpensive parliamentary or executive procedure. But in fact incorporation could not be easily obtained, not because of complications and expenses inherent in the procedure itself, but rather because of the working of interest groups and politicians. Now that the desirability of incorporation in early industrial England has been established, the question remains whether men of business and lawyers could get along without it, using surrogates. The next chapter deals with this question.

[66]The entry barrier created by the legal framework of business organization had implications not only in the economic and legal spheres. The forced cooperation of entrepreneurial interest groups with Parliament encouraged ties between these groups and certain MPs but not with others. This had implications also on the development of the political sphere that cannot be discussed here.

6

Trusts, Partnerships, and the Unincorporated Company

Many legal and economic historians consider the development of the unincorporated company to be one of the best examples of the flexibility and adjustment of the English legal system to the changing needs of the growing and industrializing English economy. These historians, often unknowingly, join their voices to the functional paradigm of the relationship between the law and economic growth. What they are saying, in fact, is that despite a prohibitive legal doctrine, the Bubble Act, and the law of corporations in general, there was a loophole within the English legal system which made the system more instrumental to the needs of business. These historians perceive the unincorporated company to be a distinct form of business organization, based on a coherent legal concept. According to this view, the unincorporated company, which acquired almost all the characteristics and privileges of the business corporation, served as an adequate substitute for it and made possible the development of large-scale concerns at a time when incorporation by Parliament or the Court was very rare, before the mid-nineteenth-century reform in company law.

The present chapter examines this view, with an intention to refute it. I do not deny that unincorporated associations existed and played important roles in academic, professional, charitable, and other areas. However, when applied to profit-maximizing business enterprises, with freely transferable interests, liquid assets, intensive managerial tasks, and loose social and moral connections between members, the unincorporated form of business organization had many impediments. It is my argument that because, in fact, the unincorporated company could not serve as a viable alternative to the business corporation, this sphere of the English law did not manifest much functionality.

I begin by discussing the legal structure of the unincorporated company and the bodies of legal doctrines that applied to it. I then examine the implications of its not having a separate legal personality; that is, the

137

difficulties caused by the fact that this form of business organization was composed of its members' individual legal personalities and not of a single personality. The suitability of the trust device as a core component in the structuring of the unincorporated company is then questioned. Finally, the fate of the unincorporated company as a type of partnership, in common law and Chancery courts, is evaluated.

A final methodological remark, before moving on: I do not delve too deeply into doctrinal examination. I do not aim to explain precisely what the law said, or what the Lord Chancellor, a common pleas judge, senior barrister, or leading equity lawyer thought it said, but rather what an average attorney, entrepreneur, potential trustee, or investor thought it was saying. Thus, while I do not dismiss the elite perspective, which relies on thorough analysis of court judgments, it is the lower perspective, utilizing mediocre legal literature and practical business manuals as sources, that is stressed in this chapter.

The historiographic line of thought praising the unincorporated company originated with Maitland early in this century, and was supported, variously, by DuBois, Cooke, Ashton, Deane, Cottrell, Manchester, and Daunton, to name but a few.[1] Maitland states that "in truth and in deed we made corporations without troubling King or Parliament though perhaps we said that we were doing nothing of the kind."[2] He further claims that the equity trust "in effect enabled men to form [unincorporated] joint-stock companies with limited liability, until at length the legislature had to give way."[3]

Cooke, writing in 1950, fully develops this line of argumentation. To Maitland's often quoted phrases, he adds:

After the Bubble Act the position was that either a grant of incorporation or a recognized prescriptive right to be a corporation established a legal entity which could own property, sue and be sued, and possess transferable shares. But beyond this field, and out of the reach of the legal prohibition of spontaneous corporate form, a second class of companies grew in number. These companies were linked to the two equitable forms of group association, the partnership and the trust. They developed within the bounds of equitable jurisdiction and did not trouble the common law courts with the problem of their existence.[4]

[1]Maitland, "The Unincorporate Body," 128–140, and "Trust and Corporation," 141–222; DuBois, *English Business Company*, 215 ff.; Cooke, *Corporation, Trust and Company*, 83–88; Ashton, *Economic History*, 119; Deane, *First Industrial Revolution*, 222; Cottrell, *Industrial Finance*, 39 ff.; Manchester, *Modern Legal History*, 350; M. J. Daunton, *Progress and Poverty: An Economic and Social History of Britain 1700–1850* (Oxford University Press, 1995), 239–240.

[2]Maitland, "The Unincorporate Body," 139.

[3]Ibid., 135.

[4]Cooke, *Corporation, Trust and Company*, 85.

Thus, according to Cooke, a clear and distinct legal concept of the unincorporated company was developing within the realm of equitable institutions and reasoning. This concept, and the technique that utilized it, developed during the eighteenth century and reached its peak in the early nineteenth century.[5]

THE APPROPRIATE LEGAL FRAMEWORK

There is considerable confusion in the literature regarding the legal framework appropriate for an analysis of the nature of the unincorporated company. Cooke claims that both the partnership and the trust were equitable forms of association, and that the unincorporated company was linked to both.[6] Cottrell believes that the partnership was developed within the framework of common law, while the unincorporated company was a separate equitable concept.[7] Hadden talks of the unincorporated partnership.[8] Manchester, on the other hand, distinguishes the unincorporated company from the partnership, and holds the trust to be a central device within the former.[9] Finally, DuBois views the unincorporated company as a stepchild of the law, one which did not fit properly into any of the contemporary categories.[10] Was the unincorporated company based on the partnership or on the trust? Was it an equitable or a common-law doctrine? Was it a legal or an extralegal form of association?

As a first step to approaching these questions, we can observe the interaction among the components, agents, and processes which gave birth to this form of organization. A prototypical advanced unincorporated company, such as one of the insurance companies referred to in Chapter 4, was formed by entrepreneurs and their attorneys. It was based on an initial agreement, oral or written, between these entrepreneurs, followed by a call on other, possibly more passive investors. The initial entrepreneurs and all joining members were required to sign a second, more formal, detailed, explicit contract drafted by the original entrepreneurs and their attorneys. This constitutive agreement, in the form of a deed of settlement, specified the joint-stock capital of the company, its division into shares, their transferability, and the manner in which the capital would be raised. It also determined the composition, election, and powers of the various organs of the company: the general

[5]Ibid., 87.
[6]Ibid., 85.
[7]Cottrell, *Industrial Finance*, 41.
[8]Hadden, *Company Law*, 17.
[9]Manchester, *Modern Legal History*, 350.
[10]DuBois, *English Business Company*, 217.

court, the court of directors, and the major officers. It also usually included the formation of an explicit trust comprising all the capital and assets of the company, designated the first trustees, and defined arrangements regarding replacement of trustees, the terms of the trust, and so on. It supposedly acquired the common holding of assets, transferability of interests, hierarchical managerial structure, and a degree of limitation of liability, without having to resort to the State for granting incorporation as a separate legal personality. This prototypical, advanced unincorporated company was developed in a learning-by-doing process by consecutive teams of attorneys and businessmen during the second half of the eighteenth century.

The legal framework in which the unincorporated company functioned in the late eighteenth and early nineteenth century was indeed, as this spontaneously evolving model suggests, complicated and controversial. The following attempt to clarify it demonstrates the complexity of the contemporary framework. The unincorporated company was subject to several legal realms in the different stages and aspects of its activity. First, partnership law doctrines were applicable to this type of association because it had the element of profit sharing, and thus, from a partnership law perspective, the unincorporated company was not distinguishable from any other partnership. Second, the deed of settlement, the contractual agreement between members to form and regulate the company, was subject to contract law. Contract law also governed the deals between the members and third parties: customers, suppliers, and employees. Third, though corporate law as such was not applicable to unincorporated companies because they were not State-sanctioned legal entities, structures borrowed from corporate law and from acts of incorporation of specific companies were used by unincorporated companies. Fourth, the relationship between officers and shareholders as well as some other relationships among internal organs were subject to agency law. Last, the trust, an equitable doctrine, was employed by unincorporated companies as a device to overcome some of the deficiencies they faced due to lack of legal entity.

Above these five areas of law which governed the unincorporated company, and on a different level, stood one notorious statute, the Bubble Act. The act has already been discussed in detail in Chapter 3, and need only be briefly mentioned here. Its effects were limited only to the formation and legality, and not to the regulation of structure and activities, of unincorporated companies, but as such, it seemed omnipotent to many contemporaries and historians.

From a jurisdictional perspective, matters were also quite complicated. Due to procedural limitations and considerations that are examined below, the unincorporated company's litigation in the realm of partnership law could find its way, in different circumstances, both to the common-law courts and to Chancery. In the contractual realm, litigation was more likely to take place in common-law courts. In the realm of the trust device, jurisdiction was with the Court of Chancery. The fact that much of the litigation had to be conducted in Chancery was detrimental to the unincorporated company, as I argue in the last part of this chapter.

Any attempt to generalize and define the unincorporated company solely as a partnership or a trust, or as an equitable or common-law doctrine, will reduce the complex reality to dogmatic legal anachronism. Equitable doctrines and jurisdictions intermingled with those of the common law in the unincorporated company. This conceptual disorder should not come as a surprise, first because the English law of this period was itself dominated by form and not substance: by writs and remedies, procedures and institutions, induction from case to case, fictions, and a limited reporting system. There was a scarcity of generalizing, abstracting, and systematizing in the contemporary legal literature. But it is manifest in this case in particular because the unincorporated company was not a concept formed "from above" by judges in courts, but rather a construction of various components assembled by practical entrepreneurs and solicitors, for their own business needs, far from the courtrooms of Westminster and the Inns of Court. It was a distinctive example of evolution "from below," at the margins of the legal system.

THE LACK OF LEGAL ENTITY

The unincorporated company was not "a body politick and corporate." The unincorporated company, which was spontaneously created in the private sphere without explicit State permission, could not be a corporate entity. Like the partnership, it was an association between individual and natural entities – the shareholders – and did not amount to the creation of a new and aggregate legal entity. In that period, only the State, via the Crown or Parliament, could grant corporate status.[11] This lack of legal entity resulted in many legal and practical inconveniences for both the partnership and the unincorporated company. Four of the major inconveniences resulting from lack of legal entity – want of continuity, unlimited liability, problems of governance, and standing in court litigation – are considered below in some detail. The potential of the

[11]See Chapters 1 and 4.

trust to ease these inconveniences is not examined here; it receives its due attention in the following section.

Continuity

In every case of death, retirement, incapacity, or bankruptcy of even one of the partners, the partnership was terminated and a new, reorganized partnership had to be formed.[12] The same was true whenever one of the partners wanted to retire for either personal or professional reasons. Reorganization was a major and recurrent problem.

Two examples give some indication of the frequency of partnership reorganization in the period under discussion. The pharmaceutical partnership of the Howard family of London passed from one generation to the next, and was dominated by only two individuals – the father, Luke Howard, and his son, Robert Howard – over a fifty-year period. The partnership, however, went through no less than ten reorganizations within these two generations.[13]

The Parker family solicitors' office in Sheffield frequently dealt with reorganization of partnerships. For the period between 1792 and 1811, 23 deeds of partnership, 26 deeds of dissolution of partnership, and seven deeds for other organizational changes, such as admission or withdrawal of partners, survive in the firm's records.[14] Of the 23 newly formed partnerships, ten underwent organizational change within these two decades and four even underwent two stages of change.

Thus, from the perspective of men of both business and the legal profession, partnership reorganization was frequent. The legal requirement for the formation of a new partnership with every change in the identity of any of the partners placed a heavy burden on those who organized their business in the form of a partnership. They had to resort to legal services for preparing the deeds and drafting all the rest of the required documents, and had to arrange for a notice in the London Gazette in case of dissolution. This involved time and especially money, in the form of solicitors' fees and other expenses.

In unincorporated companies, the number of partners tended to be much larger than in regular partnerships – hundreds or even more – and, furthermore, shares were easily transferable. The likelihood of replacement of partners-shareholders made the need for reorganization a daily

---

[12]Basil Montagu, *A Digest of the Law of Partnership: With a Collection of the Cases Decided in the Courts of Law and Equity upon That Subject* (1815), 86–93.

[13]Greater London Record Office, Acc. 1037/1–12, Acc. 1037/15–16, Acc. R 1979 (1798– 1849).

[14]Sheffield City Archives, Parker Collection, P.C. 744–849, Feb. 16, 1792 – March 4, 1811.

matter. There was no way of bypassing the problem of absence of continuity in either the partnership or in the unincorporated company, because neither was a legal entity apart from its members.

Liability

Toward the end of the eighteenth century, limited liability emerged as an integral outcome of separate corporate entity, as demonstrated in Chapter 5. The lack of separate legal entity for the partnership was coupled with the general principle which stated that each partner was individually liable for all the debts of the partnership. In one case, an ex-partner who neglected to withdraw his name from the deed of an Essex banking partnership was found liable for its debt and was forced to surrender his entire fortune, £32,000, leaving him with only £100 and his watch.[15] In the words of the author of a partnership-law treatise in 1815: "The members of unincorporated trading companies are liable to third persons, as general partners in the concern for which the company is formed. . . . Such companies are merely partnerships."[16] Thus, because of the large scale of these concerns, the impersonal connections, and the frequent transferability of interests, shareholders of unincorporated companies were exposed to even higher risks than partners in ordinary partnerships, due to the lack of limited liability.

Indeed, inter se partners could limit their liability by including clauses to this effect in the partnership deed. But such clauses had no effect on third parties. Partners could also insert clauses into contracts with third parties, granting each of the partners limited liability vis-à-vis the contracting third party. In the insurance sector this became common practice with the inclusion of such clauses in insurance policies. But the attempt to ensure limited liability in the relationship with third parties met with only partial success. The insured persons could refuse the inclusion of such clauses, or alternately could negotiate for a lower premium, because they could obtain policies without such clauses from other companies or individuals. Furthermore, it was not practical, due to transaction costs, to include express contractual limitations in every individual deal. Express limitation could be included in uniform deals or ones of high value, but not in numerous lesser deals, oral or implicit, made in the course of daily business. Noncontractual claims, based on torts, negotiable instruments, and the like, were also not affected by contractual limitation of responsibility. Thus, even in the insurance sector, the limitation of liability was only partial, and in other sectors, in which there was no practice

[15]Davidoff and Hall, *Family Fortunes*, 201.
[16]Montagu, *Law of Partnership*, 6.

of drafting standard written agreements, almost no limitation was in fact achieved.

Governance

In common law, acts executed by any partner, in the name of the partnership, were seen as acts of the partnership and were binding on the rest of the partners. A partner could destroy or dispose of partnership property or bind the partnership in bad bargains, and such acts were binding even when done in the face of majority objection. As the partnership lacked a separate legal entity, there was no separation of ownership and control nor any legally enforced arrangement for appointment and delineation of responsibilities of officeholders, and for assemblies, reports, votes, and the like, as was the case in the corporation. The unincorporated company, like the partnership, lacked separate legal entity, but here the problem of governance and control were more troublesome because of the more complex structure of organization and management. The solution of copying managerial structures from corporations was only partial, because it was performed on a contractual and not a constitutional level. Third parties were in the dark, in many circumstances, as to the status of the person they were dealing with. They could not be certain whether a person pretending to be a director, officer, or clerk could act for the company, its capital, or its shareholders.

Litigation Using Common Name

Because a partnership had no legal entity, it did not enjoy independent standing in court litigation. This dictated that in actions brought by or against third parties, and in suits between partners, all partners had to be joined as parties to the action. In large unincorporated companies of many members, this became a very cumbersome requirement. George mentions an example in which a person bought goods on credit on twenty-five different occasions from an unincorporated company and failed to pay when the credit expired. The proper partners had to join an action against the debtor for each of these twenty-five occasions. This involved locating and invoking the cooperation of all the partners who bought or sold shares in this unincorporated company during this time period, some of whom might have died or otherwise disappeared.[17] Ker describes another problematic situation, with the unincorporated com-

[17]John George, *A View of the Law Affecting Unincorporated Companies*, 2d ed. (1825), 15.

pany as the defendant, not the plaintiff. In this case each of the 300 shareholders could file a separate defense with which the plaintiff would have to deal. Furthermore, any alteration in the share-holding required that the plaintiff revive his suit.[18] Clearly, litigation involving large partnerships and especially unincorporated companies with many shareholders was cumbersome, expensive, and inefficient.

Statutory and Other Implications

The formation of a large and heterogeneous organization lacking a separate legal personality created difficulties in applying various other legal arrangements: taxes, regulations, grants, and execution procedures to or by the unincorporated company. These difficulties have been relatively neglected by the few historians of the unincorporated business company. They are revealed here by examination of court litigation records and statutory clauses.

Taxes and duties were assessed differently for individuals of different status, so when individuals associated themselves in an unincorporated company, it became unclear whether the company should be treated as a separate entity for tax purposes or, if not, which of its members' status should dominate. This problem can best be explained through an example. The Golden Lane Brewery was an unincorporated company. It paid excise tax at a lower rate which took into account waste permitted to brewers, though not to retailers. Three years after its establishment, the brewery was sued by the Board of Excise for £43,000, because 120 of its 600 members were publicans-retailers. The board argued that the brewery as a whole should pay the higher rate reserved for retailers rather than the lower one, allowing waste, reserved for brewers.[19] Had Golden Lane been a separate corporate entity, its tax status would also have been separate from that of its shareholders, and no such dispute would have arisen.

The Elizabethan Statute of Artificers[20] demanded a seven-year apprenticeship for individuals wishing to enter specific crafts and trades. A

---

[18]This would be the case, for example, when dissolution or other remedy against the company itself is sought. In other cases, the plaintiff might have to hold his suit against shareholders no longer connected to the company. See H. Bellenden Ker, "Report on the Law of Partnership," *Parliamentary Papers* 44 (1837), 248.

[19]*Attorney General v. Brown, Parry, and Others*, Excise Trials 584, 599 (1808), and see Chapter 7 for other difficulties faced by the Golden Lane Brewery. Eventually, after going through the Commissioners of Excise and the Court of Exchequer, a final decision was given in favor of the brewery in the Court of Exchequer Chamber. But this was achieved only after heavy legal costs and business disturbances were suffered by the company during the litigation.

[20]5 Eliz. c.4 (1562).

problem arose when partnerships or unincorporated companies, in which some partner-members fulfilled the apprenticeship requirement while others did not, wished to enter these controlled crafts and trades.[21] It was argued that all members of such an association, including the passive investors, had to serve as apprentices before the association could enter that trade or craft. Such an argument could not have been raised against a business corporation, where the qualifications of the shareholders were not relevant to the status of the corporation vis-à-vis the Statute of Artificers.

As a rule, patents for invention included a proviso voiding them if they were assigned to, or in trust for, more than five persons. An unincorporated company formed by a large number of individuals for the purpose of becoming assignees of two patents was given a judgment in court that the assignment was illegal.[22] Corporations, on the other hand, were not subject to such limitations because they were seen as legal entities separated from their members, and because the Statute of Monopolies[23] treated them differently from individuals.

The Annuity Act[24] required that all deeds granting life annuities should be enrolled in the Court of Chancery. It required that each of these registrations include the names of all parties to the deed granting the annuity. According to Francis Baily, a contemporary observer:

This being the case, it would be almost impossible for any of those societies, of the nature of [unincorporated] joint-stock companies, to deal in this kind of securities; since the names of all the proprietors (amounting to some hundreds, or perhaps even to some thousands) must be inserted in the deed; and it would in fact be difficult, if not impossible, to collect all those names, at the time of making any one contract, owing to the fluctuating state of the proprietary.[25]

Two additional examples can be mentioned briefly: Shareholders of the unincorporated company had to join together in applications for State licensing for various matters; and the question arose whether shareholders in unincorporated companies which did not engage in trade on their own account should be treated as traders according to bankruptcy law, or as nontraders according to general insolvency law.

The cases above, of apprenticeship requirements, excise payment, shares in patents, registration of annuities, licensing, and bankruptcy are only a few examples of a large number of impediments encountered by

[21]*Raynard v. Chase*, 1 Burrow 2 (1756).

[22]*Duvergier v. Fellows*, 5 Bing 248 (1828) and 10 B.&C. 826 (1830). See also H. I. Dutton, *The Patent System and Inventive Activity During the Industrial Revolution: 1750–1852* (Manchester University Press, 1984), 152, 163ff.

[23]21 Jac. I c.3 (1623).

[24]17 Geo. III c.26 (1777).

[25]Baily, *Life Assurance Companies*, 40–43.

unincorporated companies because they lacked legal entity. These impediments became apparent mainly when difficulties led to disputes which reached the courts and judicial records; instances that did not result in litigation are simply not known to us. From all these cases, it is clear that the lack of legal entity caused the unincorporated companies and their shareholders a wide range of difficulties, prohibitions, expenses, and uncertainties. The final result was higher transaction costs imposed on unincorporated companies connected to these aspects of their activities, compared with business corporations involved in similar activities.

THE ROLE OF THE TRUST

The trust was portrayed by Maitland and Cooke, cited above, and by others as the cornerstone of the unincorporated company. Manchester explained the mechanism:

The property of the company was vested in trustees who were required to further the covenants which were set out in the deed of settlement. In this way it was possible to provide both for the company to sue and be sued and also for the transferability of shares. It was possible even to provide for a form of limited liability, at least as between the partners.[26]

The more cautious DuBois agreed that "the trustees device thus served effectively to give the unincorporated association at least some of the ease and effectiveness in dealing with property and court procedure that were the characteristics of the corporation."[27]

The Evolution of the Trust

Could the trust device fulfill the heavy burden placed on it by historians of business organization? I argue that because the trust evolved in the context of real property, it was not suitable in the late eighteenth and early nineteenth century to efficient functioning in the service of the unincorporated company. Trust doctrine went through substantial modification in modern times, as the employment of trusts branched out beyond the narrow landed class and real estate context. However, this adaptation of the trust device to the administration of nonreal assets and to the needs of the middle classes, of men of business and entrepreneurial aims, came only in the second half of the nineteenth century and in the twentieth century. It took a century or more for the Court of Chancery and the legislature to react to the gradual change in the context of the

[26]Manchester, *Modern Legal History*, 350.
[27]DuBois, *English Business Company*, 221–222.

employment of trusts. Thus, the modification took place too late to affect the fortune of the unincorporated company during the crucial period before 1844, in which industrializing England was subject to prohibitive methods of incorporation. By the time equity, and, after 1873–1875, the fused English legal system responded to the changing reality, Parliament had already enacted free incorporation and general limited liability. Thus, from the point of view of timing, the unincorporated company had the misfortune of being one of the earliest employments of the trust outside the landed context, while nineteenth- and twentieth-century employments of the trust were more fortunate in having a more accommodating trust law.

To substantiate this argument we turn to the origins of the trust device and its later modifications. I do not survey the history of the trust at length or discuss the law of trusts in depth, as this has been done elsewhere. I aim here only to present the timing argument and analyze those elements of early trust law (actually, only of express private trust law) that constrained the adaptation of the trust to the unincorporated form of business organization during the eighteenth century.

The Origins of the Trust

The trust grew out of the "use" which originated in the realities and constraints of the feudal system.[28] In crude modern terms, the formal common-law proprietor held the land for the use of a beneficiary who had an equitable interest in that same land, thus splitting the bundle of ownership rights between them. Uses were made for monasteries, crusaders, minor aristocratic heirs, and others. One of the main motives for the creation of uses, as fiscal feudalism advanced, was the evasion of feudal dues. The massive expansion of land held in use led to a sharp decline in the profits of feudal landlords, and especially of the lord of all lords, the King. In one of several attempts to revive fiscal feudalism, Henry the VIII pushed forward the Statute of Uses in 1536.[29] Innovative lawyers found a way of bypassing the Statute by forming a use upon use, which was by then called a trust.

The common-law system did not recognize the use and the equitable rights it gave rise to. From the common-law perspective, all that existed

---

[28]For a much fuller survey of these developments and further references see J. L. Barton, "The Medieval Use," *Law Quarterly Review* 81 (Oct. 1965), 562–577; J.M.W. Bean, *The Decline of English Feudalism: 1215–1540* (Manchester University Press, 1968); S.F.C. Milsom, *Historical Foundation of the Common Law*, 2d ed. (London: Butterworths, 1981), 166–239; A.W.B. Simpson, *A History of the Land Law*, 2d ed. (Oxford: Clarendon Press, 1986), 173–192; Baker, *English Legal History*, 283–295, 318–336.

[29]27 Hen VIII c.10 (1535).

was the legal rights of the trustees. The rights of the beneficiaries conflicted with the legal rights over that same land and were simply ignored altogether. For this reason, the arrangements regarding the use, and later the trust, were not recognized or enforceable in courts of common law. As early as the late fourteenth or early fifteenth century, the Lord Chancellor was called upon to serve justice to damaged beneficiaries. He gradually acquired judicial supervision over disputes concerning arrangements between beneficiaries and trustees. This was one of the important fields of dispute in which the Lord Chancellor developed his first judicial functions (as described in Chapter 1), on the way to establishing Chancery as a separate court, distinct from the common-law courts, with special norms – equity – distinct from the common-law norms. By the late fifteenth century, the use had become, in the hands of the Lord Chancellors, a relatively coherent equitable doctrine. Cases regarding uses and trusts came to comprise a considerable share of the total litigation within the jurisdiction of Chancery and to shape it as a judicial institution in competition with common-law institutions.

The Strict Settlement Trust

In the generations that followed the enactment of the Statute of Uses, as the feudal system declined sharply, the trust ceased to be utilized as a device for overcoming feudal dues. However, around the middle of the seventeenth century, zealous lawyers and landowners adapted this equitable device to the contemporary needs of the landed class. During the next two centuries, the trust was widely employed for a new purpose: control and division of family assets, as a component of the strict settlement.[30] The strict settlement and the trust served two ends. One was to ensure the passage of family estates from generation to generation without disturbance by greedy, mentally disabled, or improvident elder sons, who might try to dispose of the entire estate and thus terminate the family's landed social status. The second was to ensure that part of the family's estate income be distributed to widows, younger sons, and

[30]W. R. Cornish and G. de N. Clark, *Law and Society in England: 1750–1950* (London: Sweet and Maxwell, 1989), 123–132, 166–172; L. Bonfield, *Marriage Settlements, 1601–1740: The Adoption of the Strict Settlement* (Cambridge University Press, 1983); Eileen Spring, "The Family, Strict Settlement and Historians," in G. R. Rubin and David Sugarman, eds., *Law, Economy and Society, 1750–1914: Essays in the History of English Law* (Abingdon: Professional Books, 1984); Lloyd Bonfield, "Strict Settlement and the Family: A Differing View," *Economic History Review* 41, no. 3 (1988), 461; F.M.L. Thompson, *English Landed Society in the Nineteenth Century*, London: Routledge and Kegan Paul, 1963; Eileen Spring, *Law, Land, and Family: Aristocratic Inheritance in England, 1300 to 1800* (University of North Carolina Press, 1993), 123–147.

daughters. During this period, the trust still developed within the context of real property and the landed classes, and suited the landed estates, the dynastic needs of families of these classes, and the desire of these classes as a whole to secure their exclusivity as the English elite. These needs were economically, socially, and legally different from the needs of entrepreneurial businessmen who tried to form unincorporated companies during the eighteenth and early nineteenth centuries.

The Investment Trust

Michael Chesterman convincingly demonstrates the unsuitability of the trust device, as shaped by the landed society reality, to the new needs of the rising middle classes with their new forms of wealth and investment.[31] He then describes some major modifications that took place in recent centuries, in a process in which "numerous new questions requiring legal regulation presented themselves," and in response, the courts of equity, and to a lesser degree the legislature, developed from a "very meager starting point" what they believed were appropriate legal rules for the new context. In Chesterman's words: "While doubtless the basic concept of the trust and the broad outlines of modern trust law owe their origins to the reasonably well-documented phenomenon of feudal conveyances of land to uses, the bulk of the law relating to trust administration stems from this virtually overlooked process" which took place during the period from 1750 onward.[32] The modern investment trust is distinct from earlier landed trusts in four respects: It was employed chiefly by middle class and nouveau riche upper-class families, rather than old landed families; it held mixed property, a large portion of which was nontangible property such as government stock and corporate shares, rather than predominantly real property; it had a relatively high turnover of assets, according to changing market opportunities, not fixed estates to be held in specie by the same family for generations; and, last, as a consequence of these three differences, trustees were expected to be active managers of the trust assets, or to employ and supervise agents with professional and managerial capacities, rather than to be merely titular owners of land or passive watchers over heirs. Joshua Getzler, referring to a wide range of modern trusts holding intangible property, focuses on the problem of delegation and employment of professional agents in relation to fiduciary duties. He concludes that during the nine-

---

[31]M. R. Chesterman, "Family Settlements on Trust: Landowners and the Rising Bourgeoisie," in G. R. Rubin and David Sugarman, eds., *Law, Economy and Society, 1750–1914: Essays in the History of English Law* (Abingdon: Professional Books, 1984), 124–167. See also Graham Moffat and Michael Chesterman, *Trust Law: Text and Materials* (London: Weidenfeld and Nicholson, 1988), 32–39.

[32]Chesterman, "Family Settlements," 150.

teenth century, a few major cases, later codified in trust legislation, modified the relevant equitable doctrines, and states that "one of the great discoveries of English jurisprudence was to allow the ancient equitable institution of the trust to be applied to modern intangible forms of property."[33]

Chesterman and Getzler eloquently describe the process, often neglected by legal historians (who traditionally focus on earlier periods), by which the trust doctrine was transformed, from premodern to modern, to suit the needs of trusts holding intangible assets. The issue of precise timing was not central to their needs. However, the timing of this transformation is crucial when considering whether it could be in any way instrumental to the shaping and advancement of the unincorporated company. Though Chesterman and Getzler identified some minor changes in the doctrine of the trust before the mid-nineteenth century, the more radical transformation occurred only from that period on, with *Saunders v. Vautier* (1841), *Speight v. Gaunt* (1883), the Trustee Acts of 1893 and 1925, and the Trustee Investments Act of 1961 as landmarks.[34] In the long run, the trust device was indeed functionally adopted for new purposes, but for a considerable time in the mid-run it reflected a degree of autonomy.

The unincorporated trust was quite similar in its characteristics to the investment trust, and both were radically different from the strict settlement trust or the feudal trust. Medieval landed trusts were clearly unsuited to modern forms of wealth, but the change came only after the mid-nineteenth century, when incorporation was readily available to the business community, after the heyday of the unincorporated form of business organization. The relatively late modification of trust law, compared with the development of corporation law, is not merely a contingent. The railway booms of the 1830s to 1850s and the permissive corporate legislation of 1844 and 1856 dramatically expanded the share market, legitimized investment in intangible assets, encouraged the formation of the investment trust, and eventually motivated the modification of trust law.[35] The late modification of trust law was a result partly

[33]Joshua Getzler, " 'Gentlemen Do Not Collect Rents': Fiduciary Obligations and the Problem of Delegation" (forthcoming).

[34]*Saunders v. Vautier*, 4 Beav. 115 (1841); *Speight v. Gaunt*, 9 App. Cas. 1 (1883); Trustee Act 56 & 57 Vict. c. 53 (1893); Trustee Act 15 & 16 Geo. V c.19 (1925); Trustee Investment Act 9 & 10 Eliz. II c.62 (1961).

[35]As argued in Chapters 2 and 5, the share market was not a mid-nineteenth century invention, but rather one of the late seventeenth century, which expanded substantially after the middle of the eighteenth century. But its diffusion to new social groups was slow. It was a matter of time before a large number of investment trusts were created, a demand for share investment appeared, and litigation of a new sort reached the courts and affected trust law.

of the relative autonomy of the law, and partly of the fact that the social and economic context in which the trusts were employed was slow to change. The unincorporated company trust was a pioneer and as such encountered unsuitable equitable doctrines. In conclusion, I argue that studies of the modification of the trust to other modern purposes support my conclusion that the eighteenth-century trust could not adequately serve the needs of the businessmen involved in the unincorporated companies.

THE UNINCORPORATED COMPANY TRUST

In this section I focus on the employment of the trust in the context of the unincorporated joint-stock company. I analyze some of the major practical and conceptual difficulties resulting from the late adaptation of the trust doctrine and practice for nonlanded needs, focusing on those elements that were distinctively manifest in the unincorporated company of late eighteenth and early nineteenth century. I analyze difficulties first regarding the nature of trust assets, then regarding the trustees, and finally regarding the beneficiaries. I then examine the possibility that express clauses in trust deeds could replace doctrinal adaptation to lessen these difficulties. In this section I do not survey in any general or comprehensive manner the trust law of the period.

The Assets to be Vested in the Trust

Because traditionally trustees were supposed to hold specific real assets (normally the landed estate of one family), they did not typically deal with the sale, purchase, and substitution of assets. In fact, it was assumed that "a trustee cannot but in one instance injure the estate of *cestique* trust [beneficiary], by alienation."[36] Thus, to control trustees and prevent breach of duty, severe limitations were placed on the transferability of trust assets. Generally, land could not be turned into money,[37] and money had to be invested in the most secure form, 3 percent Treasury consols. The lending of trust money on personal credit or on partial security was also considered to be a breach of trust.

Chancery money was, as a rule, invested exclusively in this government stock, and trustees were expected to follow Chancery in this practice. Discussions in eighteenth-century Chancery cases and trust treatises revolved around questions such as whether Bank of England annuities

[36]Francis William Sanders, *An Essay on the Nature and Laws of Uses and Trusts* (1791), 255.
[37]Even relatively minor changes in trust assets, such as in the terms of land lease, or cutting down timber, were prohibited and considered to be a breach of trust. See *Witter v. Witter*, 3 P. Wms. 100 (1730); *Bromfield ex parte* 1 Ves. Jun. 453 (1792).

or well-secured real estate mortgages are an acceptable form of trustee investment. The doctrine of authorized investments gradually replaced the view of land as the dominant or even exclusive trust asset. However, the list of authorized investments was short and conservative. It was stated in most definite terms by Lord Chancellor Hardwicke in 1746 that "Neither South Sea stock nor Bank stock are considered as a good security, because it depends upon the management of governors and directors, and are subject to losses."[38] Lord Eldon determined fifty-six years later that "Bank Stock is as safe, I trust and believe, as any Government securities: but it is not Government security; and therefore this Court does not lay out, or leave the property in Bank Stock; and what the Court will decree it expects from trustees and executors."[39] And it was still the commonly held view in the 1830s that "a trustee may not invest the trust-fund in the stock of any private company, as South Sea Stock, Bank Stock & c." If this was Chancery's attitude to the moneyed companies, the smaller and riskier canal and insurance companies and the like, not to mention bubble companies, were out of the question. It seems that the financial revolution and the rise of the stock market had not yet reached Chancery. Or that the days of the South Sea Bubble, during which both Chancery clerks and trustees were tempted to invest in shares, and thus lost most of their trust assets, were still a vivid reminder for the Lord Chancellors. After the middle of the nineteenth century, the list of authorized investments was gradually extended, and eventually also included corporate shares (subject to some limitations), but this modification was too late to affect the unincorporated company.

Newly established unincorporated companies had no intention of burying all their joint-stock in low-yield government stock. This mode of investment was available to each of the members on his or her individual account. The companies were formed in order to invest high-yield venture capital in relatively speculative projects. The shareholders of the company expected money to be invested in forms not permitted to trustees according to equity doctrine. This conflict between business practice and legal doctrine created a serious problem.

The Trustees' Perspective

From the perspective of trustees, several new problems arose when the trust device was employed for the first time in the formation of unincorporated companies. In this section, I consider three of these. First, in this

---

[38]Thomas Lewin, *The Law of Trusts and Trustees* (1837), 305–317, citation from 308. See also Grant Harding, *Advice to Trustees and to Those Who Appoint to That Office* (1830), 47.

[39]*Howe v. Earl of Dartmouth*, 7 Ves. Jun. 137, 150 (1802).

business context, risks were considerably higher and the issue of trustees' liability more disturbing. Second, because in the unincorporated company trustees represented diversified shareholders and varied interests, there was a tendency to increase the body of trustees, thus the decision-making process within this body became more problematic. Third, the new, more active, managerial role played by trustees in this enterprising environment forced them to delegate powers to company officers and to employ professional agents.

By the early eighteenth century, trustees were exposed to liability toward beneficiaries as well as toward third parties, as the doctrine of trustees' fiduciary obligation crystallized.[40] However, unlike contemporary corporations and their officers and directors, they did not enjoy the privilege of limitation of liability.[41] Trustees as a body were not a legal entity, separate from the legal personality of the individual trustees, and trust assets were not considered to be legally separated in any sense from other, personal, assets of trustees. Because of this, liability incurred on trustees as such intermingled with their nontrust liabilities and could affect their personal, nontrust assets. In the words of a contemporary author, "Trustees merely acting as such, cannot discharge themselves of the legal liabilities which would have attached to them as individuals placed in similar situations." This exposure to liabilities was not merely theoretical. Trustees could become liable toward third parties, particularly in common law, in various instances including misrepresentation in sale of property, failure in the performance of contracts, tortorious acts, and claims based on bills of exchange. On the other hand, they were also liable vis-à-vis the beneficiaries. "Where a loss would have fallen upon trust property through the negligence of the trustees," they would carry the responsibility.[42] Negligence, not fraud, was all that was required at that stage for holding a trustee in breach of his duties, and entitle the beneficiaries to equitable remedies.

Because trustees were exposed to a double-edged, personal and unlimited, liability toward third parties and beneficiaries, it is not surprising that Grant Harding, the author of a popular 1830 trustees guidebook, advised them that "carrying on of trade or business for the object of a trust estate is a very hazardous expedient, for the trustee may easily make himself responsible for various losses."[43] This is exactly what trustees of unincorporated companies were expected to do. They were

---

[40]For a notable statement of the obligation to avoid conflict between self-interest and duty as trustee, a typical fiduciary obligation, see *Keech v. Sandford,* Sel Cas T King 61 (1726).

[41]For the development of corporate limited liability, see Chapter 5.

[42]Harding, *Advice to Trustees,* 66–67.

[43]Ibid., 75.

required to carry on trade on behalf of the company, and thus to subject themselves to personal responsibility for losses. Whereas responsibility toward beneficiaries could possibly be waived by wide authorizing clauses (with the collateral consequence of giving up beneficiaries' control over trustees), and was in fact reduced by a gradual judicial lowering of fiduciary obligation standards (from absolute – strict – liability to negligence to fraud), the responsibility toward third parties could not be contractually limited for several types of liabilities (torts, transferable bills).[44]

A typical feudal or strict settlement trust would involve a handful of trustees, senior members of other branches of the dynasty, friends or neighbors of aristocratic or gentry standing, and possibly the family attorney. The main reason for having more than a single trustee in the landed context was to create a perpetual body. In the unincorporated company the scheme would usually include the appointment of a relatively large number of trustees, directors, or representatives on behalf of some of the major shareholders. This created a new set of problems concerning the relationship between the trustees. Cotrustees were expected as a rule to act together, in attendance, as one body. Voting was not an acceptable mode of decision-making among trustees in the traditional landed context and the majority could not bind the minority or the trust assets. Harmony and unanimity were expected. However, this expectation was not realistic in the context of the unincorporated company trust, in which the number of trustees was large and the actions they had to perform were numerous and had to be taken on short notice. This dissonance did not exist in the real-estate trusts, and thus was not resolved by the equitable doctrine, at its eighteenth-century state. Gradually, but again too late for our purposes, the doctrine was relaxed to allow majority decisions in public and charitable trusts, and by way of express permission in other types of trusts.[45]

Why would anyone want to be a trustee under such circumstances? Trustees of real-estate trusts were often kin or friends of the beneficiaries. They were not exposed to high risks, within a regime of unlimited liability, and were not involved in day-to-day managerial duties. They

[44]After the middle of the nineteenth century, the law in these respects was somewhat modified to give certain effect to express trustee exemption clauses (in trust devices and in contracts with third parties) to allow trustees to recoup out of trust assets their trust liabilities, and to lower the standard of trustees' conduct, the breach of which would make them liable toward beneficiaries.

[45]For early examples, validating majority decision making, in the context of dissenters' chapels trusts, see *Blacket v. Blizared,* 9 B. & C. 851 (1829); *Wilkinson v. Malin,* 2 C. & J. 636 (1832). Yet as late as 1875, the general rule that a majority of the trustees could not bind the minority was confirmed in *Luke v. South Kensington Hotel Company,* 11 Ch. D. 121 (1875).

were willing to serve as trustees for altruistic motives, rooted in gentlemanly culture. Alternately, their service might be viewed as a thriving gift economy, based on an exchange between kin and friends of comparable social rank.[46] The service as a trustee was seen as "a burden upon the honour and conscience of the person intrusted, and not undertaken upon mercenary views."[47] The rule was that trustees were allowed expenses but not "trouble and care." Again, none of these characteristics applied to trustees of unincorporated companies where the body of trustees was larger, more socially diverse, profit-motivated, and potentially of conflicting interests. An honorary, or gift-exchange, relationship seems less suitable to a shrewd and competitive business culture. Furthermore, there was a problem of who would select the trustees. In the landed trust, a father was in a position to select the best available trustees for his sons and daughters. In the unincorporated company, various shareholders might have conflicting interests in this respect. After the initial appointment of trustees, other problems could arise, such as rotation, death, travel, insanity, and the like. In an unincorporated company, there was objection to authorizing trustees to appoint new trustees, as this could lead to a change in the delicate balance of power between shareholders. Since the joint body of trustees was not as homogeneous as in the family trust, the solution was to order the remaining trustees, in the initial trust agreement, to resort to the beneficiaries. In such a case, all the shareholders – the beneficiaries, in legal terms – became involved in the appointment of new trustees. The problems stemming from the selection of trustees agreeable to all shareholders, and willing to be exposed to liabilities at no charge, further complicated the use of the trust device for the unincorporated company.

The Beneficiaries' Perspective

As long as trustees were rigorously restricted in their ability to alienate rights in, or decrease the value of, trust assets, due to the landed nature of most trust assets and the doctrine of authorized investment, they could not expose the beneficiaries to high risks. Trustees were also restricted in their ability to damage beneficiaries due to other, related trust doctrines: Trustees had to act unanimously, were themselves subject to

---

[46]For a general discussion of the gift economy and of reciprocated gifts, see Avner Offer, "Between the Gift and the Market: The Economy of Regard," *Economic History Review* 50, no. 3 (1997), 450–476. For a suggestion to view the trust in this light, see Joshua Getzler, "Patterns of Fusion," in Peter Birks, ed., *The Classification of Obligations* (Oxford: Clarendon Press, 1997).

[47]*Ayliffe v. Murray*, 2 Atk. 58 (1740) per Lord Hardwicke. This was the common wisdom even fifty years later. See Sanders, *Uses and Trusts*, 256, for a similar statement.

unlimited liability toward third parties, were not allowed to employ agents or delegate powers, and were prohibited from making personal profit out of trust assets or dealings. This legal framework of trusts, with the fiduciary relationship at its core, worked well in the landed context of the early eighteenth century where it provided a reasonable solution to principal-agent and related problems. But this legal framework had to be modified (as seen above) when trusts were employed in the business context and this modification augmented agency problems. One potential course of trust law modification was through the introduction of express authorizing clauses into trust deeds.[48] Such clauses allowed trustees to purchase intangible assets, to take majority decisions, to employ agents, and the like. However, in this way, the beneficiaries lost much of their control over trustees. The dilemma was that on one hand beneficiaries wanted, in the business – profit-maximizing – context, to relax the doctrine and allow trustees more flexibility in order to enable them to maximize trust assets; but on the other hand, wider authorization meant less supervision.

Drafting such clauses may be viewed as merely inverting the default trust law rules, the way a default contract clause can be inverted (contracted out or disposed of, in legal jargon). However, such inversion could injure the beneficiaries themselves. This can be argued in terms of standards (generalized principles) and rules (narrower and detailed norms). The core of trust law, the relationship between trustees and beneficiaries, began as a handful of general standards. Over a period of some 400 years, it developed through the accumulation of equity judgments into a thick weave of concrete rules. These rules were well suited to deal with disputes between beneficiaries and trustees in typical landed trusts. But when trust default clauses are contracted out, the accumulated detailed rules become irrelevant. All that remains of trust law, once again, as 400 years earlier, are a few general standards that cannot solve concrete disputes. By agreeing to contract out the default clauses, and thus render trust rules irrelevant, beneficiaries give up the power to supervise trustees. Inversion of default clauses by a large number of trusts would eventually lead to the evolution of new, detailed, judge-made rules to suit the new litigation reality, but this was bound to be a long process.

Take, for example, the issue of delegation of trustees' duties, or employment of agents.[49] Traditionally, trust doctrine (the default) did not

---

[48]I have not come across sufficient evidence to indicate that this means was indeed widely used in unincorporated companies' trust deeds, as some argue. But I am willing, for the sake of the debate, to deal with this argument.

[49]Admittedly, my evidence here is scant, and the argument, accordingly, is rather speculative and based on theoretical postulations.

allow it. During the pre-eighteenth-century period, there were no rules that dealt with the nature of liability of delegating trustees. The early clauses permitting agency were apparently drafted during the eighteenth century in the context of the unincorporated company trust with the employment of professionals as agents. The effect of such clauses, in the absence of relevant rules of liability, was that delegating trustees were acting in a legal vacuum, and could theoretically escape any liability for damages caused the assets or beneficiaries by their agents and delegates. The expected reaction of cautious beneficiaries might have been to min-imize the use of such empowering clauses. The expected reaction of conservative judges might have been twofold: narrow interpretation of the empowering clauses in order to check delegation, and the evolution of new, judge-made rules to ensure strict vicarious liability. It took the doctrine more than a century to develop in a fashion suitable to the new context of trusts, balancing between the growing need of trustees to employ agents and the growing need of beneficiaries to supervise trus-tees.[50] Since my argument here is confined to timing, the fact that the doctrine was not firmly settled and based on thick and workable rules prior to 1883 is conclusive. In summary, the shift from the landed trusts to the new context of business trusts, coupled with the broad permissive clauses that inverted the default doctrine, left some fields of trust law with abstract standards and lacking well-defined workable rules. It took over a century for the relevant rules to be defined and accumulated. During this century, the supervision of managers (as trustees) by share-holders (as beneficiaries) in unincorporated companies was, at best, par-tial.[51]

The Role of the Trust: A Reappraisal

The concept of the trust was used in some cases and to some degree by businessmen and solicitors who organized unincorporated companies with transferable shares. It was not the sole or fundamental basis of such

[50]*Ex parte Belchier*, Amb 218 (1754); *Turner v. Corney*, 5 Beav 515 (1841); *Speight v. Gaunt*, 22 Chan. D. 727 (1883); *Learoyd v. Whiteley*, 12 App. Cas. 727 (1887); Trustee Act 15 & 16 Geo. V c.19 (1925). See also Getzler, "Fiduciary Obligations."

[51]I briefly mention another possible dimension of supervision: the unilateral termi-nation of a trust by beneficiaries before its time of expiration. Unilateral termination contradicted the basic aspiration of landed society to preserve estates and lineages. Only in 1841, in *Saunders v. Vautier*, Cr. & Ph. 240 (1841), was the doctrine that allowed beneficiaries to terminate trusts and acquire their assets satisfactorily settled. However, the efficacy of this means of supervision is dubious because of its severity. It is an emergency means, equivalent to the dissolution of a corporation or a partner-ship, rather than a conventional means of supervision.

companies, but only one of many building blocks and legal devices used to ease the problems caused by lack of incorporation. While the trust was able to solve for the unincorporated company some of the problems it was originally intended to solve, such as holding real estate property, it was of no service in many other, more commercial and managerial aspects of the activities of the unincorporated company. Furthermore, because trust litigation lay within the jurisdiction of Chancery, the litigants suffered from high costs and delays, as I demonstrate below. The trust was by no means an omnipotent device in the context of the unincorporated company and did not reduce the costs and uncertainties involved in its operation to any considerable extent. It thus did not turn this form of organization into the first choice of the business community.

THE UNINCORPORATED COMPANY IN COURT LITIGATION

Partnership as a Common-Law Conception

The law of partnership was partly borrowed from Roman and medieval civil law and partly from the law merchant.[52] In England, it was first received by merchant and municipal courts at the outports, London and other cities and boroughs, and in the Court of Admiralty. Gradually, between the fourteenth and sixteenth centuries, as part of the royal common-law courts' efforts to centralize the legal system and increase the volume of litigation in their halls, they extended their judicial review over these inferior courts.[53] Consequently, partnership law was gradually accepted or, rather, assimilated into common-law jurisdiction, forms, and doctrine. At this stage, it was the principles of common law which determined the legal formation and dissolution of partnerships, and this reflected on the application of other norms of common law on the partnership. Only later did partnerships make inroads into the Courts of Equity, due to the rigidity of the common law. But the equitable jurisdiction over these affairs was only supplementary to the common-law jurisdiction, and was limited to specific remedies. Therefore, the partnership should not be perceived as an equitable form of business organization, as Cooke claimed.[54]

[52]See Chapter 1.
[53]This was done primarily by the Court of King's Bench, exercising judicial review over the inferior court, based on technical defects, by way of writ of error and writ of certiorari. For the process in general, see Baker, *English Legal History*, 26–33, 141–143, 155–173.
[54]Cooke, *Corporation, Trust and Company*, 85.

In common law, a partnership consisted of the communion of profits and losses among individuals.[55] Thus, every unincorporated company with a sharing element constituted a partnership in common law. As a result, unincorporated companies faced even greater legal difficulties than those facing smaller and less complex partnerships in common law, due to their unique characteristics, such as an extremely large number of partners. The major difficulty faced by unincorporated companies was in the sphere of litigation between partners. Though, as we have seen, a wide range of disputes between partners or shareholders existed, available remedies were very limited in common law. There were no adequate legal forms of action or remedies for litigation of this sort.

The Obsoleteness of Common-Law Account Action

Relationships between partners existed on a continuing basis. Partners invested in the partnership account and divided profits at different points of time. Each partner paid out and received sums of money from customers, suppliers, and the like, both as an agent for the partnership as a whole, and also privately for other partners and himself. Whenever one partner brought a claim against another partner, stating that money was owed in a certain case, the defendant could raise a counterclaim for money the plaintiff owed in a different affair, but which also constituted part of the ongoing and complex activity of the same partnership. The practical result was that any claim inter se in partnerships required a detailed and comprehensive settlement of numerous claims, counterclaims, and accounts among all partners.

Common law did not offer efficient methods for settling such accounts. The antiquated, personal, quasicontractual action of account originated around the year 1200, during the formative period of the common law. In the thirteenth century, its scope was extended by court judgments from a bailiff–lord relationship to various types of personal relationships: receivership, agency, and partnership, and the action became popular for a while. As time passed, and more complicated account actions were litigated, the procedural rigidities of this form of action turned out to be more detrimental. Common-law account was divided into two related stages. The first primarily involved a question of law and fact: the accountability of the defendant to the plaintiff, or, in other words, the extent to which the relationship between the litigants fitted into the action of account. Only in the second stage, if reached, were the

---

[55]In some circumstances, sharing of profits alone, without sharing of losses, could constitute a partnership. See Andrew Bisset, *A Practical Treatise on the Law of Partnership* (1847), 2–36, for a discussion of what kind of sharing arrangements constitute a partnership.

actual accounts settled, again a matter that involved questions of both fact and law. Common-law judges had neither the time nor the competence to settle complicated accounts, and as a result the second stage was conducted by appointed auditors. However, the auditors could not resolve legal disputes or perform a wager of law when the facts were in dispute. Thus, many actions went back and forth between judges and auditors. The action of account became time- and money-consuming. In the fourteenth century it went into a prolonged decline. At first, other common-law actions – debt and later also assumpsit – were used whenever possible, instead of account. Later, equity became the target of plaintiffs in accountable relationships. By the seventeenth century, the common-law action of account, like other ancient personal actions, was obsolete.[56] Common-law action on the case of assumpsit, a relatively late offspring of the writ of trespass, provided fertile ground for seventeenth- and eighteenth-century developments in contract law, but not in partnership law. Because assumpsit involved trial by jury, it was not suitable for the unraveling of accounts, which was time-consuming, involved documentation, and required expertise.[57] The future of account, and of much partnership law litigation, was in Chancery.[58] The driving forces for the decline of the common-law account and for the rise of equitable account were not economic or social, but rather legal, reflecting the relative autonomy of this aspect of the law. It is important to note that the procedural rigidities, which caused the decline of common-law account, had nothing to do with partnerships or substantive law as such. They resulted from the adversarial nature of common law in general, the limits of common-law fact-finding methods, and the formality of its system of forms of action. They were fueled by forms, procedures, competition between institutions, and legal traditions in general.

The decline of common-law account, which began in the late fourteenth century, had, by the early nineteenth century, implications far beyond the procedural sphere. As H. Bellenden Ker said in his 1837 report on partnership law, "although actions are permitted to be brought by partners against their co-partners in particular cases, yet the general rule at law is, that where no account has been settled between the partners, no action lies between them in respect of a partnership, but that resort must be had to equity."[59] The internal dynamics of the

---

[56]For specific problems of the account see S. J. Stoljar, "The Transformation of Account," *Law Quarterly Review* 80 (April 1964), 203–224; Milsom, *Historical Foundations*, 275–282; Baker, *English Legal History*, 412–413.

[57]Ibid., 414–415.

[58]For the contrast between the adversarial characteristics of common law and the inquisitorial nature of equity see Getzler, "Fiduciary Obligations."

[59]Ker, "Law of Partnership," 246.

common law created the above general rule and in most cases prevented inter se litigation between partners in common-law courts.

The Rise and Limitations of Equity Account

The process by which a considerable portion of the litigation concerning partnership disputes found its way to the Courts of Equity is explained by the Commissioners on Courts of Common Law in their Second Report:

> The method of trial by jury, however well adapted to the determination of questions of fact in general, is peculiarly ill suited to the minute and patient investigation necessary to ascertain the balance of an account involving various items on both sides. Among our ancient forms of action is one provided for the express purpose of enabling the Courts of Law to authorize the examination of such matters by auditors appointed under their authority; but the mode of proceeding in an action of *Account* has been found so inconvenient in practice, that this remedy has quite fallen into disuse; and the Courts of Equity, in consequence of the inadequacy of relief afforded by the Courts of Law, have long exercised a jurisdiction over matters of mutual account; and that, even in cases where the items constituting the account are founded on obligations purely legal.[60]

The need for settling accounts was particularly manifest in dealings between partners inter se, where the continuous relationship created a complex set of accounts.

Partnership litigation came into the Courts of Equity not because of substantive innovation within equitable conceptions, but rather because of the procedural rigidity of the common-law system. The legitimization for this extension of a concurrent Equity jurisdiction was an old one, in fact the motor which moved Equity from its inception, that "a court of Law could not give so complete a remedy as a court of Equity."[61] Equity indeed offered more in terms of forms of action and remedies for litigation of partners against third persons, and especially between partners. This is evident in the space devoted to equitable remedies in early treatises on the law of partnership, published from 1794 onward.[62] Equitable remedies also included the appointment of receivers and the issue of injunctions, but account was the most commonly sought remedy in partnership and unincorporated company litigation. Chancery, it should be remembered, also handled trust litigation.

---

[60]P. 25, cited by ibid., 256.

[61]Henry Maddock, *A Treatise on the Principles and Practice of the High Court of Chancery*, 2d ed., 2 vols. (1820), 85

[62]William Watson, *A Treatise on the Law of Partnership* (1794); Montagu, *Law of Partnership*, 47–53; Niel Gow, *A Practical Treatise on the Law of Partnership* (1823), 117–140; Bisset, *Law of Partnership*, 131–154.

Mitigating the internal relations of partnerships in extreme cases, such as frauds and embezzlements by a partner that led to the destruction and dissolution of a partnership, could also be well served by account and equity in general. "The benefits of a resort to equity are, however, in many cases greatly, and it is submitted, injuriously narrowed by a rule ... that equity will not interfere in the concerns of a partnership, unless a dissolution is prayed."[63] Lord Chancellor Eldon was very clear on this subject in *Waters v. Taylor* (1808): "This Court does not interfere for the management of a joint concern, except as incidental to the object of the suit, to wind up the concern and divide the produce."[64] A few years later he reiterated this policy in *Forman v. Homfray* (1813), explaining that "if a partner can come here for an Account merely, pending the partnership, there seems to be nothing to prevent him coming annually."[65] By this time, Chancery was not competing for increased business, but rather for reduction of its load, as we see in the next section, and the possibility of annual suits alarmed Eldon. Thus, the internal governance of unincorporated companies could be regulated and enforced in equity only in severe cases when the entire future of the company was at stake. In other cases of disputes between individual members, when the intention of the partners was to retain their ongoing business, the Court of Chancery did not avail itself to litigants.

The Crisis at the Court of Chancery

This judicial policy of Lord Eldon might better be understood in the wider context of the status of the Court of Chancery in the late eighteenth and early nineteenth century. Chancery had considerably expanded its jurisdiction during previous centuries due to its flexible procedures, in sharp contrast to rigid common-law forms of actions and procedures. By this time, Chancery jurisdiction had spread beyond trusts and accounts to remedies of injunction and specific performance, guardianship of infants, idiots, and lunatics, and to bankruptcies and frauds.[66] It was involved in an unmanageable conglomerate of legal doctrines, rights, remedies, and general principles and maxims. By the eighteenth century, in parallel to the jurisdictional expansion, Chancery, under Chancellor Hardwicke, had also gone through procedural reform which

[63]Ker, "Law of Partnership," 246.

[64]*Waters v. Taylor,* 15 Ves. Jun. 10 (1808). There were a few cases in which accounts between partners were handled in Chancery without dissolution, but in most cases, particularly when this point was disputed, Lord Eldon's doctrine was upheld. See Ker, "Law of Partnership," 246.

[65]*Forman v. Homfray,* 2 V. & B. 329, 330 (1813).

[66]See the two-volume, over 1,300-page treatise required for covering this expanded and disordered court jurisdiction: Maddock, *High Court of Chancery.*

formalized and complicated petitions, hearings, deliberations, and judgment writing. Despite this huge expansion and formalization, Chancery
remained a one-man court from the fourteenth century until 1813.[67]
This one man was not a full-time judge, because as Lord Chancellor, he
held other significant positions: head of the upper house of the Legislature (the House of Lords), senior member of the executive branch (the
Cabinet), and head of the legal profession (the Bar).

As a result of all these, by the early nineteenth century, there could be
up to 20,000 pending cases, and a plaintiff could expect to wait as long
as thirty years for a final judgment.[68] Furthermore, fees in Chancery
were extortionary because the numerous Chancery clerks lived off fees,
rather than fixed salaries.[69] The Court, and Lord Eldon himself, became
targets of public animosity and, later, of official inquiries. In light of the
overburdening of Chancery, it is not surprising that Eldon was not
inclined to involve his court in disputes regarding the daily running of
partnerships and unincorporated companies, a highly complicated, detailed, and time-consuming matter. Dealing with the winding up of
partnerships was quite enough for him.

All these factors made the Court of Chancery, by the late eighteenth
century, a place to be avoided if at all possible. Shareholders in unincorporated companies facing inter se partnership litigation or trust litigation
did not consider themselves very fortunate. Their route to the courts of
common law was blocked by procedural obstacles, and in Chancery they
could expect nothing but expenses and delays. The jurisdictional classification, which was an advantage to partnerships and trusts in the early
days of the Court of Chancery, and may have been a slight disadvantage
in the seventeenth century, became, by the late eighteenth century, a
considerable practical expediency. The unincorporated company, han-
dling both trust and partnership litigation in Chancery, rather than in
the common-law courts, was considerably disadvantaged compared with
corporations, whose litigation only rarely reached Chancery. This disadvantage was the result of internal dynamics within the legal system

[67]In that year a Vice-Chancellor was appointed; in 1842, two more. In 1833, the
Master of the Rolls was formally given judicial powers (though there are some
examples before that date of a Master of the Rolls' judicial, rather than administrative, decisions). Yet throughout the period, even cases not heard by the Lord Chancellor in the first instance could reach him sitting in appeals. His limited free judicial
time remained the bottleneck of Chancery until the judicature reform of 1873–1875
that integrated Chancery and the common-law courts.

[68]For long-term trends in chancery litigation, see Henry Horwitz and Patrick Polden, "Continuity or Change in the Court of Chancery in the Seventeenth and Eighteenth Centuries?," *Journal of British Studies* 35, no. 1 (1996), 24–57.

[69]Manchester, *Modern Legal History*, 137–39; Baker, *English Legal History*, 128–
132.

and its institutions, unaffected by economic developments and considerations, but which in turn did affect economic change.

CONCLUSION

The unincorporated company was a practice shaped by the needs of various entrepreneurs dissatisfied with organizing their undertakings along traditional closed partnership lines, and who could not obtain, for one reason or other, a grant of incorporation from the State. However, this form of business organization faced various conceptual, but mainly practical and procedural, limitations which prevented it from becoming a highly preferable alternative to the business corporation.

To overcome these limitations, solicitors and men of business developed various arrangements to ease the problems. Through contractual devices, the unincorporated company achieved arrangements among its members regarding governance and transferability of shares, without affecting the status of third parties. The trust device enabled it to handle its real property in common, but was not a very efficient method for dealing with other types of assets and activities. By obtaining a specific Act of Parliament, the unincorporated company could gain the right to sue and be sued using a common name.[70] Through these acts, unincorporated companies indeed overcame some of the inconveniences inherent in litigation, but without affecting the basic rights and liabilities of the shareholders and without solving all the technical problems at the stage of judgment execution. Furthermore, each company had to carry the costs of pushing its act through, with no guarantee of success. If they were already turning to Parliament, considering these costs and uncertainties, companies could go one step further and venture application for full incorporation.

Some of the basic problems proved to be insoluble. Unincorporated associations could not achieve separate legal entity, except by obtaining full incorporation from the State. They were still under the province of the Bubble Act, which from time to time cast a shadow over their legality. They could not find a convenient legal arena for the litigation of internal disputes. They often found themselves involved in lengthy and costly litigation in the Court of Chancery.

[70]After 1807, several unincorporated companies sought a parliamentary solution to the problem they faced in common-law litigation. They obtained acts of Parliament that allowed them to sue and be sued using a common name, usually that of the secretary, treasurer, or other manager. By 1815, thirty such acts had been passed (25 for insurance companies) and more acts for the same purpose followed (based on *Commons' Journal*, vols. 62–70 for the years 1807–1815).

These problems are not considered only in retrospective analyses; they were evident to contemporaries as well. Practical men were skeptical about this form of organization. If a satisfactory substitute for the business corporation were available, one would expect more enterprises to adopt it as a first, not a second, choice.[71] Prominent contemporary lawyers stressed the limitations of the unincorporated company. The first two comprehensive accounts of early nineteenth-century unincorporated companies were not enthusiastic. In 1825, John George, a barrister of the Middle Temple, published *A View of the Existing Law Affecting Unincorporated Joint Stock Companies.*[72] H. Bellenden Ker of Lincoln's Inn issued a "Report on the Law of Partnership" to the president of the Board of Trade in 1837. In sharp contrast to later historical accounts, both these accounts stressed the limits and shortcomings of the unincorporated company. The courts, beginning with the Dodd case (*The King v. Dodd*) of 1808, raised serious doubts as to the legality of the unincorporated company and its benefits to the public at large.[73] Debates in Parliament over bills for incorporation and the use of a common name in court litigation skillfully emphasized the limits of the unincorporated company.[74]

To reiterate my introductory qualification, I do not argue that unincorporated associations played no role in English history. They did, as Maitland insisted.[75] They included learned bodies such as the Society of Antiquaries and the Royal Academy, professional societies such as the Inns of Court and the Law Society, and organized marketplaces such as Lloyd's and the Stock Exchange. John Baker, who closely analyzed the consequences of lack of incorporation for the Inns of Court, found many inconveniences. He could, however, conclude that "the advantages of corporateness were never sufficiently overwhelming to induce the lawyers to give up the freedom they possessed in managing their own affairs." But this was true for the specific context of the Inns of Court in which each association held a few fixed assets, was engaged in limited transactional and litigation activity, and was "expected to work through general consent" and "to prevent awkward questions from coming to

[71]As seen in Chapters 4 and 7, the unincorporated company did not become a very popular and widespread phenomenon. It could be found in large numbers in only two sectors: insurance and the Birmingham metal and related industries.

[72]John George, *A View of the Existing Law Affecting Unincorporated Joint Stock Companies,* new ed. (1825).

[73]See Chapter 9 for *The King v. Dodd,* 9 East 516 (1808) and the subsequent judgments.

[74]See, for example, the case of the Globe Insurance Company, detailed in Chapter 4.

[75]Maitland, "Trust and Corporation," 186–213.

the fore."[76] In such a context, the unincorporated company could survive, but in the context of profit maximizing joint-stock organizations with freely transferable shares, its disadvantages overwhelm any possible advantage.

In conclusion, through the industrious work of imaginative lawyers and businessmen, the unincorporated company was able to advance beyond the organizational characteristics of the closed partnership, and to gain some ability to handle transferable joint stock. But it could not offer most of the features inherent in the joint-stock business corporation: separate legal entity, transferability of interest, and limitation of liability. The moderate achievements were subject to the need to apply many complicated and limiting devices, to follow lengthy procedures, to negotiate and draft documents involving high legal costs, and to arrive at a final outcome which was less than satisfactory, because many legal doubts and practical uncertainties still remained. This final outcome was also less than satisfactory for the individuals involved – the entrepreneurs and investors – and it is important to remember that it was also less than satisfactory in terms of overall social costs, efficient allocation of resources, and eventually the rate of growth of the English economy.

[76] J. H. Baker, "The Inns of Court and Chancery as Voluntary Associations," *Quadreni Fiorentini,* 11–12 (1982–85), 9–38, citations from 38.

7

The Progress of the Joint-Stock Organization

In previous chapters, I surveyed the emergence of two models of business organization during the eighteenth century, the joint-stock business corporation and the unincorporated company. I demonstrated the entrepreneurs' preference for the corporation over the unincorporated company and showed the growing advantages of the corporation toward the end of the century, due to its personality, transferability, and liability features. In addition, I claimed that the unincorporated company could not, due to legal deficiencies, serve as a surrogate form of organization. But these three assertions taken together do not say much about the position of these forms of joint-stock organization in the economy as a whole. Was joint stock a marginal or a central phenomenon in eighteenth-century England? Did eighteenth-century joint-stock organizations have any significant impact on the contemporary economy, or is their study worthwhile only because they were precursors to the late nineteenth-century corporate economy? These questions were initially touched on in Chapter 4, which dealt with transportation and insurance, two significant sectors. The present chapter aims to broaden the perspective by dealing with the following questions: Was the development of the joint-stock undertaking during the eighteenth century confined to these two major sectors? Did other sectors pursue the paths of either transport or insurance, or did they follow other models of organization? What, if any, were the effects of the Bubble Act on the spread of the joint-stock form of association after 1720? What was the role played by vested interests, particularly those of existing undertakings, in creating barriers to entry into the joint-stock form of organization? The present chapter attempts to answer these questions by presenting a sectoral survey of much of the English economy from the perspective of business organization, with an emphasis on the different kinds of joint-stock investment.

The progress of the joint-stock undertaking from the passage of the Bubble Act and up to the first decade of the nineteenth century is pre-

168

sented in three stages: First, the total number of joint-stock companies and their capital, early in the period (around 1740), is established. Next, a sectoral survey of the development of business organization roughly between 1720 and 1810 is presented. This section elaborates on sectors and subsectors in which joint stock played an important role, such as wool milling, fishing, brewing, flour milling, shipping, and mining, but does not discuss insurance or transport and only briefly touches on overseas trade and banking, all of which are treated elsewhere in this book.[1] Some of the above-mentioned sectors were relatively neglected in earlier literature because they were wrongly classified as lacking this feature. This is likely because the joint-stock undertakings in these sectors were not legally based, or were based on concepts outside the realm of the common law. Finally, the spread of joint-stock undertakings toward the end of this period, the first decade of the nineteenth century, is evaluated.

This chapter relies partly on unexplored primary sources and also utilizes secondary accounts that surveyed various sectors from the conventional perspective of organization of production, labor, and capital, but these are examined here for unconventional purposes. The combination of the legal–organizational approach with newly exploited sources enables me to reach some surprising conclusions. First, the weight of joint-stock organizations in the English economy as a whole was much greater than hitherto believed. Its percentage increased dramatically, reaching a quarter, and later even a third, of England's "relevant" capital stock. Second, that the rise in joint-stock capital did not occur evenly among the sectors. The moneyed companies, which comprised most of the joint-stock capital early in the period, retained their nominal capital throughout the period, thus declining dramatically in their relative weight. The growing industrial sectors, cotton and iron, did not undergo significant joint-stock organization. The total increase was mainly affected by a sharp increase in joint stock in the transportation, insurance, shipping, utilities, and traditional industries. Third, that the impact of joint-stock organizations on the economy cannot be measured only by their capital weight. The entrance of a new joint-stock enterprise into a sector effects the structure of the market, competitive practices, and political lobbying throughout the sector. The examples of flour milling and brewing are illuminating in this respect. Fourth, to reveal the importance of joint stock in this period, one has to go beyond the classic legal categorization. Only by delving into the financial and managerial nature of enterprises can one get the broader view. Thus, in addition to business

---

[1] Transportation and insurance are discussed in Chapter 4, overseas trade in Chapter 2, and banking in Chapter 8.

corporations and unincorporated companies, this chapter also deals with joint-stock wool mills, shipping part-ownership, cost-book mining partnerships, and turnpike trusts.

THE STARTING POINT: CIRCA 1740

A good starting point for studying the expansion of the joint-stock company after 1720 is William Maitland's *The History of London*, published in 1739. It surveyed various aspects of the political, economic, and social life of London of his period, and is the most comprehensive account of joint-stock companies in the years after the South Sea Bubble.[2]

Accounts of the earlier period included, inevitably and in large numbers, bubbles and short-lived companies formed in the 1690s and especially in 1720. As seen in Chapters 1 and 2, there were about 150 joint-stock companies in existence in 1695, and in 1719–1720 alone, some 190 schemes for the formation of companies were promoted. However, most of these companies disappeared as swiftly as they had appeared, and left no lasting mark. These large numbers indicate that many individuals of the period aimed at quick financial gain more than at the initiation of serious economic activity. They thus do not exemplify long-term trends, or companies with a bearing on the economy in general, which Maitland's account, not written in or around a boom year, reflects.

In Maitland's time, there were eight trading companies (Merchant Adventurers, Russia, Eastland, Levant, East India, Royal African, Hudson's Bay, and South Sea), five fire assurance offices (Friendly Society, Hand-in-Hand, Sun, Union, and Westminster), three water supply companies (Chelsea, London Bridge, and New River), two marine insurance companies (Royal Exchange and London Assurance), two metallurgical companies (English Copper and Lead), one life insurance company (Amicable), the Bank of England, the York Buildings Company, and the Charitable Corporation.[3] Altogether, twenty-six joint-stock companies are included in Maitland's account (see Table 7.1). This number does

---

[2] William Maitland, *The History of London: From Its Foundation by the Romans, to the Present Time* (1739).

[3] York Buildings Company was established for building and operating waterworks, then expanded into finance, trade, and landowning. The Charitable Corporation was originally formed for granting loans to the industrious poor, later engaged for a short while in insurance, and, by Maitland's time, was involved in fraudulent financial speculations. For a fascinating account of these companies, and of the small group of individuals that controlled them both (and were pioneers in developing white collar criminal practice), see A.J.G. Cummings, "The York Building Company, A Case Study in Eighteenth Century Mismanagement," Ph.D. thesis, University of Strathclyde (1980).

Table 7.1. *Joint-stock companies, c. 1740*[a]

Sector	Number of companies
Moneyed companies: Bank of England, East India, South Sea	3
Other overseas trading companies: Eastland, Hudson's Bay, Levant, Merchant Adventurers, Royal African, Russia	6
Fire insurance: Friendly Society, Hand-in-Hand, Sun, Union, Westminster	5
Marine insurance: London Assurance, Royal Exchange	2
Life insurance: Amicable	1
Water supply: Chelsea, London Bridge, New River	3
Metal companies: English Copper, Lead	2
Miscellaneous: Charitable, York Buildings	2
Total	24

Source: Maitland, *History of London*

[a] This table represents my arrangement of the companies listed by Maitland. I did not include the Mines Royal and Mineral and Battery Works, which did not seem to be active after their charters were exploited by insurance undertakings in the late 1710s, or the Georgia Company, because other colonial companies were not included by Maitland (by this time, they probably could not be viewed as business concerns, certainly not ones that were managed from London).

not include corporations only, as some of the insurance companies were unincorporated. Even if this list was incomplete, the number of joint-stock companies in 1739 was not far from the above.[4] To Maitland's numbers for 1740 one should add two sectors that were disregarded by Maitland, river navigation and turnpike trusts.[5] By 1740, some thirty-five river improvement acts and ninety-five turnpike acts were passed.[6] These high figures, however, are misleading: Most of the river navigation projects and the early turnpikes – the Justices of Peace turnpikes – should

[4] Maitland correctly did not account for the Million Bank, which was formally a joint-stock association, but in practice was only an investment fund and not an active business company.

[5] Maitland disregarded these sectors because his concern was with the London trade.

[6] Ward, *Canal Building*, 164.

be viewed as branches of local government, and not as joint-stock undertakings.

Maitland did not offer any capital figures for the companies he surveyed. The capital of the three moneyed companies during this period is well known from other sources. It totaled about £15.82 million, less than their total capital in 1717, which was about £18.7 million. This is attributable to the fact that the capital of the South Sea Company decreased considerably after the crisis of 1720, though the total loss was partly offset by the increase in the capital of the Bank of England. The total capital of the twenty-one other companies listed by Maitland can be estimated only by forward and backward extrapolation.[7] This places the capital of Maitland's twenty-one nonmoneyed companies within the range of £2 million to £2.5 million. The actual capital investment in early joint-stock transport undertakings can only be guessed. These undertakings were tiny in terms of capital, a few thousand pounds per project on the average.[8] Accounting for these reservations, a rough estimation of total river and turnpike joint stock in the range of £200,000 to £400,000 seems plausible for 1740. A total capital estimation for these two categories ranging between £2.5 million and £3 million seems to me quite conservative. This is a slight increase over the about £1.9 million in nonmoneyed companies in 1717.[9] Thus, if we ignore the ups and downs of 1720, there is an insubstantial decline in total capital of joint-stock companies during the period 1717–1740. The share of the nonmoneyed companies increased slightly during this period, but their capital still comprised no more than 15 percent of the total, while only three companies, East India, Bank of England, and South Sea, held the rest of the capital. The progress of the joint-stock form of organization up to 1810 should be based on this very modest and moneyed companies-oriented starting point.

[7]Based on Scott's figures for 1720, English's figures for 1825, and Fenn's figures for 1837. See Scott, *Constitution and Finance of Joint-Stock Companies*, vol. 3, p. 462ff.; English, *Joint-Stock Companies*; Fenn, *English and Foreign Fund.*

[8]The huge investments per project and in absolute numbers came only with the longer turnpikes of the 1750–1770 mania, with the early canal schemes of the 1760s and 1770s (in which investments were in six digits), and with the canal mania of the 1790s that overwhelms all earlier figures. See Chapter 4 for more on capital accumulation in the transportation sector.

[9]These estimates do not include ship ownership and mining not referred to in Maitland's account. According to Feinstein and Pollard, the net capital stock of these sectors in Great Britain in 1760, the first year of his survey, was £3,000,000 (see Charles H. Feinstein and Sidney Pollard, eds., *Studies in Capital Formation in the United Kingdom: 1750–1920* (Oxford: Clarendon Press, 1988), 437, col. 2, 439, col. 8). By extrapolating, we can place the numbers for England alone in 1740 at less than £2,000,000, and in 1720, at over £1,000,000, but these are unsubstantiated figures.

SECTORAL SURVEY

The picture outlined in earlier chapters focused on three sectors: overseas trade, transport, and insurance, and did not present any significant industrial joint-stock companies. It is often assumed that joint-stock companies were limited in this period to canals, utilities (docks, water supply, bridges, gas supply), and insurance.[10] This assumption builds on another assumption, already discussed in Chapter 3, according to which the Bubble Act arrested the development of the joint-stock company for more than a century. It is widely believed that the industrial sectors played no role in the shaping of the joint stock company. Conversely, it may be claimed that the joint-stock company played no role in the development of the industrial sectors. Taking this further, one can argue that considerations of business organization in general, and the joint-stock form of organization in particular, played no significant role in the industrial revolution. The validity of these arguments is examined in this sectoral survey.

Textile Industries

Silk: Large-scale mechanized production first appeared in England in the silk subsector. By the 1720s, the Lombe family constructed a large and unique silk-throwing machine located in a huge building, and employed 300 workmen.[11] Lombe had made a spying journey to Italy, thus saving the cost of developing new technology, and on his return, he constructed the machine using family capital. Within fifteen years, the family made a fortune of at least £120,000 which could provide for any future capital needs without resorting to external sources. By the 1760s, several other silk-throwing factories emerged, employing a few hundred workers each. But these remarkably large factories by contemporary standards did not use joint stock. As the Lombe case demonstrates, the silk industry was exceptional: It imported technology; used machinery in only one stage of production and based the rest of the production on a capital-saving putting-out system; was relatively localized and isolated; and did not undergo any further technology or market leap. It could, and did, remain organized in a few sole proprietorships and family firms.

Cotton: Cotton textile manufacturing became a growth industry in the last quarter of the eighteenth century and is considered the leading sector of the early industrial revolution. Diffusion of machinery and

[10]Deane, *First Industrial Revolution*, 180; Ashton, *Economic History*, 119.

[11]Paul Mantoux, *The Industrial Revolution in the Eighteenth Century: An Outline of the Beginnings of the Modern Factory System in England*, new and rev. ed. (London: Jonathan Cape, 1961), 193–197.

concentration of production occurred, most notably, in Lancashire. Yet the family firm, based on mercantile capital, plowed-back profits, country banks, and networks of friends and relatives, was able to survive without having to resort to the joint-stock form of organization.[12] A detailed examination of the reasons for this phenomenon are beyond the scope of the present study and its sources. At first glance, it seems that an explanation might be found in the pattern of technological innovation and in the rate of diffusion of new technology. Relatively low cost and adaptability to cottage use of some of the early hand-powered gadgets enabled them to spread fast, while patenting, high construction costs, and complicated operation delayed the diffusion of the more sophisticated engine-powered machines until well into the nineteenth century. These factors enabled the cotton manufacturing sector to increase its output without an immediate revolution in financing methods, organization of production, or the use of novel forms of business organization. The more gradual transformation of the structure of the textile sector conforms with recent studies which emphasize gradual growth during the industrial revolution together with the presence of nonfactory manufacturing and of protoindustry well into the industrial era.[13] No profound motivation for resorting to joint-stock organization emerged in the first generations of industrialization in this sector.

There were, however, a few exceptional endeavors of joint-stock textile manufacturing. The first of them, in 1764, was outside the cotton sector. It was the English Linen Company "for manufacture of cambricks and lawns" which obtained an act authorizing the Crown to grant a charter of incorporation. However, it did not obtain the charter itself.[14] In 1779, a petition was made to the House of Commons for "establishing a manufactory, for making and printing cotton and linen cloths upon a more extensive plan than has hitherto been practiced . . . but such manufacture cannot be established . . . without a very large capital or joint stock." It was argued by the petitioners that companies for similar manufacture had been established in Switzerland and other countries, on a larger scale than individual English manufactures.[15] Leave was given

---

[12]Seymour Shapiro, *Capital and the Cotton Industry in the Industrial Revolution* (Ithaca: Cornell University Press, 1967), esp. 204–207.

[13]Crafts, *British Economic Growth*; Hudson, *The Industrial Revolution*, 27–29, 111–121; Roger Lloyd-Jones and M. J. Lewis, *Manchester and the Age of the Factory: The Business Structure of Cottonopolis in the Industrial Revolution* (London: CroomHelm, 1988).

[14]See the report in *Lords' Journal* 30 (1764), 556, 557, 559, 578, 581, 582, 585; 4 Geo. III c.37 (1764); and DuBois, *English Business Company*, 27, 96, 98. This company should not be confused with the British Linen Company incorporated by charter in 1746, which actually acted as a bank in Scotland.

[15]*Commons' Journal* 37 (1779), 108, 147.

to bring a bill for incorporating such a company, but the bill was never brought in. In 1788, a petition for a charter, proposing to incorporate a company to promote cotton manufactures, was rejected by the Privy Council. The sole long-lasting joint-stock company in the cotton industry was organized only twenty-five years later.[16] Rare cases of attempts at joint-stock organization in the cotton textile industry only confirm the general picture that the industry lacked, and did not strive for, this form of organization. In this period the cotton industry did not adopt joint-stock factories, as was the case in some parts of the woolen industry, to which we now turn.

Wool: Woolen textile was the major industry in the eighteenth-century English economy, both in terms of value-added and of export.[17] Though other sectors, such as cotton and iron, grew faster toward the end of the century, the woolen industry retained its supremacy in absolute terms. The growth in the woolen sector was concentrated geographically around the West Riding of Yorkshire, where the share of the national production rose from 20 to 60 percent during the century.[18] This growth at times created bottlenecks in finishing and at other times in spinning and weaving. The few existing public mills could not supply the growing demand. In the 1780s and 1790s, a solution emerged to the grievances of local clothiers. They took the initiative and organized in unincorporated joint-stock company mills. By the first decade of the nineteenth century, there were numerous company mills, especially in the Leeds and Wakefield areas. Pat Hudson, in her comprehensive study of the West Riding woolen industry, was able to identify by name no less than thirty-one company mills that first appeared in the period 1785–1840.[19]

The major motive for joint-stock mills was financial. The introduction of machinery and water, and later also steam power, in some stages of the production increased the incentives but also the capital demands imposed on erecting mills to the point where they were beyond the reach

---

[16]From 1815 to 1834 an unincorporated cotton-printing firm, Spencer and Company, known as "The Long Firm," was in existence. In 1813, Robert Owen reorganized, with six distinguished partners, the New Lanark mills into an unincorporated joint-stock company, the only long lasting joint-stock company in the cotton industry. See Shapiro, *Cotton Industry*, 159–163. The first joint-stock corporation in the cotton industry was formed in 1845, and only in 1860 did incorporation in significant numbers began in Lancashire itself. See D. A. Farnie, *The English Cotton Industry and the World Market, 1815–1896* (Oxford: Clarendon Press, 1979), 215–227, esp. table 13.

[17]Crafts, *British Economic Growth*, 22, table 2.3, 143, table 7.2 (the figures are for Great Britain rather than England).

[18]Hudson, *The Industrial Revolution*, 16.

[19]Pat Hudson, *The Genesis of Industrial Capital: A Study of the West Riding Wool and Textile Industry, c. 1750–1850* (Cambridge University Press, 1986), 79, table 3.6.

of individuals or of underfinanced local authorities. In using joint stock, three types of schemes appeared: one in which a mill already built was rented by a company; another in which both merchants and clothiers cooperated; and a third in which only clothiers shared the finance.[20] The third type, which was probably the most common, usually limited its membership to clothiers of the neighboring region. Regulation of these mills included, either explicitly or implicitly, a proviso to the effect that the shareholders send all their milling work to their own mills. Thus, the company mills had an element of mutuality, as the owners of the mills were also their customers. The number of shareholders in company mills ranged from ten to fifty, with forty being a common number.[21] Each of the members could hold more than one share, typically nominally priced at £25 or £50, and the total subscribed capital of a mill could reach several thousand pounds.

From a legal perspective, these joint-stock company mills were not a unique form of business organization. Unlike in the shipping or the mining sectors, no separate jurisdictions or regional customs had a legal impact on this sector. The company mills were subject to the general common-law doctrines. Because none of them obtained a charter, they were viewed not as corporations, but merely as partnerships. Like other partnerships with large numbers of partners and transferable shares, they were actually unincorporated companies which tried to achieve some of the privileges of incorporation through the use of the trust. Yet, like other unincorporated companies, they were "subject to all the inconveniences arising from the law of partnership."[22] These legal inconveniences, as detailed by contemporaries, included the inability to sue and be sued using a joint name, the lack of power to proceed in common law against one partner, the fact that one partner could bind the whole against their will, the difficulty of getting rid of an unwanted partner, and generally the ease of fraud amongst partners.[23] Many of these legal inconveniences were not unique to company mills, but were common to all unincorporated companies, as is discussed in Chapter 6. Much of the success of the joint-stock company mills "depended on the mutual trust and co-operation of the clothier communities."[24] These could be attained be-

---

[20]J. Goodchild, "The Ossett Mill Company," *Technology History* 1 (1968), 1; mentioned in Hudson, *Genesis of Industrial Capital*, 77.

[21]Companies that settled for renting rather than constructing a mill had a considerably smaller number of shareholders.

[22]*Parliamentary Papers* (1844), vol. 7, p. 349.

[23]From letters sent in 1843 to the Select Committee on Joint-Stock Companies, one written by a cloth manufacturer, the other by a factory inspector, see *Parliamentary Papers* (1844), vol. 7, pp. 349, 351–352. Though the letters referred to the nineteenth century, they well represent the difficulties of the previous century. Many of the early company mills, as these writers knew them, had no partnership deeds, printed regulations, or organized bookkeeping, and their legal difficulties were even more severe.

[24]Hudson, *Industrial Capital*, 81.

cause the mills were of regional character and their shareholders lived in the vicinity and knew each other personally, and because the owners had a direct interest in the functioning of the mills, as they were customers as well as owners.

Metal Industries

Iron: Together with cotton, iron is considered to be one of the leading sectors in the early stages of industrialization. The early ironworks were potentially more capital-consuming than the early spinning and weaving machines. Yet despite the more capital-intensive nature of this sector, it was dominated by family firms and small partnerships of fewer than eight partners. Joint-stock companies were practically nonexistent until the boom of 1825. From that time and until 1844, fifteen iron companies, mostly speculative, were established.

The major explanation for the scarcity of joint-stock companies in the iron sector is the fact that it was relatively centralized and based on long-existing and well-established firms. These firms were able to grow during the industrial revolution by reinvesting their profits, resorting only marginally to external sources of capital.[25] The Coalbrookdale firm was valued at £4,200 in 1718, £16,000 in 1738, £40,000 in 1798 and £165,000 in 1815. The Dowlais ironworks whose initial capital was £4,000 in 1760, were valued at £20,000 in 1782, £61,000 in 1798, and £503,200 in the 1850s. The Carron Company began with £12,000 in capital in 1760, reached £150,000 in 1771 and £270,000 in 1815.[26] The fifteen largest firms combined, including those above, accounted for 53 percent of the coke pig-iron output by 1815. They were large and successful enough to rely on plowed-back profits as the major source of growth, without needing to resort to the joint-stock form of business organization.

Other Metal Industries: Three unincorporated joint-stock metal companies (and one timber company) were established in Birmingham in the 1780s and 1790s with a total capital of £200,000. These were the Birmingham Metal Company, Birmingham Mining, and Copper Company, Rose Copper Company, and the Birmingham Timber Company.[27]

[25]Birch Alan, *The Economic History of the British Iron and Steel Industry 1784–1789: Essays in Industrial and Economic History with Special Reference to the Development of Technology* (London: Frank Cass, 1967), 196–212.

[26]Charles K. Hyde, *Technological Change and the British Iron Industry, 1700–1870* (Princeton University Press, 1977), 64–65, 124–125, 178–179. Though some of the large ironworks used the term "'company" as part of their tittle, they were not organized as joint-stock companies. The only exception was the Carron Company, which was originally established as a partnership but in 1773 was incorporated in Scotland.

[27]DuBois, *English Business Company*, 231–235.

All four companies had an identical model of organization and many of the same individuals were involved in their establishment. They inspired the formation and the structural organization of other unincorporated joint-stock companies in the Birmingham area in the 1790s: the Birmingham Flour and Bread Company and the Birmingham Coal Company.[28] There may have been other unincorporated metal companies scattered around England in 1810, but they are not mentioned in the available records.

Food Industries

Flour Milling and Bread: In the early 1780s, the improvement of the steam engine – the double acting engine – reached a stage where some contemporaries considered it conceivable to attempt to use the power of steam engines to rotate millstones. James Watt, the engine's innovator; his business partner, Matthew Boulton; Samuel Wyatt, the architect and mill builder; and other wealthy individuals took the initiative to construct a steam-powered flour mill, the Albion Mill. By November 1783, after the planning stages were completed, it was felt by the investors that the business organization structure of the undertaking should be formalized. The capital of the undertaking was fixed at £60,000 and divided into five shares of £12,000, each subject to further subdivision, based on mutual agreement. "The proprietors of the Albion Mill were anxious to secure their personal property, and accordingly decided to apply to the Crown for a Charter of Incorporation. The advice of Kenyon [at that time Attorney-General, and later Chief Justice of King's Bench] was obtained; and it was felt that there was every likelihood of a successful application."[29]

Yet things did not go as smoothly as had been hoped. A caveat was entered by a group of private millers in and around London against the application for a charter to incorporate the Albion Mill Company. They argued that the Albion Mill would be too big, that it would crush its smaller competitors (individuals and partnerships), create a monopoly, and raise the price of flour. The counterargument, that the millers were those who held an effective monopoly, and that Albion Mill would lower prices and benefit the nation as a whole, was in vain.[30] In April 1784, the application was rejected after a hearing of counsel by the Law

[28]Birmingham Central Library, Birmingham Coal Company Minutes of Annual General Meetings, May 4, 1795 – June 3, 1862.

[29]O. A. Westworth, "The Albion Steam Flour Mill," *Economic History* 2, no. 7 (Supplement to the *Economic Journal*) (1932), 383.

[30]Birmingham Public Library, Matthew Boulton Papers, Albion Mill Box, ms. 1–5; Boulton and Watt Papers, box 25, Albion Mill.

Officers. The large scale of the mill, valued at fifteen times more than any other mill in the London area, and the unfamiliar technology must have been major reasons for the opposition and the refusal to grant a charter. The undertakers of the Albion Mill had to settle for second best, a partnership deed. The mill began operation in 1786. It went through several crises during its existence, some of them due to its organization as a partnership, but the final blow was a fire that destroyed the mill in March 1791. The failure to obtain a charter must have deterred Boulton and Watt from future attempts to incorporate any other of their businesses.

The Birmingham Flour and Bread Company, also known as the Union Mills Company, was formed on a totally different basis from the Albion Mill. It was formed as an unincorporated company, by an Article of Association in 1796, with joint stock of £20,000 in £1 shares, in which no individual could hold more than twenty shares.[31] It was a mutual company in the sense that only shareholders had the right to purchase flour from the company at a fixed low price. The legal status of the mills was vague, most likely deliberately: The Article of Association declared that its signers made themselves into "a society, company or copartnership." The number of subscribers for shares was 1,360 in the first stage and kept growing. The article stated that "shares may be sold or transferred, but to such only as will enter into covenants for the performing of these articles." Thus, the Union Mills Company was clearly a joint-stock company with transferable shares, a huge number of shareholders, and a representative governance mechanism. Yet the company was not and did not aim to be a corporation or to hold the exclusive corporate privileges.

The company was not a marginal one; on the contrary, it was estimated that the mills could supply the needs of between 18 and 24 percent of the estimated Birmingham population of 70,000 at that time.[32] A large part of the population of Birmingham probably became familiar with the joint-stock company as a form of business organization toward the turn of the century, thanks to the establishment and activities of the Union Mills Company.

In 1800, a new initiative for joint-stock flour milling emerged, fundamentally different from the earlier schemes of 1783 and 1796. The scale of its stock was much larger: £120,000, divided into 4,800 shares of £25

---

[31] *Article of the Birmingham Flour and Bread Company* (Birmingham, 1796).

[32] *Copy of Examination Taken Before the Privy Council on 4 March 1800 Respecting the Birmingham Flour and Bread Company, or Union Mills* (Ordered to be printed on June 9, 1800). Reprinted in Sheila Lambert, ed., *House of Commons Sessional Papers of the Eighteenth Century*, Vol. 131: *1731–1800* (Wilmington, Del.: Scholarly Resources, 1975), 69–82.

each. The number of subscribers in the first stage reached 164. Many of these subscribers were from London's upper and middle classes: nine peers (including the Duke of Bedford), six MPs, numerous professionals, officers, and businessmen (including Matthew Boulton and Samuel Wyatt of Albion Mill).[33] The bill of incorporation that followed was known in the contemporary press as the "Earl of Liverpool's Bill." The bill faced strong opposition, expressed in petitions from bakers and millers in London and Westminster.[34] After lengthy debates that included the appointment of committees in both Houses, the calling of counsel, and examination of witnesses, the bill passed, and the London Company for the Manufacture of Flour, Meal, and Bread was incorporated.[35] A proviso was added by the Commons, according to which the managers of the company would lay annual reports on their activities before each House of Parliament, but otherwise, the well-placed undertakers had their way against the weaker millers and bakers.

Within two decades, at the close of the eighteenth century, the flour milling sector experienced three major efforts in joint-stock enterprise. In the first, entrepreneurial inventors played a dominant role; in the second, poor consumers; and in the third, rich investors. The first aimed at incorporation by charter and failed; the second settled for an unincorporated form; and the third aimed again at incorporation, this time by act of Parliament, and was able to secure it. By the time the London Flour and Bread Company was established, the experience of Albion Mill and the Birmingham Union Mills was well known, and was used by adherents and antagonists alike. The large number of shareholders, of individual millers who opposed the companies, and of consumers brought the issue of joint-stock milling companies to public debate. Thus, this relatively unexplored sector was important both in the advance of the joint-stock company and in shaping public opinion regarding this form of business organization at a key point in its history, the turn of the nineteenth century.

Brewing and Distilling: A revival of the speculation in stocks and a sharp rise in the price of port drew the attention of both entrepreneurs and speculators to the brewing industry in the early 1800s. In 1804, a group of newcomers to the industry, headed by William Brown and Joseph Parry, decided to establish a new brewery.[36] They realized that

---

[33]House of Lords Record Office (hereafter referred to as H.L.R.O.), Main Papers, H.L., July 9, 1800.

[34]*Commons' Journal* 55 (1800), 626, 632, 633.

[35]*Cobbett's Parliamentary History*, vol. 35, pp. 454–465; H.L.R.O., Main Papers, H.L., July 9, 23, and 24, 1800; *The Times*, July 22, 1800, p. 2.

[36]For an authoritative survey of the brewing industry, with reference to the episode of Golden Lane Brewery, see Peter Mathias, *The Brewing Industry in England, 1700–1830* (Cambridge University Press, 1959).

the strong position of the established interests in this sector, wealthy and influential private brewers, would create severe difficulties for any new-comer. They thought that in order to improve their chances in this competitive market, they should aim at a large-scale brewery with the ability to produce beer of better quality and at lower prices than the individual brewers. The only way to achieve this scale of production was, in their opinion, to establish a brewery by way of raising substantial joint stock.

A prospectus was circulated for establishing a joint-stock brewery, the Genuine Beer Brewery of Golden Lane, and a subscription list opened for share units of £50 and £80. The new undertaking was well received, and by 1806, two years after the brewery was launched, 600 copartners had subscribed over £250,000. Golden Lane Brewery was an immediate success in all respects. Its shares were traded at 60 and even 100 percent premiums. By 1808, Golden Lane already ranked third in barrel production of London's breweries. By 1809, its capital had reached £327,500. The brewery, however, never attempted to incorpo-rate, but rather was organized as an unincorporated company.

Powerful individual brewers were alarmed by the success of the newly established brewery and soon exploited the organizational disadvantage of Golden Lane Brewery to the utmost. They brought to the attention of the Commissioners of Excise the fact that some of the copartners of Golden Lane were publicans, and consequently the company as a whole should not enjoy the excise exemption reserved only for brewers and not for retailers. The commissioners demanded extra duty, the payment of which could prevent the brewery from surviving the competition. The legal argument was that, because the brewery lacked corporate entity, it was not entitled to an exemption to which any of its copartners was not entitled.[37] After long litigation and heavy legal costs, the brewery re-ceived a judgment in its favor in 1808. In the following years, the brewery faced endless legal attacks, including the claim that it was a nuisance within the Bubble Act.[38] In an attempt to overcome some of its organizational limits, the brewery twice brought bills to enable it to sue and be sued by common name. Such bills had been easily obtained by other unincorporated companies during this period but, both in 1809 and in 1814, the backstage lobbying of the private brewers caused Golden Lane's bills to be shelved.

The promotion of the Golden Lane Brewery and its apparent success motivated others to try to establish joint-stock companies in brewing,

---

[37]The proceedings and the evidence were published in the pamphlet *Golden Lane Brewery: The Attorney General versus Brown, Parry, and Others* (1808).

[38]*Brown and Another v. Holt,* 4 Taunt. 587 (1812). For a fuller discussion of the 1800s prosecutions based on the Bubble Act, see Chapter 9.

distillation, and similar sectors. A list of proposed subscriptions of companies in the speculations of 1807 includes no less than six breweries, four distilleries, five wine companies, and two vinegar companies.[39] Some of these proposed companies were undoubtedly of a speculative or even fraudulent character; however, a few represented a genuine attempt to establish joint-stock undertakings. Only one of these companies, the British Ale Brewery, was quoted for a time on the Stock Exchange List.[40] One interesting case was that of the London Distillery Company. The company was promoted by Ralph Dodd, a well-known business innovator. A subscription was opened for capital of £100,000, divided into 2,000 shares of £50 each. Suitable premises were purchased and managers and other officers were employed. No attempt was made to obtain incorporation and a solicitor was engaged to draft a deed of trust.[41] Within a short time this decision proved fatal to the future of the undertaking. In 1808, a case was brought for criminal information in the Court of King's Bench against Dodd for promoting a scheme for a company with transferable shares in violation of the Bubble Act. The court refused to interfere and grant the information; however, its judgment cast a serious doubt as to the legality of the company and its future prospects, and may have caused its failure.[42] The legal implications of this judgment are discussed at a later stage. In the present context, the importance of this litigation is that it opens a window into the unfamiliar world of promotions in this sector.

Promotion of joint-stock breweries and distilleries first appeared in the opening decade of the nineteenth century. Some of the promotions never passed the prospectus stage and others faced difficulties on the way to completion, yet in a few cases, beer and spirits were actually produced. Private brewers and distillers could no longer ignore the joint-stock form and were forced to learn its business abilities as well as its legal status. The flour milling and brewing sectors refute the assertion that joint-stock companies made no inroads into manufacturing.

Utilities

Utility companies are comparable in some respects to transportation companies. They require lump-sum investment and land appropriation, and may enjoy a natural monopoly. As the transportation sector has

---

[39]Tooke, *A History of Prices*, 278–280.

[40]Mathias, *Brewing Industry*, 244 n. 1.

[41]*Arguments in the Court of Kings Bench Against Ralph Dodd* (1808), esp. "A Prospectus of the Intended London Distillery Company" and "Report of Mr. Dodd, delivered to the Directors," 95–102.

[42]*The King v. Dodd*, 9 East 515 (1808).

already been discussed in detail, I settle here for a brief survey of this significant sector. The first water supply companies emerged in the seventeenth century. Maitland reported on three companies supplying water to London in his time: New River, London Bridge, and Chelsea. The number of water supply companies increased during the century, and by 1811, some eight waterworks were listed in the *Course of the Exchange*. The first of the dock companies established around the turn of the nineteenth century were the Commercial Docks in London. These were followed in 1800 by the huge West India Docks with capital of almost £1.4 million, and in the following year by the even more impressive London Docks with capital of more than £3.2 million. Two more docks were constructed by 1810: East County Docks and East India Docks. The first gas light company, the Chartered Gas Company, was incorporated in 1810. On the *Course of the Exchange*, we find joint-stock companies for two other types of utilities: harbors and bridges. Only two of each were listed, but there may have been more companies of this type in the provinces, which were unknown on the London Market. In conclusion, toward the turn of the century, the joint-stock form of organization became a dominant form in those massive utility projects, into which large capital investments were sunk.[43]

Banking

Due to the corporate monopoly of the Bank of England, the banking sector was dominated by private and family banks and by small partnerships, both in the country and in London. The only exception, and a most significant one, was the Bank of England itself, which had a unique position within the banking system and in relation to the State. We return to the bank and to the banking sector in general in Chapter 8.

Overseas Trade

Overseas trading corporations were in decline after their early Stuart heyday, as demonstrated in the Chapter 2. Individual traders and trading houses replaced them as the century progressed. The decline of the trading corporations continued during the eighteenth century, most notably in the case of the Levant Company and the Royal African Company. During this period, the South Sea Company ceased functioning as a trading company and its sole activity remained the administration of a portion of the national debt. The newly formed Sierra Leone company

[43]For more on the utilities sector, see James Forman-Pack and Robert Millward, *Public and Private Ownership of British Industry, 1820–1990* (Oxford: Clarendon Press, 1994), 29–41.

was a short-lived adventure of the closing years of the century. Hudson's Bay Company was still active in North America but it was relatively small in terms of capital and revenues. The only exception was the East India Company, a megacompany in size and importance in terms of trade, overseas policy, and public finance.

Fisheries

The English government had a traditional interest in fisheries for strategic reasons: It viewed them as a training ground for seamen, a source of extra boats in wartime, and a frontier in the naval–economic battle against other nations, especially the Dutch. It is not surprising that side by side with other State interventions in this field (such as taxes on foreigners, subsidies and bounties to English fishermen, and regulation of the smallest details), monopoly and incorporation emerged as the path taken by the government to serve its ends.[44] The desire for joint-stock investment, especially in the long-range fishing of Greenland, Newfoundland, and the South Atlantic, is quite understandable. Fishing required an investment in large fleets of boats and in coastal facilities, and the risks were high because of changing fish populations, unpredictable weather conditions and currents, growing foreign competition, and the intervention of hostile navies. Thus, the policy of the English government and the needs of the fishing industry went hand-in-hand and made the fisheries a likely field for the development of joint-stock corporations.

The first joint-stock fishing company appeared in 1632. Other companies were established during the seventeenth century, but by the 1720s, joint-stock fishing had disappeared, to reemerge only in the second half of the eighteenth century.[45]

[44]A. R. Michell, "The European Fisheries," in G. E. Rich and C. H. Wilson, eds., *Cambridge Economic History of Europe*, Vol. 5: *The Economic Organization of Early Modern Europe* (Cambridge University Press, 1977), 178–182.

[45]The first joint-stock fishing company to appear in the seventeenth century was the Association for the Fishing, chartered by Charles I in 1632. After the Restoration, in 1661, an act was passed in the Parliament of Scotland authorizing the establishment of companies for promotion of fisheries. A charter was issued in 1664 to the Royal Fishery Company, which was replaced in 1677 by a new letters patent. The company was dissolved in 1690 and revived in the years 1692–1698. An attempt to form a new company based on its patent failed in 1717, and a scheme for promoting the New Royal Fishery in 1720 ended in failure like many other schemes in that year. In 1692, the Greenland Company was formed with exclusive monopolistic privileges that lasted until 1707. See John R. Elder, *The Royal Fishery Companies of the Seventeenth Century* (Glasgow: Maclehose, 1912), 48–50, 55, 71, 81–84, 90–92, 97–115; Scott, *Constitution and Finance of Joint-Stock Companies*, vol. 2, pp. 372–376, 379.

In 1749, a bill passed Parliament authorizing the chartering of the Free British Fishery Company, and on October 10, 1750, a royal charter was issued. Frederick, Prince of Wales, was made governor of the company.[46] The act and the charter authorized raising up to £500,000, prohibited the transfer of shares for the first five years, and gave the company subsidies and benefits, but not exclusive monopoly of any branch or region of the fisheries.

In 1786, an Act of Parliament incorporated a new joint-stock company, the British Society for Extending Fisheries. The act authorized raising £150,000, in £50 shares, with a maximum holding of £500 per person. This, in addition to the limit on use of proxy and on the number of votes per person, reflected the intention to spread control of the company over as many individuals as possible. It was argued by the initiators of the company that while the older Free British Fishery (which by then was known as the British Herring Company) was a trading company, their company was intended to promote facilities for expanding fishing. While the old company was formed for maximizing private profit, the new one, it was argued, was established for public advantage, at private expense. To prove this, a clause was added to the act of incorporation which excluded the company from trade, and its directory was filled with notables: seven peers and seven MPs. Nevertheless, as a hint to potential subscribers, a clause limiting their liability to the sums they subscribed was added to the act, and they were told that the money they invested would not diminish, "on the contrary."[47]

In 1789, a petition by the Duke of Northumberland and others was made to Parliament to incorporate a company "for the purpose of extending and increasing the British Fishery." Several arguments were used to support the petition: that the company would increase national navigation, that it deserved national protection, that limited liability would encourage subscription, and that inconveniences would be removed if the company were enabled to plead and defend its property in any dispute of law as a corporate body. The bill passed both Houses, and the Northumberland Fishery Society was incorporated that same year with capital of £50,000.[48]

Fisheries are a relatively neglected field of study in economic history in general, and in the history of the joint-stock company in particular.

---

[46]*Lords' Journal* 27 (1749), 434, 440, 450, 452–454; 23 Geo. II c.24 (1749); the charter itself was printed and published in London in 1750.

[47]26 Geo. III c.106 (1786); *Lords' Journal* 37 (1786), 553, 558, 562, 566, 571; *The Substance of the Speech of Henry Beaufoy to the British Society for Extending the Fisheries at their General Court, 25 March 1788* (1788), 77–79.

[48]29 Geo III c.25 (1789); *Commons' Journal* 44 (1789), 163, 167, 171, 425, 426, 487; *Lords' Journal* 37 (1789), 377, 379, 402, 413, 419, 432, 434, 435, 439, 465.

Yet this was a sector in which, particularly in its long-range subsector, joint stock had a substantial presence. Interestingly enough, the second half of the eighteenth century was a period of initiatives in this sector as well.

SECTORS OUTSIDE THE REALM OF COMMON LAW

Two important eighteenth-century sectors, ship ownership and mining, were outside the realm of the common law insofar as the legal framework of business organization was concerned. Both these sectors developed from early times within local jurisdictions, stannary courts and merchant courts, which resisted integration into the centralized legal system for several centuries. The different institutional context of their early development led to a unique path of development in each. The outcome was that none of the three basic conceptions, partnership, trust, or corporation, was adopted in these sectors, and that the alignment of the four features of organization, personality, transferability, governance, and liability, was different in these sectors from those of the central system.[49] In both these sectors, associations with joint stock could be formed without resorting to the State for a charter or an act and without falling into the disadvantaged forms of the unincorporated company or the common-law partnership. Thus, neither sector was confined to the two paths paved by the transport and insurance sectors. Furthermore, both these sectors were unaffected by the Bubble Act and had no need to develop in its shadow, as other sectors did after 1720. The complicated and peculiar legal framework that applied to each of these sectors left them on the margin of research on the development of the joint-stock company. Yet these sectors, which were of major importance in the eighteenth century and among the first to employ joint stock, suggest two interesting legal alternatives for the joint-stock corporation. In the long run, historically the business corporation won, and these alternatives were marginalized and disappeared.

Ship Ownership

The legal framework of the business organization of ship ownership was unique from its inception. It did not develop as part of the mainstream of the English legal system. Its origins could be found in civil law and international maritime practice.[50] Litigation was placed under the juris-

---

[49]For a discussion of the origins of the conceptions and the alignment of the features, see Chapter 1.

[50]Ralph Davis, *The Rise of the English Shipping Industry in the Seventeenth and Eighteenth Centuries* (London: Macmillan, 1962), 82–83.

diction of the High Court of Admiralty when that court appeared in the fourteenth century.[51] Thus, the ownership of ships was not subject to general common-law principles nor was it regulated by common-law courts.

A basic principle of partnership in ships, or of part-ownership, the term used by contemporaries, was that it was not personal or general in its nature, not a relationship between partners concerning property, but a relationship which focused on the ship. While ownership relations between partners regarding common-law partnership assets were inspired by the property-law concept of joint tenancy, the part-ownership of ships drew on, or was closer in content to, the property-law concept of tenancy in common.[52] The consequences of these distinctions, which seem at first sight to be minor and technical in nature, are quite far reaching.[53] The part-ownership of ships could develop on a totally different course than a partnership and could acquire some of the characteristics of the joint-stock corporation, out of reach for partnerships. Although the intellectual origins of the part-ownership are difficult to comprehend, its practical outcomes are much simpler, as is shown below.

Ownership of a ship was divided into equal parts, called shares; customarily, but not necessarily, eighths, sixteenths, or thirty-seconds. The shares, though not identical in their legal status to the shares of joint-stock companies, were, like them, freely transferable. The division of the ownership of ships into shares served two economic ends. The first was of sharing the burden of raising the capital required to build and equip the ships, capital beyond the reach of the average mariner. The second, and probably the more dominant, was of spreading the risk of loss of a ship over several individuals, at a time when the availability of marine insurance was limited.[54] Shares in ships during the eighteenth century were held by merchants, mariners, shipwrights, and suppliers of ship equipment, as well as by gentlemen, widows, and other wealthy individuals who had no special connection to the sea.[55] Many sharehold-

[51]Baker, *English Legal History*, 141–143.

[52]I can try to explain this distinction, insofar as it is relevant to our matter, using modern terms. In joint tenancy, the property as a whole was both owned and possessed, without any division whatsoever, by all tenants; that is, each tenant could sell his abstract part of the ownership rights, or make use of any of the possessory rights for a specific purpose, only in cooperation with all other joint-tenants. Tenants in common, on the other hand, had some separation on the ownership level, that is, their part-interest could be transferred relatively freely, though none of them was entitled to the exclusive use of any part of the property, which was undivided on the possession level.

[53]Watson, *Law of Partnership*; Montagu, *Law of Partnership*, 172.

[54]Davis, *English Shipping Industry*, 86–88.

[55]Ibid., 100.

ers held small shares in several ships.[56] Thus, part-ownership facilitated the use of passive capital, or capital that could have been used in other sectors, within the shipping industry, and at the same time provided a mechanism for the well-to-do investors to diversify their holdings and spread their risks over several ships. During the eighteenth century, an active market in ships' shares could be found in London as well as in the major ports. Shares were transferred by bills of sale, and after the Registration Act of 1786 (26 Geo. III c.60), the names of the original owners of each ship were recorded. A combination of the two gave some protection to buyers of shares as to the validity of their title. This flourishing share market reached its zenith in the eighteenth century, and decreased afterward as a group of professional ship owners emerged. By this time, a group of individuals had abandoned the actual trade in goods and concentrated their fortunes in ships they fully owned. They could afford this after previous generations had accumulated wealth in overseas trade, and because risks in the shipping industry lessened after the end of the French wars and with the advance of marine insurance.

The unique form of business organization dominating the shipping industry was not limited to one aspect, the availability of freely transferable shares. The realities of eighteenth-century business raised other problems, such as management, liability, and litigation, and demanded new solutions, some similar to those of joint-stock companies. The fact that ships were divided into small shares held by many individuals, none of whom held a majority of the shares, left the question of governance and management open. Who would determine whether a ship should take part in the risky and highly profitable East India trade, or in the less ambitious Baltic timber trade? Would a London widow come down to Bristol port to inspect the hiring of a crew for an Atlantic vessel? The solution to this problem was twofold, on the practical and on the legal level. On the practical level, a ship's husband, usually one of the owners, was elected by majority of the part-owners (per their shares). The ship's husband was empowered to conduct the daily routine business of the ship. Yet when disputes between the part-owners occurred, the husband had no mechanism to resolve them, nor to determine which of the part-owners he should obey. Such disputes found their way to litigation at the Court of Admiralty, and, from case to case, a body of legal principles emerged.[57] It was decided that ship's husbands would

---

[56]Simon P. Ville, *English Shipowning during the Industrial Revolution: Michael Henley and Son, London Shipowners, 1770–1830* (Manchester University Press, 1987), 2; Davis, *English Shipping Industry*, 106.

[57]For the various cases and principles discussed below, see Watson, *Law of Partnership*; Montagu, *Law of Partnership*, 172–181; John Collyer, *A Practical Treatise on the Law of Partnership* (1832), 666–693.

be authorized, without having to resort to the co-owners, to outfit and man the ship, to repair it, to deal with merchants and to contract with them to engage the vessel, and to keep its books. However, the court determined that an explicit decision by a majority of the part-owners was required in order to borrow money or to insure the ship. Thus, much of the day-to-day management of a ship was in the hands of the husband. Once they elected a husband, the part-owners who preferred to do so could remain relatively passive. Yet a majority of the part-owners could always force the husband to submit to their will, since they could choose another husband, if they made the effort to convene. At the same time as the Court of Admiralty vested powers in the hands of the husband and of the majority part-owners, it also protected the minority rights. It was decided, in order to prevent deadlocks, that the majority could overrule the dissenting minority and employ the ship at its will. The minority did not have to bear the expenses of a voyage it opposed; however, it was precluded from sharing in the profits of that specific voyage. The minority could also obtain a security from the majority, by order of the Court of Admiralty, for restoring the ship and for covering damages to it. Finally, based on the principles of part-ownership, the majority could not force the minority to sell its shares in the vessel, even when an attempt was made to sell the vessel as one unit to new owners.

When there was need for litigation, part-owners of a ship found themselves in a better position than partners in a common-law partnership. In most cases, they turned to the High Court of Admiralty where the procedure was different from that of the common-law courts. In some cases, a ship, as such, had standing in court, and in others, one of the part-owners could sue in the name of all the part-owners. Part-owners could sue each other for remedies in Admiralty without having to call for dissolution of the partnership, as was the case in common law. Nevertheless, there were causes in which all part-owners had to be joined, as when a third party sued for breach of contract.

Unlike shareholders in a modern business corporation, part-owners of a ship did not enjoy a general limitation of their liability. Yet they were better protected than partners in a general partnership because their liability was limited in some respects. Liability was principally attached only to debts connected to the ship, and not to any other debts. Debts that incurred due to the construction of the ship could be settled in Admiralty by seizing the ship. Loss of a ship on a voyage was in most cases covered by insurance, and the liability of the owners was limited by law to the loss of cargo and not to other damages.[58] Dissenting part-

---

[58] 7 Geo. II c.15 (1734).

owners could, as mentioned above, obtain security in Admiralty for damages they could suffer when the ship was employed against their will. When a ship's husband, or one of its part-owners, acted in breach of his authority, the rest of the part-owners were not liable. Altogether, the actual probability that the private assets of a part-owner would be subject to debts incurred by the ship was minimal.

All these developments, we must remember, took place while the Bubble Act and its sanctions were supposedly shadowing the fate of the business organization. It seems that the act should have had some effect on this form of organization because it had many of the characteristics of the corporate bodies, most notably, division into transferable shares, a practice condemned by the act. Yet, either because Article 25 of the act excluded trade in partnership from the act, or because ships were under the jurisdiction of the High Court of Admiralty, the Bubble Act was not considered as applicable to the part-ownership system.

In conclusion, a combination of maritime practice and admiralty law developed a unique form of business organization in the shipping industry. This form, the part-ownership of ships, was, on the whole, closer in its characteristics to the joint-stock corporation than to either the general or limited partnership. It included freely transferable shares, separation of ownership from management, sleeping or passive investment, a mechanism for settling disputes and for protecting minority rights, a degree of limited liability, and a degree of accessibility to courts that partners in common-law partnerships lacked. The shipping industry grew during the eighteenth century at least as rapidly as did the foreign trade, and probably faster than most other sectors of English economy. The shipping industry was engaged in opening new challenging and risky sea routes, and yet it was able to raise substantial capital resources from a wide range of social groups, while developing an alternative to both the partnership and the joint-stock company.

Mining

From the point of view of business organization, the mining sector was in some respects similar to the shipping sector. A unique form of business organization, the cost book system, developed outside the realm of the common law in this sector as well. The origins in both cases were antiquated, yet of different roots. The origins of the mining cost book company lay not on the Continent but in the tin mines of Cornwall and Devon. There they developed under local custom and the separate jurisdiction of the local stannary courts. From the tin mines, the cost book system spread to other metalliferous mines in Cornwall and Devon, to neighboring counties in the Southwest, and eventually to metalliferous mines in other regions. The cost book system did not make substantial inroads into mines of other types, such as coal mines.

The cost book company cannot be easily classified in modern terms. It had some of the characteristics of the partnership and some of those of the joint-stock company, yet it was distinct from both.[59] The cost book company was originally divided into eight or sixteen shares held by working miners. However, by the eighteenth century, the demand for capital grew and with it companies were further subdivided into 32, 64, 128, 256, or 512 parts, and some of the shares were held by investors rather than active miners. The main feature of the cost book company was that it had joint, yet not fixed, capital and that it was managed on the principle of ready money. The adventurers (partners or shareholders) in the company were called on to contribute more capital or to receive dividends on a frequent basis, according to the needs and fortunes of the company. This process involved frequent settling of accounts based on the company's cost book. Adventurers had to contribute only as much as the company actually needed in the short term; however, there was no limit to the amounts they could be asked to contribute in the long term. The capital of the cost book company could thus go up and down periodically. In this respect there is some similarity between its capital flow and that of the early joint-stock trading corporations, which raised ad hoc capital for each voyage.

The fact that adventurers could be called on to pay money that in some cases they could not afford must have contributed to the development of a mechanism for exiting the company. Adventurers had the right to transfer their shares in a cost book company without the consent of their associates. They even had the right to relinquish their interest upon written notice and withdraw their share in cash, whose value was usually left to arbitration. This alternative was not available even in the joint-stock company. Unlike a common-law partnership, the cost book company continued to function as shares changed hands and even when the number of adventurers was reduced.

The key figure in the company was the purser, who was in charge of the cost book, the expenses, and the calls. He was assisted by the committee of management. Separation of management and control, a feature not existing in the common-law partnership, surfaced in the cost book company. The purser had the power to enforce contributions upon adventurers, suing them in the name of the company in Stannary court, and to exclude defaulters from participating in the profits. The purser

[59]For the legal characteristics of the cost book company, see G. R. Lewis, *The Stannaries: A Study of the English Tin Mines* (Cambridge: Mass.: Harvard University Press, 1924), and Robert R. Pennington, *Stannary Law: A History of the Mining Law of Cornwall and Devon* (Newton Abbott: Davis and Charles, 1973).

could sue third parties in the name of the company and could be sued for debts of the company. An updated register of adventurers was kept, the absence of which in partnerships caused legal complications. Conceptually, the adventurers' interest lay not in the company's capital but in the mine itself. In addition to liability to meet the calls made by the company's purser, adventurers had direct liability for debts incurred by the company to external creditors. In principle, their liability was joint and individual and entirely unlimited.[60] A single adventurer could be sued for the entire debt of the company.

Because characteristics of the cost book system were established on a case-by-case basis and not on the basis of a codification or a general doctrine, in some cases confusion and contradictions existed within the system. Nevertheless, it is evident that the cost book system was a unique form of business organization fundamentally different from the joint-stock corporation, from the common-law partnership, and from the unincorporated company. It could survive side by side with the general forms because it was sheltered under a separate jurisdiction. Under that jurisdiction, it was protected not only from the common law of partnership but also from the Bubble Act. When adopted outside the Stannary jurisdiction, it faced considerable legal and institutional difficulties. However, when based in the mines of Cornwall and Devon, its shares could be held and traded throughout England, and indeed mine share markets flourished in London and the Southwest during the eighteenth century and in the first half of the nineteenth century.

In coal mining, the growing demand for capital, the withdrawal of landowners from active involvement in mining on their estates with the development of leasing, and the limited resources of the miners who leased these mines all motivated a search for new forms of organization in this subsector. Cost book companies were rare in coal mining because the mines were outside the Stannary jurisdiction. Business corporations were nonexistent in mining after the charters of the Elizabethan Mines Royal and Mineral and Battery Works were abandoned. Incorporation in the mining sector reappeared only in the boom year of 1825. There were a few cases of unincorporated joint-stock companies, such as the Grand Allies, the Banbury Company, and the Hetton Coal Company, but most of the mines not operated by their landowners were leased to relatively small and closed partnerships.[61] That was the case at least until

---

[60]See Roger Burt and Norikazu Kudo, "The Adaptability of the Cornish Cost Book System," *Business History* 35, no. 1 (1983), 30, esp. 34–36, for an argument according to which in practice, there were ways to reduce liability and risks.

[61]Michael W. Flinn, *The History of the British Coal Industry*, Vol. 2: *1700–1830, the Industrial Revolution* (Oxford: Clarendon Press, 1984), 36–42, 206–211; Roy

the 1820s and 1830s when changing law and technology exposed coal mining to joint-stock enterprise.

THE END POINT: CIRCA 1810

Aggregate Estimation

We have seen that the use of joint-stock capital became more popular during the eighteenth century. There was a dramatic increase in the diffusion of this form of investment and business organization in many sectors throughout the English economy. Can these qualitative and impressionistic observations be translated into a more solid quantitative assessment of the total capital of joint-stock undertaking?

The year 1810 is the target year for the following estimation because in 1800, many projects initiated during the 1790s, such as canals, insurance promotions, and docks, were still incomplete. My interpretation of joint-stock undertakings, in this context, is wide. It includes not only joint-stock corporations but also unincorporated companies, such as those in the insurance sector; part-ownership of ships; cost-book partnerships in mining; and turnpike trusts. Yet it covers only undertakings which employed joint stock, and no other forms of business organizations, such as large partnerships.

Based on my survey of studies of specific companies, on different sectors of the economy, on the stock market, and on capital formation in the economy, I selected what seem to be the best available figures and estimations of the capital of the various joint-stock undertakings scattered over the English economy in 1810. For undertakings whose capital was fully paid up, I used, to the extent that I could find them, the nominal capital figures. For undertakings whose capital was only partly paid, I used paid-up capital figures, insofar as these were available. In other cases I used estimations of total capital investment, which were more readily available, at least in some of the sectors, than paid-up figures. The sources, calculations and assumptions, as well as their limitations, are detailed in Appendix 2. The actual numbers, listed by sectors, are given in Table 7.2.

The total capital of joint-stock undertakings, based on the above estimations, increased by about 500 percent during the period 1740–1810, from approximately £18–19 million to more than £90 million (see Table 7.2). Second, the weight of the three moneyed companies in this total decreased dramatically, from about 85 percent in 1740 to

Church, *The History of the British Coal Industry, 1830–1913* (Oxford: Clarendon Press, 1986), 121–132.

Table 7.2. *Joint-stock undertakings in England, c. 1810*

Sector	Capital (in thousands of pounds, at current prices)
Canals and rivers	17,200
Turnpike trusts	15,970
Insurance	4,000
Water works	1,340
Docks	5,660
Gas light	600
Shipping	22,000
Mining	800
East India Company	6,000
Bank of England	11,642
South Sea Company	3,663
Miscellaneous	1,582
Total	90,457

Source: See Appendix 2.

about 24 percent in 1810. The increase in the capital of the rest of the companies was thus much more significant than the total suggests, reflecting an increase of 2,300 percent or even 2,760 percent between 1740 and 1810, from about £2.5–3 million to £69 million.[62]

The Importance of the Joint-Stock Organization in the Economy at Large

The joint-stock sector increased not only in absolute terms, but also in terms of its weight in the whole English economy, which, one has to remember, itself grew considerably during this period of industrialization. Table 7.3 presents a rough estimate of the weight of the capital of joint-stock companies in England's aggregate capital stock. Because there are no available aggregate capital stock estimations for 1740, the starting point of the table is 1760, the first year for which such an estimate, by Feinstein and Pollard, is available.[63] Although the table takes us beyond

[62]The two growth percentages are a result of the variation between minimum and maximum estimations for 1740.
[63]Feinstein and Pollard, *Capital Formation.*

Table 7.3. *The percentage of joint-stock capital in England's aggregate capital stock: 1760, 1810, 1840 (Stocks in £ million at current prices).*

		1760	1810	1840
1[a]	Net reproducible fixed stock	133	649	856
2[b]	"Relevant" stock	70	305	586
3	Total capital of joint-stock companies	20	90	210
4[c]	Capital of moneyed companies	17	21	21
5	Capital of nonmoneyed companies	3	69	189
6[d]	Capital of transport companies	0	17	75
7	Capital of nonmoneyed, nontransport companies	3	52	114
8	% line 3/1	15	13.9	24.5
9	% line 5/1	2.3	10.6	22
10	% line 7/1	2.3	8	13.3
11	%,line 3/2	28.6	29.5	35.8
12	% line 5/2	4.3	22.6	32.2
13	% line 7/2	4.3	17	19.5

Source: See Tables 7.2 and 8.4 and Feinstein and Pollard, *Capital Formation.*

[a] Net stock of domestic reproducible fixed assets, Great Britain (£ million at current prices).
[b] [Line 1 − nonrelevant sectors (agriculture + dwellings + public and social services) + nonfarm stocks and work in progress (fixed at 30% of total based on 1800) + overseas assets] × 80% (England's share in Great Britain based on population ratio).
[c] East India Company, Bank of England, South Sea Company.
[d] Canals plus railways.

1810, to 1840, a detailed discussion of the growth of the joint-stock sector in the period 1810–1844 is given below, in Chapter 8.

My dilemma was deciding which aggregate capital stock figures to use in this table. The solution was to offer two figures, an inclusive one (line 1) and a smaller one of "relevant stock," which includes only the capital of sectors in which joint-stock organization is common in modern times (line 2). I then sliced the capital of joint-stock companies (lines 3–7) to separate the growing and stagnant sectors from each other. Finally, I presented my weighted findings, based on the two aggregate capital figures (lines 8–10 and 11–13), in a manner that stresses the overall increase, and the uneven sectoral pattern of rise, of the weight of joint-stock companies in the English economy as a whole.

The total capital of joint-stock companies comprised some 13.9 percent of Great Britain's net reproducible fixed stock in 1810 and 24.5 percent by 1840 (line 8), and, even more remarkably, 29.5 percent of England's "relevant" stock in 1810 and 35.8 percent of its "relevant" stock (line 4) by 1840. When we turn our attention from absolute share in the economy to the rate of increase over the whole period, the most dramatic figures are to be found when we put aside the three old moneyed companies and focus on the nonmoneyed companies. The rate of increase of their share in these aggregate capital figures over the period 1760–1844 is stunning, 800 to 1,000 percent (lines 9 and 12). Though a considerable portion of this increase was attributed to the emergence of the transport sector, canals, and later railways, a striking increase could nevertheless be found outside these sectors (lines 10 and 13), and nonmoneyed and nontransport companies held about 17 percent of England's "relevant" stock by 1810.

The employment of joint-stock capital in various legal frameworks became widespread particularly during the late eighteenth century, as demonstrated above. The two leading sectors which utilized various forms of business organization and used joint stock on a regular basis were the transport sector (in canals, turnpikes, and river improvement projects) and the insurance sector. But the use of joint stock went far beyond these sectors. It was found in various manufacturing subsectors such as woolen company mills, the metal industry, flour milling and bread baking, and the brewing and spirits industry. It was found in that often neglected sector, fishing. Joint-stock concerns were found in the great moneyed companies, the Bank of England, the East India Company, and the declining South Sea Company. It was still found in other trading companies and, subject to different legal frameworks, in the ship ownership and the mining sectors. It was found in public utilities, such as water supply, and by the early nineteenth century also in docks and gas light. Thus, joint-stock undertakings were almost everywhere in the English economy, with the exception of agriculture. This is not to say that the joint-stock form became more popular than the family firm or the closed partnership. It did not, and in many sectors not surveyed in the present chapter, such as hardware, construction, pottery, black-smithing, shoe making, and other crafts and trades, the old forms of organization were still dominant in 1810 and beyond.

The joint-stock form of business organization became familiar to two groups beyond those entrepreneurs who invested their own capital and activities and were considered above. These included individuals personally connected to the companies as passive shareholders and as employees and officers, and the even larger group of competitors, adversaries, and consumers who out of necessity became familiar with this form of business organization. Not many in England of the early nineteenth century remained unaware of the new phenomenon or unmindful of its consequences.

The number of shareholders in joint-stock undertakings in early nineteenth-century England must have been myriad. An attempt at quantitative estimation, at the present level of historical research on these issues, seems premature. But without getting into specifics, it is quite clear that shareholders were found everywhere, and in large numbers: the local shareholders of canal companies in the Northwest and the Midlands, part-owners of ships in the outports and London, the cost book partners in Cornwall, Devon, and other mining districts, the shareholders of company mills in West Riding, and of course the shareholders of the Bank of England and the East India Company in the City of London and all over England. Shareholders were found in a wide variety of social classes and groups, from peers and gentlemen, through high financiers, merchants, and lawyers, manufacturers and inventors, mariners and tradesmen, widows and minors, down to the miners of the cost book partnerships and the poor of Birmingham who owned the Union Flour Company. Quite a few of the above were more than passive investors, and at one point or another held offices in the companies in which they owned shares. Thus, individuals all over England, from all classes, acquired first-hand experience as owners and managers of joint-stock undertakings.

The presence of joint-stock companies was felt far beyond their own yards. In many cases, the form of industrial organization, competition and discourse of an entire sector was shaped by the existence of even one joint-stock company in that sector. The entire banking sector was shaped by the corporate monopoly of the Bank of England and the struggles over its continuation. All the millers of London were familiar with the scheme for the London Flour and Bread Company, had petitioned against it, and had to change their business practices after the scheme was approved by Parliament. The brewers of London went through the same traumatic experience a few years later when the first joint-stock brewery, Golden Lane Brewery, was promoted. Mine owners and miners all over England were familiar with the business organization of the cost book partnerships of Cornwall and with their advantages, and tried as far as possible to enjoy these advantages outside the stannary jurisdiction. The canal age caused vast groups of landowners whose lands were crossed by canals, and traders whose cargo was carried on the canals, to become familiar with this new form of undertaking. They had to learn how to cooperate and counter, to contract and litigate, with joint-stock companies.

CONCLUDING REMARKS

Four factors may have misled some scholars into thinking that joint-stock companies were of marginal importance throughout the eighteenth century and especially in the early stages of industrialization. First, the fact that joint-stock companies were of no importance in the two growth sectors of the industrial revolution, the cotton and iron industries, created the impression that they were of no importance in industrialization in general. Second, the fact that the great trading companies which symbolized the joint-stock form of business organization in the sixteenth and seventeenth centuries had been in decline for several generations supported the misconception that joint-stock companies in general were in retreat. Third, the fact that two of the major sectors of the eighteenth-century economy, shipping and mining, were outside the realm of common law and subject to separate legal jurisdiction, the High Court of Admiralty and stannary courts, and to unique forms of business organization, disguised for the nonlegal eye the fact that the joint-stock form dominated these key sectors. Fourth, the misconception that the Bubble Act was intended to block the future development of the joint-stock company in general, and that its effects actually achieved that aim, led some scholars to believe that the employment of joint stock under its century-long shadow was rare. Although these four factors may serve as a partial explanation for the common wisdom, this wisdom is certainly not based on a survey of a wide range of sectors.

Joint-stock businesses were much more widespread in England by 1810 than they had been in 1740, and their impact on the economy as a whole during this growth and industrialization period should not be overlooked. Furthermore, their everyday problems could not be ignored by the State for long. As we shall see in Chapters 8 to 10, starting around 1805 and more so during the 1820s, the courts, Parliament, and the government were forced, one by one, to deal with the totally new scale of the employment of joint stock by the business sectors and with all the problems related to this new phenomenon.

PART III

1800–1844

8

The Attitudes of the Business Community

The business community was not monolithic in its attitude toward the joint-stock company and the concepts attached to it. Several studies have emphasized the division within the business-oriented middle class between the northern industrialists and the City merchants and financiers, and the dominant position of the City in politics and in the economy.[1] This chapter argues that as far as the attitude toward the joint-stock company is concerned, an additional dimension should be added, the division within the City of London between various groups of businessmen.[2] This chapter first deals with the social and economic identity of the promoters of joint-stock companies and their adversaries. The rival interests over the question of trade and corporate monopoly are then studied. The advance of the joint-stock company into new sectors during market booms and with the introduction of new technology is then surveyed. Finally, the change in negative attitudes toward the share market is explained in light of the advance of the market and the widening circle of investors.

---

[1]W. D. Rubinstein, *Men of Property: The Very Wealthy in Britain since the Industrial Revolution* (London: CroomHelm, 1981); Geoffrey Ingham, *Capitalism Divided? The City and Industry in British Social Development* (London: Macmillan, 1984); P. J. Cain and A. G. Hopkins, "Gentlemanly Capitalism and British Expansion Overseas – I. The Old Colonial System, 1688–1850," *Economic History Review* 39, no. 4 (1986), 501–525, see also P. J. Cain and A. G. Hopkins, *British Imperialism: Innovation and Expansion, 1688–1914* (London: Longman, 1993).

[2]A few recent studies have called into question the notion of the City as a coherent interest with unified opinion on economic policy, as opposed to the landed and the industrial interest. See M. J. Daunton, " 'Gentlemanly Capitalism' and British Industry, 1820–1914," *Past and Present* 122 (Feb. 1989), 119–158; A. C. Howe, "Free Trade and the City of London: c. 1820–1870," *History* 77 (1992), 391–410. The argument in the present chapter is in line with these studies.

THE PROMOTERS OF THE NEW COMPANIES AND THEIR FOES

A considerable number of joint-stock entrepreneurs appeared near the turn of the nineteenth century. They were concentrated in London and involved in the promotion of the dock and water supply companies of that period. In the boom year of 1807, some forty-two new companies were formed, most in London, and mainly in the fields of insurance, brewing, food production, and metal manufacturing. By this time, a distinct group of middle-class joint-stock promoters could be identified. Among its more famous members were Frederick Eden of the Globe Assurance Company, William Brown and Joseph Parry of the Golden Lane Brewery, and Ralph Dodd of the London Distillery Company, who all wrote pamphlets in support of their undertakings and of companies in general. The promoters were connected to one another socially and through business. They employed the same bankers and solicitors, arranged promotional meetings in the same coffee shops, and shared the same legal difficulties and hostile attitudes from their rivals.

None of the newly promoted companies was well received by the business community as a whole. The Golden Lane Brewery was harassed by private publicans and brewers. The London Flour Company was opposed by private millers. The Globe Assurance Company faced opposition from the monopolistic marine insurance companies, the unincorporated fire and life companies, and Lloyd's underwriters.

The number of those involved in the promotion of joint-stock companies increased from a few dozen around 1807 to at least several hundred in 1825. The number of promoted companies at that time was no less than 624, each with designated directors, managers, secretaries, and auditors. The group of solicitors, bankers, and parliamentary agents who specialized in establishing these companies was also concentrated primarily in the City of London, around the Stock Exchange, the alleys, coffeehouses, and pubs.

A few examples demonstrate the complex attitudes of the business community to these new promotions. The West India Company was promoted by plantation proprietors and opposed by abolitionists and antimonopolistic small merchants. The Pasco-Peruvian Mining Company was promoted by adventurers who desired the legendary fortunes of South America, and resisted by radicals who decried it a scam for trapping innocent investors and by adventurers who held rights to neighboring mines. The Liverpool and Manchester Railway Company was opposed by two major interest groups: landowners and shareholders in the canal companies that connected the two cities. The group that promoted St. Catherine's Dock Company was challenged by the other dock companies, particularly the London Dock Company, and by part of the establishment of the City of London.

The entrepreneurs who attempted to promote new joint-stock companies in the first quarter of the nineteenth century faced opposition on two fronts. On one hand, they were attacked by Lloyd's insurance underwriters, family banks, small merchant houses, and individual brewers and millers who held a privileged position as long as family fortunes were the major source of business finance and who worried that they would be driven out of the market by the competition of large joint-stock concerns. On the other hand, they were confronted by the well-established joint-stock companies, the monopolistic Bank of England, East India Company, Royal Exchange Assurance and London Assurance, the naturally monopolistic water, gas lighting, and dock companies, and the nonmonopolistic fire and life insurance companies which aimed at creating entry barriers to newcomers. Thus, financiers, merchants, and manufacturers could be found on both sides of each conflict.

THE CONFLICT OVER THE OLD MONOPOLIES

By 1800, most of the monopolies held by corporations were a thing of the past. With the exception of the East India Company, almost all the great trading companies had been dissolved or had had to abandon their monopolistic privileges. The Bank of England still retained its 1708 chartered monopoly on corporate note issuing, thus practically precluding country banks from employing the joint-stock form of business organization. The Royal Exchange Assurance and the London Assurance still held their corporate marine insurance monopoly of 1720. The trade monopoly of the East India Company and the corporate monopoly of the two marine insurance companies came under heavy attack during the first decade of the nineteenth century. The attack on the Bank of England's monopoly would come in the 1820s.

The conflict over the trade monopoly of the East India Company was primarily a conflict between London merchants and industrialists, and merchants in the outports and the growing industrial towns. The struggle over the corporate monopoly in marine insurance was concentrated within the City, between a coalition of vested interests of monopolistic corporations and of Lloyd's underwriters on one side, and newcomers with limited financial means who had to resort to joint stock on the other. The clash over the Bank of England's corporate monopoly had elements of both conflicts; it brought together country bankers, private London bankers, and newcomers who joined against the mighty Bank of England.

Trade Monopolies and the East India Company

As shown in Chapter 2, the heyday of the monopolistic joint-stock companies was in the late Elizabethan and early Stuart days. After the civil war and the Interregnum, the monopolistic system was in retreat. The general trend throughout the second half of the seventeenth century and the entire eighteenth century is unmistakable. One by one, monopoly privileges were surrendered, entry barriers into monopolistic companies were lowered, trading companies were dissolved, and overseas markets were opened to individual merchants. The monopolies of Merchant Adventurers (1662), Eastland Company (1673), Russia Company (1698), South Sea Company (1750), Royal African (1752), and Levant Company (1753) were all curtailed, surrendered, or abolished altogether.[3] By the late eighteenth century, the only surviving overseas monopolies were the Hudson's Bay Company and the much more significant East India Company.[4]

However, the fact that the monopoly system had been in decline since the 1630s and was practically nonexistent by Adam Smith's time did not remove it from the public agenda. To many, including Smith, the association of the joint-stock corporation with monopoly remained. The widespread hostility, anger, and envy toward the East India Company on the part of those excluded from sharing in the legendary fortunes of India and China were translated into antagonism toward monopolies and merchant companies, and ultimately led to the condemnation of the joint-stock corporation as a legitimate form of business organization. The abolition of the monopoly could play a role in creating a more favorable atmosphere for the joint-stock company as a form of organization.

In 1744, the anonymous *Essay on the Causes of the Decline of Foreign Trade* stated that exclusive and monopolistic companies were a major cause of the decline in England's foreign trade. They reduced exports or imports in order to raise prices, concentrated only on high-yield goods and destinations, paid high salaries, discriminated between

---

[3]The dates given in the text are of the effective cessation of each trade monopoly, not necessarily of the official abolition of its monopolistic charter or the ultimate winding-up of the corporation.

[4]A few monopolistic trading companies were formed after the Restoration: the Royal African (1662), Hudson's Bay (1670), and the South Sea (1711), but both the Royal African and the South Sea were soon to lose their privileges, whereas Hudson's Bay was marginal in terms of capital and revenues.

directors and servants on one hand and ordinary members on the other, neglected the provinces in favor of London, and used corrupted practices.[5] The essay equated the monopolistic trading companies to "the dog in the manger, not eating themselves, but preventing those who would." Josiah Tucker proposed in *An Essay on Trade* in 1750 "to lay open and extend our narrow and restrained companies."[6] Tucker discussed all the justifications for the formation of monopolistic companies, or, to use his term, exclusive companies, and came to the conclusion that they were no longer valid by his time. Adam Smith in *The Wealth of Nations* surveyed the monopolistic merchant companies of the last few generations, both regulated and joint-stock, and came to a clear conclusion:

These companies, though they may, perhaps, have been useful for the first introduction of some branches of commerce, by making, at their own expense, an experiment which the state might not think it prudent to make, have in the long-run proved, universally either burdensome or useless, and have either mismanaged or confined the trade.[7]

Adam Smith directed much of his criticism at the East India Company, the only great trading company to survive until his day, and the most powerful of them all. He called for the termination of its charter and said:

The East India Company, upon the redemption of their funds, and the expiration of their exclusive privilege, have a right, by act of parliament, to continue a corporation with a joint stock, and to trade in their corporate capacity to the East Indies in common with the rest of their fellow-subjects. But in this situation, the superior vigilance and attention of private adventurers would, in all probability, soon make them weary of the trade.[8]

He thus linked the mere existence of the East India Company to its monopoly. Without State intervention in the form of monopolistic privileges, the inferiority of the company vis-à-vis the individual merchants would be manifest. The superiority of the individual over the business association is inherent and stems from human character, the hierarchical structure of the company, and the functioning of the market.

   James Mill continued Adam Smith's attacks on the East India monopoly in the early nineteenth century. He called for separation of the

[5]In J. R. McCulloch, ed., *A Select Collection of Scarce and Valuable Tracts on Commerce* (1859), 187–199. McCulloch attributes this essay, though not without hesitation, to Matthew Decker (see ibid., viii).
[6]Josiah Tucker, *An Essay on Trade* (1750), reprinted in McCulloch, *A Select Collection*, 360.
[7]Smith, *The Wealth of Nations*, 691.
[8]Ibid., 713.

company's territorial functions from its trade functions and for transfer of the India trade to private hands.[9]

In the last decades of the eighteenth century, the trade monopoly of the East India Company, as well as its newly acquired territorial governance, were under constant attack not only by the political economists but also by ministerial officials who resented the company's growing influence over foreign and domestic policy and by commercial and manufacturing interests in Parliament, mainly the representatives of the outports and of the northern industrial towns.[10] In a way, the writings of the political economists were used by these groups to advance their own ends. This broad coalition gradually got its way. In 1767, in an attempt to limit the exploitation of the company's monopoly by its proprietors, the Dividend Act, the first of a series of regulatory acts to fix a maximum rate of dividends, was passed. The Regulation Act of 1772 created a Governor-General and a Council in Bengal with some supervisory powers over the company's affairs. The India Act of 1784 set up a Board of Control in London with authority over political and military matters and extended the executive powers of the Governor-General. The huge personal fortunes made by the company's representatives in India, the nabobs, did not improve its public image. Warren Hastings's impeachment trial, which began in 1787 and lasted for seven years, was another source of public hostility toward the company, its monopoly, and the joint-stock corporation as a form of business organization. His ultimate exoneration from accusations of misconduct as Governor-General could not reverse the damage to the company's image. An act of 1793, which extended the company's charter for twenty years, forced the company to allocate shipping space to private traders. Thus the company's monopoly and its unique powers were eroded over the course of a few decades.

In the years 1812 to 1813, some thirty pamphlets were circulated and 130 petitions were presented to Parliament against the renewal of the East India Company's charter, most originating in Liverpool, Birmingham, Bristol, Hull, and other provincial towns.[11] The India lobby in Parliament was as strong as ever: thirty-eight MPs with a company interest and sixty-one with an Indian interest.[12] Yet, in 1813, during the troubled times of the Napoleonic and American wars, the Continental System and the Orders in Council, when trade with the Continent and with North America was seriously disturbed, the interests of the provin-

---

[9]William J. Barber, *British Economic Thought and India, 1600–1858: A Study in the History of Development Economics* (Oxford: Clarendon Press, 1975), 133ff.

[10]See Sutherland, *East India Company*; C. H. Philips, *The East India Company: 1784–1834*, 2d ed. (Manchester University Press, 1961).

[11]Ibid., 182–184.

[12]Ibid., 323–325.

cial towns and of the government coincided.[13] The writings of the political economists in favor of free trade in general, and with India in particular, were utilized to the utmost by these antimonopolistic interests. Under these unique circumstances, the India interest was defeated and the trade monopoly with India abolished. The company was able to retain its China monopoly for two more decades before it too was finally abolished in 1833.

The Marine Insurance Corporate Monopoly

The corporate monopoly in marine insurance was formed with the incorporation of the Royal Exchange Assurance and London Assurance in 1720. Throughout the remainder of the century, this monopoly was not attacked by any significant group. Individual marine insurance underwriters sat regularly at Lloyd's coffeehouse, which eventually became a marketplace for marine insurance coverage. The underwriters, known as the names, acted in their own legal capacity and enjoyed no limitation on their liability. Thus Lloyd's was not a corporation or any other form of business organization. The value of property insured at Lloyd's increased dramatically over the century, and by the end of the century, its underwriters were to control most of the market for marine insurance.[14] Entrepreneurs who wished to organize themselves in joint-stock companies turned to other branches of the insurance sector, fire and life, avoiding the marine insurance business.

The first attack on the marine insurance monopoly was made by the Globe Insurance Company and its chief promoter Frederick Eden. In 1799, the Globe obtained an act to enable its incorporation by charter. From that point on, for about eight years, it was in direct confrontation with the monopolistic companies. On one hand, it was argued that the incorporation of the Globe for the purpose of marine insurance, among other things, "would be an infringement upon the rights of the London and Royal Exchange Insurance Companies," rights that were purchased for valuable consideration.[15] This is clearly a promonopolistic approach.

---

[13]Anthony Webster, "The Political Economy of Trade Liberalization: The East India Company Charter Act of 1813," *Economic History Review* 43, no. 3 (1990), 404–419. Whereas previous studies stressed the role of the provincial interests, Webster integrates into his explanation the role of government change of policy.

[14]It was estimated that the number of underwriters at Lloyd's reached 1500 by the turn of the century. Individual underwriters, mostly Lloyd's names, were dominant in the marine insurance business. They paid more than 95 percent of the policy stamp duties in London in 1809, compared with less than 5 percent paid by the chartered companies (this is the best available indication as to their market share). See *Hansard's Parliamentary Debates*, vol. 15, pp. 405–406, Feb. 14, 1810.

[15]*Hansard's Parliamentary Debates*, vol. 7, p. 812, June 24, 1806.

On the other hand, it was argued that the large capital of the Globe, its wide scope of activities and its powers and privileges as a corporation, would make it into a monopoly within a few years. "Each of these powers necessarily operates as a restraint and an abridgment of the rights and privileges of all other members of the community."[16] Yet the writer of this antimonopolistic statement, George Stonestreet, the founding father of the Phoenix, would claim a few pages later in that same pamphlet, when arguing that existing insurance undertakings are sufficient, that "the argument 'competition is always good for the public' . . . as a general proposition, it is, however, by no means founded . . . When the number of competitors exceeds the public want . . . the public is not better, but worse supplied, sometimes much worse."[17] So we see that Stonestreet's attitude toward the relationship of monopoly and incorporation changed considerably between 1782, when he was promoting the Phoenix, and 1800. He employed the same arguments used against the Phoenix, but this time he turned them against the promotion of the Globe.

Eden and his supporters argued that the market for marine insurance had grown several-fold since 1720, that the original charters of the two marine insurance corporations had been obtained using manipulative means, that these charters were unprecedentedly unlimited in time and coverage, and that the two utilized their monopoly and charged higher premiums than Lloyd's.[18] Eventually the strong vested interest of the monopolistic corporations on one side, Lloyd's on the other, and the established fire and life insurance companies on top blocked the attempt of the Globe to curtail the marine insurance monopoly or even to incorporate itself by an act or a charter.

In 1810, another attempt to confront the marine monopoly took place when the New Marine Insurance Company was initiated. This was intended to be huge, by contemporary standards, with capital of £5 million, and it was supported by many leading merchants and financiers in the City.[19] The battle for the incorporation bill was made along two fronts, one facing the monopolistic chartered companies, the other facing the individual underwriters of Lloyd's. The arguments of the promoters of the Globe against the marine monopoly were reiterated by the supporters of the new company when its petition for incorporation was debated in the Commons in a lengthy session in February 1810.[20] The

[16]George Griffin Stonestreet, *The Portentous Globe* (1800), 7.
[17]Ibid., 31.
[18][Frederick Eden], *On the Policy and Expediency of Granting Insurance Charters* (1806), 11–48.
[19]Supple, *Royal Exchange Assurance*, 194.
[20]*Hansard's Parliamentary Debates*, vol. 15, pp. 399–424, 495–496, Feb. 14, 1810.

direct attack on the anachronistic privileged monopolies was accompanied by an attack on Lloyd's, arguing that the individual underwriters could not offer coverage for large amounts, that dealing with a large number of underwriters would be cumbersome, and that underwriters of limited means could become insolvent when faced with disasters. The matter was referred to a select committee, which, after surveying the drawbacks of the marine monopoly in an age of economic growth and freer trade, recommended "that the exclusive privileges for marine insurance of the two chartered companies should be repealed."[21] When the bill for incorporating the New Marine Insurance Company returned for a second reading, after the positive report was submitted, it was nevertheless defeated by a margin of one (25 to 26).[22] Thus the marine insurance monopoly narrowly escaped repeal in 1811, and was able to carry on until the next and final attack in the mid-1820s.

Joseph Marryat (a future chairman of Lloyd's), who spoke in the Commons against the New Marine Insurance bill, is one of the best examples of the contemporary confusion concerning the relationship between incorporation and monopoly. He said:

The supporters of this petition are in a situation of some embarrassment as well as awkwardness; for they must first persuade the House that insurance companies, possessing exclusive or particular privileges, are prejudicial to the public interest, in order to induce us to deprive those now existing of their chartered rights; and then, requesting us to forget all they have said on this subject, they must take up the contrary side of the argument, and persuade us that such companies are advantageous to the public interests, in order to induce us to establish their intended new company on the ruins of the old companies.[23]

Marryat, aware that the new company did not ask for any specific monopoly, insisted that, by petitioning for doing what "the law as it now stands prohibited them from doing," and for enjoying privileges that were "not enjoyed by the community at large," the company was in fact asking for monopolistic privileges. The core of this somewhat confused argument is that every corporation embodies monopolistic privileges, and thus places the individual in an inferior position. The identification of incorporation with monopoly originating in Elizabethan and early Stuart days, which seemed to have disappeared with the decline of the monopolistic system in the second half of the seventeenth century, had returned by 1810. Companies that asked for no monopolistic privileges, such as the Sierra Leone, the Globe, and the New Marine

---

[21]"Report from the Select Committee on Marine Insurance," in *Hansard's Parliamentary Debates*, vol. 17, Appendices: Parliamentary Papers, clxxvii–cxci (1810).

[22]*Hansard's Parliamentary Debates*, vol. 19, pp. 117–119 (1811).

[23]*Hansard's Parliamentary Debates*, vol. 15, p. 401, Feb. 14, 1810.

Insurance Company, were nevertheless identified with monopoly by their foes.

The political economists of the time, most notably Adam Smith, did not help in clearing up the relationship between joint-stock corporations and monopoly. Smith himself was used as an oracle by Marryat when speaking against the New Marine Insurance in 1810, whereas just four years earlier Eden had resorted to Smith's authoritative standing when writing in favor of incorporating the Globe.[24] Was Smith inconsistent, or were his readers biased? Both statements seem to be correct.[25] Smith was indeed in favor of joint-stock companies in some sectors, namely, banking, insurance, canals, and water supply, but not in others. However, he did not state a rationale for this distinction. Many of Smith's readers took his antagonism to exclusive privileges to apply to all corporations, believing that incorporation, in itself, is an exclusive privilege. Smith became renowned among his contemporaries for his hostility to joint-stock companies. Entrepreneurs like Eden, who identified with the general ideology of Smith's political economy, found themselves in a dilemma when trying to reconcile it with what was perceived to be his opinion on joint-stock companies.

Eden seems to have been ahead of his time when he said that "the creation of Joint-Stock Companies is not connected to the question of monopoly."[26] He could not undermine the 200-year-old belief that corporations and monopoly were inevitably linked. The fact that this had not been the case for more than a century did not erase the collective anxiety kept alive, at least in part, by interested parties.[27] Eden was not able to disconnect the link, but he was able to place the issue, as he rephrased it, on the agenda for the next generation.

The assault on the monopoly of the Royal Exchange and London

---

[24][Eden], *Granting Insurance Charters*, 11.

[25]There is growing interest in recent years in Adam Smith's views on the joint-stock company, an aspect of Smith's writing that was only superficially dealt with in the past. See Gary M. Anderson and Robert D. Tollison, "Adam Smith's Analysis of Joint-Stock Companies," *Journal of Political Economy* 90, no. 6 (1982), 1237; James P. Henderson, "Agency or Alienation? Smith, Mill and Marx on the Joint-Stock Company," *History of Political Economy* 18, no. 1 (1986), 111; Michael N. Hayes, "Mercantile Incentives: State Sanctioned Market Power and Economic Development in the Atlantic Economy, 1553–1776," Ph.D. dissertation, University of California, Davis (1986), 51–117. The present chapter does not aim to offer a conclusive statement of Smith's interpretation, but only to indicate its influence on Smith's contemporaries.

[26][Eden], *Granting Insurance Charters*, 10.

[27]Even one of Eden's supporters, John Sinclair, suggested revival of the old-style chartered company. He favored the incorporation of insurance corporations in return for receiving half of their net profit as public revenue. He was willing to renew the vanished link between incorporation and public finance. See John Sinclair, *History of Public Revenue of the British Empire*, 3d ed., 3 vols. (1803–1804), vol. 3, p. 292.

Assurance did not achieve its aim in the 1800s or 1810s. However, having narrowly escaped the abolition of their privilege in face of the Globe and the New Marine Insurance in the previous decades, the two marine insurance corporations met a strong rival in 1824. In the spring of that year, a new insurance company was formed, the Alliance. Only life and fire insurance were mentioned in its original prospectus. Yet with a very strong City representation, including Nathan Rothschild, Moses Montifiore, Alexander Baring and Hudson Gurney, the new company could not resist the temptation of entering the marine insurance business.[28] With powerful parliamentary representation, active lobbying, and the favorable intervention of some senior ministers, most notably Huskisson, the Alliance promoters moved for the abolition of the marine monopoly. Once again the two chartered companies on one hand, and Lloyd's on the other, opposed the bill. But this time the supporters of the bill, both those with vested interest in the Alliance and those who truly believed in advancing the idea of free trade, overwhelmed the defenders of the monopoly. The Alliance bill passed 559 to 159 on the third reading in the Commons.[29]

The corporate monopoly in marine insurance had been granted in 1720 to the Royal Exchange and London Assurance in return for paying the King's Civil List, to the amount of £300,000 each. It was secured by the Bubble Act of that year. It determined the structure of business organization of this sector for more than a century and contributed to the emergence of that unique coffeehouse turned marketplace, Lloyd's, and to the prosperity of its individual undertakers. To defeat this monopoly and pave the way for the spread of joint-stock marine insurance companies, the new spirit of free trade combined with an extremely strong vested interest, headed by Baring and Rothschild in 1824. By this time, however, the presence of Lloyd's was a lasting factor.

The Bank of England Monopoly

The banking sector had grown considerably since the middle of the eighteenth century. The rise in the number of provincial banks was remarkable: from just a handful of country banks in 1750, their number rose to over 100 in the 1780s, almost 400 by 1800, and about 600 in the boom year of 1825.[30] The number of London banks more than doubled in this period to about sixty. Yet the chartered monopoly of the

[28]Supple, *Royal Exchange Assurance*, 198–199.

[29]*Hansard's Parliamentary Debates*, vol. 11, pp. 766–775, 842–843, 920–933, 1086–1089, 1202 (1824).

[30]L. S. Pressnell, *Country Banking in the Industrial Revolution* (Oxford: Clarendon Press, 1956), chap. 2.

Bank of England prevented either joint-stock corporations or partnerships with more than six partners from entering the note-issuing banking sector.[31] Thus, with the exception of the Bank of England, all the English banks of the eighteenth and early nineteenth centuries, both country and London banks, were family firms or closely held partnerships, composed of just a handful of partners. For quite some time prior to 1825, the difficulties of running large-scale partnerships and unincorporated companies were apparent, as shown in Chapter 5. The doubts about running banks by partnerships increased with every cyclical wave of bankruptcies of country bankers. The crisis of 1793 resulted in twenty-two bankruptcies within one year. In the years 1814–1816, no less than eighty-nine bankers went bankrupt.[32] Altogether, about 300 private banks failed in the three decades prior to 1825. It became evident that the limited capital resources of the small country banks made them vulnerable, particularly during times of crises and of runs on them by the public. The absence of limited liability exposed the bankers personally to the risk of liquidity shortages. Any disagreement between the government and the Bank of England over monetary policy raised anew the issue of justification of its monopoly. Thus, by the early 1820s, the proposal for reform which would stabilize country banks, widen the range of activities of London banks, and limit the powers of the Bank of England, was placed on the agenda.

The assault on the Bank's corporate monopoly was launched by country bankers, a few of the London private bankers, and entrepreneurs who aimed at establishing new joint-stock banks in the provinces and in London. It was led by Thomas Joplin, a Newcastle timber merchant, aspiring political economist, and joint-stock bank promoter. He circulated several pamphlets in the early 1820s attacking the Bank's monopoly. He saw it as

a right which confers no advantage upon it, while it loosens the whole frame of commercial credit, of which banks are the pillars and support. To call it, therefore, a right, with respect to the country, is improper; legally it may be termed a right, but equitably it is nothing but a wrong.[33]

Joplin took two courses of action: promoting a note-issuing joint-stock country bank with £500,000 capital in Newcastle and its vicinity,[34] and

---

[31]The bank's monopoly was first granted in 6 Anne c.22 (1707), and was renewed on several occasions. The Charter Renewal Act in effect in the period under discussion was 39 & 40 Geo. III c.28 (1800).

[32]Emlyn Thomas, "The Crisis of 1825," M.Sc. thesis, University of London (1938), Appendix, p. 22, based on *Parliamentary Papers*, vol. 6, Appendix 101 (1831–1832).

[33]Thomas Joplin, *Essay on the General Principles and Present Practices of Banking*, 4th ed. (1823), 63.

[34]Ibid., 36.

promoting a nonissuing joint-stock bank in London with £3,000,000 capital.[35] He argued that the London bank could be promoted without any alteration of the Bank of England's charter. He suggested that "in lieu of the clause enacting, that not more than six partners shall enter into other banking concerns, it be enacted that no banks shall issue notes within the boundaries of the present monopoly."[36] This would enable note-issuing provincial banks and nonissuing London banks to organize with joint stock, while not harming the Bank of England, which issued notes only in London.

Joplin and other opponents of the corporate monopoly of the Bank of England could find support in the success of joint-stock banking in Scotland and Ireland. Three large chartered banks were operating in Scotland by the late eighteenth century: the Bank of Scotland, the Royal Bank of Scotland, and the British Linen Company. Side by side with them were, outside Edinburgh, provincial banks not limited to six partners, many of which had large proprietorships. The Irish experience was even fresher. Following the severe financial crisis of 1820, acts were passed in 1821, 1824, and 1825 to limit the privileges of the Bank of Ireland to a radius of fifty miles around Dublin, and permitted the formation of partnerships of over six partners and of joint-stock banks outside Dublin.[37]

Yet the Bank of England objected to the adoption of the Scottish or Irish models in England, and Joplin's proposals were thus premature. It took one more major crisis before some of Joplin's ideas were realized. In the aftermath of the collapse of the shares, the Latin American bonds, and the commodities in the summer of 1825, the entire English banking system was shaken. In late October 1825, a run on country banks began. As the run continued in November and some banks shut their doors, a rush on gold was imminent. The reserves of the Bank of England fell considerably, and the bank reduced its credit and discount services to a minimum. The panic in the money market grew during early December, and more country banks went bankrupt. On December 12, a first London bank, which carried business for forty-four country banks, had to close its doors. The next day another City bank failed, and two more had to close their doors the following day. The Bank of England's reserves on December 14 were even lower than during the 1797 crisis, and its directors came to the conclusion that payment suspension was unavoidable. Yet the government refused the bank's suspension request,

---

[35]Thomas Joplin, *Prospectus of a Joint-Stock Banking Company with £3,000,000 of Capital to Be Established in London* (1823).

[36]Joplin, *General Principles of Banking*, 66.

[37]See Michael Collins, *Money and Banking in the U.K.: A History* (London: CroomHelm, 1988), 12–14.

and with no other alternative, a complete reversal of policy seemed to be the only hope. The bank decided to increase discounts, grant new loans, issue notes, and buy Exchequer bills. That day, December 14, was, in retrospect, the peak and turning point of the crisis. By the next day the panic had allayed, the run on City banks ceased, and no new failures of London banks were registered.[38] Yet many country banks never recovered; eighty went bankrupt in 1825–1826, no less than sixty-three of these during the two worst months, December 1825 and January 1826.[39]

The crisis of the banking system, followed by many business failures and an economic depression, made the government more resolute than ever to repeal the bank's monopoly. The bank, at that point of weakness, could not show much resistance.[40] The bank's role in the crisis was debated in Parliament from several aspects, including its role in the monetary system, its relationship to the government, and its function in the note-issuing network, all not relevant to our discussion. Much of the debate, however, revolved around the justification of the corporate monopoly of the Bank of England. The issue was first debated in the Commons, then again when a reform bill was introduced in the Lords, and on several other occasions in both Houses throughout the first half of 1826.[41] Eventually, on May 26, 1826, a law was passed permitting the formation of corporations and partnerships with any number of partners for carrying on business as bankers in England.[42] It prohibited such corporations and partnerships from issuing notes within sixty-five miles of London and fixed a procedural and substantive framework for the activity of these corporations and partnerships, some of which are examined below. As part of the compromise that was made, the Bank of England, in return for giving up its corporate monopoly, received the right to "empower agents"; in other words, to open branches any place in England.[43]

The enactment of this law became possible only in 1826, for several reasons: The deficiency of small-scale country banks became more evident than ever during the crisis of late 1825; the Bank of England had

---

[38]Thomas, *Crisis of 1825*, 351–392.

[39]Ibid., Appendix, pp. 22–24.

[40]Clapham, *Bank of England*, vol. 2, p. 107.

[41]*Hansard's Parliamentary Debates*, vol. 14, pp. 165, 245, 368, 450, 556, 866 (1826); vol. 15, p. 236 (1826).

[42]7 Geo. IV c.46 (1826).

[43]The Bank had opened six provincial branches by 1827, and three more by 1829. See Dieter Ziegler, *Central Bank, Peripheral Industry: The Bank of England in the Provinces: 1826–1913*, trans. Eileen Martin (Leicester University Press, 1990); David J. Moss, "The Bank of England and the Country Banks: Birmingham, 1827–33," *Economic History Review* 34, no. 4 (1981), 540–553.

to yield to public pressure after being on the brink of payment suspension in December; the experiments in joint-stock banking in Scotland and Ireland seemed quite successful; and free trade conceptions and liberal-Tory policies had become a dominant factor by this time.

The Bank Charter Act of 1833 clarified a legal dispute over the interpretation of the 1826 act and confirmed the view that nonissuing joint-stock banks were permitted even in London.[44] Following this act, a first joint-stock bank was established in London in 1834, the London and Westminster. Other nonissuing banks were soon established in and around London. The only remaining restriction was that London joint-stock banks were precluded from issuing notes.

Conclusion

Thus, in a series of acts in 1824, 1826, and 1833, the corporate monopolies in two key sectors, banking and marine insurance, came to an end. The trade monopoly of the East India Company came to an end at about the same time, in 1813 for India itself and in 1833 for China. A combination of factors resulted in the end of the monopoly: first, attacks by rising manufacturers, traders, and bankers of the industrializing provincial towns; second, the revolt of underprivileged, less disciplined, and more ambitious groups of entrepreneurs within the City of London; and third, specific historical circumstances – the wars of 1813, the speculative boom in 1824, and the severe financial crisis of 1826.

By 1833, the monopolistic feature so strongly linked to the business corporation finally disappeared. As we have seen, the perception in this respect lagged behind the actual and attributed monopolistic tendencies to corporations in general, long after most companies held no monopolistic privileges. Only this final stage of the abolition of monopolistic privileges, coming about two centuries after the beginning of the process of separation, could create the conditions for their separation in all minds.

The repeal of the monopolies resulted in increased competition in these sectors. Their effect on the structure of business organization was varied. The termination of the Indian monopoly served individual merchants and small merchant houses. The abolition of the marine insurance and banking corporate monopolies, on the other hand, advanced new joint-stock companies at the expense of the large corporations but also of the individual insurance underwriters and the family banks. Freer trade did not inevitably advance the business company, but in this case it opened the way to the formation of many new joint-stock companies

[44]Clapham, *Bank of England*, vol. 2, p. 134.

in the financial sector. This sector held a key position in the 1820s, both for the future development of the joint-stock company and for the emergence of a second wave of industrialization which gathered momentum with the coming of the railway.

The Early Nineteenth Century

The growth of the English economy during the last decades of the eighteenth century placed new financial, technological, and managerial requirements on traditional forms of business organization. This stimulated the more extensive employment of new forms of business organization, more complex than the family firm and the closed partnership, toward the turn of the nineteenth century. These included the business corporation, the unincorporated joint-stock company, the mutual association, the building society, and others. All these, particularly those with an element of joint stock, had spread considerably. They were now found in the canal sector, in insurance, in water supply, dock building, and other utilities, and had begun to appear in manufacturing. As demonstrated in Chapter 7, their weight in the English economy as a whole was more considerable by 1810 than ever before. The legal and economic advantages of the business corporation over the partnership and the unincorporated joint-stock company became clearer than ever. Attempts to further develop the unincorporated company as a substitute for the business corporation were approaching a dead end.

The French wars provided ups and downs which served the interests of the more speculative entrepreneurs. One of the periodical waves of speculation in company shares began after 1805. The number of new promotions reached a peak of forty-two in 1807. Unlike in the previous boom, the canal mania of the 1790s, this time, proposed companies could be found in a wide range of sectors, from insurance to vinegar manufactory, from brewing to copper, and from a medical laboratory to a company for purchasing canal shares.[45] The price of the leading shares, Bank of England and East India, rose as well (the first by more than 100%) between 1803 and 1809. In the 1800s, for the first time since 1720, wide circles of society showed interest in the shares of joint-stock companies throughout the English economy, not only in those of the moneyed companies or of a specific sector, and in speculative promotions.

The number of joint-stock companies kept growing in the 1810s. They entered a new developing sector, gas lighting, which from its origins was based to a considerable degree on joint-stock undertakings. The

[45]Tooke, *A History of Prices*, 278–280.

gas light sector joined insurance, docks, and water supply as the sectors in which the number of joint-stock companies grew most remarkably after the turn of the century.[46]

The Boom of 1825

The first sign of the beginning of a new wave of speculative joint-stock promotion came with the first Latin American loans. The newly independent Latin American states were looking for financial sources for their activities, while European financiers and businessmen were seeking new investment opportunities and markets as they recovered from the Napoleonic wars. The meeting of the two led to the development of an active loan market centered in London. The first loans, to the amount of £3,384,000, were floated in 1822, but the real rush came in 1824 with £11,386,000 in South American loans issued in London. In 1825, an additional £5,980,000 were raised.[47] In 1824–1825, more than £25 million was raised in London's foreign bond market, including loans to European states. The Latin American loans were well received in London in 1824 and early 1825. Interest rates were high and paid promptly. Loans were oversubscribed and bond prices rose.

The feeling of optimism and enthusiasm soon spread from the bond market to the share market. The first joint-stock companies to be promoted in 1824 were the South American mining companies. Promoters were encouraged by the success of the loans. They tried to attract investors by reinforcing the widespread belief in ancient treasures and unexploited minerals presumably hidden in the jungles and mountains of South and Central America, and for the first time open to the English after more than four centuries of Spanish conquest. This notion was well received by the more adventurous English investors. The number of new projected companies rose daily. By January 1825, six South American mining companies were quoted regularly on the Stock Exchange lists; by March, their number was seventeen and by August, thirty-four.[48] The

[46]M. E. Falkus, "The British Gas Industry before 1850," *Economic History Review* 20, no. 3 (1967), 494; D. A. Chatterton, "State Control of the Nineteenth Century: The London Gas Industry," *Business History* 14, no. 2 (1972), 166; P. J. Rowlinson, "Regulation of the Gas Industry in the Early Nineteenth Century: 1800–1860," Ph.D. thesis, Oxford University, 1984.

[47]Frank G. Dawson, *The First Latin American Debt Crisis: The City of London and the 1822–1825 Loan Bubble* (New Haven: Yale University Press, 1990), appendix, "Table of Loans Floated in London." The above amounts do not include loans to European states in these years, notably Russia, Denmark, Greece, and Naples, nor loans raised in financial markets other than London, all of which are detailed in the table.

[48]Thomas, *Crisis of 1825*, appendix, p. 32. The numbers are based on Wetenhal's records.

success of the South American company flotations inspired the promotion of more domestic and foreign mining companies. Altogether, no less than seventy-four mining companies were projected in the years 1824–1825.[49] The snowball rolled fast, and, inspired by the popularity of mining companies, new companies of all kinds soon appeared. These included gas, insurance, canal, railroad, steam, investment, and many others of any imaginable, or unimaginable, business. These projected companies numbered 624, an astonishing number, even compared with the optimistic days of the South Sea Bubble, certainly impressive when compared with only 156 companies in existence before 1824.[50] The total nominal capital of these companies was even more amazing, by contemporary standards: £372,173,000.[51]

THE PROGRESS OF THE JOINT-STOCK COMPANIES: 1826–1844

The repeal of the Bubble Act, the abolition of the corporate monopolies in marine insurance and in banking, the diffusion of new technology and of economy of scale all contributed to the spread of the joint-stock companies in England during this period. Table 8.1 follows the listing in the *Course of the Exchange* from the point when its format was extended in the first issue of 1811 (see Chapter 5) until 1834. Except for 1811, the listings are for the first issue of May of the relevant year. The *Exchange* of this period is one of the better indicators of the number of joint-stock companies traded on the London market. The table figures do not include the three moneyed companies (East India, Bank of England, and South Sea), which were listed separately. There is a general trend of increase in the number of companies listed in the *Exchange*, taking into account the short-lived boom of 1825.[52] Increase in the number of joint-stock companies in the transport and utility sectors, namely canals, docks, water supply, and bridges, occurred mainly before 1810. In the period under discussion, increase in these sectors was moderate. In the insurance sector, the increase was more considerable. The joint-stock mining sector expanded in 1824–1825. The gas light companies appeared on the list for the first time in 1815, and their number increased dramatically by 1825. The first iron railways to appear on the

---

[49]English, *Joint-Stock Companies.* Not all of these actually reached maturity, thus their share prices were never quoted.

[50]Ibid., 30–31.

[51]Compared with a total capital of the joint-stock companies in existence prior to 1824 which was £47,936,486 (not including the three moneyed companies), ibid., 31.

[52]The increase between 1811 and 1815 is partly attributed to a change in editorial policy, which broadened the coverage of the *Exchange.*

Table 8.1. *Companies listed in the* Course of the Exchange, *1811–1834*

Sector	1811	1815	1820	1825	1830	1834
Canals	27	61	64	58	64	65
Docks	7	8	10	8	8	9
Insurance	11	19	19	35	28	28
Water supply	8	18	16	16	12	12
Bridges	2	3	4	6	4	4
Roads	1	5	5	7	7	7
Mines		7	9	22	22	19
Gas light		1	18	36	33	34
Iron railways	1	3	5	15	4	11
Literary	2	3	3		3	4
Miscellaneous	2	7	6	55	21	23
Total	61	135	159	258	206	216

Source: Course of the Exchange, Jan. 1, 1811; May 2, 1815; May 2, 1820; May 3, 1825; May 4, 1830; May 6, 1834.

lists were not operated by steam engines, and only a partial picture of the growth in this sector after 1825 is reflected in this table.

In 1834, the stock market entered a new mania of company formation that lasted for about three years, as seen in Table 8.2. The rate of survival of these newly formed companies was low. In fact, many of them never actually went into business. This company formation mania, like previous ones in the 1690s, in 1720, and in 1824–1825, did not really reflect the depth of the stock market or the penetration of the joint-stock form of business organization into the English economy. It only gives some indication of the public's willingness to enter into financial speculation, and which areas of investment seemed more promising or popular. Table 8.2 shows that almost 70 percent of the nominal capital offered during the boom of 1834–1836 concentrated in two sectors: railways and banking. The importance of the railway and the banking sectors for the advancement of the joint-stock form of business organization in the period 1825–1844 is clear from Table 8.3.

Joint-stock banks made their appearance after the abolition of the Bank of England's corporate monopoly in 1826. Their number increased gradually in the late 1820s, more quickly in the early 1830s, especially as nonissuing banks were formed in London after the Act of 1833, and jumped again in 1844. The railway sector followed the path paved by

Table 8.2. *Joint-stock companies promoted, 1834–1837*

Sector	Number of companies	Nominal capital
Railways	88	69,666,000
Mining	71	7,035,200
Navigation	17	3,533,000
Banking	20	23,750,000
Conveyance	9	500,000
Insurance	11	7,600,000
Investment	5	1,730,000
Newspaper	6	350,000
Canal	4	3,655,000
Gas	7	890,000
Cemetery	7	435,000
Miscellaneous	55	16,104,500
Total	300	135,248,700

Source: Appendix no. 4 to Report on Joint-Stock Companies, *Parliamentary Papers*, vol. 7 (1844).

the canal companies and was wholly based on the joint-stock form from its origins. It made a slow start in the early 1820s with the Stockton & Darlington Railway, received much attention in the boom of 1825, but really gathered momentum only after the completion of the Liverpool and Manchester Railway in 1830. The mileage of railway lines opened annually is a better indicator of this pattern of development of the railway sector than the number of acts passed annually. New company formations peaked in two boom periods, one in 1835–1837 and the other beginning in 1843 and culminating toward the end of the decade.

The best contemporary calculations and estimates for the capital invested in joint-stock companies on the eve of the Act of 1844 is probably the one published by Spackman and presented in Table 8.4. In this table, Irish and Scottish banks traded in London were subtracted from Spackman's original numbers. The list prepared by Spackman is more updated and comprehensive than that prepared by Fenn a few years earlier.[53] Yet even this list did not include joint-stock companies not traded at all on

[53]Fenn, *English and Foreign Fund.*

Table 8.3. *Railway and joint-stock banks*

	Railway[a]		Joint-Stock Banks Established[b]	
	Acts passed[c]	Miles opened	Issuing	Nonissuing
1820	1			
1821	2			
1822				
1823	1			
1824	3			
1825	8	26.75		
1826	10	11.25	6	
1827	1	2.75	1	
1828	6	4	3	2
1829	7	6.25	4	
1830	6	46.5	3	
1831	7	42.5	7	1
1832	6	26	10	
1833	9	42.25	12	1
1834	9	89.75	5	3
1835	15	39.75	35	10
1836	30	65.5	7	4
1837	24	137		
1838	5	202.25		5
1839	7	227.25	3	2
1840	3	527.75	2	
1841	3	277.5	1	2
1842	7	163.75	1	1
1843	11	105		1
1844	35	192		19
Total	216	2,235.75	100	51

Source: Railways: M. C. Reed, *Investment in Railways in Britain: 1820–1844—A Study in the Development of the Capital Market* (Oxford University Press, 1975), 2. Banking: Ziegler, *Central Bank*, 10.
[a]Refers to the U.K.
[b]Refers to England.
[c]Includes some acts of extension of lines, not only of new companies.

Table 8.4. *Capital of companies known on the London market, c. 1843*

Sector/Company	Number	Subtotal	Total capital
Bank of England	1	10,914,750 ⎫	
Provincial joint-stock banks ⎱	110[b]	15,000,000[a] ⎬	32,348,250
London joint-stock banks ⎰		6,433,500 ⎭	
East India Company	1		6,000,000
South Sea Company	1		3,662,734
Turnpike trusts			8,774,927
Railways	70		57,447,903
Foreign mining	24		6,464,833
British mining	81		4,500,000
Assurance companies	102		26,000,000
Canals: Main lines ⎱	59	14,362,445 ⎱	17,862,445
Canals: Branches ⎰		3,500,000[a] ⎰	
Dock companies	8		12,077,237
Gas light	27		4,326,870
Water companies	11		2,536,122
Bridge companies	5		2,123,874
Literary institutions	4		1,003,125
Shipping	72		
Land	24		
Asphalt	5		
Cemetery companies	10		25,000,000[a]
Loan companies	15		
Salt	7		
Miscellaneous companies	83		
Total	720		210,128,320

Source: W. F. Spackman, *Statistical Tables of the U.K.* (1843), 157.
[a] Approximate figure.
[b] Based on Ziegler, *Central Bank*, 10.

the London market, nor probably cost-book mining companies, ships whose shares were held under the part-ownership system, or woolen company mills. Returns made to Parliament in 1846 list 947 companies registered following the Act of 1844 as having been in existence before its passage.[54] Like Table 8.4, these returns include many unincorporated

[54]*Parliamentary Papers* (1846), vol. 43, p. 119 ff.

companies that had only started to surface as they received legitimacy. Unfortunately the parliamentary returns did not include any information on capital, thus there is no basis for comparison of the two sources.

The increase in the number and capital of joint-stock companies during the period of 1810–1844, from about £90 million to about £210 million, was linked to the repeal of restrictions, the introduction of new technology, and cyclical booms. One by one, new sectors were conquered by the joint-stock business company, which became a more familiar and integral component of England's economic success and identified with it. This helped to ease the hostility toward investment and trading in shares, as we see in the next chapter. Yet in times of crisis, a finger was pointed at this new creature, its legal status was examined, and it was pushed into contact with the State. The various branches of the State, unwillingly, had to learn how to deal with the business company, both with the growing number of petitions for incorporation and with the growing number of newly formed unincorporated companies that simply ignored the State monopoly over incorporation. Between 1808 and 1812, the courts had to deal with the business company, as is seen in Chapter 9. In 1824–1825, Parliament and the administration had to deal with it for the first time, and then again in 1834–1837 and 1841–1843, as discussed in Chapter 10. These contacts became necessary because of the unsolved legal problems that manifested themselves toward the end of the eighteenth century due to the continuing progress of this form of organization. The timing of the contacts and the character of public discourse were determined primarily by the periodical booms and crises on the share market.

HOSTILITY TO SPECULATION IN SHARES

Hostility to speculation in shares was deeply rooted in several circles in England during the eighteenth and into the nineteenth century. The government did not favor the development of alternatives to its stock, which had become the major tool of management of the national debt and, according to some historians, the sinews of Britain's power and imperial expansion after the Glorious Revolution. The moneyed companies were certainly not interested in competition which would divert investment from their shares and from the government stock they administered. The Bubble Act was the best reflection of these attitudes. Hostility to share speculation resulted also from a paternalistic outlook aimed at saving the poor from the dangers and losses of the share market. Stock speculation was still equated by many with other kinds of gambling, such as the lottery, betting at the races, the *tontine* (an insurance scheme in which the survivor takes all), and the insurance of other people's lives, in terms of both probability of gain and moral condemnation. "Ought the private market of the Stock Exchange to be suffered to exist another moment?" asked an anonymous pamphleteer as late as 1814, referring to it as an evil whose gains fall into "the pockets of gamblers."[55] A similar attitude was held by landowners and other rentiers who were more than willing to settle for the security of the 3 percent fixed interest on government stock, and were suspicious of any risky and short-range investment. A different outlook emphasized the damage to society at large from the diversion of money and time from productive activities into trading in papers. The present section examines the manifestation of this hostility during this period, and its decline in the railway age.

Waves of speculation in shares were a frequent occurrence in England after the Glorious Revolution. A boom of joint-stock company formations took place in 1692–1695. This boom was accompanied by an active speculative market in company shares and ended in the crash of 1695.[56] The unfolding of the South Sea Company's national debt conversion scheme in the years 1719–1720 coincided with the promotion of a large number of unincorporated joint-stock companies, often without any economic base, known as the small bubbles. The South Sea bubble burst in the summer of 1720 as the price of South Sea stock crashed and with it the rest of the market.[57] An outburst of speculative activities in East India stock, following rumors of Lord Clive's success in Bengal, pushed up its price in Change Alley by almost 70 percent between early 1766 and early 1768. The crash that followed, and Clive's active involvement in manipulating share prices, did not improve the image of either the East India Company or of the share market in general.[58] The canal mania, a period of numerous promotions of new canal companies and of a high volume of trade in the secondary share market, reached its peak in 1792. In 1793, this speculative boom too, ended in a crash.[59] Stock market crashes and panics had also taken place in 1733, 1745, 1761–1763 and 1772–1773, in which government stock, rather than company shares, played a leading role.[60]

---

[55]*Stock-Exchange Laid Open, the Cause of the Rise and Fall of the Public Funds Explained* (1814), iii–iv.

[56]Scott, *Constitution and Finance of Joint-Stock Companies*, vol. 1, p. 326ff.

[57]See the discussion in Chapter 3 on the South Sea Bubble for a detailed survey.

[58]Huw V. Bowen, "Lord Clive and Speculation in East India Company Stock, 1766," *Historical Journal* 30, no. 4 (1987), 905–920.

[59]Ward, *Canal Building*, 86–96.

[60]The literature of financial crises is quite extensive. For a contemporary account, see John Francis, *Chronicles and Characters of the Stock Exchange* (1849). Three recent accounts of eighteenth-century crises are: Mirowski, *Birth of Business*, 215–258; Hoppit, "Financial Crises," 39–58; Neal, *Financial Capitalism*, 166–179.

Most of these periodic stock market crashes were followed by an outcry bringing the question of the development of the stock market to the public agenda and eventually to Parliament. The first statutes to limit the new practices of the stock market were passed in 1697, following the crash of the mid-1690s. These were to limit the number of brokers in the City of London and to place restrictions upon dealings in Bank of England stock.[61] The statute regarding brokerage was extended once in 1700, and again, in a modified version, in 1708.[62] Following the burst of the South Sea Bubble, in December of 1720, a bill was brought in "for the better Establishment of publick Credit by preventing, for the future, the infamous Practice of Stock-Jobbing." In February 1721 [O.S.], another bill was petitioned "for preventing Frauds in Transferring of Shares in the Capital Stock of any Company or Companies established by Act of Parliament."[63] The crash of 1733 facilitated the passage of "An Act to prevent the infamous Practice of Stock-jobbing" in the following year. The Act of 1734 was made perpetual three years later, in 1737.[64] These acts aimed at prohibiting various types of dealings in options, futures, and on margins. It also made it compulsory for brokers to record transactions in their books. Sir John Barnard, "the chief apostle of financial purity," was to lead a battle that lasted more than two decades against the stock market.[65] He was the sponsor of no less than five bills during that period, the two that led to the Acts of 1734 and 1737, and bills in 1733, the crisis year of 1745, and 1756 that did not go through.[66] The speculation in East India stock in 1766 led to an act the following year that limited the fictitious splitting of shares and the manipulation of voting qualifications. The high volume of trade in the stock market and the eventual crash led to two more bills in 1771 and 1773. In 1793, as the canal mania was gathering momentum, a bill "to Regulate the Transfer of Shares in all Undertakings for making Navigable Canals" was introduced, once again in an attempt to prevent speculation in shares.[67]

The growth of the stock market, and especially the appearance of speculative trading in stock, and of a group of specialized stockbrokers and stockjobbers, was not very well received in England of the eighteenth century. Until the last decade of the century, attempts were made to prohibit "the infamous practice of stockjobbing" and to check the

[61]8 & 9 Wm. III c.20 (1697) and 8 & 9 Wm. III c.32 (1697).
[62]11 & 12 Wm. III c.13 (1700); 6 Anne c.68 (1708).
[63]*Commons' Journal* 19 (1720), 392; 19 (1721), 740.
[64]7 Geo. II c.8 (1734); 10 Geo. II c.8 (1737).
[65]Dickson, *Financial Revolution*, 519.
[66]*Commons' Journal* 22 (1733), 10, 133, 201; 25 (1745), 88; 27 (1756), 546.
[67]The bill was ordered to be printed on April 24, 1793.

development of the share market. Mistrust of the stock market reached new peaks after each of the crashes that occurred during the century. This is not to say that the market did not advance, but that along with its advance, a persistent nucleus of hostility remained.

The origins of animosity toward stockbrokers can be found in the late seventeenth century. An anonymous pamphleteer of 1724 was clear in his animosity to stockjobbing: "The irregular method of acquiring riches by stock-jobbing . . . [is] contrary to the natural and clear dictates of reason . . . and sacred rules of truth, justice and equity."[68]

Postlethwayt in his *Universal Dictionary of Trade and Commerce* in 1774 gave no less than eight reasons why stockjobbing is still "detrimental to the commerce of this nation."[69] Speculation in shares

turns most of the current coin of England out of the channels of trade, and the heads of all its merchants and traders off their proper business. It enriches those who are instrumental to bring no reaches into the nation by fair and honourable traffic, and it ruins the innocent. . . . It hath changed honest commerce into bubbling; our traders into projectors; industry into tricking.[70]

Thomas Mortimer declared in the preface to his best-selling *Everyman His Own Broker* that the grand object of his work was to persuade the investors to transact their own business, because this would be "the only effectual method that can be taken to reduce the great number of stock-jobbers; to diminish the extensive operations of stock-jobbing."[71] The late editions of Mortimer's book carried his message into the early nineteenth century.

Hostility to stock speculation contributed to the strict regulation of brokers' admittance and activities by the City of London. Francis Baily tried to fight these regulations in the first decade of the nineteenth century, in his *The Rights of Stock Brokers Defended*.[72] But when he took his case to court, both in the City and in Westminster, he lost and was prohibited from engaging as a stockbroker, without being admitted by the Court of Aldermen and fulfilling the other conditions set by the City.

An antiquated common-law doctrine held that some forms of manipulation of prices in the market – forestalling, engrossing, and regrating – were illegal. This doctrine was originally directed at the market for essential food supplies, particularly corn. Yet there were attempts to apply it, or at least its general spirit, to the trade in shares. It was argued

---

[68] *An Essay on the Practice of Stock-Jobbing and Some Remarks on the Right Use and Regular Improvement of Money* (1724), 83.
[69] Malachy Postlethwayt, *The Universal Dictionary of Trade and Commerce*, 4th ed. (1774), see "Stock-Jobbing."
[70] Ibid., see "Actions."
[71] Mortimer, *Every Man His Own Broker*, 18.
[72] Francis Baily, *The Rights of Stock Brokers Defended* (1806).

that speculation in shares was, by its nature, manipulative and led to artificial market prices of shares. According to the concept, this manipulation was illegal, just as manipulation in food prices was illegal. Thus, in addition to the statutory limitations on the share market, a common-law limitation was argued to apply as well.[73] Adam Smith, himself a strong opponent of these common-law doctrines and their statutory backing, was aware of the public opinion in this regard: "The popular fear of engrossing and forestalling may be compared to the popular terrors and suspicions of witchcraft."[74] An early nineteenth-century pamphleteer wrote that these doctrines were established "when Russia was almost unknown, and its Czar a half-clothed calmuck," yet his call for abandoning them in the face of the new reality of commerce was still in vain.[75]

By the early nineteenth century, suspicion of speculation in shares, professional dealers in stock, and the stock market itself were still widespread. This suspicion turned to hostility toward the form of business organization that gave rise to all of these, the joint-stock company. This did not amount to a legal ban on the share market as such, and not everyone joined in resentment of the share market. But as it was clear that further advancement of the joint-stock company would result in further development of the share market, many objected to both.

The objections to the development of the share market were eased as the holding of shares in some of the more respectable sectors of the economy became widespread. The first of these sectors was canals, particularly following the canal mania of the 1790s and the introduction of preference canal shares after 1800. The number of canals, their capital, and the number of shareholders all increased dramatically in this period. The expansion of canal share-holding and the legitimization of this sort of investment were primarily a provincial phenomenon, though there were, undoubtedly, many holders of canal shares in London, and some trading in these shares did take place in the metropolis.[76] The next sectors in which the share-holding became relatively widespread were the various utilities: docks, waterworks, and gas lighting, in the early

[73]Joseph Chitty, *A Treatise on the Laws of Commerce and Manufactures, and the Contracts Relating Thereto*, 4 vols. (1820–1824), vol. 2, pp. 259–263. Interestingly, Chitty discussed these common-law offenses and the Bubble Act under the same section, "Of the Protection of Trade from Injuries." By an Act of 1772 (12 Geo. III c.71), the ancient statutes that fixed penalties for these common-law offenses were repealed; however, the common-law offenses themselves remained in force until 1844. See, for example, *Rex v. Waddington*, 1 East 143 (1800).

[74]Smith, *The Wealth of Nations*, 500–501.

[75]*Lawyers and Legislators; Or, Notes on the American Mining Companies* (1825), 83.

[76]Ward, *Canal Building*.

decades of the nineteenth century. London was to lead the process of widening the base of share-holding in these sectors. London was also the focus of vast public investment in shares of South American loans and newly promoted companies in the boom year of 1825. Investment in joint-stock banks was allowed in 1826 and became common, first in the provinces and after 1833 also in London. But the most significant breakthrough came with the railway age, starting in the mid-1830s. Gourvish was eloquent about the effect of this new age: "It was in the buying and selling of marketable securities that the railway extended the geographical and occupational base of investment, thereby transforming the Victorian capital market."[77]

The railway age turned the London Stock Exchange from one whose main business was trade in government stock, as had been the case since the early financial revolution, to one more oriented toward company securities. The railway age also gave rise to the formation of institutionalized stock exchanges in the major provincial towns, Liverpool and Manchester in 1836 and Leeds, Glasgow, and Edinburgh in 1844–1845.[78] The London capital market and provincial markets became more integrated in this period, as London capital was invested in provincial railways, and improved communication eased the flow of information.[79]

The major argument made in the present context is that the hostility to speculation in shares was defeated primarily from below. A relatively small group of middle-class entrepreneurs promoted new projects, in upward swings of the business cycle and primarily in boom years. They were helped by the repeal of old monopolistic restrictions and by the introduction of new technology. They were able to present an alternative to government stock which was better-yielding (in most years), not too risky (except in full-scale market crashes), and invested in relatively respectable undertakings (infrastructure and other tangibles) that were considered to benefit the general public. Promotions by this group of entrepreneurs were well received as a legitimate pattern of investment, particularly by traders, professionals, and manufacturers, but also by some gentlemen and aristocrats.[80] Thus, within a relatively short period

[77]T. R. Gourvish, *Railways and the British Economy: 1830–1914* (London: Macmillan, 1980), 17. See also M. C. Reed, *Investment in Railways in Britain: 1820–1844 – A Study in the Development of the Capital Market* (Oxford University Press, 1975), and Seymour A. Broadbridge, *Studies in Railway Expansion and the Capital Market in England: 1825–1873* (London: Frank Cass, 1970).

[78]Thomas, *Provincial Stock Exchanges.*

[79]Reed, *Investment in Railways*, 99ff; R. C. Michie, "The London Stock Exchange and the British Securities Market: 1850–1914," *Economic History Review* 38, no. 1 (1985), 61. However, see also Moshe Buchinsky and Ben Polak, "The Emergence of a National Capital Market in England: 1710–1880," *Journal of Economic History* 53, no. 1 (1993), 1–24, for a recent study which suggests strong links by the 1820s.

[80]See Reed, *Investment in Railways*, chaps. 4–7, and Broadbridge, *Railway Expansion*, chap. 4.

of time, the number of investors in railway companies overturned old hostilities. This was accomplished without any significant support from above: the government, the moneyed companies, the political economists, or the more reactionary component of the landowning elite.

9

The Joint-Stock Company in Court

Chapter 3 left the history of the Bubble Act shortly after its enactment in 1720. Chapter 6 described the difficulties that the unincorporated company faced during the eighteenth century in common law and in equity, with only a glimpse at the Bubble Act. It is now time to combine the two stories, as, in 1808, the unincorporated company and the act meet in court for the first time since 1721. I argue in this chapter that this first meeting, and the frequent litigation that followed, turned the courts into a major playing field between 1808 and 1844. Though the only form of organization disputed was the unincorporated company, results of the litigation eventually had a considerable affect on the fate of the business corporation as well. This judicial playing field also greatly affected a parallel field: Parliament. The two major pieces of legislation of this period, the repeal of the Bubble Act in 1825 and the General Incorporation Act of 1844 (which are discussed in Chapter 10) were a reaction to dramatic shifts in judge-made law. They cannot be understood without a full account of their judicial context. This context includes judge-made doctrine produced in a stream of formal court decisions. These decisions, in turn, cannot be understood without an awareness of the institutions in which they were given – the courts – and the personages that shaped them – the judges. The present chapter begins with an examination of the social and intellectual origins of the English judiciary in the early nineteenth century.[1] It then analyzes the cases that interpreted the Bubble Act and applied it to various unincorporated associations up to 1825. Finally, it explores the means by which some judges tried to revive or invent a common-law prohibition on the formation of unincorporated companies following the repeal of the Bubble Act, and how other judges countered this conservative drive.

---

[1]The institutional background, and the different characteristics of common-law courts and of Chancery, have been discussed in Chapter 1 and are not repeated here.

THE JUDICIARY

Around the turn of the nineteenth century, the English judiciary was still gentlemanly and isolated from the business community. The social origins of its superior court judges were predominantly the landowning class or the respectable professions: sons of barristers, clergymen, and doctors. A very small number of judges came from merchant families, and it was only after 1790 that the first son of a businessman made his way to the bench.[2] The relative isolation of judges from the business community continued during their educational career, in the great public schools where many of them acquired secondary education, and the elite colleges of Cambridge and Oxford, attended by 65 to 70 percent of the future judges, and persisted in the four Inns of Court, a mandatory station for common-law barristers and thus for future judges in the common-law courts.[3] Their professional careers took them even further from the business class. They met daily at the courts, socialized in the dining halls of the Inns, and had only limited contact with their business clients, as solicitors mediated between clients and barristers. By the time they were appointed to the bench from their prominent positions at the top of the Bar, as Law Officers, King's Counsel, or Serjeants, they were entrenched in the social network of the gentlemanly profession and in the ethos of the landed class. Most of the judges (73 percent) were landowners, with property comparable in value to that of the gentry, and some left sizable fortunes of more than £100,000.[4] Their sons were born into the landed class and those of them that had to develop a nongentlemanly career tended to enter the upper professions; almost none became merchants or businessmen.[5]

If the upward mobility of some middle-class groups during the eighteenth century was slow in affecting the House of Commons, a somewhat representative political institution, it was even slower in affecting

[2]In the period 1727–1760, 45% of the appointed judges were sons of landowners, 25%, sons of professionals (mostly barristers and clergymen), and only 7% sons of merchants. In the period 1760–1790, 26% of the judges were sons of landowners; 56% sons of professionals, and only 6% sons of merchants. In the period 1790–1820, 17% were sons of landowners, 41% sons of professionals, 17% sons of merchants, and, for the first time, 10% were sons of businessmen. The rise of the sons of merchants and businessmen was not as dramatic in the latter period as one might think, because they numbered only eight judges and some were appointed only in the closing years of the period. Only toward the middle of the nineteenth century did their weight became more significant. Daniel Duman, *The Judicial Bench in England: 1727–1875 – The Reshaping of a Professional Elite* (London: Royal Historical Society, 1982), 51.

[3]Ibid., 38–40, 43, 45.

[4]Ibid., 126–128, 142–143.

[5]Ibid., 165–167.

the judiciary. A merchant who made a fortune in the India trade could buy his way into Parliament but not into the judiciary. Even his son, if not brought up properly from an early age, could not be assimilated into the socially and professionally demanding higher echelons of the Bar and thus make his way into the exclusive judiciary. The gap between the mercantile and early industrial social changes and their reflection in the judiciary could be of two, three, or even more generations. The long and traditional process of professionalization and socialization leading to the judiciary resulted in the fact that the few judges of business origins who made it acquired a conservative landed and legal ethos. The detachment of the judiciary from the practice of commerce and manufacturing, and from daily problems faced by men of business, was total.[6]

Only toward the middle of the nineteenth century did things begin to change. A professional ethos gradually replaced the gentlemen's ethos. Judges began to invest more of their fortunes outside the land and to divide their estates in a middle-class manner rather than using the landed-class family settlement which favored the elder son, and their sons turned less to land and more to the bar and other upper professions.[7] This corresponds to the tendency of barristers, beginning in the 1830s, to invest in the bond and share market in addition to investment in land. But even in the mid-nineteenth century, most barristers who invested in personal property were only passive investors, and less than 10 percent took an active role as directors of business companies.[8] Solicitors and other attorneys had stronger middle-class social characteristics and were undoubtedly more involved in active business from an earlier period, but they were not part of the bar–bench complex. They were involved in the formation of unincorporated companies, in raising money for all sorts of enterprises, and in the drafting and lobbying of incorporation bills in Parliament. Their important role in the development of the business company was partly discussed elsewhere in this

[6]Lord Mansfield, despite his landed origins, was able, as a mature chief justice, to reach out into the City. He was highly exceptional in this respect.

[7]Duman, *Judicial Bench*, 142–144, 166, 169.

[8]Daniel Duman, *The English and Colonial Bars in the Nineteenth Century* (London: CroomHelm, 1983), 163–164. For a more adaptive view of the bar, arguing for an earlier opening to capitalist influence, see David Lemmings, *Gentlemen and Barristers: The Inns of Court and the English Bar 1680–1730* (Oxford: Clarendon Press, 1990). However, Lemmings focuses mainly on institutional changes in the relationship between the Inns of Court and the bar, and does not indicate a significant social or cultural shift. In addition, his survey ends in 1730, early in the period discussed here, and may reflect the revolutionary bar of the seventeenth century and not the more conservative bar of the eighteenth century. For a fully referenced survey of the state of the research on the legal professions, see Sugarman and Rubin, "Towards a New History," 84–99.

book and deserves further research.[9] From the middle of the century, connections were forged between sections of the legal profession and business enterprise, as a growing number of barristers joined the solicitors and built their careers and fortunes around the rise of the railway and business in general.[10] But these developments in the legal profession, and later also in the judiciary, are beyond the temporal framework of this book.

Turning from generalizations about the bench to the individual judges who shaped decisions during this period, we first focus on the Court of Chancery, which was, as seen in Chapter 6, the major arena for litigation in matters of partnerships, trusts, and unincorporated companies. The two Lord Chancellors with the longest terms during this period, Philip York, Lord Hardwicke (1737–1756), and John Scott, Lord Eldon (1801–1806, 1807–1827), were both conservatives and both stressed the systematization and application of general principles, proper procedures, and past precedents at the expense of achieving the fairest and most equitable outcome in each specific case.[11] Both valued land as the fundamental basis of the society and to a large degree supported the status quo favoring the landowners. Both were of middle-class origins: Hardwicke was the son of a Dover attorney, and Eldon, the son of a Newcastle-upon-Tyne coal factor whose aim was assimilation into the landed class. Both were ardent guardians of upper-class values. They invested the fortunes they made as chancellors in the purchase of huge landed estates.[12] Eldon was also a very openly devoted ultraconservative Tory

[9]For recent important contributions to this field of research, see David Sugarman, "Simple Images and Complex Realities: English Lawyers and Their Relationship to Business and Politics, 1750–1950," *Law and History Review* 11, no. 2 (1993), and "Bourgeois Collectivism, Professional Power and the Boundaries of the State. The Private and Public Life of the Law Society, 1825 to 1914," *International Journal of the Legal Profession* 3, no. 1/2 (1996), 81–135.

[10]Kostal, *English Railway Capitalism.*

[11]See Clyde Elliot Croft, "Philip Yorke, First Earl of Hardwicke: An Assessment of His Legal Career," Ph.D. thesis, Cambridge University, 1982; Horace Twiss, *The Public and Private Life of Lord Chancellor Eldon* (1844). Eldon's reputation as a conservative is well known, and some of his judgments are discussed elsewhere in the present work. Hardwicke received a more mixed press. But Croft concludes his dissertation, the best available study on Hardwicke, with a clear and convincing evaluation. "The maintenance of settled rules of property was essential to the preservation of the social order, an aspect of preservation of the *status quo* which appears to have been foremost in Hardwicke's mind. . . . Thus Hardwicke's conservatism, his extreme care to follow precedent, even at the expense of his own views, mitigated against all but the most technical development of equity doctrine; and in most areas of equity these 'property' and 'family' considerations were ever uppermost in his mind" (Croft, "Philip Yorke," 476).

[12]Duman, *Judicial Bench*, 129–130.

who did not hesitate to exploit his position by politicizing judicial appointments and dominating the House of Lords. Their conservatism resulted in a reactionary attitude toward innovation and a less than favorable atmosphere toward men of business in the Court of Chancery. This was unfortunate for those entrepreneurs who had no alternative but to organize their concerns in the form of the unincorporated joint-stock company. As we shall see, when we turn to specific cases, Lord Chancellor Eldon was the key figure in questioning the legality of the unincorporated joint-stock company in statute law and common law and the one who destabilized the prevailing practice of men of business in that respect.

Ironically, the common-law Court of King's Bench, inspired by its Chief Justice William Mansfield (1754–1788), was more responsive in the second half of the eighteenth century to the new needs of commerce and industry.[13] Mansfield preferred to spend much of his King's Bench judicial time conducting trials involving City of London businessmen, at Guildhall (while avoiding the lengthy journeys of the assizes to the country). In Guildhall, he developed the practice of having special merchant juries determine facts and customs in commercial litigation. It is even rumored that he actually sat in City coffeehouses discussing business practices with their attendants. Indeed, his interest in business practices enabled him to bring about reform in several fields of law, notably insurance, negotiable instruments, and patents. Mansfield was, however, exceptional and his era was atypical. Indeed, even Mansfield was conservative, both in his jurisprudential conceptions and in his doctrinal judgments in fields of law such as property, bankruptcy, and, what interests us, corporations and partnerships (fields not often discussed by his court). The misfortune of the unincorporated company was that, for systemic and structural reasons, it much more often fell within the jurisdiction of the more conservative of the two branches of the English legal system of the period.

Mansfield's successors as Chief Justices of King's Bench, Lord Kenyon (1788–1802) and Lord Ellenborough (1802–1818), were notoriously conservative in their jurisprudential notions and opposed modernization

---

[13]For Mansfield's reformist and innovative impact on commercial law, see David Lieberman, *The Province of Legislation Determined, Legal Theory in Eighteenth-Century Britain* (Cambridge University Press, 1989), 99–121; James Oldham, *The Mansfield Manuscripts and the Growth of English Law in the Eighteenth Century*, 2 vols. (University of North Carolina Press, 1992), vol. 1, pp. 44–160, 195–208; Gerald J. Postema, *Bentham and the Common Law Tradition* (Oxford: Clarendon Press, 1989), 8–9, 34–36. For an evaluation of Mansfield's legal perception, that views it as more conservative, see Michael Lobban, *The Common Law and English Jurisprudence 1760–1850* (Oxford: Clarendon Press, 1991), 98–115.

of legal reform through common law.[14] Though Ellenborough was originally a Whig and even served as a cabinet member in the Whig-dominated "Ministry of all the Talents," he deserted the party and later in life moved toward the more conservative wing of the Tory party. Ellenborough, who delivered some of the major judgments concerning unincorporated companies between 1808 and 1812, was considered to be almost as reactionary in his judicial outlook as Eldon. He objected to any legislative intervention in the province of common law and rejected many of the novel doctrines presented before him in court.

THE REVIVAL OF THE BUBBLE ACT

The wave of new joint-stock promotions and of speculations in shares during the first decade of the nineteenth century raised echoes of 1720. The history of the South Sea Bubble remained in the public eye for more than eighty years, mainly through the works of William Maitland and Adam Anderson.[15] These works narrated the events of the bubble year as part of larger chronological surveys, without analyzing the exact causes and effects of either the crash or the Bubble Act. Shortly after the turn of the nineteenth century, as speculations in the financial markets gathered momentum, the memory of the South Sea Bubble was revived. The old narratives were referred to, reprinted, and circulated, and the events of 1720 became better-known in the 1800s than they probably had been at any time since the 1720s.[16] The bubble was used by foes of the joint-stock company and the stock market to awaken suspicion of both. Entrepreneurs who promoted and invested in these companies and their supporters found themselves on the defensive. It was for them to convince the public that the companies of the 1800s were different from and better than those of 1720.[17]

This awakening interest in the South Sea Bubble brought the Bubble Act into the limelight, and by the early nineteenth century, the act was mistakenly considered by many contemporaries to have been a reaction to the market crash of 1720. The highest legal authority of the late eighteenth century, William Blackstone, expressed this fallacy clearly in his *Commentaries* of 1765–1769.[18] He was joined in this misconception

---

[14]Atiyah, *Freedom of Contract*, 361–369.

[15]Maitland, *History of London*; Anderson, *Origin of Commerce*.

[16]David Macpherson, *Annals of Commerce: Manufactures, Fishing and Navigation* (1805); *An Account of the South Sea Scheme and a Number of Other Bubbles . . . With a Few Remarks upon Some Schemes Which Are Now in Agitation* (1806).

[17]Philopatris, *Observations on Public Institutions, Monopolies and Joint-Stock Companies* (1807); Henry Day, *A Defense of Joint-Stock Companies* (1808).

[18]Blackstone, *Commentaries*, vol. 4, p.117.

concerning the timing and rationale of the Bubble Act by other jurists and men of business. Many perceived the Bubble Act as having been an effective remedy for the evils of 1720 and, thus, just as effective a remedy for the ills of the 1800s.

Litigation: 1808–1812

By 1808, opponents of the unincorporated joint-stock company moved from warning the unwary public against a flood of new schemes to concrete legal action. An anonymous individual with an interest in proclaiming illegal two recently promoted companies – the London Paper Manufacturing Company and the London Distillery Company – decided to take the matter to court. That individual may have had a business dispute with the promoter of these companies. A normal course of action in such a dispute would have been to sue the promoter, or the companies, based on a common-law action that suits best the circumstances of the dispute (be it in contract, tort, etc.). Instead he chose to resort to an old statute, the Bubble Act. Even when reviving this old act, he could sue the promoter of these schemes, a business adventurer named Ralph Dodd, in a civil action for treble damages, an action available through Clause 20 of the Bubble Act. Yet he chose the less obvious path, which placed the State and the Law Officers on his side. Based on Clause 19 of the act, he initiated criminal proceedings by way of information, a method not very common in King's Bench by that period. Thus, it was not new government policy, but rather private vested interests that revived the Bubble Act. The Attorney General was forced to pull the act out of the statute books for the first time since 1722 because of the initiative of that private informer.[19] Thus, in 1808, the Attorney-General moved for criminal prosecution against Ralph Dodd, the publisher of the prospectus for the two promotions, on the grounds that the promotions, which offered subscriptions to transferable shares, were in violation of the Bubble Act.

The King v. Dodd reached the Court of King's Bench in May 1808.[20] Dodd's counsels argued that the Bubble Act calls for a distinction between mischievous and advantageous schemes and defines only the former as criminal. In addition, they argued that the act was obsolete, that

---

[19]To be precise, the second part of the act. The first part of the act that deals with the two marine insurance companies was resorted to on several occasions during this period. See *Watts v. Brooks,* 3 Ves. Jun. 612 (1798); *Knowles v. Haughton,* 11 Ves. Jun. 168 (1805). In these two cases an interesting question arose, whether a partner in a marine insurance partnership, supposedly illegal according to the marine monopoly clause of the Bubble Act (s. 12), was entitled to equitable remedy of account against other partners.

[20]*The King v. Dodd,* 9 East 516 (1808).

by subscribing for shares the informer had lost his goodwill, and that such a severe criminal prosecution should not be initiated by a private informer. The Attorney General argued that the act was not in use because the evil it was intended to cure had indeed been cured after 1720. Thus the act itself was not obsolete; there simply had been no need to employ it for eighty-seven years, and now that the evil resurfaced, it was again called for. In addition, he argued that the act made no distinction, in terms of purpose, between the various unincorporated joint-stock companies. All such companies were considered mischievous and were prohibited by the act. The court, led by Lord Ellenborough, sought a pragmatic decision, avoiding an authoritative interpretation of the act or criminal sanction to the defendant. It decided not to interfere for the time being, explaining that the statute had not been in use for eighty-seven years, that the Attorney General could still prosecute ex officio at a later stage if necessary, and that the informer himself had not personally been adversely affected by the project. However, Ellenborough stressed that "it is not because we think that the facts brought before us are not within the penalty of the law."[21] Furthermore, the Court added this warning: "as a matter of prudence to the parties concerned . . . they should forbear to carry into execution this mischievous project, or any other speculative project of the like nature, founded on joint stock and transferable shares: and we hope that this intimation will prevent others from engaging in the like mischievous and illegal projects."[22]

The obiter in the Dodd case, though it had no direct impact on the parties involved, nor did it serve as an interpretative precedent for future employment of the Bubble Act in other cases, shocked the English business community.[23] The Bubble Act, considered to be obsolete or inapplicable for generations by practical businessmen, if not by more formalistic jurists, was alive again. How should it be interpreted in light of its ambiguous wording? Would it apply to all unincorporated joint-stock companies established since the middle of the eighteenth century and to the dozens of new projects being promoted after the turn of the nineteenth century? The practice of business organization of at least two generations had been placed under severe legal doubt and was now being examined by the courts and at their mercy.

The dramatic consequences of the decision in the Dodd case were best

---

[21]Ibid., 527.

[22]Ibid., 528.

[23]For a recent comparison of the Dodd and later cases with the legal position of the joint-stock company in contemporary France, see Alceste Santuari, "The Joint Stock Company in Nineteenth Century England and France: *The King v. Dodd* and the *Code de Commerce*," *Legal History* 14, no. 1 (1993), 39–52.

appreciated and explained in 1808 by Henry Day, a solicitor for the British Ale Brewery, the next company in line for court litigation:

When it is considered that property to the vast amount of nearly one hundred and fifty millions is involved in this contest, and that, if the doctrine insisted upon as the true construction of the 6th George I [the Bubble Act] be correct, (to say nothing of rendering some of the noblemen and commoners of the realm subject to indictments,) not only the breweries and distilleries . . . but all the manufacturing and other companies, which are organized merely by a deed of trust, although they have been permitted by the legislature to grow to most productive maturity, will be swept in the general wreck.[24]

Day went on to explain that even without being swept away altogether, the unincorporated companies "are necessarily paralyzed and placed in a state of anxious suspense, not only for their property but their persons (this act inflicting criminal punishments,) until the court shall declare their construction of the act in question."[25]

A stream of cases regarding the applicability of the Bubble Act and the legal status of unincorporated companies followed the Dodd case. The British Ale Brewery (*Buck v. Buck* (1808)),[26] Philanthropic Annuity Society (*Rex v. Stratton* (1809)),[27] Globe Insurance Company (*Metcalf v. Bruin* (1810)),[28] Birmingham Flour and Bread Company (*The King v. Webb* (1811)),[29] Greenwich Union Building Society (*Pratt v. Hutchinson* (1812)),[30] and Golden Lane Brewery (*Brown v. Holt* (1812))[31] were all subject to court litigation within five years of the Dodd case. For the first time, the courts had the chance to express and elaborate their opinions on matters of business organization as they stood in statute and common law.

After the harsh warning by Ellenborough (in the Dodd case) and the decisions regarding the British Ale Brewery (by James Mansfield in Common Pleas – the Buck case) and the Philanthropic Annuity Society (by Ellenborough in King's Bench – the Stratton case) finding them within the Bubble Act and thus without legal standing, the legality of the unincorporated company seemed to be doomed. Both common-law courts offered strict prohibitive interpretations of the wording of the act. They were not willing to be instrumental to economic developments and interpret the act in keeping with the changing reality between 1720 and 1808.

[24]Day, *Joint-Stock Companies*, 2.
[25]Ibid., 3.
[26]*Buck v. Buck*, 1 Camp. 547 (1808).
[27]Referred to in ibid., 549.
[28]*Metcalf v. Bruin*, 12 East 400 (1810).
[29]*The King v. Webb*, 14 East 406 (1811).
[30]*Pratt v. Hutchinson*, 15 East 511 (1812).
[31]*Brown v. Holt*, 4 Taunt. 587 (1812).

Yet in 1810, in *Metcalf v. Bruin*, the Court of King's Bench showed the first signs of retreat and of a more positive approach to the legality of unincorporated companies. Though it was argued that Globe Insurance was an unincorporated body, the court ignored its doubtful legality in light of the Bubble Act. It did not declare that all business transacted by the trustees in the name of the company was void by virtue of being made on behalf of an unincorporated company, but rather skipped to an examination of the specific disputed bond. Unlike the two previous cases, where the illegality of the company determined the final outcome, in this case the question was bypassed. What may have made the difference was the fact that the Globe was a more significant and respectable company which had already obtained an act to sue and be sued using a common name three years earlier, thus giving it some degree of recognition in law.

The case of *The King v. Webb* in 1811 continued the same trend. It was the first case in which the Bubble Act was discussed in detail and interpreted narrowly by the Court. Lord Ellenborough, who delivered the judgment in this case, seems to have changed his mind considerably since issuing his general warning in the Dodd case some three years earlier. It may, however, have been a conservative rather than an innovative approach which led to this shift. He may have realized that the decision in *The King v. Dodd* caused a scare far beyond what he had intended, and that such a scare could lead to a much more radical change than he wanted to bring about. In any case, in *Webb*, Ellenborough examined in detail the wording of Sections 18 and 19 of the act. He came to the conclusion that the enacting part of Section 18, as well as Section 19, should be interpreted as subject to the qualifications of the preamble to Section 18. In simple words, not every association that pretends to act as a body corporate, or every undertaking with transferable stock, is meant to be illegal by the Bubble Act:[32]

Upon this view of the statute we think it impossible to say, that it makes a substantive offence to raise a large capital by small subscriptions, without any regard to the nature and quality of the object for which the capital is raised, or whatever might be the purpose to which it was to be applied.

Only those of the above undertakings that also met the general description of the preamble, an undertaking "which manifestly tended to the common grievance, prejudice and inconvenience," should be held as illegal, according to Lord Ellenborough in *Webb*. In this case, the company under discussion, the Birmingham Flour and Bread Company, was considered to be beneficial; it supplied large quantities of cheap bread to the lower classes of Birmingham, and the act therefore did not apply to

[32]*The King v. Webb*, 14 East 406, 420 (1811).

it. Ellenborough, who was probably not completely convinced by the above narrow interpretation of the Bubble Act, added another factual argument to support his conclusion. The transferability of shares in the company was, in fact, qualified by various conditions, and irrespective of favoring a wide or a narrow interpretation of the act, the company was out of its scope.

In *Pratt v. Hutchinson* (1812), the question of the legality of a Building Society, the Greenwich Union, was raised. The defendant, who was in debt on bond to the society, raised the argument that the society was illegal according to the Bubble Act, and thus his obligation to the society was void. Ellenborough and his fellow judges at King's Bench again used the two lines of argument used in *Webb*. By noting that the society was not prejudicial to the public and that its shares were not freely transferable, they bent again to the factual component and relied on the consideration of the jury. In not declaring all the unincorporated companies illegal, but at the same time not legalizing them altogether, they avoided a conclusive and authoritative interpretation of the Bubble Act.

In that same year, the Court of Common Pleas was called on for a similar matter in *Brown and Another v. Holt*. The defendant, once again, tried to escape his obligation by arguing that the plaintiffs were actually the trustees for the Golden Lane Brewery, which was an unincorporated company with transferable stock and thus guilty of nuisance under the Bubble Act. The court took the same approach as the King's Bench had taken in Pratt's case, that is, turned the problem into a factual one. "They refused however, in a matter of so great importance, considering how much property was at this time embarked in speculations of a like nature, to entertain the [general] question upon this summary proceeding."[33]

Within a short five years, between 1808 and 1812, at least seven cases concerning the scope of the Bubble Act and the legality of the unincorporated business undertaking reached the superior courts of common law. This is indeed a striking number as compared with not even one reported case on these issues throughout the preceding eighty-seven years. This phenomenon is explained, at least in part, by the unprecedented expansion of the unincorporated company in the closing decades of the eighteenth century. When the development of the unincorporated company combined with a new wave of promotions and speculations, the conditions for court litigation arose. The first stage was a revival of the collective memory of 1720, coupled with public debates on the Bubble Act; the second was a decision by the Attorney General in one specific case to support a private informer and try to enforce the act in

---

[33]*Brown v. Holt*, 4 Taunt. 587 (1812).

criminal proceedings; and only then, in the third stage, was there a flow of civil actions of private litigates wishing to benefit from the revival of the act. The seven cases discussed above did not develop logically and linearly from one to the next. The first three judgments in 1808 and 1809 gave the impression that the Bubble Act was to be actively revived and given a wide interpretation. The fourth case, in 1810, in a way the turning point, bypassed the act. The last three cases, in 1811 and 1812, sought a way to limit its applicability. They served as an attempt to block the flow of litigation in which parties tried to avoid obligations toward unincorporated companies with which they had transacted.

Despite the change of tone in the approach of the common-law courts in the later cases, no coherent doctrine had emerged by 1812 regarding the appropriate interpretation of the act. It became clear that the act was not a dead letter and that some unincorporated companies were illegal according to the act. But to the crucial question of which unincorporated companies were void and illegal and which were legal, no conclusive answer was offered by 1812. If it were left to the jury to decide, on a case-to-case basis, whether or not a specific undertaking was of mischievous purpose, predictability as to the legal outcome of dealings with unincorporated companies would be lost. If, on the other hand, the court were to decide conclusively on the proper interpretation of the act, what would be the fate of all the undertakings which would only then realize that they had been illegal for years? The more respectable and public-spirited a company was, the more assured its members could feel about its legality, but no unincorporated company could be certain of being held as legal. It should be noted that doubts regarding the legality of the unincorporated company within the Bubble Act only added an additional layer of uncertainty to this form of organization. As shown in Chapter 6, many other uncertainties and limitations were associated with the unincorporated company because, among other things, it lacked legal personality and limitation of liability. The cases of 1808–1812 again placed the Bubble Act and the question of the legality of the unincorporated company on the public agenda.

Litigation During the Boom of 1825

Only one case concerning the applicability of the Bubble Act to unincorporated companies was decided between 1812 and 1825. This was *Ellison v. Bignold*, in 1821, and related to the National Union Fire Association, a mutual fire insurance company that had been formed two years earlier. The National Union was a typical unincorporated company of the first quarter of the nineteenth century: formed by a deed, using the trust device, having a managerial hierarchy from president, trustees, and directors to secretaries and servants, joint stock based on the annual premium payment, and about 2,000 policyholders–shareholders. *Ellison v. Bignold* was the first reported case directly concerning the Bubble Act to be discussed in the Court of Chancery. The case reached Chancery by way of a bill for account and injunction for misconduct sought against the most active director by the other directors. The case demonstrates well the position of the unincorporated company in Chancery on the eve of the 1825 boom. It combines the equitable trust and partnership doctrines, difficulties of the unincorporated company,[34] with the statutory difficulties that appeared as a result of the revival of the Bubble Act in common law during the previous decade, and now reached Chancery. Lord Chancellor Eldon said that the National Union, as a mutual association, seemed to have nontransferable shares. But associations with "assignments and transfers of the shares" are illegal according to Eldon in an obiter to this case.[35] This obiter, which applied to most unincorporated companies, was soon to become Eldon's main judicial policy.

Interest in the Bubble Act grew again in the wake of the speculative boom of 1824–1825. Once more the story of the South Sea Bubble was rewritten and circulated; the Bubble Act was exploited by opponents of new promotions.[36] Just as the 1807–1808 boom led to numerous disputes between promoters and investors, intensive court litigation, and some leading judgments on the interpretation of the Bubble Act, so did the 1824–1825 boom.

On February 4, 1825, the Court of King's Bench held, in *Josephs v. Pebrer*, that the Equitable Loan Bank Company was to be considered illegal within the operation of the Bubble Act.[37] The company had petitioned Parliament, but, because the matter was debated in the Lords for many months, it did not await incorporation, and opened subscription books.[38] The defendant argued that a contract for the purchase of shares in the company was void because the company itself was illegal. The court based its decision on the evidence that though the company presumed to act as a corporate body, it had a mischievous effect (it charged a usurious 8 percent interest) and its shares were transferable. The court did not determine whether all three elements had to be fulfilled concur-

---

[34]See Chapter 6.

[35]*Ellison v. Bignold*, 2 Jac. & W. 503, 510 (1821).

[36]*The South Sea Bubble . . . Historically Detailed as a Beacon to the Unwary Against Modern Schemes . . . Equally Visionary and Nefarious* (1825).

[37]*Josephs v. Pebrer*, 3 B. & C. 639 (1825).

[38]See *Hansard's Parliamentary Debates*, vol. 11, p. 1339 (1824); vol. 12, pp. 1194, 1350 (1825); vol. 13, pp. 164, 899, 1061, 1163, 1349 (1825). The bill was defeated on the third reading in June 1825, after having been debated for over a year.

rently in order for a company to be illegal. The judges distinguished this case from the Webb and Pratt cases, in which the relevant companies were not declared illegal because the purpose of the society was not in grievance to the public and because restrictions had been placed on the transferability of shares.

In March 1825, a month after the Equitable Loan Bank was pronounced illegal by the King's Bench, and the rush of incorporation bills to Parliament began, the Court of Chancery examined the legality of the Real del Monte Company. The Real del Monte, like the Equitable, was a product of the boom years. Like the Equitable it aspired to incorporation but, while waiting for the completion of the legislative process, began its business, mining in Mexico, as an unincorporated company. At one point, the company resolved to divest itself of the rights to the Bolanos mine in favor of the defendant, who was one of its promoters. The plaintiff argued that this resolution denied him his fair share in the mine. The matter was brought to Chancery as *Kinder v. Taylor*, and both parties argued about the interpretation of the deed of settlement to determine whether the company's resolution was valid.[39] Lord Eldon astonished Counsel by turning his attention from the content and interpretation of the deed to the question of the legality of the company altogether and "the right of any persons claiming as proprietors in such a company, to have the aid of a court of justice." Counsel for both parties contended, in surprising harmony, but in vain, for the legality of the company. Eldon, however, insisted upon shifting the case to the Bubble Act and questioning the legality of the company. He did not see how the Real del Monte was not acting as a corporate body: "If the Bank of England, the East India Company, or the South Sea Company, wanted a new charter, they could not do better than copy the deed of regulation of the Real del Monte Company."[40] He took the opportunity to criticize the common-law courts for not considering the Bubble Act fully and not determining conclusively what constituted action as a corporate body. His main target was Ellenborough, who had not done so in the Webb case.[41] He thought that the interpretation of the Bubble Act was a matter that the Court of Chancery could determine only incidentally, and that it should be settled in the courts of law. Neverthe-

---

[39]*Kinder v. Taylor,* Law Journal Reports, old series 3, Cases in Chancery 68 (1824–1825).

[40]Ibid., 78.

[41]Ellenborough, unlike Eldon, was not enthusiastic about discussing the effects of the Bubble Act. In *Davies v. Hawkins*, 3 M. & S. 488 (1815), the question of the legality of the British Ale Brewery, an unincorporated company with transferable shares, was raised by counsel, yet Ellenborough avoided it and decided the case on other grounds.

less he applied a broad interpretation to the Bubble Act and inclined to view the Real del Monte, as well as other unincorporated companies, as illegal.

Eldon shook any certainty still left regarding the legality of the unincorporated company. He attacked the unincorporated company on what is believed by many scholars to have been its home court, the Court of Chancery. On his own initiative, he raised a matter that was incidental, if not immaterial, to the dispute between the parties. They talked trust and contract, he replied in corporate law and the Bubble Act. He added one last surprising blow:

Now, the statute supposes, and he himself confidently believed, that to act as a corporation, not being a corporation, was an offence in common law . . . we have a common law as well as statute law; and that what may not be within the comprehension of the statute, may, nevertheless be within the prohibition of the common law.[42]

In this, Eldon established a second line of defense: Even if the Bubble Act were interpreted narrowly by the common-law courts, or were repealed by Parliament, the common law would be on Eldon's side and would prevent the slide toward uncontrolled speculation and chaos. This line of defense was formed just at a time when Eldon felt that the statutory prohibition was subject to growing criticism in Parliament and elsewhere.[43]

The growing relevancy of the Bubble Act as a result of these judgments and the intensive public debate on the legitimacy of unincorporated companies had an interesting by-product: a renewed interest in the history of the South Sea Bubble and especially in the rationale behind the enactment of the Bubble Act. This history was based on the outlook of contemporary historians. The conventional wisdom upheld by the champions of the act was that the act came to remedy the evils of the South Sea Bubble and that it should remain in force as a remedy against the evils of the new bubble of 1824–1825. The opponents of the act argued that this was not the case. One of them said:

Ask 99 persons out of a 100 what the Bubble Act is? They will think that it was a statute somewhat strict to be sure, not altogether suited to the spirit of these times, but nevertheless, a statute passed by wise statesmen immediately *after* the bursting of the infamous South Sea bubble and its less glittering companions, and tending to prevent any such ruin from again recurring. Never let them forget

---

[42]*Kinder v. Taylor*, 81.

[43]Interestingly, Eldon's final judgment was delivered on March 29, 1825, the day that Peter Moore presented his first bill for repealing the Bubble Act in the Commons (see Chapter 10). For a fuller discussion of this case in the wider context of the 1825 events, see Ron Harris, "Political Economy, Interest Groups, Legal Institutions, and the Repeal of the Bubble Act in 1825," *Economic History Review* 50, no. 4 (1997).

that it was a statute smuggled through the Houses by the promoters and projectors of the South Sea scheme itself.[44]

Thus, history once again served as a tool in a contemporary debate. The misconception as to the reason for the enactment of the Bubble Act which developed in the later part of the eighteenth century survived until the late twentieth century, and was certainly a major factor in the 1825 litigation.

THE REINVENTION OF THE COMMON LAW

Lord Chancellor Eldon's statement in *Kinder v. Taylor*, in March 1825, that "to act as a corporation, not being a corporation, was an offence in common law" became operative shortly after it was delivered.[45] The Bubble Act was repealed a couple of months later, and what seemed to be a theoretical question at the time Eldon delivered his judgment in March became an acute legal problem in May 1825, just as Eldon intended it to be. Were unincorporated companies illegal even after the repeal of the Bubble Act? Were the parameters for determining the illegality of a given company similar to the ones employed by the prerepeal courts based on the wording of the Bubble Act?

The argument was basically that the Bubble Act only declared in a statute what was already illegal in common law before 1720, and thus its repeal only revived the common law. This line of reasoning was raised in other contexts as well, and was not unique to the repeal of the Bubble Act. It was argued at about the same time that in common law, engrossing and regrating were criminal and that combination of workers was illegal, even after the repeal of prohibitive statutes in these fields. This argument can be interpreted as a manifestation of judicial activism, in which judges compensated for the withdrawal of the legislator from the regulation of a specific issue by applying their own prohibitive policies. A conservative judiciary, and in this case the ultraconservative Lord Eldon, attempted to block a more liberal government and Parliament. The tactic was a retreat from statute law to a revived common law.

The argument for the illegality of unincorporated companies was not abandoned when their chief foe on the bench, Lord Eldon, retired from the chancellorship in 1827. In 1828 Lord Chief Justice Best of the Court of Common Pleas said, in *Duvergier v. Fellows*, that "there can be no transferable shares of any stock, except the stock of corporations or of

---

[44]*Lawyers and Legislators; Or, Notes on the American Mining Companies* (1825), 89.

[45]*Kinder v. Taylor*, 68, 81.

joint-stock companies created by acts of Parliament."[46] He declared the Patent Distillery Company, an unincorporated company with transferable shares, illegal.[47]

In 1837, in *Blundell v. Winsor*, Vice Chancellor Shadwell held the Anglo-American Gold Mining Association illegal. He said that the deed of association of the company:

is not only illegal because it trenches on the prerogative of the King, by attempting to create a body not having the protection of the King's charter, the shares of which might be assigned without any control or restriction whatsoever; but also because it holds out to the public a false and fraudulent representation that the shares could be so assigned.[48]

From 1825 onward, through the above cases, a new and extensive common-law construction emerged to block the creation and the legal enforceability of unincorporated companies.

Yet a competing approach appeared during the chancellorship of the reforming Whig Henry Brougham (1830–1834), according to which the raising and transferring of stock as such was not a nuisance at common law. In *Walburn v. Ingilby* (1833), Lord Chancellor Brougham was urged to declare the Potosi la Paz and Peruvian Mining Association, an unincorporated company formed during the boom of 1824, illegal, or a mere partnership. The counsel of a director in the company used this legal argument to rescue their client from a fraud bill by a shareholder. The counsel relied on a long line of precedents, from *The King v. Dodd* to *Kinder v. Taylor*. Nevertheless Brougham held an opinion opposite to that held by his predecessor Lord Chancellor Eldon in the Kinder case, just eight years earlier:

To hold such a company illegal would be to say that every joint stock company not incorporated by Charter or Act of Parliament is unlawful, and indeed, indictable as a nuisance, and to decide this for the first time, no authority of a decided case being produced for such a doctrine.[49]

He refused to declare the company illegal though it had a transferable stock, and was not even willing to view the clause in the company's deed that pretended to limit the liability of its members as a means of deception. This new favorable approach toward unincorporated companies

---

[46]*Duvergier v. Fellows*, 5 Bing 248, 267 (1828).

[47]This judgment was affirmed on error by King's Bench in 1830, and on appeal by the House of Lords in 1832. See *Duvergier v. Fellows*, 10 B. & C. 826 (1830); *Duvergier v. Fellows*, 1 Clark & Finnelly 39 (1832). In this case the illegality of the company was argued on two grounds: that it acted as a corporate body, and that it intended to hold a patent which could not be assigned by law to more than five persons.

[48]*Blundell v. Winsor*, 8 Sim. 601, 613 (1837).

[49]*Walburn v. Ingilby*, 1 My. & K. 61, 76 (1833).

emerged in Chancery, of all places, and indicates that the dispute between Brougham and Eldon had crossed institutional boundaries and arose from jurisprudential, legal, and political disagreement.

In 1843, Chief Justice Tindal of the Court of Common Pleas, in two quite similar cases, *Garrard v. Hardey* and *Harrison v. Heathorn*, three months apart, refused to hold the Limerick Marble and Stone Company and the Anglo-American Gold Mining Company illegal. He distinguished these cases from *Duvergier v. Fellows*, in which a patent was assigned illegally and infected the discussed company with illegality. He also defined narrowly the illegality of "presuming to act as a corporation," and held it to include only using a common seal. Tindal concluded that "the raising of transferable shares of the stock of a company can hardly be said to be of itself an offence at common law."[50] It is interesting to note that the second of these cases dealt with the same gold mining association that was the subject of *Blundell v. Winsor*. However, whereas the Vice-Chancellor declared the Anglo-American illegal in 1837, Chief Justice Tindal decided in 1843 that the same company was legal.

Whereas the more prevalent opinion in the judiciary followed Eldon and held the unincorporated company as illegal in common law even after the repeal of the Bubble Act, a rival doctrine, led by Brougham, held the unincorporated company legal in many circumstances. The prohibitive-conservative opinion had three major lines of reasoning: constitutional law, the law of frauds, and public benefit policy considerations. The constitutional law objection to the unincorporated company was based on the old notion of the King's prerogative. It was the King's constitutional discretionary privilege to grant incorporation. Acting as a corporation while breaching the King's privilege was subject to common-law sanctions. The old prerogative writs of *quo warranto* and *scire facias*, not used or mentioned explicitly in this context since 1720, were the original means for enforcing this privilege. To this was added fraud as a second argument. The argument was that the presentation, even implicitly, of any unincorporated company as having transferable shares or limitation of liability was fraudulent and thus illegal, because neither of these features could be secured without full State incorporation. Third, it was argued that any company for mischievous purpose and any bubble company (that is, a company with no real economic activity) is illegal by virtue of being detrimental to the public in general. The common law, according to this argument, protects unwary investors by

---

[50]*Garrard v. Hardey*, 5 Man. & G. 471 (1843), and *Harrison v. Heathorn*, 6 Man. & G. 81 (1843). For post-1844 cases, see the references in Ronald R. Formoy, *The Historical Foundation of Modern Company Law* (London: Sweet and Maxwell, 1923), 32, nn. e and f.

outlawing such companies for paternalistic reasons. According to the conservative interpretation, the common law views these associations as partnerships. Thus, conservative judges strictly applied partnership doctrine to these associations, including the requirement to have all shareholders as parties in litigation, to have all of them sign the original deed itself while purchasing shares, and to allow litigation among members (in the form of account) only in the eventuality of dissolution. In practice, this view left the unincorporated company with no legal framework, because the partnership form of organization did not suit this large, open, and complex form of organization. Shareholders, officers, and third parties could not rely on the courts to enforce their deals, protect their expectations, and grant them remedies in times of crises, when they needed them most.

Led by Brougham, the judges who favored reform in the common law in general to make it more instrumental to the growing economy advocated recognition of the unincorporated company. Ironically, these judges employed a traditional, or a formalist, form of reasoning in order to shape a more functional and responsive common law. They emphasized the centrality of precedents in common-law adjudication. They argued that there was not even one single case prior to 1825 that discussed the common-law position on the formation of unincorporated companies, hence there was nothing on which Eldon and his school could rely. They could find no rationale in the enactment of the Bubble Act if it merely reflected and reasserted the pre-1720 common law. They held that the Bubble Act created a new, though confined, prohibition that was removed with the repeal of the act. All the pre-1825 judgments that held unincorporated companies illegal were based on the Bubble Act and not on the common law. An interesting line of reasoning was that the practice of forming joint-stock companies was relatively new, and thus could not be prohibited by ancient common-law doctrines. Thus, conservative jurisprudential reasoning, based on a static and archaic representation of the common law, on precedent as the major normative source, on a clear distinction between common law and statute law, and on the relatively passive role of the judge enabled Brougham and his allies to advance reformist legal outcomes in the present context, at a stage when free incorporation by parliamentary legislative reform was not attainable.

Therefore, an interjudicial conflict that was viewed by outsiders as a massive zigzag existed between 1825 and 1843: prohibitive judgments in King's Bench, Common Pleas, and Chancery in 1825–30, a permissive judgment in Chancery in 1833, a prohibitive one in Chancery in 1837, and two permissive ones in Common Pleas in 1843. The legal rule was not settled and the outcome of concrete disputes was not predetermined.

No solicitor in the period 1826–1844 could definitely advise his clients whether to organize into an unincorporated company, aim at full incorporation, or refrain from being involved in joint-stock enterprise altogether. He could not assure them that the deed of association he would draft at their request would be held legal in court. It was mainly the identity of the sitting judge which determined the outcome, and unincorporated companies could expect to find themselves declared illegal in most instances throughout most of this period.

The inconsistent court decisions created repeated shocks in two directions, that of business and that of politics. The only way to assuage these shocks and to overcome the uncertainties and the persistence of reaction to the joint-stock company throughout the conservative-dominated judiciary was through legislation. The turn to legislation was not unique to company law. The days of Mansfield and Blackstone were over, and the limited scale of reform that could be achieved through common law became more evident as Bentham and the law reform movement of the early nineteenth century demonstrated. The province of legislation was being determined and Parliament became the target of reformers in criminal law, procedure, and other fields. We turn to Parliament in the next chapter.

10

The Joint-Stock Company in Parliament

Having studied the attitude toward the joint-stock company in the business community and in the judiciary, we are now in a position to turn to an examination of the range of opinions in Parliament and in the government itself toward this form of business organization. While the company had become more popular with entrepreneurs and investors alike beginning in the late eighteenth century, it was not well received by the dominantly conservative judiciary, and the split between the economic reality and the legal framework reached a critical point. As a result, in 1824–1825, Parliament was forced to put the issue on its agenda for the first time since 1720, and to try to deal with the two conflicting outlooks.

The present chapter examines the debates in Parliament in 1824–1825 which led to the repeal of the Bubble Act. The Whig attempts at reform between 1830 and 1841 are studied next. The limited effectiveness of these attempts is examined in the context of the debate on the role of liberal ideology and the administrative competency of the Whig governments of this period. Finally, this chapter turns to Gladstone's Select Committee and the Joint-Stock Companies Act of 1844, which was based on the committee's recommendations. Gladstone's role in this reform is examined in the context of his early career. The act itself and accompanying legislation are analyzed in terms of laissez-faire and State intervention.

THE BOOM OF 1824–1825 AND THE REPEAL OF THE BUBBLE ACT

Liberal Toryism and the Parliamentary Background

By the time the issue of joint-stock companies first appeared on the agenda of Parliament, in the 1824 session, Lord Liverpool's Tory government had been in power for thirteen years. His leading ministers that year were Frederick Robinson, Chancellor of the Exchequer; William Huskisson, President of the Board of Trade; George Canning, Foreign Secretary; and Robert Peel, Secretary of the Home Office. In 1820, against the backdrop of the postwar social upheaval leading to Peterloo, the budget deficit, growing national debt, and higher taxation, Lord Liverpool was the first Prime Minister to declare free trade as his favored policy. The appointment of Robinson and Huskisson to their positions in 1822, some argue, transformed his ministry from "reactionary Toryism" to "liberal Toryism." Other historians attribute this transformation to the growing influence of Ricardo as a scholarly authority and as the mentor of statesmen. According to this interpretation, by adopting free trade, Liverpool's government hoped to achieve the economic growth and national wealth promised by the political economists. Others attribute the transformation to an attempt to shift the electoral base of the Tory party from what was perceived to be the declining landed gentry to the rising middle class. Yet others stress that the retrograde outlook of the liberal Tories aimed only at providing food and employment, in order to preempt riots by a rapidly growing population, while attempting to contain social and economic change.[1]

Though the motives are controversial, the manner in which the new policy was implemented is manifest. From the turning point of 1820–1822, the government took various steps to relax the severe legal and economic restrictions that had been in force because of the war. In the years 1822–1825, duties were lowered, taxation was reduced, the budget transformed from deficit to surplus, and the national debt decreased. Many limitations on trade, especially on foreign trade and shipping, were eased by, for example, liberalizing navigation laws, lowering dues and opening duty-free warehouses to foreign ships in British harbors, and simplification as well as reduction of tariffs. Peel introduced an extensive program of criminal law reform, amending and consolidating laws and reducing the number of capital offenses (but not the number of actual executions). The Combination Acts of 1799, which had limited the organization of workers, were repealed in 1824, though a modified version of these acts was introduced a year later.

[1] The outline of the political agenda of Liverpool's ministry in the 1820s is based on Barry Gordon, *Political Economy in Parliament: 1819–1823* (London: Macmillan, 1976) and *Economic Doctrine and Tory Liberalism, 1824–1830* (London: Macmillan, 1979); William R. Brock, *Lord Liverpool and Liberal Toryism: 1820 to 1827*, 2d ed. (London: Frank Cass, 1967); Boyd Hilton, *Corn, Cash, Commerce: The Economic Policies of the Tory Governments, 1815–1830* (Oxford University Press, 1977), and "The Political Arts of Lord Liverpool," *Transactions of the Royal Historical Society* 38 (1988), 147–170; and Norman Gash, *Aristocracy and People: Britain 1815–1865* (London: E. Arnold, 1979).

Despite the government's transformation from conservative Toryism to liberal Toryism in the early 1820s, a significant element of High or ultra-Tories remained in Parliament. These were found in the House of Lords and among back-bench landed gentry in the Commons, which at that time numbered about 200 on the Tory side alone. Ideologically, they were not uniform: They included agriculturists and other protectionists, and opponents of Catholic Emancipation, dissenters, legal reform, and parliamentary reform. In short, this group included supporters of the status quo and reactionaries of different sorts. Their prominent speakers included Lord Eldon, the Earl of Westmorland, the Earl of Lauderdale, Thomas Gooch, Sir Edward Knatchbull, and Thomas Lethbridge, and, on some issues, the Duke of Wellington and John Harries.

The Tory Ministry of 1825 was still too committed to its agrarian power base to support the repeal of the Corn Law. However, it accepted other measures to increase corn imports and was able to mitigate the political controversy over this issue and postpone the inevitable crisis for several years. Another issue that threatened Tory solidarity, and led to the fall of the Tory administration in 1830, was parliamentary reform. In the mid-1820s, however, this was not yet high on the agenda. The only burning controversy in 1825, both within the administration and between Tories and Whigs, was the question of Catholic emancipation, which was connected to the Irish crisis and related to political activities and national demands in Ireland. In terms of political excitement, the debates on joint-stock companies were second only to the debates on the various aspects of the Irish problem in 1824–1825. In terms of parliamentary time-consumption, the debates over the joint-stock company were undoubtedly first.

The paucity of major disputes in the early and middle 1820s can well explain the low profile of the parties in parliamentary politics. The liberal Tories, who dominated their party in this period, were close to the liberal Whigs on many questions, including the adoption of free trade politics. The liberal Whigs could not, therefore, oppose them on these issues. The Tory majority in the Commons was overwhelming: 411 members for the government and only 198 for the opposition.[2] The Whig party was in decline; MPs were less active and less united and

---

[2]Based on an analysis of the 1818 elections. There is no comparable detailed study of the 1820 elections, the last general elections before 1826; however, changes were minor. Of a total of 658 members, there were also 32 Independent, 11 Grenvillite, five doubtful, and one neutral member. See *The History of Parliament: The House of Commons 1790–1820*, Vol 1: *Introductory Survey* (London: Secker and Warburg, 1986). The volumes for the period 1820–1832 of this important project are still in preparation.

many found common interests with Tories.[3] Whig morale was low, as they could not hope to return to power in the near future, barring dramatic changes, not likely in this period, such as parliamentary reform or effective popular agitation. The disputes over the emergence of a modern party system, over the degree of representation of voters by their MPs, and over MPs' independence have long been debated by historians. Without going into these problems, one can quite safely argue that party organization in the 1820s was not yet developed, and that MPs were less dependent on the party for reelection, less loyal to the party, and less committed to its policy than in the decades to come. The conclusion from all the above is that, where joint-stock companies were concerned, party affiliations were not the dominant factor in shaping individual MPs' positions; rather, their other private and group financial interests played a major role.

In view of this, the social and economic background of the individual MPs gain importance as possible factors in shaping their interests and positions in Parliament on the question of the joint-stock business company. Estimates of the number of members of the House of Commons with landed interests are not precise, but they range between one-half and three-quarters of the MPs, an absolute majority by all accounts. After the 1820 elections, 216 MPs were baronets or sons of peers, indicating the presence of considerable landed interests. The next most-represented social group in Parliament was the professionals. Between 1790 and 1820, 144 military officers and 112 members of the legal profession, as well as other professionals in lower numbers, sat in the House of Commons.

While representation of the commercial interests was on the rise, only 150 MPs, less than one-quarter, had such interests in 1820. More than two-thirds of the commercial interests in the House were London-based. Between 1790 and 1820, thirty-two MPs were directors in the East India Company and thirteen in the Bank of England.[4] In 1820 some fifty MPs had interests in the East India trade (company directors as well as nabobs and shipowners) and thirty-three had interests in the West India trade. Thus, much of the business representation in Parliament was of the merchant and financial interests of the City of London, and it is not surprising that twenty-seven of the City's aldermen were MPs during this period.[5] Studies of the distribution of wealth in England at this time

---

[3]See Austin Mitchell, *The Whigs in Opposition: 1815–1830* (Oxford: Clarendon Press, 1967), 171–193.

[4]Gerrit P. Judd, *Members of Parliament: 1734–1832* (New Haven: Yale University Press, 1955), 54–77, 84–85, 88–89.

[5]*The History of Parliament: The House of Commons, 1790–1820*, Vol. 1: *Introductory Survey*, 278–356.

indicate that a very large portion of the wealthiest, nonlandowning men were from the City of London.[6] They were indeed well represented in Parliament, whereas the less wealthy provincial businessmen captured only a small number of seats.

Yet along with the overwhelming weight of the City and its merchants and high financiers, other business interests began to claim their share. Only nine of the MPs in our period were manufacturers, but even this figure was higher than in previous Parliaments. Some ten MPs were London bankers, other than Bank of England directors, and eight were country bankers.[7] A new phenomenon was the involvement of MPs in joint-stock companies other than the moneyed companies, beginning in the 1790s. MPs held 110 seats in directorships of London insurance companies (most of them unincorporated), twenty-five seats in London dock companies, and a few seats in gas, copper, linen, and other minor companies during the period 1790–1820.[8] During the boom of 1824–1825, an unprecedented number of MPs took positions as directors in the newly promoted companies, a phenomenon which is discussed below.

The House of Lords is not included in the above analysis, because economic interests there were less complex; that is, most peers had inherently landed interests. Some were elevated to the peerage due to service to the administration, the military, or the judicial system. The number of peers with commercial interests grew as industrialization advanced, yet in this period it was still relatively small, though greater than once thought.

The Lords had a less intensive agenda than the Commons. Both Houses sat only between February and midsummer. But while the Commons sat four to five days a week for long hours, the Lords sat no more than twice a week and their productivity was considerably smaller. It is not surprising that the Lords were not as interested in economic issues as the Commons, and that only a few bills on joint-stock companies were transacted in the upper chamber.

The Rush on Parliament

The new wave of speculative joint-stock promotions began in 1824. By the opening of Parliament in February 1825, some 160 new schemes had already been publicized, and by the end of the year, their number

---

[6]See Rubinstein, *Men of Property*, 56–116.
[7]Brock, *Lord Liverpool*, appendix A.
[8]*The History of Parliament: The House of Commons 1790–1820*, Vol. 1: *Introductory Survey*, 322–323.

reached 624.[9] Unlike the boom years of 1720 and 1807, in 1825 most projectors sought parliamentary incorporation. This can be explained by the judgments of 1808–1812 and particularly the King's Bench decision on February 4, 1825, in the case of *Joseph v. Pebrer*,[10] and Lord Eldon's Chancery decision on March 25 in *Kinder v. Taylor*,[11] which raised serious doubts as to the legality of unincorporated companies with transferable stock.[12] In March 1824, in the early stages of the boom, some seventeen bills of incorporation were pending in Parliament, many more than in previous years. But the real rush on Parliament came in 1825, as the boom advanced and the issue of illegality loomed, with 438 requests for forming new companies.[13] Not all the promoters really desired incorporation as a shield against prosecution, or in order to benefit from the legal features it provided; some were only after the publicity and respectability that could be achieved from encounters in Parliament, and had no intention of completing the legislative process. Yet no less than 286 of the applications resulted in an incorporation act from Parliament.

Toward the end of March 1825, shortly after Eldon's alarming decision, the burden of private company bills on the House became unprecedentedly heavy. The pressure was evident from the need to call a debate on the "want of accommodation" for private committees, committees which examined the company bills between readings in the House. The atmosphere in the House as reflected in this debate was colorful: 150 persons sitting in the body of the House transacting business for several private committees, two committees sitting at the same time in one small room, 100 MPs mixed with witnesses, counsels, and strangers in a crowded committee room, forty different committees on incorporation bills meeting in one single day. One can imagine that at that point, when the House lost some of its gentlemanly qualities, and looked more like a

---

[9]For a list of schemes including dates and capital, see *Parliamentary Papers* (1844), vol. 7, appendix no. 4 of the "First Report of the Select Committee on Joint Stock Companies," 334–339. The lists include, in addition to the 160 companies mentioned above, 83 companies promoted after January 1825, and 100 companies that were advertised but did not progress any further. See also *Remarks on Joint Stock Companies by an Old Merchant* (1825), 28, which lists a total of 153 promotions until the end of January and 68 in January alone. For more detail on the market boom, see Chapter 8.

[10]*Joseph v. Pebrer*, 3 B. & C. 639 (1825).

[11]*Kinder v. Taylor*, Law Journal Reports, old series 3, Cases in Chancery 68 (1824–1825).

[12]See Chapter 9.

[13]According to Thomas, *Crisis of 1825*, 211–215. He calculates a total of more than 500 applications for the period 1824–1826. Hunt, *Business Corporation*, 52, reaches a slightly different figure: 488 incorporation petitions for the years 1825–1826, to which we should add the bills of 1824.

coffeehouse in the alleys of the City, that even some of the back-bench country gentlemen started showing interest in the joint-stock question.[14]

Parliament did not place the issue of joint-stock companies on its agenda voluntarily, from any political or public benefit consideration. It was dragged into debating these issues by shocks from the courts and the stock market that drove promoters to crowd its doors and halls. The House devoted most of its time to debates on specific incorporation bills and not to discussions of general measures. Nevertheless, these debates on specific companies are very useful, as from them we can learn a great deal about the opinions of a wide spectrum of MPs and ministers on the more general problems.[15]

The Debates in Parliament

The 1824 session of Parliament closed at the end of June. By the time the King opened the 1825 session on February 3, the stock market hysteria was at a new height, and many speculators were awaiting the opening of the new session. The dramatic developments after the end of the preceding session forced Lord Chancellor Eldon to rise after the King's speech and refer with even greater urgency to what he had said at the close of the previous session:

> that he would, in the course of the present session, move for leave to regulate a system which was now going on to a most mischievous extent – he meant Joint-Stock Companies not yet formed, and which never might be formed.[16]

Eldon opposed promoters' selling the shares of any company before it was duly incorporated, because this was illegal and exploited innocent share buyers. Eldon, the conservative jurist and longtime member of Liverpool's cabinet, opposed parliamentary incorporation, not to say free incorporation, and aimed at returning to a royal chartering system, which had declined over the past century. He favored strict enforcement of either the Bubble Act or, preferably, a more prohibitive statute; he opposed unincorporated companies and rejected any compromise that would give them the privileges of corporate bodies.[17] Eldon believed in the old social order, by which he, a coal factor's son, had done well, and

---

[14]Home Secretary Peel and the Speaker promised that if the press of private business continued they would look for a solution for the next session, and meanwhile the private committees were allowed into the House itself. See *Hansard's Parliamentary Debates*, vol. 12, pp. 1032–1034 (1825).

[15]For an analysis of the legislative process in the theoretical framework of regulation, collective action and interest groups, see Harris, "Political Economy."

[16]*Hansard's Parliamentary Debates*, vol. 12, p. 31 (1825).

[17]Ibid., vol. 11, pp. 791–792 (1824); vol. 12, pp. 31, 127–128 (1825).

in the professional ethos that stressed formalistic thinking, the rule of law, past precedents, and stability.

He rose on that first day to give proper notice to promoters of future schemes. "With respect to the past, he would either leave it to be dealt with according to the common law as it at present stood, or he would introduce into the bill a declaration as to what he conceived to be the intent of the common law on the subject."[18] Whether it was to his relief or not, the Lord Chancellor, in his judicial capacity, found himself involved in the above mentioned *Kinder v. Taylor* case which dealt with an unincorporated speculation, and used this as a pretext to avoid any legislative initiative as long as this case was pending. He said it to be improper for him to further declare his position in the Lords on the state of the law or on required legislation, matters about which he was hearing arguments in the Court of Chancery.[19] Thus Eldon could terrorize the market, exploiting his multiple capacities, without drafting a bill or putting his ultra-Tory ideas to the test of a parliamentary vote.

Other High Tories, including Westmorland, Lauderdale, and Redesdale, shared Eldon's belief that nontangible holdings, speculations, and paper transactions hindered real trade and individual traders, did not contribute to the wealth of the nation, and endangered public finance in wartime.[20] The "fiscal-military" apparatus was based on the market for State securities.[21] The High Tories may have sensed that the emerging share market was competing successfully for investors' money, and that, by the next war, the government might not be able to mobilize private resources and consequently troops, as it had in the past. These aristocrats were not concerned with Eldon's legal niceties, but they reached the same operative conclusion: The rise of the joint-stock company should be checked.[22]

---

[18]Ibid., vol. 12, p. 31 (1825).

[19]Ibid., vol. 12, p. 1196 (1825). The Lord Chancellor was presiding over the House of Lords; at the same time he was the head of the judicial hierarchy, the senior judge of the Court of Chancery, the head of the legal profession, and a member of the cabinet. Nevertheless, he was expected to maintain, somehow, a degree of separation between these various capacities.

[20]For the High Tories in government, and particularly in the Lords, see Brock, *Lord Liverpool*, 231–232.

[21]Dickson, *Financial Revolution*; Mathias and O'Brien, "Taxation in Britain," 601; Brewer, *Sinews of Power*.

[22]In May 1824, the Earl of Lauderdale, the ex-Whig and now ultra-Tory, suggested a Standing Order, a procedural order, to prohibit a second reading of each incorporation bill before four-fifths of the company's capital had been paid up. His intention was to prevent speculators from obtaining incorporation and selling their shares in profit, without actually investing the capital declared in the prospectus in the company. On June 2, the Standing Orders were agreed to (reducing the capital requirement from four-fifths to three-fourths). The Standing Orders were probably a major obstacle for promoters, and explain the fact that from then on almost no company

On this simplified spectrum of opinions, the High Tories are located on one extreme, and a group of bankers and businessmen, including Hudson Gurney, the Whig banker from Norwich; Mathias Attwood, the liberal Tory banker from Birmingham; and Alexander Baring, the international City financier, on the other. All three were prolific speakers on economic issues and usually rose above their private points of view, at least when the issues did not touch on banking policy. They all realized that the joint-stock form of business organization was there to stay and would expand within the economy, and judged this as a positive development because the joint-stock company made possible the development of capital-intensive projects: canals, docks, and other infrastructures that individuals could not, and the government should not, construct or administer.

Mathias Attwood, the liberal Tory banker from Birmingham (brother of the reformer-radical Thomas Attwood), glorified the businessmen and their unincorporated companies:

Millions of capital, hundreds, perhaps, of millions, were employed in this country by those associations, honourably, profitably, usefully to the country; and were totally without the pale or protection of the law. The parties were a law for themselves, their character was their law.

Attwood attacked those lawyers (the Lord Chancellor and his officers) who tried to delegitimize and prosecute the unincorporated joint stock companies:

Those individuals would have better consulted their own character, and have rendered better service to the country, if, instead of attempting to influence the conduct of the mercantile operations, of which they knew nothing, they had applied themselves to remedy the absurd and disgraceful state of the law itself, which fell within their own province.[23]

Hudson Gurney, the Whig banker from Norwich, called for:

one general law for the formation and regulation of all joint stock companies – whether the introduction of a law of registration of partnerships, with limited responsibility, as in France, and many other states of the continent, he was not competent to say. . . . He hoped the president of the Board of Trade, would take the matter into his own hands. . . . The common law was what grew up in an entirely different state of society, when there was little or no commerce; and the Bubble act was passed in a moment of national phrenzy – assuredly, when there was no wisdom.[24]

private bill was initiated in the House of Lords. Instead, all the promotions found their way to the Commons first. Eldon may have wanted to extend this Order to the House of Commons, improve it, and give it the powers of a statute. *Hansard's Parliamentary Debates*, vol. 11, pp. 856–857, 1076–1077 (1824).
    [23]Ibid., 1068.
    [24]Ibid., vol. 12, p. 1060 (1825).

Alexander Baring, the international financier and a leading Whig speaker on economic issues, found himself in a dilemma:

The evil was certainly one which deserved to be checked; though he hardly knew how the check could be applied. The remedy would be worse than the disease, if, in putting a stop to this evil, they put stop to the spirit of enterprise.[25]

Baring said that he was still waiting for "a learned person of great influence in the cabinet" (the Lord Chancellor) to fulfill his promise of the first day of the session, to invent a remedy for the evil. He called on William Huskisson, the president of the Board of Trade, to take the initiative himself and come to the House with a general rule. Yet Baring did not say whether that rule should grant free incorporation.[26]

Gurney and Attwood may have been inspired by several proposals for new legislation circulated in London in 1825, most notably that of John George.[27] These proposals called, among other things and in some variations, for free incorporation, standard clauses of deeds of association, proper disclosure, and regulation of public offerings. They were probably the first to raise some of the modern aspects of company law, aspects which were to remain on the agenda in the decades to come. These pamphlets, as well as the three MPs, were inspired by the experience of other countries, particularly France, where there were more permissive legal frameworks of business organization. They all shared the perception that the law of business organizations was an anachronism, its common-law component was shaped "in an entirely different state of society, when there was little or no commerce," and its legislative component – the Bubble Act – was passed "in a moment of national phrenzy – assuredly, when there was no wisdom." They favored legislative intervention for the purpose of removing past restraints and encouraging economic growth. They were all practicing men of business, in fact, banking, and were in disagreement not only with the conservative landed ultra-Tories, but also with the mainstream liberal Tories in cabinet, who favored inaction. We now turn to this highly influential group of leading cabinet ministers, who were positioned between these two groups and opposed both restrictive and permissive intervention.

While debating some of the incorporation bills, Huskisson found it necessary to redefine his general position on joint stock companies, a position he had already stated late in the 1824 session:

Parliament had very properly put an end to the system of gambling by lotteries; but many of these companies led to much more destructive consequences than

---

[25]Ibid., 1063–1064 (1825).
[26]Ibid., 718.
[27]George, *Law Affecting Unincorporated Companies*, 66–72. *Remarks on Joint Stock Companies by an Old Merchant* (1825), 95–98.

even that. It would surpass any powers which he possessed, or any leisure he could bestow upon it, to probe to the bottom the merits of the various speculations, and to be able to decide which was likely to be a beneficial undertaking, and which a bubble.[28]

He saw danger in the ongoing speculation and was tired of debating the hundreds of private bills. He joined in Eldon's opinion that all petitioners should seek a charter rather than an act and should bother the Law Officers rather than Parliament.[29] He was not willing to grant parliamentary limited liability to any of the new promotions, but saw no reason to reject their applications to sue and be sued using a common name. Unlike Eldon, the ultraconservative jurist, Huskisson, the political economy-conscious liberal Tory, did not think that stricter legislation or stricter enforcement of existing legislation was needed. He said: "You can form yourselves into what companies you please," and meant: As long as you do not bother Parliament. "With the exception of bankers he did not see that there was any thing in the law [of partnership] to limit the number of persons who might choose to associate, for the purpose of carrying on any particular trade."[30] Huskisson concluded in the noninterventionist (some would say laissez-faire) spirit, of which he was one of the finest spokesmen in the ministries of the 1820s:

The high-raised hopes of many who embarked in such speculations would, in the end, vanish into thin air, and leave those who entertained them nothing but regret and disappointment. At the same time that he gave this as his opinion of many of the speculations afloat, he did not see how the Parliament could at present interfere.[31]

On March 25, while debating the Equitable Loan Company Bill in the House of Lords, Lord Liverpool decided to break his long silence in this matter and state his opinion in the face of a growing storm:

In a country like this, where extensive commercial interests were constantly at work, a great degree of speculation was unavoidable, and if kept within certain limits, this spirit of speculation was attended with much advantage to the country. [Furthermore], he would be one of the last men ever to interfere, by legislative provision, . . . to prevent men from spending their own money as they pleased.[32]

[28]*Hansard's Parliamentary Debates*, vol. 12, pp. 717–719 (1825).

[29]Eldon's reasoning was more legal. He explained that if a company acted improperly a charter could be withdrawn immediately, whereas a company formed by an act could be deprived of its incorporation only by a repealing act. Ibid., 792 (1825). Huskisson's opinion was more practical. Parliament had neither the tools nor the time to distinguish between "'good" and "'bad" schemes.

[30]Ibid., vol. 11, p. 530 (1824).

[31]Ibid., vol. 12, p. 1076 (1825).

[32]Ibid., 1195.

This was indeed a laissez-faire speech by the Tory Prime Minister, who was in line with Huskisson in this matter.[33] However, Liverpool did not go a step further; he refused to call for the abolition of the existing interfering legislation, namely, the Bubble Act.

Thus, by the end of March 1825, a wide array of opinions emerged in Parliament (mainly during the debates on specific incorporation bills) concerning the attitude toward joint-stock companies and the desirable reaction of Parliament to the mounting wave of speculations and promotions. On one extreme stood Eldon and other ultra-Tories who thought that the Bubble Act should be enforced and even enhanced by new legislation, and that Parliament should not approve any of the incorporation bills now pending. On the other extreme were men of business of both parties, such as Gurney and Attwood, who called for repeal of the out-of-date Bubble Act, legitimization of the unincorporated companies, and the passage of a new general law for the formation and regulation of companies, preferably based on the liberal French law. Not far from them stood Baring, a high financier, and as such more cautious and responsible. He was in favor of legislative intervention but was not certain how, as he wanted to encourage beneficial promotions while at the same time checking illusory ones. The leading members of cabinet, the liberal Tory holders of major economic portfolios, and the prime minister himself, were against any intervention whatsoever. The ways in which individuals were to organize their business and invest their money was not, according to them, a matter for State concern. The government should initiate legislation only to secure food supply, public order, national defense, and the like, but not in this field. It seems that the liberals in cabinet believed that the natural state of things was one in which no special privileges were to be granted to associations beyond those available to every individual. Privileges granted to corporations represented undesirable intervention by the State. The reformers, Gurney and Attwood, seemed to hold that limitation on free incorporation created in past generations, including by the Bubble Act, comprised undesirable intervention by the State. To remove this intervention and return to the natural state of things, general legislation would be required. As long as the government's position prevailed the status quo was protected, and the Bubble Act was not expected to be repealed, or replaced either by an act that would totally block company formation or, conversely, would allow free incorporation.

[33]For the liberal Toryism of Liverpool's administration, and its inclination toward free trade economic policy, see J. E. Cookson, *Lord Liverpool's Administration: The Crucial Years, 1815–1822* (Edinburgh: Scottish Academic Press, 1975); Brock, *Lord Liverpool*; Gordon, *Economic Doctrine*; Hilton, *Economic Policies*; Mitchell, *Whigs in Opposition*.

Peter Moore's Bubble Act Repeal Bill

By late March, the speculative boom was still gathering momentum with no signs of a crisis. Debates over specific incorporation bills and general measures still took most of Parliament's time, the Lord Chancellor had not yet proposed the prohibitive bill he promised on the first day of the session, and other cabinet members were unwilling to initiate legislation. Until that stage, the legislative framework of business organization seemed to be as stable as it had been throughout the century before the boom.

On March 29, on the same day in which Eldon delivered his Chancery judgment, and four days after Liverpool's speech in the Lords, Peter Moore decided to take the initiative and rose in the Commons to bring forward a proposition "for defining and ascertaining the law relating to joint-stock companies." He stated:

At present the law in respect to these companies was very obscure and ill-understood; the common law, from its antiquity, being but little applicable to them, and the statute known as the "Bubble Act" being so full of penalties and contradictory enactments, that it was, in fact, a dead letter. The necessity of settling a question of so much importance was placed beyond question, by the amount of capital which was daily investing in these speculations, and which he would be safe in estimating at upwards of 160 millions.[34]

Moore concluded his speech by asking leave to bring in a bill to repeal the Bubble Act.

Was Peter Moore ideologically motivated in his move for the repeal of the Bubble Act? Was he a reformer who wanted to bring about modern economic legislation, or was he acting for the Lord Chancellor in advancing a restrictive measure? In the context of 1825, Peter Moore was none of these. As one of the most active MPs in the field of company promotions, he had a vested interest in the repeal of the Bubble Act. He gave his name to many companies as a director, held their shares which he usually received at no cost, and helped them as much as he could through parliamentary committees. He stated openly that "he had himself the honour to belong to some of these companies, and he pledged himself that there was as much integrity in their views, as in those of the company of the Bank of England."[35] Moore had even been involved, as chairman of one of his promotions, the British Annuity company, in a Chancery case, in which the legality of this promotion and of his conduct were questioned.[36] Interestingly enough, his draft bill was circulated in

---

[34]*Hansard's Parliamentary Debates*, vol. 12, p. 1279 (1825).
[35]Ibid., 1280.
[36]*Van Sandau v. Moore and others*, 1 Russ. 441 (1826).

London by Wilks and Verbeke, solicitors to many of the new schemes, whose interest in keeping the speculative wave alive was overt.[37] Moore was characterized by a contemporary observer as "director of a considerable number of joint-stock companies, every one of which, we venture to prophecy, must, from their very nature, in the course of 12 months, be dissolved or insolvent, perhaps both."[38] Indeed, within less than a year, Moore's promoted undertakings collapsed, and he had to flee to Dieppe to escape arrest while surrendering much of his fortune to investors who had lost all their money in his companies.[39] Thus, the motive behind his repealing bill was not very different from that of the initiators of the Bubble Act some 105 years earlier: It was simply greed. His end, like that of some of the South Sea directors and officers, was life in exile in France. For Moore, Eldon's policy of strong enforcement of the Bubble Act, coupled with his and Huskisson's objection to further granting of parliamentary incorporation acts, meant the end of his promotion business. By the way, Moore's fellow in preparing the bill, Pascoe Grenfell, also had a strong interest in the promotions of 1824– 1825, especially in the Latin American mining companies, but was able to survive the ultimate collapse.[40]

Moore and Grenfell were certainly not the only MPs with an interest in the ongoing speculative boom. Members often accused one another, during debates on bills of incorporation, of having private interests in specific companies and of voting accordingly. Attention was called in the Commons to an example in which sixteen members of a committee held shares, in sums of up to £30,000, in the joint-stock company whose incorporation bill was pending in that same committee.[41] One member referred to the custom of "offering shares to members – advertising them by preference as directors, to entrap the unwary; and as directors, giving

---

[37]Goldsmiths' Collection holds a copy of the pamphlet, *A Copy of the Bubble Act and Notes on Praemunire from Blackstone and Comyn's Digest and Draft Bill Proposed, to Be Introduced by Peter Moore* (1825), with an inserted note "with Messrs. Wilks and Verbeke's compliments," dated April 25, 1825. Wilks and Verbeke were solicitors to at least seven of the newly promoted companies, Wilks Sr. to nine more. See English, *Joint-Stock Companies*. Wilks Jr. was the solicitor of the British Annuity Company, of which Moore was chairman, and both were codefendants in *Van Sandau v. Moore and others*. This opens a small window into the networking of solicitors, company promoters, and MPs typical of 1825.

[38]*Lawyers and Legislators; Or, Notes on the American Mining Companies* (1825), 78.

[39]*Dictionary of National Biography* (Oxford University Press, 1885–).

[40]See entries in *Dictionary of National Biography* and *The History of Parliament: The House of Commons, 1790–1820*, Vol. 4: *Members* (London: Secker and Warburg, 1986), 84–85, 627–630. One of the mining companies, the Pasco-Peruvian, was rumored in the City to be named after him.

[41]Joseph Hume in *Hansard's Parliamentary Debates*, vol. 11, p. 913 (1824).

them shares to sell at a profit in the Bubble-market."[42] Another member mentioned that "it was well known that in most of the speculations now afloat in the city, some thousand shares were reserved for the use of members of Parliament."[43] Matters in Parliament deteriorated to such a level in 1824–1825 that Henry Brougham made it a rule not to vote on private bills, and Joseph Hume brought in a motion for a standing order that would restrict voting on a private bill by members who had an interest in that bill.[44] Peter Moore might have been the most renowned MP as far as company promotions were concerned but he was certainly not alone. Many other members had an interest as far as the repeal of the Bubble Act was concerned.

Moore did not initiate a repeal bill in 1824 or early in the 1825 session, but only in late March. Parliamentary control on the entrance to the corporate form suited him well and increased his income as a broker for legislation. But by late March, Eldon threatened company promoters, and Moore's business was in danger. The Attorney General, John Copley, the Lord Chancellor's representative in the Commons, opposed the repeal of the Bubble Act. He was rushed into the House and warned that the act dealt with a variety of matters including the incorporation of the two marine insurance companies and could not be repealed altogether. Home Secretary Peel and Huskisson came to his aid, and, using the procedural argument that a bill brought for the repeal of an act cannot be altered into a bill amending it, advised Moore to withdraw his motion, without referring to its merits.[45] Moore was coerced into withdrawing his motion and promised to bring a new bill after the holidays. In April, a pamphlet was circulated with a draft of Moore's amended bill.[46] As the government took no initiative, Moore did just what he promised and on April 29 he presented a new bill, this time to amend the Bubble Act. Leave was given to bring in the bill, Moore and Grenfell prepared it, and the next day it passed the first reading and was ordered to be printed.[47] Moore's bill went beyond repealing the relevant clauses of the Bubble Act. It aimed also at regulating the initial stage of company promotion and subscription.[48] However,

[42]Hudson Gurney in ibid., vol. 12, p. 982 (1825).

[43]Alexander Robertson in ibid., 986.

[44]Ibid., vol. 11, pp. 910–918 (1824); vol. 12, pp. 635– 641, 973–986 (1825). Hume's motion was withdrawn in May 1824 and, when presented again in the next session, was defeated in March 1825. See also Alexander Mundell, *The Influence of Interest and Prejudice upon Proceedings in Parliament* (1825), for a detailed deliberation of the defects in parliamentary proceedings and the ways by which these are exploited by interested MPs and result in inappropriate legislation.

[45]*Hansard's Parliamentary Debates*, vol. 12, pp. 1280–1285 (1825).

[46]*A Copy of the Bubble Act and Notes on Praemunire from Blackstone and Comyn's Digest and Draft Bill Proposed, to Be Introduced by Peter Moore.*

[47]*Commons' Journal* 80 (1825), 358–359.

[48]*Parliamentary Papers* (1825), vol. 1, April 29.

the second reading scheduled for May 13 was deferred and the bill went no further.[49]

The Repeal of the Bubble Act

Less than three weeks after Moore's bill was buried in the Commons, Attorney General Copley presented his own bill for the repeal of the Bubble Act on June 2. Whereas Moore's bill filled no less than ten pages, the new bill was laconic and included only two operative clauses, one repealing the relevant part of the Bubble Act, the other empowering the King to grant charters without limited liability.[50] Copley's reasoning for repealing the Bubble Act was mainly legal: "[I]ts meaning and effect were altogether unintelligible," it incurred "the heaviest penalty," and it had become a "dead letter." To this he added a practical consideration: Many of the unincorporated joint-stock companies said to be illegal had been formed for useful and laudable purposes and were advantageous to the public. Copley's bill seems a preemptive measure: first, to block Moore's bill; second, as a response to recurring shocks from both the court system and the stock market.

In addition to the repealing clause, the only other clause gave the Crown discretion to grant charters without full limited liability. This, Copley believed, would make the Law Officers more willing to grant charters, and would encourage promoters to apply for charters rather than for parliamentary acts of incorporation. Any further legislative measures "would be at once difficult, unwise and impolitic."[51]

In the House of Commons, the Attorney General, at least in theory, represented the Lord Chancellor (who sat in the Lords). It is not likely that the bill as such was in harmony with the Chancellor's policy of strong enforcement of the Bubble Act or measures for curtailing future speculative activities. Colonel Davies, who rose after Copley, expressed his fear that the bill "might encounter opposition in another place, from a learned Lord who already expressed his opinion on this subject." That learned Lord, unmistakably Eldon, "had uttered a general exclamation against all joint-stock companies." Davies concluded that even if Eldon "had spoken intelligently as a lawyer it was palpable that he had spoken with utmost possible ignorance, both as a statesman and a political economist."[52] This is one of the many examples of the widening gap between conservative lawyers and men of economic and business outlook during this period of economic change.

Davies also criticized Eldon for not adhering to Ellenborough's deci-

[49]*Commons' Journal* 80 (1825), 414.
[50]*Parliamentary Papers* (1825), vol. 1, June 6.
[51]*Hansard's Parliamentary Debates*, vol. 12, pp. 1018–1020 (1825).
[52]Ibid., 1020–1021.

sions, given in King's Bench in 1808–1812, regarding the interpretation
of the Bubble Act. Eldon's judgment in Chancery in early 1825 created
the uncertainty that led to the need to repeal the Bubble Act.[53] Huskisson
did not agree on this point. He did not doubt the legal reasoning behind
Ellenborough's interpretation of the Bubble Act, but thought that this
interpretation left to the jury the question of whether a company was
prejudicial to the public interest. According to Huskisson, it was not
Eldon who confused things and not even Ellenborough, it was the wording of the act. "Where persons had embarked large properties in a
speculation, ought they not be guaranteed by some secure provision of
the law, instead of having their interests left to the eloquence of counsel,
or to the discretion of a jury?"[54]

Whether Eldon was responsible for the legal and economic uncertainties of that year or not, it is clear that Copley did not introduce the bill
promised by Eldon on the first day of the session, some four months
earlier, and even spoke explicitly against such a measure. Interestingly,
Copley's bill passed the House of Lords in late June without any reported objection from Eldon or any of the other ultra-Tory Lords. How
can we explain the Lord Chancellor's silence in view of the apparent
break between him and his Attorney General? Why did he not use his
authority in the Lords to block the bill? Eldon must have realized that
he was on the weaker side, both in Cabinet and in Parliament, at least
among the active participants in the debate. It seems that, starting with
his judgment in Chancery in March 29, Eldon had revised his tactics. He
contemplated retreating into his judicial capacity and the safe haven of
judge-made law. On four separate occasions, on May 27, June 7, June
14, and, in particular, on June 24, Eldon revealed his modified approach.
If the Bubble Act is repealed "he should not much care, for he could tell
their lordships that there was hardly anything in that act which was not
punishable by the common law." Eldon induced the judges of the common-law courts to interpret the common law as he did and asked Parliament not to consider incorporation bills submitted by illegal associations.[55] Just as Moore retreated to his second option by moving for the
amendment of the Bubble Act, so did Eldon retreat from absolute objection to the repeal to his next option, the declaration or invention of a
common-law substitute for the act.

[53]For Ellenborough's decisions, see the preceding chapter; for Eldon's, see above in
this chapter.
[54]*Hansard's Parliamentary Debates*, vol. 12, p. 1021 (1825).
[55]Ibid., vol. 13, pp. 900–902, 1061–1062, 1135, 1349–1350 (1825). All these
addresses were made while the Lords were debating the Equitable Loan Company
bill. Eldon was against the consideration of the bill if, as was his opinion, the
company had acted illegally as a corporate body before applying to Parliament. He
presumed that most incorporation bills were made in similar circumstances and thus
should be barred.

On July 5 the bill received royal assent as 6 Geo. IV c.91 (1825).[56] Thus, 105 years after the Bubble Act was passed at the height of a speculative boom, its second part (the first part dealt with the formation of the two marine insurance companies) was repealed at the height of another speculative boom.

Ideological considerations played only a minor role in the process that led to the repeal of the Bubble Act. The discourse on the issue in 1824–1825 was not initiated by the theoretically confused political economists in Parliament nor was it initiated by the emergence of a new economic policy. Liverpool's administration of 1825 favored minimum interference in the status quo, and did not act positively or decisively to diminish existing State intervention in the economy or to strengthen individual autonomy. The debates over the massive incorporation phenomenon and the repeal of the Bubble Act demonstrate the limits of applying a laissez-faire paradigm to the 1820s. The term itself was not used in the contemporary debate and the concept was not employed coherently.

The parliamentary upheaval was ignited by an exogenous shock, the independence of Spain's Latin American colonies, and the ensuing stock market boom. When these took place, the political economists and statesmen in Parliament left the arena relatively open to manipulation by the representatives of interest groups. The function of the interest groups and the private interests of MPs in the decision-making process in Parliament in our context was pervasive. It is true that interests can usually be proven when searched for meticulously and that they do not always provide the key to politicians' opinions, but saying this does not make the discussion of their actual role in a specific context redundant. The question is why and by what mechanism interests rose to dominance at a specific point in time and in relation to specific issues. The above narrative aimed at explaining the reshuffling of interest groups and the dynamics of their lobbying that eventually led to the repeal of the Bubble Act.

In addition to interest groups, the judiciary – the legal culture in general and the personality of Lord Eldon in particular – also considerably influenced the final outcome. Lord Eldon, a key figure in 1825, was a typical outgrowth of a social and educational system and, in turn, of a legal ethos, that stressed the importance of legal precedents, ancient legal conceptions, formalistic legal thinking, and an autonomous legal realm. His objection to the suggested regulatory transformation was motivated not by interest-group pressures nor by an articulated economic outlook, but rather by his legal ideals. His action in two of his capacities, in Chancery and in the House of Lords, drove the interest groups to seek

---

[56]*Commons' Journal* 80 (1825), 483, 523, 545, 552, 554, 627. There is no report in *Hansard's Parliamentary Debates* or any other conventional source as to whether there was a debate in the Lords on the repeal bill.

legislation in the first place. His conservatism eventually prevailed as he retreated safely to the common law and declared the illegality of associations according to it, the repeal of the Bubble Act not withstanding. To conclude, the events in Parliament in 1825 culminating in the repeal should be understood as a result of the interplay between interest groups and the Lord Chancellor, interplay in which political economy and economic policy should be viewed as taking a back seat.

Between the passage of the repeal act, late in the hectic 1825 session, and the opening of the next session, in February 1826, the market lost its momentum and eventually crashed. During the summer, after some negative reports were published, turnover in the stock exchange diminished. In October, many of the newly promoted companies were traded for the first time below par, and even prices of East India and Bank of England shares took a downward turn. On October 25, a run on country banks began and by December the entire banking system was on the verge of collapse.

Aftershocks of the crisis were felt well into 1826. Altogether, eighty country banks went bankrupt, most by January of 1826, as did a large number of businesses in the following months. By mid-1826 none of the Latin American companies was traded above par. By 1827, only fifteen of the 624 companies formed in 1824–1825 were traded above their paid-up price, while about 500 disappeared altogether. An attempt to again raise the issue of the legal framework of business organization in Parliament and to call for an inquiry or new legislation to replace the Bubble Act was curtailed by the Ministry in 1826. The matter was excluded from the public agenda until the mid-1830s. At that point the issue resurfaced, to remain on the agenda for the next twenty years. The common-law limitation on the formation of joint-stock companies remained in force, subject to a few counterholdings, until the introduction of general incorporation by Parliament in 1844.

TORY AND WHIG GOVERNMENTS AFTER THE REPEAL: 1827–1841

After the share market collapse and the banking system crisis of late 1825 and early 1826, supporters of free trade lost some of their confidence. Ricardo's reputation as an omnipotent economist dimmed and doctrinaire Ricardianism in Parliament went into eclipse. Huskisson's free trade policy was attacked more vigorously than before. Liverpool suffered a stroke, and was not able to fulfill his duties. He had to resign in February 1827 and thereafter three short-lived Tory administrations were formed, headed by George Canning, Frederick Robinson (now titled Viscount Goderich) and the Duke of Wellington. The leading liberal Tory ministers moved to new, less economically influential offices, and some left the government altogether.

Upon Canning's death in 1827, Huskisson was induced to take over the Colonial Office in order to continue the former's policy. He thus left the Board of Trade and gave up the Exchequer to his long-time rival John Herries. In 1828, he resigned from the government because Prime Minister Wellington was not willing to commit himself to a free trade policy. Huskisson was killed by a steam locomotive on the day of the opening of the Liverpool and Manchester Railway in 1830. His death, to a great degree, represented the demise of the liberal Tory economic policy of the 1820s.

In the late 1820s, the Catholic question and the parliamentary reform controversy consumed much of the time of the by then unstable Tory governments. Under these circumstances, it is not surprising that the question of joint-stock incorporation was not placed again on the agenda, and that no further legislative measures were taken after the repeal of the Bubble Act and of the corporate monopolies in marine insurance and banking.

Wellington's government fell in 1830 over the controversy on parliamentary reform. After that time, with only a short interval in 1834–1835, the Whigs, headed by Earl Grey and later Viscount Melbourne, remained in power until 1841. This period did not bring about any significant change in the field of company legislation. It was a period of experiments and half measures, not of systematic reform based on the implementation of a concrete economic doctrine. Was the government in the years 1830–1841 liberal in its general orientation? Was the absence of reform in company law in this period exceptional in the wider context of government policy?

According to Norman Gash, the Whig governments of 1830–1841 were incompetent both economically and administratively.[57] They were aristocratic in character and were rushed around in some respects, including parliamentary reform, by a small group of radicals. Liberal ideology and doctrinaire economic policy had no real holding in these governments which were anachronistic in their outlook. In any event, due to internal manipulations and loss of seats in elections, their real power ended by 1835.[58] In light of Gash's interpretation, it is not surprising that no real reform in company law took place between 1830 and 1841, and that serious efforts at further reform were renewed as

---

[57]Norman Gash, *Sir Robert Peel: The Life of Sir Robert Peel after 1830* (London: Longman, 1972), and *Aristocracy and People*.

[58]David Southgate, *The Passing of the Whigs* (London: Macmillan, 1962), is more sympathetic toward the Whig governments than Gash, yet he also stresses their anachronistic, rather than liberal, character.

soon as Robert Peel (Gash's exemplification of liberalism and competence) returned to office in 1841.

Later interpretations are more positive in their judgment of the Whigs.[59] These focus on political and social reform as the main achievements of the Whig governments. However, even these reforms were moderate because of the difficulty for liberalism and Whigism to coexist within the Whig party. The Whig administrations did not show any particular interest in economic questions, were not influenced by the political economists, adopted no coherent economic policy, and were prone to concessions to pressure groups. In other words, the economic policies of these governments were pragmatic and compromising. From this interpretative perspective, the changes in company law that took place during this period can be viewed as moderate and pragmatic reform, rather than a sign of incompetence. Neither of the interpretations above would anticipate widescale transformation in company law during this era of Whig dominance.

With these two approaches to the wider context in mind, I turn to the actual legislative attempts of that period. Attempts at legislative reform during the Whig era took three major lines: facilitation of incorporation through letters patent (unsealed charters) issued by the Crown (in practice, the Privy Council), introduction of the limited liability partnership, and the emergence of the concept of registration as a new method for the formation of associations of several types. We now examine the novelty, realization, and effectiveness of these attempts. It can be disclosed at this stage that the third line turned out to be most successful, but only in 1844, after the Whigs were ousted from power.

Return to Incorporation by the Crown

The first line of legislative attempts during the Whig era was based on a direction initiated by the Liberal Tory government of 1825. As mentioned above, the repeal act was laconic and included only two clauses, the first repealing the relevant parts of the Bubble Act and the second, relevant to this line of development, enacting that:

In any Charter hereafter to be granted by His Majesty . . . for the Incorporation of any Company . . . it shall and may be lawful, in and by such Charter, to declare and provide, that the members of such corporation shall be individually

---

[59]Peter Mandler, *Aristocratic Government in the Age of Reform, Whigs and Liberals 1830–1852* (Oxford: Clarendon Press, 1990); Ian Newbould, *Whiggery and Reform: 1830–1841 – The Politics of Government* (Stanford University Press, 1990).

liable, in their persons and property, for the debts, contracts and engagements of such corporation.[60]

This clause was added on the initiative of Attorney General Copley and Huskisson.[61] Their opinion was that incorporation should be granted by the Crown rather than by Parliament. Parliament was overburdened by incorporation applications, whereas the Crown had the needed legal advisers to deal with such applications. They may also have been influenced by Eldon's opinion that charters can easily be withdrawn if exploited, whereas parliamentary incorporation can be abolished only by a full legislative annulling process. They insisted upon including the second clause in the repeal act in order to make legal advisers to the Crown more attentive to applications and to facilitate granting charters by the Crown. They envisioned an increase in chartered incorporation, yet in most cases without the privilege of limited liability.

In 1834, the Whig government joined in supporting this line of solving the problems of business associations through the Crown. C. P. Thomson, the president of the Board of Trade, who came from a family with an overseas trading firm, and who for some years had shown an interest in joint-stock companies as well as in finance and free trade economics, introduced a bill, the Trading Companies Act, into the House. With the objection of only one member, the act was passed.[62] It empowered the Crown

to grant to any company or body of persons associated together for any trading, charitable, literary or other purposes . . . although not incorporated by such Letters Patent, any privilege or privileges which, according to the rules of the common law . . . it would be competent to His Majesty . . . to grant . . . by any Charter of incorporation, and especially the before-mentioned privilege of maintaining and defending actions, suits, prosecutions . . . in the name . . . of principal officers.[63]

Theoretically, this clause created a new form of association, a quasicorporation, not fully incorporated but not unincorporated. This quasicorporation was referred to throughout the act as "Company, Body, or Association." In fact, after 1807, unincorporated companies had obtained specific acts of Parliament enabling them to sue in the name of an officer.[64] They thus received legislative recognition, and enjoyed some of the exclusive privileges of corporation, without being incorporated, and

[60] 6 Geo. IV c.92 (1825), cl. 2.
[61] *Hansard's Parliamentary Debates*, vol. 13, pp. 1020–1021 (1825).
[62] Ibid., vol. 25, p. 194 (1834).
[63] 4 & 5 Wm. IV c.94 (1834).
[64] See Chapter 4.

could not be classified as totally unincorporated. The real effect of the act of 1834 was to shift the responsibility for granting privileges of this kind from Parliament to the Crown. This was in line with the tendency in this direction that began with the Tory act of 1825.

It is important to note that the return to the Crown during this period had nothing to do with the seventeenth-century constitutional struggle over the prerogative of incorporation between the Crown and Parliament. Supporters of this line of reform believed that the task of examining incorporation petitions could be performed better by administrative than by legislative bodies, and that with the increase in the number of petitions it became too time-consuming a matter for Parliament, which had more important business to deal with. On the other hand, an anonymous pamphleteer objected to the rationale of the bill, because "in Parliament all must be open and straightforward . . . yet before the King, or rather his Ministers, there would be no open application – no means of opposition – no fair fighting; but back-door influence and private friendship. . . ."[65]

Shortly after the enactment, in November 1834, the Committee of Privy Council for Trade declared its policy on granting letters patent according to the new act. The committee would approve the application for limited privileges of incorporation only under special circumstances. It enumerated four types of companies that would justify such approval: those formed for hazardous business, such as the working of mines; those requiring large amount of capital, such as canals and railways; those subject to extended responsibility, such as assurance companies; and those which associate numerous members, such as literary and charitable societies.[66] Interestingly, this list was not far different from that proposed by Adam Smith some fifty years earlier.

In the wake of another wave of speculations, a new Trading Companies Act was passed in 1837 whose aim was very limited: to improve the act of 1834. The fourth section of this act made it lawful to grant letters patent to limit the liability of members of unincorporated associations "to such extent only per share as shall be declared and limited in and by such Letters Patent."[67] Following the act of 1837, the Crown was empowered to grant some of the privileges of incorporation to petitioners, notably the right to sue in the name of an officer and limitation of personal liability, without fully incorporating them. At this point, full incorporation could still be obtained only by an act of Parliament or by royal charter, yet petitioners were encouraged to take the developing

[65]*Observations on the Trading Companies Bill* (1834), 7.
[66]Minutes of the Lords of the Committee of Privy Council for Trade, Nov. 4, 1834. Printed in *Parliamentary Papers* (1837), vol. 39, p. 287.
[67]1 Vict. c.73 (1837).

course of obtaining letters patent, making do with only some of the privileges of incorporation.[68] The act of 1844 abandoned this seemingly unsatisfactory course of reform taken by the Whigs, and left no future role to the Privy Council, to letters patent, or to partial or quasiincorporation.

Limited Liability Partnership

The introduction of limited liability partnership into England resurfaced in the 1830s. The limited liability partnership had not developed within the English legal system.[69] Attempts to use settlements between partners to form de facto limited liability partnerships were not successful. The courts held these arrangements to apply only inter se, without restricting third parties from treating each partner as fully liable.

An attempt to introduce the limited liability partnership statutorily failed in the Commons in 1818.[70] By 1825, the desirability of adopting the limited liability partnership into the English system was being widely discussed both in and out of Parliament.[71] Explicit reference was made to the French and Irish models. It was argued that the limited partnership could serve as a substitute, in some cases, for the unincorporated company and even for the corporation. The French model was generally perceived as a successful one, yet some speakers were against importation of foreign legal concepts into England.

In 1836, H. Bellenden Ker, a barrister with enthusiasm for legal reform, was appointed by C. P. Thomson to "inquire into the present state of the law of partnership . . . and to consider whether it would be expedient to introduce a law, authorizing persons to become partners in trade with limited responsibility, similar to the French law of partnership, *en commandite*."[72] Ker heard mixed opinions from witnesses on this point. A. Levinger presented a comparative example to support his view: "The city of Mulhausen, on French grounds, in the department of

[68]The formal distinction between a charter and a letters patent is only technical; what makes the difference in this case is the substance of the letters patent, which did not include a clause to the effect of incorporation.

[69]See Chapter 1 for the origins of this form of organization and its earlier rejection by the common law. See also Postan, "Partnership in English," 65–91, for an unorthodox argument according to which some sort of limited liability partnership did exist in medieval England.

[70]*Hansard's Parliamentary Debates*, vol. 38, pp. 22–23 (1818).

[71]Ibid., vol. 12, p. 1060 (1825); John Austin, "Joint-Stock Companies," *Parliamentary History and Review* (1825); *Remarks on Joint Stock Companies by an Old Merchant* (1825), 92–95; Mundell, *Influence of Interest*, 133ff.

[72]Ker, "Law of Partnership." The report was reprinted as an appendix to Gladstone's report in Reports, *Parliamentary Papers* (1844), vol. 7. References in this chapter are to the reprint. See p. 245.

Haut and Bas-Rhin, which is now a second Manchester, . . . would not have risen to one-tenth part of the importance and riches it possesses now, were it not for these *commandites*."[73] Francis Baring went as far as submitting a proposed bill to Ker for the formation of limited partnerships in England.[74] On the other hand, Samuel Jones Lloyd was more patriotic: "In other countries where either capital is less abundant, as in the United States, or where the spirit of commercial enterprise is either more feeble or less generally prevalent, as in Continental countries of Europe, the case may be different."[75] In other words, what is an essential form of organization for undeveloped countries is not necessary for the entrepreneurially spirited and capital abundant world leader, England. The bottom line was that six of the witnesses (all bankers) opposed the introduction of limited liability partnerships in England, while four (three bankers and Nassau Senior) favored their introduction.[76] Ker himself did not explicitly renounce the limited liability partnership, but did not include in his recommendations any measure for its introduction in England.

When Gladstone's committee issued its report on joint-stock companies in 1844, it decided to "forbear to express an opinion [on limited partnerships], because, though highly worthy of consideration, those subjects do not appear to fall within the scope of reference which has been made to them."[77] The result was that this line of possible reform in the law of business organization, seriously considered for at least three decades, was abandoned. The issue of the introduction of the limited liability partnership in England was left outside the main discourse. After the early 1850s, discourse revolved around the question of the desirability of the granting of general limited liability to corporations, rather than to partnerships.[78] Only in 1907 was the limited liability partnership recognized by the English law, but this is well beyond the time frame of the present work.[79]

The Rise of the Concept of Registration

The rise of the concept of registration, as a substitute for the concept of petition to the State as a monopolist and discretionary incorporator, was a gradual one. It was based on an evolutionary trial and error process

---

[73] *Parliamentary Papers* (1844), vol. 7, p. 320.
[74] Ibid., 277.
[75] Ibid., 273–274.
[76] Ibid., 260. See p. 18 for a classification of the witnesses by profession.
[77] Ibid., 6.
[78] See John Saville, "Sleeping Partnership and Limited Liability: 1850–1856," *Economic History Review* 8, no. 3 (1956), 420–433.
[79] The Limited Partnership Act, 7 Edw. VII c.24 (1907).

that stretched over more than half a century. The Registration, Incorporation and Regulation Act of 1844, to which we turn in the next sections, should not be examined in isolation, but rather as a culmination of this conceptual development. In its mature form, the concept of registration offered a middle ground between public sphere (constitutional) and private sphere (contractual) formation of corporations. I begin by describing the historical evolution of the concept, beginning in 1786.

The main purpose of the Registration Act of 1786 was to enhance the implementation of the navigation laws. Yet the act also established a procedure for recording information about the shareholders and the transferring of shares in each ship under English flag.[80] An act for the Registering of British Vessels of 1825 further elaborated the mechanism for reporting and recording information on the ownership of shares in ships.[81] The Collector and Comptroller of each major port were empowered to set up a registry and receive the reports. As shown in an earlier chapter, the ownership structure of ships, division into sixty-four shares held by part-owners, is somewhat similar to the structure of joint-stock companies. Thus, in a way, the registration procedure developed in the context of ships was a forerunner of the registration of companies.

The Saving Banks Act of 1817 fixed a procedure for the formation and regulation of savings banks based on registration and submission of accounts.[82] The national debt commissioners and a barrister to be appointed by them were empowered to certify the rules of such savings banks and to receive their accounts. By 1833, there were 408 savings banks formed on the basis of the act with 425,000 depositors and capital of £14,334,000.[83]

The act of 1826 that terminated the corporate monopoly of the Bank of England and authorized the formation of joint-stock banks also required that these banks deliver returns and accounts. A schedule was annexed to the act detailing the substance of these annual returns which were to include the names of all the members of each bank. Each return was to be verified by the oath of an officer taken before any Justice of Peace. Each return was to be delivered to the Commissioners of Stamps in London.

The Friendly Societies Act of 1829 stated that it would be lawful for any number of persons to form themselves into a society for the mutual relief and maintenance of its members.[84] A barrister, the same person

---

[80] 26 Geo. III c.60 (1786).

[81] 6 Geo. IV c.10 (1825), particularly sections 31 to 35.

[82] 57 Geo. III c.130 (1817).

[83] Holdsworth, *English Law*, vol. 13, pp. 334–335.

[84] 10 Geo. IV c.56 (1829), clause 2. This act was in part a consolidation of earlier acts referred to in its preamble.

who had held the appointment for certifying the rules of savings banks in the Trustee Saving Bank Act of 1817, was appointed in England to certify the rules of each of the societies. These rules and other information were to be deposited with the Clerk of the Peace in the county in which each society was to be formed. Each clerk had to present these deposited documents to the Justices of Peace of the country in their next quarter session. Furthermore, once every five years, they had to submit returns on all the societies formed in their county to the Secretary of State and to both Houses of Parliament. An act of 1834 required an additional return on the rate of sickness and mortality to be made to the Barrister.[85]

An act of 1836 authorized the establishment of building societies to erect or purchase dwelling houses, with shares not exceeding £150.[86] The provisions of the Friendly Societies acts of 1829 and 1834 were extended to building societies formed by this act. These included rules on certifying and enrolling the societies as well as on returns made on their formation.

The Letters Patent Act of 1834 required prior notice in the London Gazette, as well as an entry on every grant of letters patent in the Gazette and in a local newspaper. It also required that a list of the members of each company formed according to the act be filed every six months with the Clerk of Patents, and be opened to inspection by any person.[87] The Letters Patent Act of 1837 was even more demanding. A form was fixed for the returns and a long list of instances requiring the filing of returns within three months was specified in the act.[88] Returns in England were to be made to the enrollment office of the Court of Chancery.

Thus, step by step, the mechanism of registration of associations, of periodical returns, of disclosure, and of publicly open records was set up for the business-oriented joint-stock company. The process was slow and initiated long before the Whigs came to power in 1830. For some decades, experiments were made concerning the frequency of the returns, the information to be included in them, the place of registration, and the degree of accessibility to the public of the records. Free information was gradually replacing paternalistic supervision, by King or Parliament, as a means of enabling the public to distinguish between good and bad associations.

One important feature of this process was that the new arrangements were first experimented with on the periphery, before being generally implemented. They were first employed in the context of ships, then

[85] 4 & 5 Wm. IV c.40 (1834).
[86] 6 & 7 Wm. IV c.32 (1836).
[87] 4 & 5 Wm. IV c.94 (1834), clauses 2 and 4.
[88] 1 Vict. c.73 (1837), clauses 6–17.

friendly societies, savings and joint-stock banks, building societies, companies formed by letters patent, and only later on joint-stock companies of all sorts. The Whig administrations were pragmatic in this respect and did not try to force the entire economy to accept or to reject the new conception altogether.

By the time Gladstone's committee on joint-stock companies sought solutions in the early 1840s, it had ample experiments in the use of registration and of periodical returns. Its decision to adopt the concept of registration and general inspection by the public, and reject the centuries-old conception of inspection and authorization by the State, was not as revolutionary as some later observers thought.[89] It was based on the experiments employing this new concept in limited sectors in the 1820s and 1830s. This is evident from Gladstone's committee minutes.[90]

The Select Committee of 1841

The boom of company promotions peaked in 1837, and was followed by the usual market crash and the collapse of companies. The Trading Companies Act of 1837 did not seem to provide a remedy against cyclical crashes, did not attract a large number of companies to seek the privileges it offered, and did not solve other fundamental legal problems facing partnerships and unincorporated companies. Disillusion with the act and the boom led to the formation of a parliamentary Select Committee in May 1841. The committee was appointed during Melbourne's second administration, shortly before the Whig electoral defeat in July 1841, and was chaired by Richard L. Sheil, vice-president of the Board of Trade. Sheil, a supporter of Daniel O'Connell, leader of the Catholic Association, was primarily interested in Irish and religious problems. He did not show much interest in economic policy or in administrative duties such as the chairing of the committee. His free time was devoted to writing plays rather than to reading literature on political economy.

The first meetings of the Select Committee seemed to follow the

---

[89]Hunt, *Development of the Business Corporation*, 94–95. Hunt says of the Act of 1844: "'On implementing Gladstone's basic insight, adequate knowledge for the investor, it initiated the policy of publicity which by gradual evolution has become an outstanding and progressively more pronounced characteristic of company regulation in England.' The act was indeed an important turning point in this respect, yet it did not initiate this policy and did not rely only on Gladstone's insight, but also on three decades of experiments.

[90]J. T. Pratt, the barrister appointed by law to certify the rules of Friendly Societies and savings banks, was examined by the committee. He testified that he certified nearly 11,000 Friendly Societies consisting of 2,000,000 members. Another witness, Charles Ansell, presented to the committee an abstract of the privileges of Friendly Societies. See *Parliamentary Papers* (1844), vol. 7, pp. 79–83, 153–155.

pattern of previous committees, inquiring into specific fraudulent cases, rather than dealing with more general cases. Such an ex-post approach could do justice to swindlers of the previous crash, but could not prevent future crashes or lead to legal reform. The committee held three meetings in May of 1841 and heard seven witnesses, four of them actuaries of insurance companies. It did not really go beyond the investigation of frauds in specific insurance schemes, and reached no conclusions. The elections and the changed composition of the cabinet probably contributed to the dead end at which this select committee arrived.

A decade of Whig domination did not bring about any fundamental change in the framework of business organization. Most attempts at reform either were not realized at all (the limited partnership) or did not fulfill the desired aims (quasiincorporation by letters patent). One investigation (Ker's) provided a set of recommendations, most of which were not adopted, whereas another investigation (Sheil's) was very limited in scope and proposed no recommendations. Yet despite the incompetence demonstrated by the Whig administrations, one important line of reform was kept alive and developed: the conception of incorporation by registration, subject to publicity of information. The experiments carried out along this line were essential to Gladstone in shaping his recommendations for reform two years after the Whig defeat.

PEEL'S CONSERVATIVE ADMINISTRATION, 1841–1844

Peel led the conservatives to victory in the elections of 1841 and was in a position to lead the most stable, independent, and talented Tory administration since Liverpool's administration of the mid-1820s. He still gathered around him some of the key figures of Liverpool's liberal Tory administration and continued its liberal and free trade policy. Peel began to unfold his plans as soon as he took office. He lowered tariffs and taxes on consumer goods and encouraged foreign trade in order to stimulate the economy. To offset the decrease in income from these sources and to reduce the large deficit, he introduced an income tax. He was able to draft a compromise on the Corn Law question, which would delay the conflict between the agriculturists and the Anti-Corn Law League for a short while. His budget for 1842 was in tune with the classical dogmatic theory of the political economists. Support of free trade seemed at its zenith as its main supporters, Richard Cobden, the Manchester school, and the newly founded *Economist*, expressed their ideas in any available arena. Yet, as political and economic difficulties mounted, Peel's administration deviated, in some respects, from a pure noninterventionist policy. This deviation became apparent in the Ten-

Hour Factory Act and the legislation on banking and railways discussed below. Was Peel's administration turning away from free trade or advancing the two contradictory policies simultaneously? When considering this question, we should not confuse free trade with laissez-faire. The administration could advance free trade while intervening in other spheres. But before proceeding to the more general discussion, we should first turn to the joint-stock company, and examine whether the administration's treatment of this issue can be seen as laissez-faire or interventionist in its outlook.

The answer to this question serves as one part of a wider picture of the character of economic policy of Peel's administration. It contributes its modest share to the more general and by now seasoned, but somewhat revitalized, debate between laissez-faire and State intervention views of mid-nineteenth-century England.[91] Was Peel's government policy toward joint-stock companies in tune with the individualistic and liberal conception of the early Victorian State, as Dicey would like us to believe?[92] Or was its policy more interventionist than the policy of the liberal Tory government of the 1820s, as Brebner, Parris, and others would argue?[93]

The Parliamentary Committee

In the early months of his administration, Peel showed no interest in the subject of joint-stock companies or in the Select Committee appointed in 1841.[94] Only when William Gladstone was promoted from vice-president to president of the Board of Trade, in 1843, and took over from Sheil the chairmanship of the committee shortly afterward, did it resume its activity.

In 1843, Gladstone was a young (thirty-four-year-old) and energetic politician, yet already an eleven-year veteran of the House of Commons. Two years earlier, when Robert Peel's second administration was formed, he had been appointed vice-president of the Board of Trade, and in May of 1843, he became president and joined the cabinet. In

[91]P.W.J. Bartrip, "State Intervention in Mid-Nineteenth Century Britain: Fact or Fiction?," *Journal of British Studies* 23, no. 1 (1983), 63–83; Philip Harling and Peter Mandler, "From 'Fiscal-Military' State to Laissez-faire State, 1760–1850," *Journal of British Studies* 32, no. 1 (1993), 44–70.

[92]A. V. Dicey, *Lectures on the Relations Between Law and Public Opinion in England During the Nineteenth Century* (London: Macmillan, 1905).

[93]J. Bartlet Brebner, "Laissez Faire and State Intervention in Nineteenth-Century Britain," *Journal of Economic History* 8 (supplement) (1948); Henry Parris, "The Nineteenth-Century Revolution in Government: A Reappraisal Reappraised," *Historical Journal* 3, no. 1 (1960), 17–37.

[94]Gash, *Sir Robert Peel*, 273–329.

1841, Gladstone admitted to having no particular interest in economic policy or in time-consuming administrative duties. He was much more interested in moral and religious questions and wanted to be involved in shaping policy on the Irish question. He was disappointed that Peel had not offered him a cabinet position and reluctantly joined the Board of Trade. He told Peel as he was offered the job: "I have no general knowledge of trade whatsoever."[95] Furthermore, he admitted to being a vowed Protectionist in 1840, an ideology that did not yet reconcile with Peel's policy, and later wrote:

The very next stage in my career was my becoming Vice-President of the Board of Trade in August 1841. That assumption was followed by hard, steady, and honest work and every day so spent beat like a battering ram on the unsure fabric of my official Protectionism. By the end of the year I was far gone in the opposite sense. . . . From one cause or another my reputation among the Conservatives on this question oozed away with rapidity: it died with that year [1842].[96]

By the time he replaced Ripon as a president of the Board of Trade in 1843, Gladstone had developed a fascination with the details of administration and a growing interest in economic policy. He came to the conclusion that "as a man in politics he might have a wider function than the ethical role he had accorded himself in the 1830s."[97]

Thus, Gladstone took over the Select Committee with a fresh free-trade ideology, enjoying the support of Peel, who had converted at about the same time to anti-Corn Law positions, with a growing standing in the cabinet and an intimate knowledge of parliamentary practices and Board of Trade functioning. He used all these in directing his committee and pushing its resolutions through Parliament.

The committee met frequently between June 1843 and March 1844. It heard the evidence of no less than twenty witnesses. It had before it Ker's report on the law of partnership.[98] Altogether, with evidence that was presented in writing, as part of Ker's report, and testimony heard by the committee in 1841, the committee had on its table the opinions of 39 persons: eight barristers, 13 solicitors (some of them practicing parliamentary agents), 12 merchants and bankers, four insurance actu-

[95]M.R.D. Foot and H.C.G. Matthew, eds., *The Gladstone Diaries*, 14 vols. (Oxford: Clarendon Press, 1968–1994), vol. 3, p. 135; see also Gash, *Sir Robert Peel*, 277.

[96]John Brooke and Mary Sorensen, eds., *The Prime Ministers' Papers: W. A. Gladstone*, Vol. 1: *Autobiographica* (London: H.M.S.O., 1971), 60.

[97]John Morley, *The Life of William Ewart Gladstone*, 3 vols. (London: Macmillan, 1903), vol. 1, p. 247ff.

[98]The first thing Gladstone did when reviving the committee on June 23, 1943, was to read Ker's report; see Foot and Matthew, *The Gladstone Diaries*, vol. 3, p. 293.

aries, one Alderman, and one locksmith.[99] Gladstone nominated new members to his committee, called on a group of witnesses familiar with the problems of joint-stock companies and of other sorts of business organization, and most important, instructed his witnesses to refer to general questions and alternative proposals for future reform, rather than discuss specific cases and past evils.

On March 15, 1844, Gladstone's committee submitted its report and resolutions to Parliament. It was entitled "First Report," but because no future reports were made, this turned out to be the final report of the committee. The committee reported briefly on a number of bubble companies, whose cases it had examined. It then turned to twenty-three resolutions, the first of which revealed their general spirit:

That in order to prevent the establishment of fraudulent companies, and to protect the interests of the shareholders and of the public, it is expedient that all joint stock companies (other than banking companies) for commercial purposes, whether future or already formed, be registered in an office to be appointed for that purpose.[100]

The twenty-third and last of these resolutions recommended that bills be prepared to carry all of the resolutions into effect.

Gladstone acted decisively. The bills were quickly drafted and by June they had passed through Commons without much debate. On September 5, 1844, the two acts that embodied Gladstone's legislative reform received royal assent. These were an act for Registration, Incorporation and Regulation of Joint Stock Companies, and an act for Facilitating the Winding Up of the Affairs of Joint Stock Companies.[101]

Gladstone may have been troubled by the lack of interest in his bills. He said in the Commons:

Though of great importance, these two measures had not been much discussed in that House; but they had obtained considerable notoriety, and so far as he could judge from communications he had received, and also from what he had observed in the papers, he judged that the principles on which the bills proceeded met with pretty general, or indeed he might say, universal approval.[102]

However, Gladstone should not really have been surprised by the low profile of the legislative process and the lack of objections to his recommendations. From the start, he employed a tactic to minimize opposition to his bill. Gladstone's Registration Act was also not as revolutionary as some might think. The concept of registration was by then well tested on a smaller scale, and not strange to the House. When shaping his

[99]*Parliamentary Papers* (1844), vol. 7, p. 18.
[100]Ibid., 7.
[101]These were, respectively, 7 & 8 Vict. c.110 (1844) and 7 & 8 Vict. c.111 (1844).
[102]*Hansard's Parliamentary Debates*, 3d ser., vol. 75, p. 475 (1844).

position, Gladstone was also well aware of the relatively unsuccessful legislation of 1834 and 1837, and abandoned the idea of large-scale Crown, or rather administrative, incorporation. Furthermore, he employed the tactic of isolating problems. He removed the hotly disputed issue of limited liability from his agenda. He decided to avoid the introduction of general limited liability as a privilege for every registered company, or of the limited partnership, and left the status quo in this matter untouched. He knew that the issue of limited liability could attract strong opposition to his bill and bury it altogether, thus he left the debates for future sessions of Parliament. These were indeed highly debated issues before the enactment of general limited liability in 1855 and 1856, as well as afterward.[103] Gladstone further separated the treatment of two of the most significant and fastest growing sectors of his time, banks and railways, from that of other sectors.[104] Railways and banking were not affected by the Registration, Incorporation and Regulation Act. Joint-stock banks had been formed by simple registration since 1826. The act to Regulate Joint Stock Banks was passed in 1844 to exclude banks from the application of the general act, and deal with this sector separately, subject to more severe regulation.[105] Railway companies in any case needed to resort to Parliament because lines could not be constructed without the powers of eminent domain to expropriate private property. Thus railways had to rely on specific acts of incorporation both before and after the Railway Act of 1844.[106] Gladstone, a relatively junior politician, maneuvered Parliament superbly, like a veteran legislator. He expanded a well-tried conception, abandoned failed Whig attempts at reform, separated and isolated problems, and avoided the treatment of disputed issues. In this way, Gladstone could expect to face weaker opposition to his reform scheme, and indeed his bills, among the most important of the era, passed through Parliament smoothly and with almost no debate.

The Companies Act of 1844 and Its Significance

The Registration, Incorporation and Regulation Act was the core of Gladstone's reform. This act proclaimed that incorporation could be

---

[103]These debates are beyond the time frame of the present work. For discussion of these debates, see Shannon, "Limited Liability," 358; Hunt, *Business Corporation*, 116–159; Boyd Hilton, *The Age of Atonement: The Influence of Evangelicalism on Social and Economic Thought, 1795–1865* (Oxford: Clarendon Press, 1988), 237ff; Christine E. Amsler, Robin L. Bartlett, and Craig J. Bolton, "Thoughts of Some British Economists on Early Limited Liability and Corporate Legislation," *History of Political Economy* 13, no. 4 (1981), 774–793.

[104]For the growth of these sectors, see Chapter 8.

[105]7 & 8 Vict. c.113 (1844). See also 7 & 8 Vict. c.32 (1844).

[106]7 & 8 Vict. c.85 (1844).

obtained merely through registration. A Registry Office was set up for the purposes of the act, and a registrar was to be appointed by the Committee of Privy Council for Trade. Each company had to register in this office, in two stages: provisional registration before its promoters could offer any shares publicly (by way of prospectus, advertisement, etc.), and complete registration after its deed was signed by the shareholders and the first officers appointed. A deed of incorporation had to include the purpose of the company, the structure of its share capital, the names of the subscribers and the amount of shares they held, and the names of the directors and auditors of the company. Upon complete registration, a company could, among other things, use a registered name, sue and be sued by its registered name, enter into contracts, purchase lands, issue shares, borrow money, hold meetings, and make bylaws. In fact, a company registered by the act enjoyed all the features of incorporation – separate personality, free transferability of shares, and hierarchical managerial structure – with but one exception: limitation of liability. An elaborate system was developed for making returns to the registrar and for annual reports by the registrar to Parliament. The directors of each company were responsible for entering all its accounts into account books. Balance sheets were to be produced to the shareholders periodically, and to be inspected by the auditors.

Examination of the act on a more conceptual level leads to the conclusion that the last mentioned requirements are probably the most innovative. The concept of formation of associations by mere registration, without specific authorization by the State, could be found, as shown above, in saving, friendly, and building societies as well as in banking, over the previous two or three decades. What was new in Gladstone's act was the scope and the sophistication. The act included 130 clauses and had ten schedules. It was much more specific and detailed than previous acts in spelling out requirements regarding registration, returns, and disclosures. Furthermore, it took a new approach which emphasized that the disclosure required in these returns was to serve not only the interests of State authorities, but especially those of the shareholders and the general public. The Registrars Office was ordered to be open to the public from 10 a.m. to 5 p.m. daily, and each company was to present its books for the inspection of its shareholders, to distribute balance sheets to shareholders, and so on.[107]

Another conceptual novelty was the distinction drawn between joint-stock companies and partnerships, where previously a distinction had been drawn between corporations and unincorporated associations. Unincorporated associations, such as unincorporated joint-stock companies

---

[107]See, for example, 7 & 8 Vict. c.110 (1844), sections 20, 33, 36.

that used deeds of settlements and the trust device, companies that obtained acts for suing using a common name, or companies that were granted letters patent by the acts of 1834 and 1837 had acquired several of the characteristics of joint-stock corporations. But by law, none was a corporation and until 1844 they could enjoy only some of the privileges of full incorporation and of the corporate entity. The act of 1844 granted all these associations incorporation by law, provided they were duly registered. At the same time, it made the formation of joint-stock companies illegal unless they were registered according to the act. The duty of registration according to the act was to apply to every partnership with transferable shares, every insurance association including mutual insurance societies (lacking joint stock), and every partnership of more than twenty-five members (including those having no joint stock).[108] The applicability of the 1844 act was even wider than that of the Bubble Act in some respects. In other words, an association could fall into the definition of either a "joint-stock company" or a "partnership." The wide sphere of intermediate forms of business organizations that had developed over the past century was wiped out by the act of 1844.

A last conceptual innovation, which by now might seem trivial, but in fact lay at the core of the longer term revolution, was the abandonment of a pure public sphere notion of the business corporation. Ever since the consolidation of the Crown as a sole sovereign, and the rise of royal jurisdiction in the late middle ages, the State had held the prerogative to form corporations. The first business corporations of the sixteenth century were formed through this prerogative. The State did not abandon this prerogative as the constitutional power of the King declined. The prerogative was gradually transferred to Parliament during the seventeenth and eighteenth centuries. Most of the newer corporations, formed between the middle of the eighteenth century and 1844, received incorporation by way of a specific act of Parliament and not by a royal charter. The act of 1844 changed all this. For the first time in at least 500 years corporations could be formed without explicit, deliberated, and specific State permission. The act was a move from the public to the private pole of the spectrum. However, registered corporations were a long way from the private pole, as their formation relied on a State statute and was subject to State regulation.

The issue of free incorporation was settled once and for all in 1844 and never seriously questioned afterward. After 1844, the question of licensing undertakings was separated from the question of their incorporation. Vested interests could not prevent the incorporation of busi-

---

[108]Ibid., section 2.

ness associations; they could only try to prevent them from obtaining a license for conducting certain activities, if these required a specific license. The entry barrier to the corporate form of business organization, as such, was finally eliminated. Every undertaking that followed the instructions of the act of 1844 could offer transferable shares and enjoy a separate legal entity and all the other privileges of incorporation, except for limited liability. Though some of the conceptions of the 1844 act were not novel, their accumulation had a considerable impact. In fact, they revolutionized the legal framework of business organization in an unprecedented and irreversible manner.

Laissez-Faire or Intervention?

The act of 1844 was brought to Parliament at a time when the case for free trade seemed to be gaining support. Once again, as in the mid-1820s, a Tory government was successfully carrying out liberal policies. Two individuals who had been involved in the repeal of the Bubble Act held key positions in 1844: Robert Peel, previously Home Secretary and then Prime Minister, and John Copley, once Attorney General and then (titled Lord Lyndhurst) Lord Chancellor. But whereas in 1825 they had both opposed any further intervention of the State in the formation and regulation of companies, and were forced reluctantly into the repeal of the Bubble Act by Moore, Eldon, and the stock market, by 1844 they no longer opposed Gladstone's interventionist measures. This may be because free-traders had become more assertive and militant as they faced a strong protectionist opposition, particularly over the Corn Law. They were willing to resort to interventionist policies in order to free the market of obstacles and facilitate economic growth. If this interpretation is correct, as far as company legislation was concerned, we can view the year 1825 as the turning point from reaction (as represented by Eldon) to status quo laissez-faire (as represented by Huskisson and the mainstream liberal Tories), whereas 1844 was the turning point to more interventionist free trade (as represented by Gladstone).

Paradoxically, Gladstone augmented the regulation of both banks and railways, while he granted other sectors free incorporation. The Joint Stock Banks Act passed in 1844 required each new bank of more than six partners to obtain a letters patent in order to carry on the business of banking.[109] The Bank Charter Act of the same year prohibited the issue of notes by newly established banks, and limited and regulated the issue of notes by the banks that existed at the time of its enactment.[110]

---

[109] 7 & 8 Vict. c.113 (1844), section 1.
[110] 7 & 8 Vict. c.32 (1844), section 10ff.

Though the promotion of new railway companies was regulated by elaborated Standing Orders of Parliament and their structure was already dictated by specific acts of Parliament, Gladstone's Railway Act of 1844 was a step in the direction of further regulation, creating a Railway Board, fixing the rates of at least one passenger service a day per line, obliging companies to present accounts, and even giving the State the option to purchase new lines twenty-one years after they were authorized.[111] Interestingly, Peel's and Gladstone's policy toward business organization had laissez-faire and interventionist elements at the same time.

In conclusion, even if the mid-nineteenth century was the heyday of laissez-faire, and I doubt that to be the case, the legislation of 1844 is not a prime example of it. On the contrary, this legislation presents a complex and mixed picture that includes assorted interventionist and regulatory elements, both in the free incorporation act itself and in the complementary banking and railway legislation.

[111] 7 & 8 Vict. c.85 (1844). For more on the railway regulation, see Forman-Pack and Millward, *Ownership*, 11–28; Ian McLean and Christopher Foster, "The Political Economy of Regulation: Interests, Ideology, Voters, and the UK Regulation of Railways Act 1844," *Public Administration* 70, no. 3 (1992), 313–331.

Conclusion

The timing of the eventual transformation in 1844 can be explained by a number of factors. First, the awareness that developed after the middle of the eighteenth century on the part of entrepreneurs in the transportation and insurance sectors that joint stock is a beneficial feature of finance at least for some sorts of enterprises. Second, the recognition, in the late eighteenth and early nineteenth century, and particularly after the court decisions of 1807–1812, that the only efficient, not to mention legal, way to employ joint stock is by combining it with the conception of the corporation to form the joint-stock business corporation. Third, the realization, after 1825, that Parliament could not deal with each incorporation individually, and in the 1830s, that the Law Officers of the Crown would not be able to take Parliament's place in that respect. Fourth, the split of the link between incorporation and monopoly between 1813 and 1833, when the East India, Bank of England, and Marine Insurance monopolies were abolished. Fifth, the legitimization of investment in shares and in the share market in general, due to the spread of share ownership during the canal era, in other utilities after 1800, and particularly in the railway era, gathering momentum in the 1830s and 1840s. Sixth, the concept of registration as a method for facilitating and regulating associations, which had developed by the 1830s outside of the pure business context. Seventh, the periodical business cycle of the late 1830s that sparked the formation of the parliamentary committee. Eighth, the formation in 1841 of Peel's government which provided an ideological and political base favorable to the concurrent advance of free trade and interventionist policies. The ninth and final factor was Gladstone's appointment to the Board of Trade and to the chairmanship of the parliamentary committee, his conversion to free trade, his growing interest in administration, and his ability to tactically reduce opposition to his proposals. This set of long- and short-term, structural and contingent, legal and economic, ideological and personal

287

factors demonstrates that the timing and pattern of the legal reform were not determined in a systematic manner solely by either economic developments or internal legal dynamics.

Within fourteen months of the passage of Gladstone's Joint-Stock Companies Registration Act of 1844, some 1,639 joint-stock companies were provisionally registered based on it.[1] This was a major break with the earlier trend. The number of companies registered in this short period of time was ten times the number of companies existing in the whole of the English economy two decades earlier, and more than twice the number in existence two years earlier. By July 1856, there were 956 complete registrations, and the number of provisional registrations had reached 3,942.[2] During the same period, 135 additional companies were incorporated with limited liability by specific acts of Parliament. Within a scarce nine years after the introduction of general limited liability in 1855–1856, no fewer than 4,859 limited companies were registered in London.[3] Thus, not only did the act of 1844 transform the legal framework of business organization, but it also led to a dramatic increase in the number of joint-stock business corporations, evidence of the lifting of a hitherto imposed constraint, changing business practices, or both.

It has been maintained by those who claim that the legal framework was not a constraint placed on the economic growth of Britain during the industrial revolution that the General Incorporation Act of 1844 did not lead to an outburst of incorporating businesses. I believe that this claim is not well founded. The enactment was a turning point in terms of the number of incorporating enterprises. Furthermore, one should not expect an entrepreneurial spirit restrained for a century by the legal framework to burst within a few years. The presence of the legal framework molded the economy in a fundamental way that could not be easily and instantly reversed. One should follow the outcome of lifting of restraints on incorporation beyond the years immediately following 1844 and beyond the mere counting of the number of incorporations. This is a prerequisite to disputing my position that the enactment of general incorporation was a highly significant turning point.

---

[1]In the period between Nov. 1, 1844 and Dec. 31, 1845. See *Parliamentary Papers* (1845), vol. 47, pp. 1ff.; *Parliamentary Papers* (1846), vol. 43, pp. 1ff. Allowance was made for the overlap in dates between the returns.

[2]The difference between the two figures is a result of the fact that railway companies (1,600 of which were promoted in this period) did not need to obtain complete registration and that many other companies had not come into maturity.

[3]Based on the Act of 1856 (19 & 20 Vict. c.47 (1856)), between July 1856 and December 1856. See H. A. Shannon, "The First Five Thousand Limited Companies and Their Duration," *Economic History* 2 (1930–1933), 396. In addition, 283 limited companies were registered between 1855 and 1856 based on the earlier act.

The longer run outcome of the general incorporation legislation is momentous, and can hardly be disputed. Business organization came to be dominated by the conception of the corporation, to which were attached the features of separate legal personality, transferable shares, hierarchical managerial structure, and limitation of liability. This unique combination was embodied in the joint-stock and limited business corporation. This form of organization gradually gained dominance in all industrialized economies, at the expense of older forms such as the individual proprietorship, the family firm, and the partnership.

While Britain was experiencing the world's first industrial revolution, England's formal legal framework of business organization remained in its preindustrial state. In some respects, the legal system became even more prohibitive during the century or so beginning in 1720 than it had been over the previous century. The first industrial revolution and, in fact, a much broader transformation of the economy took place within a legal system more restrictive in terms of business organization than almost any other system in the British Isles, in Western and Central Europe, or North America. During the industrial revolution, many in England sought to copy more permissive and novel frameworks of business organization abroad. By the mid-nineteenth century, the tide had turned, and English company law became the model for Europe. Both the new company law of 1867 in France and the company law enacted in Germany in 1870 were influenced by English legislation, and other continental countries were soon to follow. In the United States, a wave of state legislation, and state constitutional amendments passed between 1845 and 1875, partly influenced by the English model, which introduced general incorporation and prohibited incorporation by specific charters.[4] By the time the English legal system caught up with the Continent, and began to serve as an organizational model, the British economy was well into the second industrial revolution and historians with the wisdom of hindsight would argue that it was already beginning to show early signs of retardation.

Was the legal system of business organization at this stage finally efficient? Was the post-1844 English legal system more instrumental than the earlier system? Were functionalists Richard Posner, Robert Clark, and their like right after all, in the long run? The business corporation originated in the sixteenth century, acquired most of its features

---

[4]U.S. legislation was indeed only partially influenced by the new English model. One has to recognize that unique local factors, including federalism and competition among states, the emergence of an interstate railway system and a more integrated market, and the changing constitutional status of the corporation, played major roles in the American case.

during the seventeenth and eighteenth centuries, and gained gradual legal recognition in the first half of the nineteenth century to become a major phenomenon in the economy by the late nineteenth century, and the core of the corporate economy and managerial capitalism of the twentieth century. This development paralleled the rise of capitalism, in its mercantilist and industrializing phases. However, the institutional change over these four centuries was not linear or inevitable. The business corporation that came to dominate the modern economy is a product of a peculiar historical path.

From the perspective of 1500, the corporation showed no more potential for adapting to business needs than did the trust or the partnership. A complex and aggregate business organization could have relied on the adaptation of the trust conception or on the introduction of the limited partnership at an earlier stage into the English law. If either of these conceptions, the trust or the partnership, had gained a slightly earlier or more momentous start relative to the corporation, it could have become more popular with business organizations. Such popularity might have diverted the pressure exerted on the corporation to adapt to business needs, to either the trust or the partnership, in an early period, say, the sixteenth century. However, the initial decision of the English monarchs, notably Elizabeth, to use the corporation as a tool in their overseas and financial policy created path dependency.

We have seen that in the next phase, in the period up to 1630, there seems to have been an evolutionary selection, between the variations of business corporations: some regulated, some with joint stock, and some mixed. However, this selection was based not only on a competitive market mechanism. Major roles in this selection were played both by the English monarchs, Elizabeth and the early Stuarts, and by conditions in India that determined the good fortune of the institutional model of the East India Company. Furthermore, insofar as the evolutionary process led to the selection of the fitter institution, the fit was to the mercantilist environment of the past rather than to the industrial environment of the future.

In the period 1640–1720, the corporation went through a long decline and its path reached what seemed to be a dead end. This was not a result of the economic environment. The business corporation was not dying out because it could not evolutionarily adapt to the changes in the economic environment. Rather, exogenous shocks – political and constitutional crises, costly and destructive wars, and conflicts between rent-seeking interest groups – led to its decline. In the period 1750–1825, the trust and partnership were back in the picture thanks to these shocks. During this period they were widely used and significantly changed to suit the needs of businesses.

The final selection of the corporation in 1825–1856, and its subsequent rise to dominance, were mainly due to the interaction between political factions, interest groups, and judges as they reacted to external shocks and to contingent circumstances in Parliament. To this one should add the fact that at around 1825, the corporation still enjoyed its early-start adaptation advantage. Though the gap was closing, the trust and the partnership still lagged behind in the second quarter of the nineteenth century. In the case of the partnership, the lawyers' rejection of foreign influences and the institutional decay of the Court of Chancery slowed its adaptation. In the case of the trust, it was the late start in the final decades of the eighteenth century that created an adaptation disadvantage. The complex judge-made equity doctrines of the trust were, by virtue of their legal structure, slow to change. Only the accumulation of a large number of disputes in the business context, followed by the overburdened Lord Chancellor's judgments addressing these new types of disputes, could accomplish adaptation of the trust as a viable alternative to the business corporation. The trust and the partnership, and the various concrete forms of organization and features attached to them, eventually lost, not because of any inherent inferiority. It was not the initial and inherent advantages that made the corporation the big winner, but rather a particular historical path that made it dominant.

There is no reason to assume that the new framework of 1844–1856 was evolutionarily selected for the industrial economy because it better defined and enforced property rights, minimized transaction costs, or maximized efficiency in any other strong sense. One can conceive a slightly different historical path in earlier periods that would have led to a different outcome that cannot be readily evaluated as less efficient. This does not mean that the business corporation as we know it would exist today but under a different name: the "business trust" or the "joint-stock limited partnership." On the contrary, having stressed the role of legal modalities and institutions, there is no reason to hold that either the trust or the partnership would have fully converged into the business corporation model in their features. Even the business corporation itself could have acquired different features, such as a different degree of limitation of liability, different financial structure, different procedure of formation, or different regime of regulation. I do not refer here to abstract, or counterfactual, alternative features and conceptions to the real world. What I have in mind are alternatives employed in different enterprises, regions, and sectors during different periods. At least some of these alternatives were not rejected because of inherent inefficiency or inferiority in terms of evolutionary selection, but for reasons bound in time and place. This book tells the story of many of these historical alternatives.

If one accepts my claim that the business institutions that did develop during the period under discussion in this book were not necessarily the most efficient possible, one should go a step further and agree that they did to a degree shape the development of the British economy. My methodology and research approach enable me only to hypothesize that in a counterfactual world with early free incorporation, more joint-stock corporations would have been formed in the financial and in some industrial sectors; joint-stock banks would have played a more significant role in industrial finance; the aggregate rate of growth during the period 1760 to 1860, and beyond, would have been somewhat greater; managerial capitalism would have replaced the family firm in a more massive way by the mid-nineteenth century; and Britain would have entered the economic decline of the nineteenth century in somewhat different shape. Others with different aims and methodologies could pursue these directions using my study of the institutions as a starting point in the investigation of other aspects of the economy.

The case that was studied in this book, the development of the framework of business organization during England's industrial revolution, can be particularly illuminating to a more general discussion of the interaction between legal and economic developments. It focuses on a period of massive economic change. It deals with a field of law that is considered highly relevant to economic development, that of company law and business organization in general. It identifies a discrepancy between the developments in these two realms. Thus, it represents a significant challenge. Yet it is a case in which the apparent discrepancies cannot easily be dismissed. It is a case in which neither of the two conflicting interpretations of the relationship between legal and economic developments, the functionalist and the autonomous, can be reconciled with the historical process.

What I therefore attempted to offer in this book is not a coherent and monocausal interpretation of the historical process. No such interpretation can be supported by the complex nature of the interactions that molded the modern business institutions. My interpretation is rather pragmatic and dialectic. It originated in the border zone between legal history, economic history, and a variety of mainstream histories. It was inspired by theoretical insights and research concerns coming from the disciplines of economics and law. From the historical discipline, it acquired some outreach to the humanities and other social sciences by way of the narrative tool and the discourse and literary analysis; it also acquired flexibility in crossing disciplinary borders, be they between legal and economic history or between these and social, political, intellectual, and cultural histories. As history is not disciplined by general theories, it moved me toward a more context-sensitive use of insights, theories, and critical observations developed in other disciplinary discourses, and toward a perception of time as a concrete, rather than an abstract, dimension, whose relation to context and change is the core of historical exploration.

Appendix 1: The Rise and Decline of the Major Trading Corporations

Merchant Adventurers. Scott, *Constitution and Finance of Joint-Stock Companies*, vol. 1, pp. 1–10, 236–237; vol. 3, pp. 462–463. Cawston and Keane, *Early Chartered Companies*, 20–32. Hill, *Century of Revolution*, 27–29, 179–185, 224–227.

Russia Company. Willan, *Early History of the Russia Company*, 273. Scott claims that the company became regulated only in the year 1669. See Scott, *Constitution and Finance of Joint-Stock Companies*, vol. 2, pp. 15–46; vol. 3, pp. 462–463.

Spanish Company. Lipson, *Economic History of England*, vol. 2, pp. 364–366.

Eastland Company. Cawston and Keane, *Chartered Companies*, 60–66.

Levant Company. Wood mentions that he is unable to determine whether the joint-stock of the company was raised for each voyage separately or for the duration of the charter. See Wood, *History of the Levant Company*, 17 n. 2. He also claims that it is impossible to tell exactly when the company was changed into a regulated one, but assumes that it happened between 1588 and 1595. Ibid., 21–23. For the end of the company, see ibid., 200–202. Scott argues that the company was changed into a regulated one only in 1599–1600. See Scott, *Constitution and Finance of Joint-Stock Companies*, vol. 2, pp. 83–88.

East India Company. Chaudhuri, *English East India Company*, 213. Scott, *Constitution and Finance of Joint-Stock Companies*, vol. 2, pp. 89–206; vol. 3, pp. 464–467.

French Company.   Lipson, *Economic History*, 363–364.

Hudson's Bay Company.   Scott, *Constitution and Finance of Joint-Stock Companies*, vol. 2, pp. 228–237; vol. 3, pp. 472–473. Lipson, *Economic History*, 360–362.

Royal African Company.   Galenson, *Traders, Planters and Slaves*, 20–21. Scott, *Constitution and Finance of Joint-Stock Companies*, vol. 2, pp. 20–35, 67–68; vol. 3, pp. 472–473. Hill, *Century of Revolution*, 183–184, 224.

South Sea Company.   Scott, *Constitution and Finance of Joint-Stock Companies*, vol. 3, pp. 288–360, 480–481. Lipson, *Economic History*, 367–370.

Appendix 2: Capital of Joint-Stock Companies circa 1810

Canals. The best study of the finance of canals is by J. R. Ward. According to Ward, the capital raised between 1755 and 1815 for canal construction was £17,201,000.[1] This figure, with the exception of the Bridgewater canal (£300,000) refers to joint-stock canals. The figure is for England alone, in current prices, and does not cover pre-1755 investment in river improvement undertakings. A somewhat higher figure of £23,998,000 can be calculated based on Ginarlis and Pollard, who based their figures on Britain, not England.[2] For my calculations, I have used the lower figure.

Turnpikes. The best available estimate of aggregate investment in turnpikes is by Ginarlis and Pollard. A calculation, based on their annual figures,[3] brings the total investment for the period 1750–1810 to £19,962,000. The figures are of quasi-net investment; they refer only to turnpikes and not to other roads; and they give no estimates of pre-1750 investments. The figures are for Great Britain as a whole. Ginarlis and Pollard estimated that investment in turnpikes in Wales was 5 percent of the investment in England, and those in Scotland 20 percent,[4] which means that the figure for England should be reduced to 80 percent of the British total. The reduced figure, referring to England only, of £15,969,600, is used here.

Insurance. In the insurance sector the paid-up capital was only a fraction of the nominal capital of a firm (authorized in its act, charter,

[1]Ward, *Canal Building,* 74.
[2]John Ginarlis and Sidney Pollard, "Roads and Waterways: 1750–1850," in C. H. Feinstein and Sidney Pollard, eds., *Studies in Capital Formation in the United Kingdom: 1750–1920* (Oxford: Clarendon Press, 1988), 217–218.
[3]Ibid., 217–218.
[4]Ibid., 201.

or deed of settlement), typically 10 percent. We lack sufficient information regarding the market price of most insurance company shares, which were only rarely quoted, if at all, in the published price lists. Thus the paid-up capital is probably the best available indication for the value of firms in this sector. Based on Babbage and Fenn, the total paid-up capital of insurance companies established before 1810 is £2,400,000.[5] This figure includes joint-stock companies of all sorts: corporations, unincorporated companies, and mutuals. However, the number does not include three of the leading companies: Sun, Phoenix, and Royal Exchange Assurance, whose capital structure was probably too complex for Fenn to calculate. Partial data on these three companies from other sources reveals that the Sun had capital of over £100,000 as early as 1752, that the Phoenix had capital of over £500,000 in the 1820s, and that Royal Exchange Assurance had capital of £500,000 when it obtained its original charter in 1720.[6] These three companies combined held more than 50 percent of the fire insurance market in 1810.[7] The figures for the insurance sector are all based on paid-up capital and do not reflect premium, though many companies were profitable and were valued above their original capital. It was estimated that by 1824 the total capital of the insurance sector was £6,500,000.[8] All the above factors, each of which is only partially relevant to my purpose, lead me to increase the figure of £2,400,000, and to estimate the value of the joint-stock ingredient of the insurance sector in 1810 at £4 million and probably even more.

Utilities.   In joint-stock undertakings for the construction of utilities, the nominal capital was usually fully raised. The capital stock of utility companies established before 1810, based on Fenn's figures are: docks: £5,660,000; waterworks: £1,336,000; gas-light: £600,000.

East India Company.   The last increase in the stock of the East India Company before 1810 took place in 1794. This increase brought its total stock to £6 million. The shares of this company were regularly traded on the Stock Exchange and its share prices were quoted daily.

Bank of England.   The total capital of the Bank of England (after it was increased in 1781 and before it was further increased in 1816) was £11,642,400.

[5]Babbage, *Institutions for Assurance*; Fenn, *English and Foreign Fund.*
[6]Cockerell and Green, *British Insurance Business*, 65.
[7]The calculation is based on Trebilcock, *Phoenix Assurance*, 461.
[8]Ibid., 717.

South Sea Company. The total capital stock of the South Sea Company as of 1810 was £3,663,000. It was no longer an active business concern at that point. All it did was hold some of the national debt. However, it was formally a joint-stock corporation and should be included in this survey.

Shipping. Ship ownership was organized on the part-ownership system, which meant that ships were divided into transferable shares, as discussed above. As the nineteenth century advanced, a group of professional shipowners who acquired full ownership of several ships emerged. Yet early in the century, most of the ships were still divided between several part-owners, and I assume that the entire sector was organized according to this system. The net stock of British ships, according to Feinstein,[9] was £20 million in 1810.

Mining. The net stock of the mining and quarrying sector in Great Britain according to Feinstein was £4 million in 1810.[10] Our problem is to determine which part of this stock functioned under some sort of joint-stock arrangement. The cost book company spread beyond its original territory to other nonferrous mines, but it was rarely used in other mining subsectors. In 1860, 80 percent of mining was coal mining. I assume, with the lower weight of coal in the earlier period, allowing for iron mining, and taking into account some cost book companies and unincorporated companies outside nonferrous mining, that in 1810 about 20 percent of the mining stock was organized in the form of joint stock. Thus, £800,000 of the total stock of the mining sector should be added to our calculations.

Miscellaneous. The authorized capital of the three joint-stock fisheries incorporated in the late eighteenth century was £650,000. The combined capital of the London Flour and Bread Company and of the Birmingham Union Mills Company was at least £140,000. The capital of Golden Lane Brewery reached £327,500 by 1810. Hudson's Bay Company had fully paid-up capital of £200,000. There were at least thirteen woolen company mills in 1810 with an average capital of no less than £5,000 each, totaling £65,000. Four unincorporated metal and timber companies were established in Birmingham in the 1780s and 1790s with a total capital of £200,000. All the above total £1,582,500. There were other unincorporated companies scattered around England in 1810, but I was not able to learn about their capital. There were no

---

[9]Feinstein and Pollard, *Capital Formation*, 439, column 8.
[10]Ibid., 437, column 2.

less than forty-two new promotions of joint-stock companies during the speculative boom of 1807. I have accounted for some of them above, but for most, I have no information as to whether they were actually established and what their capital was. Thus, only the £1,582,500 for which I have specific evidence is included in the table.

Bibliography

PRIMARY SOURCES (TO 1850)

Manuscripts

Public Record Office
BT 31, Returns to the Registrar by Companies registered under the Acts of 1844
    and 1856.
BT 41, as above, for companies dissolved before 1860
Rail 810/1, Birmingham Canal
Rail 818/1, Coventry Canal
Rail 846/1, Leeds and Liverpool Canal
Rail 871/1, Staffordshire Canal

Guildhall Library
Ms. 8,660, Hand-in-Hand Assurance
Ms. 8,727, London Assurance
Ms. 11,656, Globe Insurance
Ms. 11,657, Globe Insurance
Ms. 15,021, London Assurance
Ms. 16,170, Atlas Assurance
Ms. 19,297/1, New Stock Exchange
Ms. 24,171, Hand-in-Hand Assurance

Greater London Record Office
Acc. 1037/1–12, 15–16, R 1979, Howard Family Partnerships
Acc. 2558/CH, Chelsea Water Works Company
Acc. 2558/LA, Lambeth Water Works Company
Acc. 2558/LB, London Bridge Water Works Company
Acc. B/GLCC, Gas Light & Coke Company

House of Lords Record Office
Main Papers
Committee Book
Parchment Collection

Birmingham Central Library
Mathew Bolton Papers, Albion Mill Box
Bolton and Watt Papers, Box 25, Albion Mill
Lee Crowder Papers
Birmingham Coal Company Minutes

Sheffield City Archives
Parker Collection, P.C. 744–849

Books, Pamphlets, and Periodicals

Place of publication is London unless otherwise stated.

An Account of the South Sea Scheme and a Number of Other Bubbles . . . With a Few Remarks upon Some Schemes Which Are Now in Agitation. 1806.

Anderson, Adam. *An Historical and Chronological Deduction of the Origin of Commerce.* 6 vols. 1764.

Arguments in the Court of Kings Bench against Ralph Dodd. 1808.

Article of the Birmingham Flour and Bread Company. Birmingham, 1796.

Austin, John. "Joint-Stock Companies." *Parliamentary History and Review.* 1825.

Babbage, Charles. *A Comparative View of the Various Institutions for Assurance of Lives.* 1826.

Baily, Francis. *An Account of the Several Life Assurance Companies.* 1810.

Baily, Francis. *The Rights of Stock Brokers Defended.* 1806.

Bisset, Andrew. *A Practical Treatise on the Law of Partnership.* 1847.

Blackstone, William. *Commentaries on the Laws of England.* 4 vols. 1765–1769. Rpt. University of Chicago, 1979.

Blount, Thomas. *A Law Dictionary.* 1670.

[Blunt, John]. *A True State of the South Sea Scheme.* 1722.

Chitty, Joseph. *A Treatise on the Laws of Commerce and Manufactures, and the Contracts Relating Thereto.* 4 vols. 1820–1824.

Coke, Edward. *Commentary upon Littleton.* 19th ed. 2 vols. 1832.

Collyer, John. *A Practical Treatise on the Law of Partnership.* 1832.

A Copy of the Bubble Act and Notes on Praemunire from Blackstone and Comyn's Digest and Draft Bill Proposed, to be Introduced by Peter Moore. 1825.

Course of the Exchange. 1697–1834.

Day, Henry. *A Defense of Joint-Stock Companies.* 1808.

The Deed of Settlement of the Equitable Society. 1801.

[Eden, Frederick]. *On the Policy and Expediency of Granting Insurance Charters.* 1806.

English, Henry. *A Complete View of the Joint-Stock Companies Formed during 1824 and 1825.* 1827.

Equitable-Papers Relating to the Dispute Between Members of the Equitable Society and the Charter-Fund Proprietors. 1769.

Essay on the Causes of the Decline of Foreign Trade. 1744.

An Essay on the Practice of Stock-Jobbing and Some Remarks on the Right Use and Regular Improvement of Money. 1724.

Fenn, Charles. *A Compendium of the English and Foreign Fund, and the Principle Joint Stock Companies.* 3d ed. 1840.

Fortune, Thomas. *An Epitome of the Stocks and Public Funds.* 8th ed. 1810.

Francis, John. *Chronicles and Characters of the Stock Exchange.* 1849.

George, John. *A View of the Existing Law Affecting Unincorporated Joint Stock Companies.* New edition. 1825.

Golden Lane Brewery: The Attorney General versus Brown, Parry and Others. 1808.

Gordon, Thomas. *A Complete History of the Late Septennial Parliament 1722: In a Collection of Tracts by John Trenchard and Thomas Gordon.* 1751.

Gow, Neil. *A Practical Treatise on the Law of Partnership.* 1823.

Harding, Grant. *Advice to Trustees and to Those Who Appoint to That Office.* 1830.

Hutcheson, Archibald. *Several Calculations and Remarks Relating to the South Sea Scheme.* 1720.

Joplin, Thomas. *Essay on the General Principles and Present Practices of Banking.* 4th ed. 1823.

Joplin, Thomas. *Prospectus of a Joint-Stock Banking Company with £3,000,000 of Capital to Be Established in London.* 1823.

Ker, H. Bellenden. "Report on the Law of Partnership." *Parliamentary Papers* 44 (1837).

Kyd, Stewart. *A Treatise on the Law of Corporations.* 2 vols. 1793–1794.

Lawyers and Legislators: Or Notes on the American Mining Companies. 1825.

Lewin, Thomas. *The Law of Trusts and Trustees.* 1837.

Macpherson, David. *Annals of Commerce: Manufactures, Fishing and Navigation.* 1805.

Maddock, Henry. *A Treatise on the Principles and Practice of the High Court of Chancery.* 2d ed. 2 vols. 1820.

Maitland, William. *The History of London: From Its Foundation by the Romans, to the Present Time.* 1739.

McCulloch, J. R. *A Dictionary of Commerce.* 1832.

Montagu, Basil. *A Digest of the Law of Partnership: With a Collection of the Cases Decided in the Courts of Law and Equity upon That Subject.* 1815.

Montefiore, Joshua. *The Trader and Manufacturer's Compendium Containing the Laws, Customs and Regulations Relative to Trade.* 1804.

Mortimer, Thomas. *Every Man His Own Broker; Or, A Guide to Exchange Alley.* 13th ed. 1801.

Mundell, Alexander. *The Influence of Interest and Prejudice upon Proceedings in Parliament.* 1825.

A New Year's Gift for the Directors, With Some Account of Their Plot Against the Two Assurances. 1721.

Observations on the Trading Companies Bill. 1834.

Phillips, J. *A General History of Inland Navigation.* 1803.

Philopatris. *Observations on Public Institutions, Monopolies and Joint-Stock Companies.* 1807.

On the Policy and Expediency of Granting Insurance Charters. 1806.

Postlethwayt, Malachy. *The Universal Dictionary of Trade and Commerce.* 4th ed. 1774.

Priestley, Joseph. *An Historical Account of Navigable Rivers, Canals, and Railways of Great Britain.* 1831.

The Proceedings of the Directors of the South Sea Company. 1721.

Remarks on Joint Stock Companies by an Old Merchant. 1825.

Sanders, Francis William. *An Essay on the Nature and Laws of Uses and Trusts.* 1791.

Shepheard, William. *Of Corporations, Fraternities and Guilds.* 1659.

A Short Account of the Society for Equitable Assurance. 1762.

Sinclair, John. *The History of the Public Revenue of the British Empire.* 3d ed. 3 vols. 1803–1804.

Smith, Adam. *The Wealth of Nations.* 5th ed. London, 1789. Rpt. New York, 1937.

The South Sea Bubble . . . Historically Detailed as a Beacon to the Unwary Against Modern Schemes . . . Equally Visionary and Nefarious. 1825.

Spackman, W. F. *Statistical Tables of the U. K.* 1843.

Stock-Exchange Laid Open, the Cause of the Rise and Fall of the Public Funds Explained. 1814.

Stonestreet, George Griffin. *The Portentous Globe.* 1800.

The Substance of the Speech of Henry Beaufoy to the British Society for Extending the Fisheries at Their General Court, 25 March 1788. 1788.

Tooke, Thomas. *A History of Prices.* 1837.

Tucker, Josiah. *An Essay on Trade.* 1750. Reprinted in J. R. McCulloch, ed., *A Select Collection of Scarce and Valuable Tracts on Commerce.* 1859.

Twiss, Horace. *The Public and Private Life of Lord Chancellor Eldon.* 1844.

Watson, William. *A Treatise of the Law of Partnership.* 1794.

Parliamentary Records

Commons' Journal, 1720–1844
Lords' Journal, 1720–1844
Debrett's Parliamentary Register, 1780–1803
Cobbett's Parliamentary History of England (to 1803)
Cobbett's Parliamentary Debates, 1803–1812
Hansard's Parliamentary Debates, 1812–1844
Parliamentary Papers

Court Cases

Andrews v. Woolward (1653)
Attorney General v. Brown, Parry and Others, Excise Trials 584 (1808)
Ayliffe v. Murray, 2 Atk. 58 (1740)
Blacket v. Blizared, 9 B. & C. 851 (1829)

Blundell v. Winsor, 8 Sim. 601 (1837)
Bromfield Ex Parte, 1 Ves. Jun. 453 (1792)
Brown v. Holt, 4 Taunt. 587 (1812)
Buck v. Buck, 1 Camp. 547 (1808)
Buckeridge v. Ingram, 2 Ves. Jun. 652 (1795)
Davies v. Hawkins, 3 M. & S. 488 (1815)
Duvergier v. Fellows, 5 Bing 248 (1828)
Duvergier v. Fellows, 10 B & C. 826 (1830)
Duvergier v. Fellows, 1 Clark & Finnelly 39 (1832)
Ellison v. Bignold, 2 Jac. & W. 503 (1821)
Ex parte Belchier, Amb 218 (1754)
Forman v. Homfray, 2 V. & B. 329 (1813)
Garrard v. Hardey, 5 Man. & G. 471 (1843)
Harrison v. Heathorn, 6 Man. & G. 81 (1843)
Howe v. Earl of Dartmouth, 7 Ves. Jun. 137 (1802)
Howse v. Chapman, 4 Ves. Jun. 542 (1799)
Josephs v. Pebrer, 3 B. & C. 639 (1825)
Keech v. Sandford, Sel Cas T King 61 (1726)
Kinder v. Taylor, Law Journal Reports, old series 3, Cases in Chancery 68 (1824–1825)
The King v. the City of London, 8 Howell's State Trails 1039 (1681–1683)
The King v. Dodd, 9 East 516 (1808)
The King v. Webb, 14 East 406 (1811)
Knowles v. Haughton, 11 Ves. Jun. 168 (1805)
Joseph v. Pebrer, 3 B. & C. 639 (1825)
Learoyd v. Whiteley, 12 App. Cas. 727 (1887)
Luke v. South Kensington Hotel Company, 11 Ch. D. 121 (1875)
Metcalf v. Bruin, 12 East 400 (1810)
Pratt v. Hutchinson, 15 East 511 (1812)
Raynard v. Chase, 1 Burrow 2 (1756)
Rex v. Caywood, 1 Stranger 472 (1722)
Rex v. Waddington, 1 East 143 (1800)
Salmon v. Hamborough Company, 1 Chan. Cas. 204 (1671)
Saunders v. Vautier, Cr. & Ph. 240 (1841)
Saunders v. Vautier, 4 Beav. 115 (1841)
Speight v. Gaunt, 9 App. Cas. 1 (1883)
Speight v. Gaunt, 22 Chan. D. 727 (1883)
Sutton's Hospital, 10 Co. Rep. 23a (1610)
Townsend v. Ash, 3 Atk. 336 (1745)
Turner v. Corney, 5 Beav 515 (1841)
Van Sandau v. Moore and others, 1 Russ. 441 (1826)
Walburn v. Ingilby, 1 My. & K. 61 (1833)
Waters v. Taylor, 15 Ves. Jun. 10 (1808)
Watts v. Brooks, 3 Ves. Jun. 612 (1798)
Wilkinson v. Malin, 2 C. & J. 636 (1832)
Witter v. Witter, 3 P. Wms. 100 (1730)

Statutes

27 Hen. VIII c. 10 (1535)
5 Eliz. c. 4 (1562)
21 Jac. I c. 3 (1623)
13 & 14 Car. II c. 24 (1662)
8 & 9 Wm. III c. 20 (1697)
8 & 9 Wm. III c. 32 (1697)
11 & 12 Wm. III c. 13 (1700)
1 Anne sess. 2 c. 10 (1701)
6 Anne c. 22 (1707)
6 Anne c. 68 (1708)
9 Anne c. 33 (1711)
10 Anne c. 2 (1712)
1 Geo. I c. 24 (1715)
3 Geo. I c. 4 (1717)
6 Geo. I c. 4 (1720)
6 Geo. I c. 18 (1720)
6 Geo. I c. 28 (1720)
7 Geo. I c. 10 (1720)
7 Geo. I c. 15 (1721)
12 Geo. I c. 38 (1726)
13 Geo. I c. 20 (1727)
1 Geo. II c. 11 (1728)
3 Geo. II c. 35 (1730)
6 Geo. II c. 9 (1733)
6 Geo. II c. 30 (1733)
7 Geo. II c. 8 (1734)
7 Geo. II c. 15 (1734)
10 Geo. II c. 8 (1737)
13 Geo. II c. 26 (1740)
14 Geo. II c. 8 (1741)
23 Geo. II c. 24 (1749)
25 Geo. II c. 12 (1752)
28 Geo. II c. 8 (1755)
4 Geo. III c. 37 (1764)
6 Geo. III c. 96 (1766)
6 Geo. III c. 97 (1766)
8 Geo. III c. 36 (1768)
8 Geo. III c. 38 (1768)
9 Geo. III c. 70 (1769)
10 Geo. III c. 114 (1770)
12 Geo. III c. 71 (1772)
17 Geo. III c. 26 (1777)
21 & 22 Geo. III (Irish) c. 46 (1782)
26 Geo. III c. 60 (1786)

26 Geo. III c. 106 (1786)
29 Geo. III c. 25 (1789)
31 Geo. III c. 55 (1791)
33 Geo. III c. 80 (1793)
34 Geo. III c. 37 (1794)
39 & 40 Geo. III c. 28 (1800)
57 Geo. III c. 130 (1817)
6 Geo. IV c. 10 (1825)
6 Geo. IV c. 91 (1825)
6 Geo. IV c. 92 (1825)
7 Geo. IV c. 46 (1826)
10 Geo. IV c. 56 (1829)
4 & 5 Wm. IV c. 40 (1834)
4 & 5 Wm. IV c. 94 (1834)
6 & 7 Wm. IV c. 32 (1836)
1 Vict. c. 73 (1837)
7 & 8 Vict. c. 32 (1844)
7 & 8 Vict. c. 85 (1844)
7 & 8 Vict. c. 110 (1844)
7 & 8 Vict. c. 111 (1844)
7 & 8 Vict. c. 113 (1844)
18 & 19 Vict. c. 133 (1855)
19 & 20 Vict. c. 47 (1856)
21 & 22 Vict. c. 91 (1858)
25 & 26 Vict. c. 89 (1862)
56 & 57 Vict. c. 53 (1893)
7 Edw. VII c. 24 (1907)
15 & 16 Geo. V c. 19 (1925)
9 & 10 Eliz. II c. 62 (1961)

SECONDARY SOURCES

Books and Articles

Albert, William. *The Turpike Road System in England, 1663–1840*. Cambridge Univ. Press, 1972.

Albert, William, and P.D.A. Harvey, eds. *Portsmouth and Sheet Turnpike Commissioners' Minute Book: 1711–1754*. City of Portsmouth, 1973.

Amsler, Christine E., Robin L. Bartlett and Craig J. Bolton. "Thoughts of some British economists on early limited liability and corporate legislation." *History of Political Economy* 13, no. 4 (1981).

Anderson, B. L. "The Attorney and the Early Capital Market in Lancashie." In J. R. Harris, ed., *Liverpool and Merseyside: Essays in the Economic and Social History of the Port and Its Hinterland*. London: Frank Cass, 1969.

Anderson, Gary M., and Robert D. Tollison. "Adam Smith's Analysis of Joint-Stock Companies." *Journal of Political Economy* 90, no. 6 (1982).

Anderson, Gary M., and Robert D. Tollison. "The Myth of the Corporation as a Creation of the State." *International Review of Law and Economics* 3 (1983).

Anderson, Stuart. "Legislative Divorce – Law for the Aristocracy?" In G. R. Rubin and David Sugarman, eds., *Law, Economy and Society, 1750–1914: Essays in the History of English Law*. Abingdon: Professional Books, 1984.

Ashley, Maurice P. *Financial and Commercial Policy Under the Cromwellian Protectorate*. 2d ed. London: Frank Cass, 1962.

Ashton, Robert. *The City and the Court: 1603–1643*. Cambridge Univ. Press, 1979.

Ashton, Robert. *The Crown and the Money Market: 1603–1640*. Oxford: Clarendon Press, 1960.

Ashton, T. S. *An Economic History of England: The 18th Century*. London: Methuen, 1955. Rpt. London, 1972.

Atiyah, P. S. *The Rise and Fall of Freedom of Contract*. Oxford: Clarendon Press, 1979.

Bagwell, Philip S. *The Transport Revolution*. 2d ed. London: Routledge, 1988.

Baker, J. H. "The Inns of Court and Chancery as Voluntary Associations." *Quadreni Fiorentini* 11–12 (1982–1985).

Baker, J. H. *An Introduction to English Legal History*. 3d ed. London: Butterworths, 1990.

Barber, William J. *British Economic Thought and India, 1600–1858: A Study in the History of Development Economics*. Oxford: Clarendon Press, 1975.

Barker, T. C. "The Beginning of the Canal Age in the British Isles." In L. S. Pressnel, ed., *Studies in the Industrial Revolution Presented to T. S. Ashton*. London: Athlone, 1960.

Barker, Theo, and Dorian Gerhold. *The Rise and Rise of Road Transport, 1700–1990*. London: Macmillan, 1993.

Barton, J. L. "The Medieval Use." *Law Quarterly Review* 81 (October 1965).

Bartrip, P.W.J. "State Intervention in Mid-Nineteenth Century Britain: Fact or Fiction?" *Journal of British Studies* 23, no. 1 (1983).

Baskin, Jonathan Barron, and Paul J. Miranti. *A History of Corporate Finance*. Cambridge Univ. Press, 1997.

Baumol, William J. "Entrepreneurship: Productive, Unproductive, and Destructive." *Journal of Political Economy* 98, no. 5 (1990).

Bean, J.M.W. *The Decline of English Feudalism: 1215–1540*. Manchester Univ. Press, 1968.

Berman, Harold J. *Law and Revolution: The Formation of the Western Legal Tradition*. Cambridge, Mass.: Harvard Univ. Press, 1983.

Birch, Alan. *The Economic History of the British Iron and Steel Industry 1784–1879: Essays in Industrial and Economic History with Special Reference to the Development of Technology*. London: Frank Cass, 1967.

Bonfield, L. *Marriage Settlements, 1601–1740: The Adoption of the Strict Settlement*. Cambridge Univ. Press, 1983.

Bonfield, Lloyd. "Strict Settlement and the Family: A Differing View." *Economic History Review* 41, no. 3 (1988).

Bouvier, John. *Bouvier's Law Dictionary and Concise Encyclopedia*. 8th ed. 2 vols. Kansas: Vernan Law Books, 1914.

Bowen, Huw V. "Lord Clive and Speculation in East India Company Stock, 1766." *Historical Journal* 30, no. 4 (1987).

Braddick, Michael J. *The Nerves of State: Taxation and the Financing of the English State, 1558–1714.* Manchester Univ. Press, 1996.

Braudel, Fernand. *Civilization and Capitalism: 15th-18th Century.* Vol. 2: *The Wheels of Commerce.* London: Collins, 1982.

Brebner, J. Bartlet. "Laissez Faire and State Intervention in Nineteenth-Century Britain." *Journal of Economic History* 8 (supplement) (1948).

Brewer, John. *The Sinews of Power: War, Money and the English State, 1688–1783.* Cambridge, Mass.: Harvard Univ. Press, 1990.

Broadbridge, Seymour A. *Studies in Railway Expansion and the Capital Market in England: 1825–1873.* London: Frank Cass, 1970.

Brock, William R. *Lord Liverpool and Liberal Toryism: 1820 to 1827.* 2d ed. London: Frank Cass, 1967.

Brooke, John, and Mary Sorensen, eds. *The Prime Ministers' Papers: W. A. Gladstone.* Vol. I: *Autobiographica.* London: H.M.S.O, 1971.

Buchinsky, Moshe, and Ben Polak. "The Emergence of a National Capital Market in England: 1710–1880." *Journal of Economic History* 53, no. 1 (1993).

Burt, Roger, and Norikazu Kudo. "The Adaptability of the Cornish Cost Book System." *Business History* 35, no. 1 (1983).

Butler, Henry N. "General Incorporation in Nineteenth Century England: Interaction of Common Law and Legislative Processes." *International Review of Law and Economics* 6 (1986).

Butler, Henry N. "Nineteenth-Century Jurisdictional Competition in the Granting of Corporate Privileges." *Journal of Legal Studies* 14, no. 1 (1985).

Cain, P. J., and A. G. Hopkins. *British Imperialism: Innovation and Expansion, 1688–1914.* London: Longman, 1993.

Cain, P. J., and A. G. Hopkins. "Gentlemanly Capitalism and British Expansion Overseas – I. The Old Colonial System, 1688–1850." *Economic History Review* 39, no. 4 (1986).

Cannadine, David. "The Present and the Past in the English Industrial Revolution, 1880–1980." *Past and Present* 103 (May 1984).

Carlos, Ann M., and Jamie Brown Kruse. "The Decline of the Royal African Company: Fringe Firms and the Role of the Charter." *Economic History Review* 49, no. 2 (1996).

Carlos, Ann M., and Stephen Nicholas. "Agency Problems in Early Chartered Companies: The Case of the Hudson's Bay Company." *Journal of Economic History* 50, no. 4 (1990).

Carlos, Ann M., and Stephen Nicholas. "Theory and History: Seventeenth-Century Joint-Stock Chartered Trading Companies." *Journal of Economic History* 56, no. 4 (1996).

Carswell, John. *The South Sea Bubble.* Rev. ed. Dover: Alan Sutton Press, 1993.

Cawston, George, and A. H. Keane. *Early Chartered Companies: A. D. 1296–1858.* London, 1896. Rpt. New York, 1968.

Chandaman, C. D. *The English Public Revenue, 1660–1688.* Oxford: Clarendon Press, 1975.

Chartres, John A. *Internal Trade in England, 1500–1700.* London: Macmillan, 1977.

Chatterton, D. A. "State Control of the Nineteenth Century: The London Gas Industry." *Business History* 14, no. 2 (1972).

Chaudhuri, K. N. *The English East India Company: The Study of an Early Joint-Stock Company 1600–1640.* London: Frank Cass, 1965.

Chesterman, M. R. "Family Settlements on Trust: Landowners and the Rising Bourgeoisie." In G. R. Rubin and David Sugarman, eds., *Law, Economy and Society, 1750–1914: Essays in the History of English Law.* Abingdon: Professional Books, 1984.

Church, Roy. "The Family Firm in Industrial Capitalism: International Perspectives on Hypotheses and History." *Business History* 35, no. 4 (1993).

Church, Roy. *The History of the British Coal Industry, 1830–1913.* Oxford: Clarendon Press, 1986.

Cipolla, Carlo M. *European Society and Economy Before the Industrial Revolution: 1000–1700.* 2d ed. London: Methuen, 1981.

Clapham, John. *The Bank of England: A History.* 2 vols. Cambridge Univ. Press, 1944.

Clark, Robert C. "The Interdisciplinary Study of Legal Evolution." *Yale Law Journal* 90, no. 5 (1981).

Clark, Robert Charles. *Corporate Law.* Boston: Little, Brown, 1986.

Clayton, G. *British Insurance.* London: Elek Books, 1971.

Clifford, Frederick. *A History of Private Bill Legislation.* 2 vols. London: Butterworths, 1885–1887.

Cockerell, H.A.L., and Edwin Green. *The British Insurance Business, 1547–1970: An Introduction and Guide to Historical Records in the United Kingdom.* London: Heinemann Educational Books, 1976.

Collins, Michael. *Money and Banking in the U.K.: A History.* London: CroomHelm, 1988.

Cooke, C. A. *Corporation, Trust and Company: An Essay in Legal History.* Manchester Univ. Press, 1950.

Cookson, J. E. *Lord Liverpool's Administration: The Crucial Years, 1815–1822.* Edinburgh: Scottish Academic Press, 1975.

Cope, S. R. "The Stock Exchange Revisited: A New Look at the Market in Securities in London in the Eighteenth Century." *Economica* 45 (February 1978).

Cornish, W. R., and G. de N. Clark. *Law and Society in England: 1750–1950.* London: Sweet and Maxwell, 1989.

Cottrell, P. L. *Industrial Finance: 1830–1914 – The Finance and Organization of English Manufacturing Industry.* London: Methuen, 1980.

Crafts, N.F.R. *British Economic Growth During the Industrial Revolution.* Oxford: Clarendon Press, 1985.

Crouzet, François, ed. *Capital Formation in the Industrial Revolution.* London: Methuen, 1972.

Daunton, M. J. " 'Gentlemanly Capitalism' and British Industry, 1820–1914." *Past and Present* 122 (February 1989).

Daunton, M. J. *Progress and Poverty: An Economic and Social History of Britain 1700–1850.* Oxford Univ. Press, 1995.

Davidoff, Leonore, and Catherine Hall. *Family Fortunes: Men and Women of the English Middle Class, 1780–1850.* London: Hutchinson, 1987.

Davies, K. G. "Joint-Stock Investment in the Later Seventeenth Century." In E. M. Carus-Wilson, ed., *Essays in Economic History.* 3 vols. London: Edward Arnold, 1954–1962.

Davis, Ralph. *The Rise of the English Shipping Industry in the Seventeenth and Eighteenth Centuries.* London: Macmillan, 1962.

Dawson, Frank G. *The First Latin American Debt Crisis: The City of London and the 1822–1825 Loan Bubble.* New Haven: Yale Univ. Press, 1990.

Deane, Phyllis. "Capital Formation in Britain Before the Railway Age." *Economic Development and Cultural Change* 9, no. 3 (1961).

Deane, Phyllis. *The First Industrial Revolution.* 2d ed. Cambridge Univ. Press, 1979.

Deane, Phyllis, and W. A. Cole. *British Economic Growth, 1688–1959: Trends and Structure.* Cambridge Univ. Press, 1962.

Dicey, A. V. *Lectures on the Relations Between Law and Public Opinion in England During the Nineteenth Century.* London: Macmillan, 1905.

Dickson, P.G.M. *The Financial Revolution in England: A Study in the Development of Public Credit, 1688–1756.* London: Macmillan, 1967.

Dictionary of National Biography. Oxford Univ. Press, 1885– .

Dietz, Frederick C. *English Public Finance, 1558–1641.* 2d ed. London: Frank Cass, 1964.

DuBois, Armand B. *The English Business Company After the Bubble Act, 1720–1800.* New York: Commonwealth Fund, 1938.

Duff, P. W. *Personality in Roman Private Law.* Cambridge Univ. Press, 1938. Rpt. New Jersey, 1971.

Duman, Daniel. *The English and Colonial Bars in the Nineteenth Century.* London: CroomHelm, 1983.

Duman, Daniel. *The Judicial Bench in England: 1727–1875 – The Reshaping of a Professional Elite.* London: Royal Historical Society, 1982.

Dutton, H. I. *The Patent System and Inventive Activity During the Industrial Revolution: 1750–1852.* Manchester Univ. Press, 1984.

Eggertsson, Thrainn. *Economic Behavior and Institutions.* Cambridge Univ. Press, 1990.

Ekelund, Robert B., and Robert D. Tollison. *Mercantilism as a Rent-Seeking Society: Economic Regulation in Historical Perspective.* College Station, Texas: A&M Univ. Press, 1981.

Elder, John R. *The Royal Fishery Companies of the Seventeenth Century.* Glasgow: Maclehose, 1912.

Evans, George Heberton. *British Corporation Finance: 1750–1850 – A Study of Preference Shares.* Baltimore: John Hopkins Univ. Press, 1936.

Falkus, M. E. "The British Gas Industry Before 1850." *Economic History Review* 20, no. 3 (1967).

Farnie, D. A. *The English Cotton Industry and the World Market, 1815–1896.* Oxford: Clarendon Press, 1979.

Feinstein, C. H. "Capital Formation in Great Britain." In P. Mathias and M. M. Postan, eds., *Cambridge Economic History of Europe.* Vol. 7: *The Industrial Economies: Capital, Labour, and Enterprise.* Cambridge Univ. Press, 1978.

Feinstein, Charles H. "Part II, National Statistics, 1760–1920." In Charles H. Feinstein and Sidney Pollard, eds., *Studies in Capital Formation in the United Kingdom: 1750–1920.* Oxford: Clarendon Press, 1988.

Feinstein, Charles H., and Sidney Pollard, eds., *Studies in Capital Formation in the United Kingdom: 1750–1920.* Oxford: Clarendon Press, 1988.

Flinn, Michael W. *The History of the British Coal Industry*, Vol. 2: *1700–1830, the Industrial Revolution.* Oxford: Clarendon Press, 1984.

Floud, Roderick, and Donald M. McCloskey, eds. *The Economic History of Britain since 1700*, Vol. 1: *1700–1860.* 2d ed. Cambridge Univ. Press, 1994.

Foot, M.R.D., and H.C.G. Matthew, eds. *The Gladstone Diaries.* 14 vols. Oxford: Clarendon Press, 1968–1994.

Forman-Pack, James, and Robert Millward. *Public and Private Ownership of British Industry, 1820–1990.* Oxford: Clarendon Press, 1994.

Formoy, Ronald R. *The Historical Foundation of Modern Company Law.* London: Sweet and Maxwell, 1923.

Freedeman, Charles E. *Joint-Stock Enterprise in France, 1807–1867: From Privileged Company to Modern Corporation.* Univ. of North Carolina Press, 1979.

Friedman, Lawrence M. *A History of American Law.* 2d ed. New York: Simon and Schuster, 1985.

Galenson, David W. *Traders, Planters, and Slaves: Market Behavior in Early English America.* Cambridge Univ. Press, 1986.

Gash, Norman. *Aristocracy and People: Britain 1815–1865.* London: E. Arnold, 1979.

Gash, Norman. *Sir Robert Peel: The Life of Sir Robert Peel after 1830.* London: Longman, 1972.

Getzler, Joshua. " 'Gentlemen Do Not Collect Rents': Fiduciary Obligations and the Problem of Delegation" (forthcoming).

Getzler, Joshua. *A History of Water Rights at Common Law.* Oxford: Clarendon, 2000.

Getzler, Joshua. "Patterns of Fusion." In Peter Birks, ed., *The Classification of Obligations.* Oxford: Clarendon Press, 1997.

Gierke, Otto. *Community in Historical Prespective.* Cambridge Univ. Press, 1990.

Gierke, Otto. *Natural Law and the Theory of Society 1500 to 1800.* Cambridge Univ. Press, 1934. Rpt. Cambridge Univ. Press, 1958.

Gierke, Otto. *Political Theories of the Middle Age.* Cambridge Univ. Press, 1900. Rpt. Cambridge Univ. Press, 1958.

Ginarlis, John, and Sidney Pollard. "Roads and Waterways: 1750–1850." In Charles H. Feinstein and Sidney Pollard, eds., *Studies in Capital Formation in the United Kingdom: 1750–1920.* Oxford: Clarendon Press, 1988.

Goodchild, J. "The Ossett Mill Company." *Technology History* 1 (1968).

Gordon, Barry. *Economic Doctrine and Tory Liberalism, 1824–1830.* London: Macmillan, 1979.

Gordon, Barry. *Political Economy in Parliament: 1819–1823.* London: Macmillan, 1976.

Gordon, Robert W., "Critical Legal Histories." *Stanford Law Review* 36, nos. 1 & 2 (1984).

Gourvish, T. R. *Railways and the British Economy: 1830–1914.* London: Macmillan, 1980.

Gower, L.C.B. " A South Sea Heresy?" *Law Quarterly Review* 68 (April 1952).

Gower, L.C.B., et al. *Gower's Principles of Modern Company Law.* 5th ed. London: Sweet and Maxwell, 1992.

Hadden, Tom. *Company Law and Capitalism.* 2d ed. London: Weidenfeld and Nicholson, 1977.

Hadfield, Charles. *The Canals of Southern England.* London: Phoenix House, 1955.

Hadfield, Charles. *The Canals of the West Midlands.* Newton Abbot: David and Charles, 1966.

Hadfield, Charles, and Gordon Biddle. *The Canals of North West England.* 2 vols. Newton Abbot: David and Charles, 1970.

Hale, Matthew. *The Prerogatives of the King.* London: Selden Society, vol. 92, 1976.

Harling, Philip, and Peter Mandler. "From 'Fiscal-Military' State to Laissez-faire State, 1760–1850." *Journal of British Studies* 32, no. 1 (1993).

Harris, J. R. "Liverpool Canal Controversies, 1769–1772." *Journal of Transport History* 2, no. 3 (1956).

Harris, Ron. "The Bubble Act: Its Passage and Its Effects on Business Organization." *Journal of Economic History* 54, no. 3 (1994).

Harris, Ron. "Political Economy, Interest Groups, Legal Institutions, and the Repeal of the Bubble Act in 1825." *Economic History Review* 50, no. 4 (1997).

Hay, Douglas, et al. *Albion's Fatal Tree: Crime and Society in Eighteenth-Century England.* New York: Random House, 1975.

Heckscher, Eli F. *Mercantilism.* Revised ed. 2 vols. London: G. Allen and Unwin, 1955.

Henderson, James P. "Agency or Alienation? Smith, Mill and Marx on the Joint-Stock Company." *History of Political Economy* 18, no. 1 (1986).

Hill, Christopher. *The Century of Revolution, 1603–1714.* 2d ed. New York: W. W. North, 1982.

Hilton, Boyd. *The Age of Atonement: The Influence of Evangelicalism on Social and Economic Thought, 1795–1865.* Oxford: Clarendon Press, 1988.

Hilton, Boyd. *Corn, Cash, Commerce: The Economic Policies of the Tory Governments, 1815–1830.* Oxford Univ. Press, 1977.

Hilton, Boyd. "The Political Arts of Lord Liverpool." *Transactions of the Royal Historical Society* 38 (1988).

Hinton, R.W.K. *The Eastland Trade and the Common Weal in the Seventeenth Century.* Cambridge Univ. Press, 1959.

The History of Parliament: The House of Commons, 1790–1820. 5 vols. London: Secker and Warburg, 1986.

Holden, J. Milnes. *The History of Negotiable Instruments in English Law.* University of London, 1955.

Holdsworth, William. *A History of English Law.* 17 vols. London: Methuen, 1956–1972.

Hoppit, Julian. "Financial Crises in Eighteenth-Century England." *Economic History Review* 39, no. 1 (1986).

Hoppit, Julian. *Risk and Failure in English Business: 1700–1800.* Cambridge Univ. Press, 1987.

Horwitz, Henry, and Patrick Polden. "Continuity or Change in the Court of Chancery in the Seventeenth and Eighteenth Centuries?" *Journal of British Studies* 35, no. 1 (1996).

Horwitz, Morton J. *The Transformation of American Law, 1780–1860.* Cambridge, Mass.: Harvard Univ. Press, 1977.

Howe, A. C. "Free Trade and the City of London: c. 1820–1870." *History* 77 (1992).

Hudson, Pat. *The Genesis of Industrial Capital: A Study of the West Riding Wool and Textile Industry, c. 1750–1850.* Cambridge Univ. Press, 1986.

Hudson, Pat. *The Industrial Revolution.* London: E. Arnold, 1992.

Hunt, Bishop Carleton. *The Development of the Business Corporation in England, 1800–1867.* Cambridge, Mass.: Harvard Univ. Press, 1936.

Hurst, James Willard. *Law and the Conditions of Freedom in the Nineteenth-Century United States.* Univ. of Wisconsin Press, 1956.

Hyde, Charles K. *Technological Change and the British Iron Industry, 1700–1870.* Princeton Univ. Press, 1977.

Ingham, Geoffrey. *Capitalism Divided? The City and Industry in British Social Development.* London: Macmillan, 1984.

Ireland, Paddy. "Capitalism Without the Capitalist: The Joint Stock Company Share and the Emergence of the Modern Doctrine of Separate Corporate Personality." *Journal of Legal History* 17, no. 1 (1996).

Jackman, William T. *The Development of Transportation in Modern England.* 2d ed. London: Frank Cass, 1962.

John, Michael. *Politics and the Law in Late Nineteenth-Century Germany: The Origins of the Civil Code.* Oxford: Clarendon Press, 1989.

Johnson, Paul. *The Birth of the Modern: World Society 1815–1830.* London: Weidenfeld and Nicolson, 1991.

Jones, S.R.H., and Simian P. Ville. "Efficient Transactors or Rent-Seeking Monopolists? The Rationale for Early Chartered Trading Companies." *Journal of Economic History* 56, no. 4 (1996).

Judd, Gerrit P. *Members of Parliament: 1734–1832.* New Haven: Yale Univ. Press, 1955.

Kelley, Donald R. *The Human Measure: Social Thought in the Western Legal Tradition.* Cambridge, Mass.: Harvard Univ. Press, 1990.

Kercher, Bruce. "The Transformation of Imprisonment for Debt in England, 1828 to 1838." *Australian Journal of Law and Society* 2 (1980).

Kostal, R. W. *Law and English Railway Capitalism 1825–1875.* Oxford: Clarendon Press, 1994.

Kronman, Anthony T. *Max Weber.* Stanford Univ. Press, 1983.

Krueger, Anne O. "The Political Economy of the Rent-Seeking Society." *American Economic Review* 64, no. 3 (1974).

Lambert, Sheila. *Bills and Acts: Legislative Procedure in Eighteenth-Century England.* Cambridge Univ. Press, 1971.

Lambert, Sheila, ed. *House of Commons Sessional Papers of the Eighteenth Century,* Vol. 131: *1731–1800.* Wilmington, Del.: Scholarly Resources, 1975.

Langford, Paul. *A Polite and Commercial People: England, 1727–1783.* Oxford Univ. Press, 1989.

Lemmings, David. *Gentlemen and Barristers: The Inns of Court and the English Bar 1680–1730.* Oxford: Clarendon Press,1990.

Lester, V. Markham. *Victorian Insolvency: Bankruptcy, Imprisonment for Debt, and Company Winding-up in Nineteenth-Century England.* Oxford: Clarendon Press, 1995.

Lewis, G. R. *The Stannaries: A Study of the English Tin Mines.* Cambridge: Mass.: Harvard Univ. Press, 1924.

Lewis, W. Arthur. *The Theory of Economic Growth.* London: G. Allen and Unwin, 1955.

Lieberman, David. *The Province of Legislation Determined, Legal Theory in Eighteenth-Century Britain.* Cambridge Univ. Press, 1989.

Lipson, E. *The Economic History of England.* 3d ed. 3 vols. London: Adam and Charles Black, 1943.

Lloyd-Jones, Roger, and M. J. Lewis. *Manchester and the Age of the Factory: The Business Structure of Cottonopolis in the Industrial Revolution.* London: CroomHelm, 1988.

Lobban, Michael. *The Common Law and English Jurisprudence 1760–1850.* Oxford: Clarendon Press, 1991.

Maine, Henry Sumner. *Ancient Law: Its Connection with the Early History of Society and Its Relation to Modern Ideas.* London: John Murray, 1861.

Maitland, F. W. *The Constitutional History of England.* Cambridge Univ. Press, 1908. Rpt. Cambridge Univ. Press, 1968.

Maitland, F. W. *Township and Borough.* Cambridge Univ. Press, 1898. Rpt. Cambridge Univ. Press, 1964.

Maitland, F. W. "Trust and Corporation." In *Maitland: Selected Essays.* Cambridge Univ. Press, 1936.

Maitland, F. W. "The Unincorporate Body." In *Maitland: Selected Essays.* Cambridge Univ. Press, 1936.

Manchester, A. H. *Modern Legal History of England and Wales 1750–1950.* London: Butterworths, 1980.

Mandler, Peter. *Aristocratic Government in the Age of Reform, Whigs and Liberals 1830–1852.* Oxford: Clarendon Press, 1990.

Mantoux, Paul. *The Industrial Revolution in the Eighteenth Century: An Outline of the Beginnings of the Modern Factory System in England.* New and revised ed. London: Jonathan Cope, 1961.

Marriner, Sheila. "English Bankruptcy Records and Statistics before 1850." *Economic History Review* 33, no. 3 (1980).

Mathias, Peter. *The Brewing Industry in England, 1700–1830.* Cambridge Univ. Press, 1959.

Mathias, Peter. "Capital, Credit and Enterprise in the Industrial Revolution." *Journal of European Economic History* 2, no. 1 (1973).

Mathias, Peter. "The Lawyer as Businessman in Eighteenth-Century England." In D. C. Coleman and Peter Mathias, eds., *Enterprise and History: Essays in Honour of Charles Wilson.* Cambridge Univ. Press, 1984.

Mathias, Peter, and Patrick O'Brien. "Taxation in Britain and France, 1715–

1810. A Comparison of the Social and Economic Incidence of Taxes Collected for the Central Governments." *Journal of European Economic History* 5, no. 3 (1976).

McCulloch, J. R., ed. *A Select Collection of Scarce and Valuable Tracts on Commerce*. 1859.

McLean, Iain, and Christopher Foster. "The Political Economy of Regulation: Interests, Ideology, Voters, and the UK Regulation of Railways Act 1844." *Public Administration* 70, no. 3 (1992).

Michell, A. R. "The European Fisheries." In G. E. Rich and C. H. Wilson, eds., *Cambridge Economic History of Europe*, Vol. 5: *The Economic Organization of Early Modern Europe*. Cambridge Univ. Press, 1977.

Michie, R. C. "The London Stock Exchange and the British Securities Market: 1850–1914." *Economic History Review* 38, no. 1 (1985).

Miles, M. "The Money Market in the Early Industrial Revolution: The Evidence from West Riding Attorneys, c. 1750–1800." *Business History* 23, no. 2 (1981).

Milsom, S.F.C. *Historical Foundations of the Common Law*. 2d ed. London: Butterworths, 1981.

Mirowski, Philip. *The Birth of the Business Cycle*. New York: Garland, 1985.

Mirowski, Philip. "The Rise (and Retreat) of a Market: English Joint Stock Shares in the Eighteenth Century." *Journal of Economic History* 41, no. 3 (1981).

Mitchell, Austin. *The Whigs in Opposition: 1815–1830*. Oxford: Clarendon Press, 1967.

Moffat, Graham, and Michael Chesterman. *Trust Law: Text and Materials*. London: Weidenfeld and Nicolson, 1988.

Mokyr, Joel, ed. *The British Industrial Revolution: An Economic Perspective*. Boulder: Westview, 1993.

Morgan, E. Victor, and W. A. Thomas. *The Stock Exchange: Its History and Function*. 2d ed. London: Elek, 1969.

Morley, John. *The Life of William Ewart Gladstone*. 3 vols. London: Macmillan, 1903.

Moss, David J. "The Bank of England and the Country Banks: Birmingham, 1827–33." *Economic History Review* 34, no. 4 (1981).

Neal, Larry. "The Finance of Business during the Industrial Revolution." In Roderick Floud and Donald McCloskey, eds., *The Economic History of Britain since 1700*, Vol. 1: *1700–1860*. 2d ed. Cambridge Univ. Press, 1994.

Neal, Larry. *The Rise of Financial Capitalism: International Capital Markets in the Age of Reason*. Cambridge Univ. Press, 1990.

Newbould, Ian. *Whiggery and Reform: 1830–1841 – The Politics of Government*. Stanford Univ. Press, 1990.

Nichols, Glenn O. "English Government Borrowing, 1660–1688." *Journal of British Studies* 10, no. 1 (1971).

North, Douglass C. *Institutions, Institutional Change and Economic Performance*. Cambridge Univ. Press, 1990.

North, Douglass C. *Structure and Change in Economic History*. New York: Norton, 1981.

O'Brien, Patrick K. "The Political Economy of British Taxation, 1660–1815." *Economic History Review* 41, no. 1 (1988).

Offer, Avner. "Between the Gift and the Market: The Economy of Regard." *Economic History Review* 50, no. 3 (1997).

Oldham, James. *The Mansfield Manuscripts and the Growth of English Law in the Eighteenth Century*. 2 vols. University of North Carolina Press, 1992.

Parris, Henry. "The Nineteenth-Century Revolution in Government: A Reappraisal Reappraised." *Historical Journal* 3, no. 1 (1960).

Patterson, Margaret, and David Reiffen. "The Effect of the Bubble Act on the Market for Joint Stock Shares." *Journal of Economic History* 50, no. 1 (1990).

Pawson, Eric. *The Early Industrial Revolution: Britain in the Eighteenth Century*. London: Basford, 1979.

Pawson, Eric. *Transport and Economy: The Turnpike Roads of Eighteenth Century Britain*. London: Academic Press, 1977.

Payne, Peter. "Family Business in Britain: An Historical and Analytical Survey." in Akio Okochi and Shigeaki Yasuoka, eds., *Family Business in the Era of Industrial Growth: Its Ownership and Management*. University of Tokyo Press, 1984.

Pennington, Robert R. *Stannary Law: A History of the Mining Law of Cornwall and Devon*. Newton Abott: David and Charles, 1973.

Philips, C. H. *The East India Company: 1784–1834*. 2d ed. Manchester Univ. Press, 1961.

Plumb, J. H. *England in the Eighteenth Century*. Baltimore and Harmondsworth: Penguin, 1968.

Plumb, J. H. *The Growth of Political Stability in England, 1675–1725*. London: Macmillan, 1967.

Plumb, J. H. *Sir Robert Walpole*. 2 vols. London: Cresset Press, 1956–1960.

Pollard, Sidney. "The Growth and Distribution of Capital in Great Britain: c. 1770–1870." In *Third International Conference of Economic History: Munich 1965*. Paris, La Haye: Mouton & Co., 1968.

Posner, Richard A. *Economic Analysis of the Law*. 3d ed. Boston: Little Brown, 1986.

Postan, M. M. "Partnership in English Medieval Commerce." In *Medieval Trade and Finance*. Cambridge Univ. Press, 1973.

Postema, Gerald J. *Bentham and the Common Law Tradition*. Oxford: Clarendon Press, 1989.

Pressnell, L. S. *Country Banking in the Industrial Revolution*. Oxford: Clarendon Press, 1956.

Rabb, Theodore K. *Enterprise and Empire: Merchant and Gentry Investment in the Expansion of England, 1575–1630*. Cambridge, Mass.: Harvard Univ. Press, 1967.

Reed, M. C. *Investment in Railways in Britain: 1820–1844 – A Study in the Development of the Capital Market*. Oxford Univ. Press, 1975.

Reeder, John. "Corporate Loan Financing in the Seventeenth and Eighteenth Centuries." *Anglo-American Law Review* 2 (1973).

Relton, Francis Boyer. *An Account of the Fire Insurance Companies . . . Established in Great Britain.* London: S. Sonnenschein, 1893.

Rice, D. G. "The Legal Nature of a Share." *The Conveyancer* 21 (1957).

Robert, Rudolph. *Chartered Companies and Their Role in the Development of Overseas Trade.* London: F. Bell and Sons, 1869. Rpt. London, 1969.

Robinson, Olivia F., T. David Fergus, and William M. Gordon. *European Legal History – Sources and Institutions.* 2d ed. London: Butterworths, 1994.

Rogers, James Steven. *The Early History of the Law of Bills and Notes: A Study of the Origins of Anglo-American Commercial Law.* Cambridge Univ. Press, 1995.

Rose, Mary B., ed. *Family Business.* Aldershot: Edward Elgar, 1995.

Roseveare, Henry. *The Financial Revolution: 1660–1760.* London: Longman, 1991.

Rostow, W. W. *The Stages of Economic Growth: A Non-Communist Manifesto.* Cambridge Univ. Press, 1960.

Rubinstein, W. D. *Men of Property: The Very Wealthy in Britain since the Industrial Revolution.* London: CroomHelm, 1981.

Rudden, Bernard. *The New River – A Legal History.* Oxford: Clarendon Press, 1985.

Santuari, Alceste. "The Joint Stock Company in Nineteenth Century England and France: *The King v. Dodd* and the *Code de Commerce.*" *Legal History* 14, no. 1 (1993),

Saville, John. "Sleeping Partnership and Limited Liability: 1850–1856." *Economic History Review* 8, no. 3 (1956).

Schubert, Eric S. "Innovations, Debts, and Bubbles: International Integration of Financial Markets in Western Europe, 1688–1720." *Journal of Economic History* 48, no. 2 (1988).

Scott, William R. *The Constitution and Finance of English, Scottish and Irish Joint-Stock Companies to 1720.* 3 vols. Cambridge Univ. Press, 1912. Rpt. Gloucester, Mass.: P. Smith, 1968.

Sedgwick, Romney. *The History of Parliament: The House of Commons, 1715–1754.* 2 vols. London: H.M.S.O., 1970.

Shammas, Carole. "The 'Invisible Merchant' and Property Rights." *Business History* 17, no. 2 (1975).

Shannon, H. A. "The Coming of General Limited Liability." In E. M. Carus-Wilson, ed., *Essays in Economic History.* 3 vols. London: Edward Arnold, 1954–1962.

Shannon, H. A. "The First Five Thousand Limited Companies and Their Duration." *Economic History* 2 (1930–1933).

Shapiro, Seymour. *Capital and the Cotton Industry in the Industrial Revolution.* Ithaca: Cornell Univ. Press, 1967.

Simpson, A.W.B. *A History of the Common Law of Contract: The Rise of the Action of Assumpsit.* Oxford: Clarendon Press, 1975.

Simpson, A.W.B. *A History of the Land Law.* 2d ed. Oxford: Clarendon Press, 1986.

Simpson, A.W.B. "The Rise and Fall of the Legal Treatise: Legal Principles and the Forms of Legal Literature." *University of Chicago Law Review* 48, no. 3 (1981).

Southgate, David. *The Passing of the Whigs*. London: Macmillan, 1962.

Sperling, John G. *The South Sea Company: An Historical Essay and Bibliographical Finding List*. Boston: Baker Library, 1962.

Spooner, Frank C. *Risks at Sea: Amsterdam Insurance and Maritime Europe, 1766–1780*. Cambridge Univ. Press, 1983.

Spring, Eileen. "The Family, Strict Settlement and Historians." In G. R. Rubin and David Sugarman, eds., *Law, Economy and Society, 1750–1914: Essays in the History of English Law*. Abingdon: Professional Books, 1984.

Spring, Eileen. *Law, Land, and Family: Aristocratic Inheritance in England, 1300 to 1800*. University of North Carolina Press, 1993.

Stebbings, Chantal. "The Legal Nature of Shares in Landowning Joint Stock Companies in the 19th Century." *Journal of Legal History* 8 (1987).

Stigler, George J. "The Theory of Economic Regulation." *Bell Journal of Economics* 2 (Spring 1971).

Stoljar, S. J. "The Transformations of Account." *Law Quarterly Review* 80 (April 1964).

Sugarman, David. "Bourgeois Collectivism, Professional Power and the Boundaries of the State. The Private and Public Life of the Law Society, 1825 to 1914." *International Journal of the Legal Profession* 3, no. 1/2 (1996).

Sugarman, David. "Legal Theory, the Common Law and the Making of the Textbook Tradition." In William Twining, ed., *Legal Theory and Common Law*. Oxford: Blackwell, 1986.

Sugarman, David. "Simple Images and Complex Realities: English Lawyers and Their Relationship to Business and Politics, 1750–1950." *Law and History Review* 11, no. 2 (1993).

Sugarman, David, and G. R. Rubin. "Towards a New History of Law and Material Society in England: 1750–1914." In G. R. Rubin and David Sugarman, eds., *Law, Economy and Society, 1750–1914: Essays in the History of English Law*. Abingdon: Professional Books, 1984.

Supple, Barry. *Royal Exchange Assurance: A History of British Insurance, 1720–1970*. Cambridge Univ. Press, 1970.

Sutherland, Lucy. *The East India Company in Eighteenth Century Politics*. Oxford: Clarendon Press, 1962.

Szostak, Rick. *The Role of Transportation in the Industrial Revolution: A Comparison of England and France*. McGill-Queen's Univ. Press, 1991.

Thomas, Peter D. G. *The House of Commons in the Eighteenth Century*. Oxford: Clarendon Press, 1971.

Thomas, W. A. *The Provincial Stock Exchanges*. London: Frank Cass, 1973.

Thompson, E. P. *Whigs and Hunters: The Origin of the Black Act*. New York: Pantheon Books, 1975.

Thompson, F. M. L. *English Landed Society in the Nineteenth Century*. London: Routledge and Kegan Paul, 1963.

Trebilcock, Clive. *Phoenix Assurance and the Development of British Insurance*, Vol. 1: *1782–1870*. Cambridge Univ. Press, 1985.

Trubek, David M. "Max Weber on Law and the Rise of Capitalism." *Wisconsin Law Review* no. 3 (1972): 720.

Tushnet, Mark V. "Perspectives on the Development of American Law: A Critical Review of Friedman's 'A History of American Law.' " *Wisconsin Law Review* no. 1 (1977).

Ville, Simon P. *English Shipowning during the Industrial Revolution: Michael Henley and Son, London Shipowners, 1770–1830.* Manchester Univ. Press, 1987.

Ward, J. R. *The Finance of Canal Building in Eighteenth Century England.* Oxford Univ. Press, 1974.

Webb, Sidney and Beatrice Webb. *English Local Government: The Story of the King's Highway.* London: Longmans, Green, 1913.

Weber, Max. *Economy and Society: An Outline of Interpretive Sociology.* Ed. Guenther Roth and Claus Wittich. 3 vols. New York: Bedminster Press, 1968.

Webster, Anthony. "The Political Economy of Trade Liberalization: The East India Company Charter Act of 1813." *Economic History Review* 43, no. 3 (1990).

Westworth, O. A. "The Albion Steam Flour Mill." *Economic History* 2, no. 7 (a supplement to the Economic Journal) (1932).

Wheeler, J. S. "Navy Finance, 1649–1660." *Historical Journal* 39, no. 2 (1996).

Willan, T. S. *The Early History of the Russia Company 1553–1603.* Manchester Univ. Press, 1956.

Willan, T. S. *River Navigation in England: 1600–1750.* Oxford Univ. Press, 1936. Rpt. London: F. Cass, 1964.

Williams, O. *The Clerical Organization of the House of Commons: 1661–1850.* Oxford: Clarendon Press, 1954.

Williams, Orlo C. *The Historical Development of Private Bill Procedure and Standing Orders in the House of Commons.* 2 vols. London: H.M.S.O., 1948–1949.

Williamson, Oliver E. *The Economic Institutions of Capitalism: Firms, Markets, Relational Contracting.* New York: Free Press, 1985.

Wood, Alfred C. *A History of the Levant Company.* Oxford Univ. Press, 1935. Rpt. London, 1964.

Wrigley, E. A. *Continuity, Chance and Change: The Character of the Industrial Revolution in England.* Cambridge Univ. Press, 1988.

Ziegler, Dieter. *Central Bank, Peripheral Industry: The Bank of England in the Provinces: 1826–1913.* Trans. Eileen Martin. Leicester Univ. Press, 1990.

Unpublished Theses and Dissertations

Avi-Yonah, Reuven S. "The Development of Corporate Personality from Labeo to Bartolus." Seminar paper, Harvard University, 1989.

Clarke, C. A. Allen. "The Turnpike Trusts of Islington and Marylebone: 1700–1825." M.A. thesis, University of London, 1955.

Croft, Clyde Elliot. "Philip Yorke, First Earl of Hardwicke: An Assessment of His Legal Career." Ph.D. thesis, Cambridge University, 1982.

Cummings, A.J.G. "The York Building Company: A Case Study in Eighteenth Century Mismanagement." Ph.D. thesis, University of Strathclyde, 1980.

Duffy, I.P.H. "Bankruptcy and Insolvency in London in Late Eighteenth and Early Nineteenth Centuries." Ph.D. thesis, Oxford University, 1973.

Haagen, Paul Hess. "Imprisonment for Debt in England and Wales." Ph.D. dissertation, Princeton University, 1986.

Hayes, Michael N. "Mercantile Incentives: State Sanctioned Market Power and Economic Development in the Atlantic Economy, 1553–1776." Ph.D. dissertation, University of California, Davis, 1986.

Hughes, John. "Organizational Metamorphosis, 1765–1865: A Study of Changing Practice and Theory in the Organization and Management of Transport Companies." Ph.D. thesis, Oxford University, 1983.

Rowlinson, P. J. "Regulation of the Gas Industry in the Early Nineteenth Century: 1800–1860." Ph.D. thesis, Oxford University, 1984.

Servian, M. S. "Eighteenth Century Bankruptcy Law: From Crime to Process." Ph.D. thesis, University of Kent at Canterbury, 1985.

Thomas, Emlyn. "The Crisis of 1825." M.Sc. thesis, University of London, 1938.

Index of Cases

Index of Statutes

General Index

action of account, 160–162
Admiralty, High Court of, 26, 187, 189–190, 198
agency, 20–21, 50–51, 140, 157–158, 160
agriculture (sector), 1, 117, 196
Albion Mill Company, 178–180
Amicable Society, 101–103, 105–106, 170
assumpsit, 161
Attorney General, 77, 104, 178, 236–237, 240, 264–266, 271, 285
attorneys, 7, 102, 104, 107, 112, 126, 138–140, 155, 232–233
autonomy (legal), 4–5, 7–9, 11, 13, 16, 151–152, 161, 267

banking (sector), 1, 29, 36, 57, 80, 117, 125, 143, 169, 183, 197, 210–215, 218–219, 258–259, 268–269, 279, 281–283, 285–286; country banks, 125–126, 174, 203, 211–214, 254, 268; London banks, 212–214, 254; note-issuing banks, 29, 212–215; savings banks 275–276
Bank of England, 29, 53, 55–56, 61–63, 66, 75, 77, 80, 119, 126, 135, 152, 170, 172, 183, 196–197, 203–204, 211–214, 218–219, 225, 243, 253–254, 262, 268, 275, 287
bankruptcy, 21, 29, 80, 106, 128–129, 131–132, 142, 146, 163, 212, 234
bar, 164, 231–232
Baring, Alexander, 211, 258–259, 261
beneficiaries, 21–22, 93, 148–149, 152, 154–158
Bentham, Jeremy, 10, 249
Birmingham, 177–179, 197, 206, 239; canal, 99; companies and sectors, 177–180, 238–239, 258

Birmingham Flour and Bread Company, 178–179, 238–239
Blackstone, Sir William, 17, 73, 111–112, 235, 249
Blunt, John, 68, 72
Board of Trade, 12, 166, 251, 258–259, 269, 271, 273, 277, 279–280, 287
bonds, 62–63, 118, 122, 213, 217, 232, 239–240
Boulton, Matthew, 178, 180
brewing (sector), 135, 169, 180–182, 196, 202, 216
Bridgewater, Duke of, 95–97
Brougham, Henry, 10, 246–248, 264
Bubble Act, 1, 4, 12, 101, 109, 117, 137–138, 198, 211, 218, 223, 256; effects of, 8, 29, 102, 104, 107, 113, 127, 140, 165, 168, 173, 186, 190, 192, 248, 284; enactment of, 8, 58, 60–61, 63–68, 71–79, 81, 258–259; litigation involving, 181–182, 235–245; repeal of 230, 247, 250, 261–270, 285
building societies, 36, 216, 238, 240, 276–277, 283

Cabinet, 9, 11–12, 164, 235, 256, 259, 261–262, 266, 278–280
canals, 1, 86, 95–100, 109, 117, 122, 133–135, 153, 173, 193, 196–197, 210, 216, 218, 220, 224–225, 227, 258, 272, 287; Birmingham, 99; Leeds and Liverpool, 99, 124–126, 133; Staffordshire and Worcestershire, 97–98; Trent and Mersey, 97–98
canon law, 21, 111
canonist school, 111
capital formation, 2, 114–117, 193
capitalism, 6, 23, 290, 292

326